WITH
SCHWARZKOPF

★ ★ ★ ★

Life Lessons of The Bear

By Gus Lee

To my beautiful Diane, for everything. You said I could write and showed me the way.

To General H. Norman Schwarzkopf

For mentoring me and caring about our character.

This book may be purchased for educational, business, or sales promotional use. For information, please write: Special Markets Department, Smithsonian Books, P. O. Box 37012, MRC 513, Washington, DC 20013

Published by Smithsonian Books

Director: Carolyn Gleason

Production Editor: Christina Wiginton

Edited by Mark Gatlin

Typeset by Scribe Inc.

Cover design by Brian Barth

Library of Congress Cataloging-in-Publication Data

Lee, Gus.

   With Schwarzkopf : life lessons of the Bear / by Gus Lee.

     pages cm

   Includes bibliographical references and index.

   ISBN 978-1-58834-529-5

   1. Schwarzkopf, H. Norman, 1934-2012–Anecdotes. 2. United States Military Academy–Biography. 3. College teachers–Biography. 4. Lee, Gus. 5. Military cadets–United States–Biography. 6. Leadership–United States. 7. Character. 8. Conduct of life. 9. United States. Army. Office of the Judge Advocate General–Biography. 10. Chinese Americans–Biography. I. Title.

   E840.5.S39L44 2015

303.3'4–dc23

Manufactured in the United States of America

19 18 17 16 15   5 4 3 2 1

TABLE OF
Contents
★ ★ ★ ★

Preface   v

1 | It's Always about
    Leadership   1

2 | Work as If It
    Matters   5

3 | Excuses Are
    Cowardly   13

4 | Make Me Look
    Good   24

5 | First, Fix Yourself   31

6 | Beware the Past   36

7 | Serve Your People   43

8 | Love the Ones
    You Lead   49

9 | Do the Right
    Thing—Regardless
    of Risk to Self   54

10 | Love Them No
     Matter How Hard   59

11 | Learn to Discern   69

12 | Know Your Fears   73

13 | Assess Need   79

14 | Solve Problems at
     Root Cause   84

15 | Inspire Change   91

16 | What You Ignore
     You Endorse   97

17 | Learn from
     History   103

18 | Be an Honorable
     Man in All Things   107

19 | Cross the River
     of Fear   112

20 | Respect All
     Persons   119

21 | You Need Reliable
     Friends   125

22 | See Your
     Limitations   130

23 | Pay the Price   134

24 | Learn Your Lesson   140

25 | Act like a Man   148

26 | Base Decisions on
Good Character   162
27 | No Right Way to Do
the Wrong Thing   170
28 | Stand Tall in the
Storm   177
29 | Do the Hardest
Right   183
30 | Recover from Loss   191
31 | Learn from History   198
32 | Remember to Sing   213
33 | Discern the
Harder Right   217
34 | Never Quit Serving 231
35 | Keep to the High
Narrow Ridge   241

36 | Courage: The
Backbone of
Leadership   247
37 | Practice, Practice,
Practice   259
38 | Farewell, TOAD   267
39 | Taps   273
40 | Echoes   281

Appendix   284
Acknowledgments   293
Notes   295
Bibliography   299
Index   302

Photographs follow page 283

Preface

★ ★ ★ ★

In 1966 America, 63 percent of the public held high confidence in government, divorce was uncommon, and academic cheating was episodic. Riding an economic boom, many expected America to solve the problems of the world.

Today, research reveals that seven percent of the public has confidence in Congress, and 75 percent of Americans in high school, college, and graduate school routinely cheat. The Government Accounting Office reports that the frauds of the 2008 subprime meltdown, designed by educated elites, cost the nation 129 percent of GNP and millions of jobs. Generals, admirals, and more junior officers are routinely fired for ethical misconduct, while sexual harassment in the military and society remains a problem. Eighty-seven percent of U.S. managers said in a national survey by certified fraud examiners that they would fabricate data to make their organizations look better.

In 1966, a young major in the United States Army named H. Norman Schwarzkopf left the new war in Vietnam to reluctantly become a temporary engineering professor at West Point. To my very good fortune, I was one of his cadets.

He was committed to my self-improvement, making the next years among the most intense of my life. After a 20-year hiatus, I invited him to join a start-up company for which I worked and we reunited in a relationship that would span 47 years. Although we originally met in academics at West Point, and worked in business, his relationship with me was fundamentally moral, for it dealt with that which is unseen. He demanded facts but was driven to live in alignment with principles, and it was his very attractive habit to inspire others to do the same. Thomas Carlyle, a 19th century philosopher wrote, "Every noble work is at first impossible." What the Bear did was noble; my struggles suggested the impossible.

Norman Schwarzkopf had once been a pudgy and self-acknowledged "un-macho" child with an alcoholic mother. Perhaps he believed in changing others because he himself had changed. In the aftermath of an historic triumph in the Gulf War, General H. Norman Schwarzkopf became one of the world's most admired individuals, was offered the top position in the Army, was knighted by the Queen, and was guaranteed high elective office. He disliked "Stormin' Norman" and enjoyed being known as "the Bear."

He was officially a genius, intercollegiate athlete, missile engineer, and a superior soldier. But his unique gift was character. He tried to pound his will and intentionality about right action into his students with the fire of a medieval blacksmith. With occasional brain-rattling roars, he inspired me to strive, laugh, learn, and change in an attempt to forge a diffident person into a courageous individual.

It is now two days after Christmas 2014. Two years ago today, General Schwarzkopf died in his home in Tampa in the company of his family and his inner staff. I am writing in our oldest daughter and husband's home in East Nashville as their six-month-old son Jude chews a green wooden block and shows great interest in my feet.

"H. Norman Schwarzkopf," I say to Jude. He looks up with a radiant smile. The Bear had a broad, infectious, almost boyish grin. When I was 20, Major Schwarzkopf filled my young mind with his ideals, cemented one principle and two rules of leadership into my heart, and altered the course of my life. I want our children's generation, and Jude and his big cousin Mikey, to have access to the same life lessons that my mentor so freely passed to me.

When he retired from the Army, he refused vast powers, uncounted riches, and greater fame to be with his family, serve desperately ill children, energetically support little-known charities, and help lead organizations in protecting the nation and the environment.

He worried more about our commitment to be a right-minded and ethical people than he did about party politics or the might of potential enemies.

Every age yearns for a hero. At the dawn of the new millennium, most of America saw that hero in General H. Norman Schwarzkopf. Brilliant and knowledgeable, his enduring excellence was not within his cranium but within his chest; it was in his character and in his uniquely fierce commitment to develop high integrity in others.

Historians can easily count the few world figures who have inspired a nation to experience a hope borne of moral heroism. Americans of today have the opportunity to remember one of those few who, until recently, was still among us.

In 1966, I was, like many West Point cadets, frenetically overscheduled and given to musings about my coming greatness. I had become attached to my fears and self-doubts and fretted over short-term results.

Because I struggled with doing the hardest right, I'd ironically become a target for reform by one of the great personalities of the age.

It's Always about Leadership

The general is the bulwark of the state; if he is strong at all points,
the state will be strong. If he is defective, the state will be weak.

Sun Tzu

On a Friday in mid-January 1991, a great war was coming in the Middle East. Early mobile phones were the size of Coke machines and cost as much as a small car, so routine communication came by the landline telephone. Ours rang with its alarm-like jangle. It was Colonel Bob "More Beer" Lorbeer, my tall, broad-shouldered West Point roommate, a wounded, decorated, and sober combat veteran whose nickname was phonetic and unrelated to his personal habits.

"Turn on the TV," he said. "It's the Bear."

The television slowly warmed up with its electric crackle of tubes. The Bear appeared on the first channel. He was on every channel. Larger than before, he spoke in his familiar, confident manner. My heart jumped in pleasant shock; it was like reuniting with family after a long absence. The Bear was four-star General H. Norman Schwarzkopf and he was in our living room, speaking to the world about a war that no one wanted and no one knew how to avoid. I felt as if I'd talked with him yesterday, yet I hadn't communicated with him for 20 years.

The Bear had served as my role model when I was a soldier and had been my external conscience when I sought to learn leadership. Now he was the theater commander in the Persian Gulf for Operation Desert Storm and the Commander-in-Chief, CINC, of U.S. Central Command. His arc of military and relational responsibility embraced the Middle East and the Horn of Africa, historically the most troubled region in the world.

Norman Schwarzkopf was eight years old when he watched his dad leave to serve in the Second World War. Young Norman so loved "Pop" that he believed his father's participation would directly bring about the defeat of Adolph Hitler and the Nazis. In 1991, I was an adult with a seven-year-old son and held an equivalent conviction that the Bear would lead the Coalition and our post-Vietnam forces to victory over a massive Iraqi army and Saddam Hussein, a man known for his love of the terror tactics of Adolph Hitler and Josef Stalin.

Captivated by the Bear's familiar low, thoughtful, and engaging voice, I remembered his trying to teach me lessons of engineering and adulthood at West Point. His presence remained magnetic, and I smiled as I recalled his fiery intent to develop callow youth into emotionally wise and trustworthy officers. His familiar frown of concentration was a hint of a ferocious anger once triggered by our immaturities. Now, as he wielded his customary pointer and managed his charts, his clear description of the air campaign returned me to our engineering section room, where his acute intelligence and polymath mastery of many topics inspired some to emulate him and others to abandon any reasonable hope of imitation; I had experienced both reactions.

Beneath the lessons, the Bear had pounded into our chests the immutable principle that life had always been about leadership, that it would always be about leadership, and as this would require our integrity and courage, we should be about the work of learning how to improve both. As leaders of character, we would be equipped to inspire others to be their best selves by modeling principled conduct under pressure. We were to deny the temptations of influencing and motivating through the easily accessible tools of control, ambition, authority, money, inducements, coercion, manipulation, and fear.

Where many general officers might wear the more formal Class A's with its rows of ribbons, he wore a common soldier's desert camouflage uniform. He was imitating two of his heroes, William Tecumseh Sherman and Ulysses S. Grant. Sherman knew how to maneuver in battle and Grant would never waver or give counsel to his fears, and neither liked the gaudiness of rank or formal dress.

In 1944, General Dwight D. Eisenhower had briefed the King and Queen of England and the Combined Chiefs on the upcoming invasion of

Nazi-occupied Europe on the beaches of Normandy. But no general in the long history of war had ever openly briefed the world—and the foe—about his campaign while combat was underway. Amazingly, this was what the Bear was doing as I watched and listened.

I sensed his thin skein of wariness. He was being candid without being tactically revelatory and being accessible without surrendering control of the room to dubious reporters. He communicated reality without exaggerating gains. His presence inspired confidence in the 33 national constituent forces of his Coalition while conveying danger to the Iraqi generals with whom he would soon do battle. He was honest in his facts while no doubt subtly confusing and misleading the enemy. The enemy, due to the proliferation of cable news, had become the most important element of his television audience. In real time they could evaluate the thinking of the general who sought their defeat.

The Bear later told me that he hated our national leadership's constant media smokescreens during the Vietnam War. It offered false projections based on an incoherent strategy and sought a political exit while our soldiers continued to die. The Bear recounted in his memoir that he would not mislead the American public; he would not let the media and the press intimidate him; he would not provide information helpful to the enemy; and he would not submit to the pressure to answer every question. Knowing him as I did, it was also clear that he would follow one of the principles of Sun Tzu's *The Art of War*: winning victory by confusing the opposing commander, which he was now doing in front of the world. He used to do magic tricks for his children; now he was doing them for his foe.

His voice and presence inspired a host of reactions. I was deeply pleased that he would lead our young troops and the soldiers of the Coalition. I was happy that he represented the rebuilt and re-professionalized United States Army that had been broken by the abandonment of the nation and handicapped by deficient national leadership. I was worried that this great athlete with whom I'd shared strain and sweat in the West Point gym had gained weight.

I am an interior and private person whose personality had suggested a successful life in a quiet monastery atop a distant mountain, but he taught me to engage the world to contribute. I am not a natural warrior and was from a disabled family. Yet I'd been gifted with a wonderful wife and two

4 · WITH SCHWARZKOPF

amazing young children and had two very safe jobs. But in that moment, hearing the voice of my first moral guide in life, I was prepared to recover my dog tags, unearth my uniforms and old combat boots, and leave my family and all I knew to march outward to wherever he directed, in complete step with the irresistible drum beat that the Bear had so long ago installed in my heart.

A familiar note played in memory. I'd heard it when he spoke to me at Trophy Point at the Academy, many years ago. It was there by the Hudson River where each of us, as 17-year old lads, had taken the solemn oath to protect the Constitution of the United States, in a promise to be more than self-serving individuals.

The old note carried his familiar watchwords in his memorably gruff voice: "Let's get this right." But seeing him before me and hearing his voice increased the intensity of the memory. It asked if I had lived up to the standards that he had set for me when we were young, when he had set a course to advance my character, and to make me merit the high fortune that had lifted me from a poor and broken immigrant Chinese family into the very American institution of West Point.

Work as If It Matters

There is a natural aristocracy among men. The grounds of this are virtue and talents.
Thomas Jefferson

In 1966, the economy was robust, jobs were plentiful, "The Sound of Music" won the Best Picture Oscar, the Beatles ruled radio, public university tuition was a $200 a year, a big-block, four-on-the-floor Corvette Stingray was a daylight robbery at $5,300, and the national debt was three percent of what it is today. Baby Boomer collegians were experimenting with a new kind of answer that included angry political activism, sex, drugs, and rock and roll.

Vietnam, a small, distant, and irksome distraction from the threat of thermonuclear war with the Soviets, would happily be a quickly ended skirmish against small, distant, and irksome Asians.

On the dark granite of the Hudson highlands, a small and isolated West Point endured tectonic shock waves of change and marched on, stubbornly holding fast to ancient virtues.

West Point was an intense monastic sanctuary whose ancient values served as inoculants against the value shifts of the 1960s. I was a junior-year cadet who took academic risks in a school that proudly expelled smarter students for failure in a single class, be it nuclear physics, boxing, survival swimming, or calculus. I had more bright and athletic friends than I deserved, resentfully did academics as an interruption of poker games, ate 2,000-calorie meals on fine china served by uniformed Irish and black waiters, wore gold stripes befitting those in the top leadership fourth of my class, could bench almost 300 pounds, and loved a girl who had rejected me. I hated West Point's required major of engineering and its five unsolved universal mysteries—Electrical Engineering, Solid Mechanics, Fluid Mechanics, Thermodynamics, and Nuclear Physics.

The Chinese call the growing of character *Táoyě qingcāo*, to forge character. West Point was the Great Furnace to forge straight spines and virtuous hearts for the defense of the nation. While I resisted change, a young major was at this moment in combat along the Cambodian border and had been ordered to return to West Point to teach.

I detested even slight emotional conflicts, but imagined being Horatio at the bridge to save the republic—the fearless protector of my mother and sisters against Chinese *dufei* bandits, and later, the rather amazing secretary of state who would create the preconditions for world peace. I also wanted to be liked. I loved West Point's impossible ideals and fiery camaraderie, and hoped that being here would help me become what I was not. But I resisted West Point's mandatory engineering curriculum by reading for fun and playing with buddies as if it were a sports camp.

Before we knew better, we were 3,000 high-testosterone males with a football team that would beat Navy, Penn State, Kansas State, and Cal, and lose only to #1 Notre Dame and #14 Tennessee. Raised in a YMCA weight room from the age of seven, I judged men by the size of their arms, and I had built mine up as my identity, a barrier against the bullies that defined my past and haunted my memories. I ignored the fact that West Point preferred morals to muscles. I was soon to be an American Army officer equipped to fight the Soviet Union or, if diplomacy failed, the People's Republic of China. It would be a paying job that would break a long family tradition of male unemployment.

West Point was a school of the middle class, and I posed as if I'd never been an underfed immigrant kid who was legally blind, tubercular, dumbstruck, motherless, occasionally crazy, and from a family for which the House of Usher would have been an upgrade. The Surgeon General of the Army had granted me four rare medical waivers that magically rendered legal blindness, asthma, scoliosis (curved spine), and pes planus (fallen arches or flat feet) non-issues so I could become a cadet.

The Academy demanded obedience, spiritual endurance, and an appreciation for math and engineering. But I disliked being controlled, was spiritually undeveloped, and thought Euclid was my personal enemy. As a teen, I worked three jobs and fed the family on two-day-old fish five days a week. But hanging with pals, going to a party, watching TV, dating, and using the phone were deemed *verboten* by Edith, my strict Germanic stepmother, whose role models had probably been convicted at Nuremberg. She'd sentenced me to my *yeh*, or karma, of loneliness, holding that my birth had caused the cancer that killed my birth mother, a sin she celebrated with song. I'd been raised by three YMCA boxing coaches who took 10 years to teach me how to fight. I feared social rejection, sought friends across all social divides, and was voted Most Popular in high school while doubting myself as a human being.

America had given our rootless Chinese family safe haven from World War II. My father sought to repay this debt by joining the U.S. Army, but they rejected him for age, absence of citizenship, and a tendency to attack people who disagreed with him. My going to West Point became the substitute payment. To be a cadet, I would need to demonstrate excellence in academics, athletics, and character, but in the last feature, my ego and fear of isolation played me like San Francisco Tenderloin con men. I practiced what Augustine of Hippo called *incurvatus in se*, the fearful bending of my small life into self-concern. In *anima*, the true inner self, I was not what President George Washington had envisioned when he urged Thomas Jefferson to form an academy to educate the guardians of the young American Republic.

We were playing touch football in the long hallway of the brand new East Barracks, aka the Cadet Hilton. Now known as Lee Barracks, it apparently was not named for me. We passed the pigskin and circulated a rumor about a big officer just back from Vietnam. To most, Vietnam was a small, distant smudge, a limited conflict that our superior competence, firepower, and tactics would end before we got there.

To escape people, I'd become an early lover of books with an emphasis on arcane Asian history, a narrow niche that offered warm sanctuary from the unwanted conditions of the present. "Vietnam" was derived from its original Chinese name "southern land of Yue foreign people." A century before *anno Domini*, when Julius Caesar was born, the Chinese Empire invaded Vietnam with a massive modern army. The Vietnamese would resist China for a thousand years in a war that curiously set the conditions for the later American experience

It was said that the new prof had Silver Stars for valor, a Purple Heart for wounds, and tons of other steel medals denoting courage under fire in Vietnam. We admired him without knowing his name. That was the good part. The bad part was that an unkempt classmate had encountered the young major and had received a royal reaming for sloppy appearance.

"¡Ay, Caramba! Un hombre muy duro," said Arturo Torres, speedy quarterback, dancer extraordinaire, and Hearts ace. "De acuerdo," I agreed, catching his stinging spiral. So the new guy was just another hard-ass in a closed and fearsome society of unamused Iron Age disciplinarians. This, in a school that happily compressed five years of engineering, military duties, athletics, and psychic restrictions into four, cramming a hundred-thousand-dollar education into our ears, a nickel at a time. Menos mal y gracias a Dios, there was only one chance in 400 that we'd get him as a prof.

"We" were Section 8, 12 second-from-the-bottom students in Solid Mechanics. Here, a mean prof could flunk you out of the Academy. Section 1's members were our freakishly bright opposites with top grades: Larry "Rap" Rapisarda, Tony "Stoney" Cerne, Jon "Tenth-grubber" Gardner, and Barry "Curve-wrecker" Hittner. West Point was America's first engineering school, whose graduates had constructed America east of the Mississippi, and the institution, despite the inflating social complexities of a post-colonial world, was so deeply loyal to its traditions that engineering remained the single major. We of Section 8 were David Lee "Snake" Sackett, Bob "More Beer" Lorbeer, Ross "Wrinkles" Irvin, Keith "Hog" Harrelson, "Gentleman" Jeff Riek, "Gustavo" Lee, and "Last Man" Rick Hawley—the Dregs Plus One, just above the flaming ninth ring of Dante's Inferno, where the cries of cadets could be heard every morning as they were flogged by the cruel Harpies of science and math. Section 9 was bottom of the barrel, manned by cadets who wore crash helmets and sat on ejection seats to await their fates. Later, humping hills in the arctic Korean tundra of the DMZ (Demilitarized Zone), I huffed, "Korea is mountains, and more mountains." West Point was engineering, and more engineering.

Not long after the War of 1812, Academy Superintendent Sylvanus Thayer established the instructional culture. Profs wouldn't lecture; they'd administer graded tests every day in every class with minimalist responses to questions after the "writs." The cadet was required to sit in his room and decode textbooks for the next day's battery of seven exams. Based on grades, cadets were periodically re-sectioned up or down, with attendant risks, as a single physical or academic failure brought immediate civilian status. I'd been an engineering cellar-dweller since the invention in India of the zero. The top man in each small section of 12 brightly scrubbed, short-haired, sleep-deprived cadets was the section leader, responsible for good order and attendance.

Section leader David Lee "Snake" Sackett bellowed, "Section, Ten-HUT!" We came to attention with the confident savoir faire of Second Classmen. Something large entered: six feet, four inches of lean, hard, and quick. He had short-cropped light-colored hair and a deep tropical tan. He'd been taller until collisions with the Earth from parachuting and war wounds borrowed an inch of his height and never returned it. It's hard to gauge shoulder width, but his appeared to touch both walls. He was a young major and had more combat decorations than we had ever seen. He had absorbed the sun and then blotted it out. He exuded anger, disapproval, and the promise of processes worse than bodily harm and threats that exceeded engineering writs. Dave's spine straightened as if he'd been a victim of one of my Electrical Engineering power lab experiments.

He saluted the officer. "Sir, the section is present and accounted for!" Shouting like a plebe.

When negative stimulus causes fear, adrenals precognitively inject stress hormones into the blood to raise pulse and temperature for fight or flight; pupils expand to capture the threat; brain blood drains to suffuse the fast-twitch muscles and causes the face to flush. Mouth and throat instantly go dry as fluids lubricate armpits for combat and excrete adhesives into the palms for grappling with an enemy. Fighting an angry bear is no time for a burger and fries, so saliva becomes fluids to pre-lubricate joints for combat. Dave's face colored and his voice squeaked. We all sympathized.

The professor would return the salute and command, "Seats." We'd sit, prepared or not, for the daily writ. We usually were not. We were "Cows," juniors, wily veterans of dodging academic bust-ups, of playing fields, hazing, boxing, wrestling, gymnastics, survival aquatics, road marches, night land navigation, field tactics, close-order drill, squad drill, parades, inspections, horribly truncated liberties, invasive inspections, ancient disciplines, and arcane punishments. I took a breath and thought, He's just a prof; no sweat!

When he wasn't looking my way, I made a covert, thumbs-up gesture, which was the West Point universal signal for a Good Deal. Bob "More Beer" Lorbeer grinned.

Schwarzkopf's father, a retired Army colonel and Academy graduate, was recalled to duty after Japan's surprise attack on Pearl Harbor and Hitler's declaration of war against the United States.

Leaving home, he charged his son to be the man of the house, giving him his West Point saber. Norman was responsible for the safety of his mother and two older sisters and the good order of a happy home.

In his memoir, Norman Schwarzkopf recounts that his father said, "Now, son, I'm depending on you. The responsibility is yours." His father kissed him goodnight. In the morning, the father was gone, and Norman said later that "nothing again was the same." His absence would accidentally trigger the collapse of their mother and the erosion of the home's happiness. The boy lay awake facing the unrealistic task and asked, "How am I going to do this?"

He was eight years old.

Major Schwarzkopf emanated danger. His breathtaking intensity and evident disapproval beamed from hot-blue eyeballs and vast, lowered dark brows in a large, boulder-like head that had been sculpted from an unnaturally square block of marble. On his chest marched rows of bright service ribbons, topped by a Silver Star with Oak Leaf Cluster, Purple Heart for wounds, Combat Infantryman's Badge, and silver U.S. Army Master Parachutist's wings and gold wings of the South Vietnamese Airborne. Radiant blue eyes burned into my carefree indifference, his pupils seizing me as if they had grappling hooks. Most of the blood in my brain had evacuated to my extremities, to my twitching muscles, to the distant rivers of China. I imagined an easier life at Cal, San Francisco State, or at one of the better institutions where folks made license plates.

"I am H. Norman Schwarzkopf," he said precisely with elevated gruffness and a snarl that belonged to a Pleistocene carnivore. "I am *not* an academic officer," as if being one was a violation of all that was right. "I'm a United States Army infantryman—and damned proud of it."

He wrote "TOAD" on the chalkboard and underlined it twice. "I am just a TOAD. TOAD is Temporarily on Academic Duty. I say again,

TEMPORARILY!" His voice melted ear wax and bounced off the mountains of Nepal. It said he didn't want to be here. That made 13 of us.

He spoke harshly, making West Point seem sterner and my conscience seem weaker. I got the sharp adrenaline jolt triggered by people who see your frailties. Slowly, like in a horror film, when the Blob flows under the door, I realized he was Teutonically cruel and unfeeling, a terrifying reminder of my stepmother, Edith Swinehart, whose actual name was beyond the imagination of the most inventive novelist. He fixed a cold, penetrating gaze on us, sniper eyes inviting us to infarct. "You're in a bottom section of the lazy, the gutless wonders, the sneaking under-achievers, the academic cowards. Why are you down here?!"

"No excuse, sir!" we cried.

We were still at attention. In a gunshot instant, it was as if our very long previous years had been reversed, and we were again tormented Plebes under the rule of Pharaoh, where struggling to survive only aggravated perpetual punishment and led to the requirement to build larger pyramids.

"Seats." We sat. He spoke, which was a surprise; our engineering profs of that day were like Calvin Coolidge, for whom three words were an inaugural address. It wasn't about Solids, which was a shock, since faculty never left the bounds of their academic disciplines. He spoke to us about character. "You are fortunate young men with a unique opportunity to learn to do hard tasks. You're to grow the guts to lead the sons of America in combat, under conditions of cruelty and hardship, to protect the Republic and the values for which it stands. And you're blowing it and mooking around with thumbs up your rear! You're close to getting found (flunking) in academics and being thrown out of here! You're supposed to *lead* others by example, not goof off and act dumb! You will NOT blow it in THIS section. DO YOU UNDERSTAND?"

"YES, SIR!" we shouted.

"Stagger desks" (Prepare to be tested). We staggered desks to eliminate an inadvertent glance at a classmate's work. This was a formality in Section 8, where answers were unworthy of even accidental observation. He gave the writ. I hazarded WAGs (wild-assed guesses)—creative and fanciful shots in the dark at an unknown moving target.

At his, "Cease work," we dropped pencils; continuing to work was an honor violation and cause for unquestioned dismissal. With alarming speed, he graded our tests. He seemed to dislike our answers: He threw them on the floor. Mouths again went dry and armpits lubed for fight or flight. I imagined fighting him, which some guys do with whomever they meet, and quickly opted for retreat.

"On your feet!" Chairs scraped and one fell backward as we leaped to rigid attention.

"You were very serious about coming here, weren't you? But now, you're not serious about work. Study tonight as if it matters. DO YOU UNDERSTAND? NOW LET'S GET IT RIGHT!"

Not long ago, in high school, imagining ourselves to be young bold Greeks crossing a wine-dark sea for the Towers of Ilium, we had all pulled oars and bent wind-seeking sails for West Point. Now we were here. Instead of feeling like seasoned cadet veterans, we feared we'd become Ulysses' doomed crew on its fated attempt to reach Ithaca. Major H. Norman Schwarzkopf, a great bonfire of an angry man, had brought heat into our lives. Like the vengeful Greek gods of the sea, this frighteningly focused warrior was about to test our innards and thin our numbers.

3

Excuses Are Cowardly

★ ★ ★ ★

Hold yourself responsible for a higher standard than anybody expects of you.
Never excuse yourself.
Henry Beecher Ward

The library upper reading room was one of my favorite places in the world. I cracked the Solids textbook. It was Urdu:

$$p_{xy} = \frac{\sum_{i=0}^{N-1} (x_i - \bar{x}) \times (y_i - \bar{y})}{\sqrt{\sum_{i=0}^{N-1} (x_i - \bar{x})^2 \times (y_i - \bar{y})^2}}$$

I retreated to the beginning of the book, seeking easier explanations, There, I found Early Urdu. I paged through inexplicable bridging problems, felt the familiar drowning in the onslaught of the incomprehensible, and folded my tent. To feel better, I read Alexander Hamilton's 1799 letter urging congressional formation of a military academy, the 1925 text on the sympathetic training of horse and man, and 1793 tracts by the Association for the Preservation of Liberty and Property Against Republicans and Levellers. I read Fairbank's *The United States and China*, a gift from gentle, 120-pound, five-foot-four-inch Uncle S.Y. Shen in distant San Francisco. Happy, I studied the origins of China's second Opium War with Great Britain, and anticipated Saturday's free time.

I realized Major Schwarzkopf was seated in front of me. Cold blue eyes burned as if I'd stolen his Corvette, drove it through a concrete barrier, and buried it in the river. My left eye began closing on its own.

I was a Chinese who had become American, a secret rebel against the authority of a dictatorial stepmother and tyrannical father, reading for fun in West Point's infamously disciplinary engineering program in which I had the skills of a penguin on a pogo stick, now exposed as an engineering derelict without a coin or a cup to beg one.

The Eschaton, in recent theology, marks the end of time and the beginning of tribulation before the remaking of the world. I was as religious as Fidel Castro, but I now believed that the Eschaton had arrived. It was time to atone before the great suffering.

"You obey Sun Tzu," Schwarzkopf said. "You confuse your enemy." He said it the American way, "Sun TSOO," and not as Uncle Shen would with a precise "*SUN Za.*"

"I have an enemy?" I asked. I thought, besides my parents?

"The engineering faculty suspects you're an idiot, and even though we dislike the idea of failing a Cow, they're getting ready to punt you out. You're in top sections in social science and humanities, where they think you're smart and will write books. Why aren't you studying?"

I made a number of revolting excuses centering on a shockingly cosmic ineptitude in mathematics. When cowardly behaviors fail, I liked to try another serving of cowardice: "Sir, it doesn't do any good. It's too hard; I'm not good at math; my slide rule tick marks are off after I dropped it," etc.

He asked and I answered his logical questions. "So," he said, "you'd hate flunking out. It'd be humiliating to you, your family, and your ancestors. Ergo, you don't study, ensuring you'll fail.

"Prepare to receive a reprimand."

"We're teaching you to work hard." He crossed large, square hands. There were little blond hairs on them. "You might be smart, but you're slack, which makes you a pain in the ass. Now, in truth, I just gave you a damned good reprimand, short, concise, to the point. You should change your ways for all time and get this right. Roger that?"

"Roger that, sir," grinning for his picaresque nature. I forgot he was not my buddy.

He bellowed at me, his exact words lost as they echoed in the library's great tall ceilings. Classmates uttered forms of, "Oh, boy," scooped books, and left, as sergeants are wont to say, with a purpose.

"After Saturday parade, report to my BOQ (Bachelor Officer Quarters), Building 607, Number 39. Bring your materials. Mr. Lee, bring the right ones." He stood. I stood. He left. I'd been in more fights than most and had lost many of the first ones. When I won, my chin was low, knees bent, waiting for vaguely perceived punching alleys, the minor openings between the opponent's guard. I kept moving, like scrambled eggs over a hot flame, driving base foot to the canvas, my body behind short punches, my recoveries quick, without leg quivers. Mine now shook. I sat. My books had lost their luster.

Major H. Norman Schwarzkopf, all 210 pounds of him, reduced from his larger original version by a year of living in Vietnam's boonies, where insects the size of lizards lived on human blood and the lizards were feral, had ordered me to his BOQ during free time. I pictured a small space with books I wouldn't be invited to read. I wished he had grinned to cut that granite expression, to soften his impact as a human avalanche on my vulnerable psyche. He was going to plumb my knowledge of Solids, which would be an exercise of short duration. On the bright side, Saturday was an away game, and spending time with this two-eyed Cyclops wasn't going to cost me a football afternoon. Arturo Torres whispered, "'You in beeg trouble now, Lucy.'"

A thousand of us had taken the oath at Trophy Point, on the banks of the Hudson, to defend the Constitution against all enemies, foreign, and domestic. The Academy grind had removed a third of us, leaving in our little lifeboat the most agile and random fugitives from the law of averages. In this society, I was a super double minority—an Asian who was bad at math—and now I'd pulled the hat trick by being the only one selected to report to an officer's quarters for serious hounding. We had little outside contact with faculty, so Major Schwarzkopf's order was mildly terrifying.

Sun Tzu wrote, *Zhī jǐ zhī bǐ, bǎi zhàn bù dài,* Know yourself and your adversary, in a hundred battles be not imperiled. I researched my adversary. His yearbook reported that "Schwartzie" had been on the varsity football, soccer, and wrestling teams, led the Cadet Choir and the German Club, was in the Weightlifting Club for four years, and had made the maximum rank of Cadet Captain as a senior. In photos he resembled a young and intense John Wayne, the mythic American male: big, strong, smart, confident, dangerous, and unbeatable in a brawl. I was identical to him except that I had failed in football, hated wrestling, feared Germans with a specificity drawn from bitter experience with a member of their tribe, couldn't carry a tune in a wheelbarrow, loathed chapel, and had never been mistaken for a matinee idol. I lifted weights, but knew that wouldn't help. I re-shined shoes and re-straightened my underwear.

Later in life, the tall and courtly Major General Leroy Suddath, a Green Beret 1st Special Operations commander, told me that Schwarzkopf had graduated 43rd out of 480 in their Class of 1956. "He could've been number one or two, but he spent his free time helping slower classmates." Leroy and Norm had been West Point roommates for all four years.

The Hudson Valley exploded in impossible yellows and unlikely reds, creating perfect crisp days for long runs through aromatic, crunching leaf fall. Cadets thought about pretty girls and the freedom to say hello to them; they did not daydream about reporting to huge, angry, hard-ass professors. Birds sang as if they had no homework. The BOQ was in Lincoln Hall, across the great Plain from cadet barracks and the Mess Hall.

In today's service academies, cadets and midshipman can connect with officer sponsors and speak freely with professors. In the 1960s, a strict social caste system sharply separated cadets from officers. Plebes treated upperclassmen as Greek gods and upperclassmen viewed Army officers as hybrid Pope-Presidents. A few cadets from military families had been adopted by military families that knew theirs, but I had never heard of a cadet visiting the BOQ. I was venturing into an inner sanctum. I removed my cap in an old building that needed carpentry and paint. His room was on an upper floor. The stairs complained with little meeping creaks, making sounds that I felt. It was a beautiful day as cadets "dragged" dates, played sports, and took snoring naps. Married officers did their unknown family-related mysteries while single officers were speeding on the Palisades in convertibles with fancy women from Manhattan.

Music seeped from his open door. It lacked lyrics and invited instant slumber, so it had to be classical. I checked my uniform for lint. I cleared my throat to smooth a raspy lung. I had reviewed the unreachable and foreign Solids problem that I'd failed to solve in class.

He was in gray Academy sweats and seemed larger. Big forearms, a watch on each wrist, the one on his right facing downward. He wrote left-handed at a desk designed for smaller humans in a miniature apartment neater than mine and filled with books intended for people with large brains. A small fan busily hummed as it rhythmically riffled ranks of thumb-tacked notes next to lesson plans on his bulletin board. I inched forward to see a tiny corner kitchenette. To the left was a small bedroom. Bookcases lined walls, shelves bowing under the weight of tomes pressed together like hardened subway patrons. I learned that as a major he merited a two-room suite. But he'd already irritated his department chair by leaving West Point to fight in Vietnam in the middle of his three-year TOAD assignment. Upon his return he had been dumped into bottom-feeder cadet sections, given inferior living quarters, and put on bad-duties rosters. I knocked.

"You were pretty quiet. No need to salute in officers' quarters."

I lowered my salute. "Sir, Chinese move quietly. *Ren-che*, one who endures." The term described a fighter that the Japanese would copy and call *ninja*. I was talking too much.

"Have a seat." Without looking up, he pointed at a chair. As a cadet, he'd been a scholar, a three-sport intercollegiate athlete, humorist, and Lothario. Girls and older women in their 20s were pulled to him as if he were a rock star with an English accent. He had the vision to see what most missed while finding pleasure in academics, sports, pranks, and dating. His intellect, force of will, warmth, compulsion for the right and a hidden complexity drew some to him while repelling others. To most, because his personality was so forcefully projective, he seemed an extrovert.

He smelled like all of us, scrubbed from a shower with a splash of Aqua Velva. His small, paint-peeling lair shrank with his presence. He looked at me, hoping for signs of spiritual and intellectual vitality. I looked for food. We were both disappointed.

"Your Regimental Sergeant Major, T.L. Dolonitz, thinks you're a fair squad leader who really cares for his men. That's good. When a tough Infantry sergeant major who beat the Nazis and survived the tragedies of Eastern Europe speaks, I listen. Why aren't you studying?"

I reflected. "No excuse, sir," I said, the practiced Plebe response, delivered truthfully.

"Thanks for a novel, no-B.S. answer. You made me puke with your excuses in the library. Excuses are cowardly, they're not worthy of anyone in the Army, and they induce air sickness." He pulled two sodas from an old vibrating fridge. I drank, glad to use trembling hands.

"We learn how to be from our fathers. What's key in life. What'd yours teach you?" God, it was a horrible question.

I stammered out artificial answers. I heard my sad exaggerations of a non-existent relationship, shuddering with the fumbling. I'd told no one that my father hated me. I hadn't told myself. My father was handsome, charismatic, aggressive, decisive, a naturally coordinated athlete, and fearless. He thought I was ugly, indecisive, and timid; he'd never seen me otherwise. Coordinated in the ring, fast on the track, or competent on the basketball court, in his presence I'd feel his dislike of me and would stammer and trip on shadows. The professor's question, as many that he put to me across the next 47 years, required hard insight. I'd used denial to hide the truth that I wasn't as worthy or as smart as I appeared.

My father, whose invasive Confucian authority had been fused into my deepest consciousness, knew my inner secrets: I disliked him and loathed the physical, emotional, and spiritual brutalities of his second wife, and I had countered his rages by hating my life. I saw achievements—class officer, academic awards, San Francisco *Call-Bulletin* Newsboy of the Month, YMCA Boy of the Year, Athlete of the Year, president of Junior Leaders, unusually well-paying childhood jobs—as miscalculations by others, random accidents or generosities driven by pity.

My father was the deeply resentful, abused second son of a cruel, sociopathic opium addict, and his anger made him virtually unemployable in America. He lacked business level English and lived desperately on sporadic income and borrowed funds with the loneliness of a man without genuine friends. My father had always been physically strong and vital, and he hated my childhood illnesses, surgeries, expensive hospitalizations, fragility and fears, and my nocturnal inability to breathe. I was nine when I got my first paying jobs and began putting cheap food on the table for our sad excuse for a family, and his sullen jealousy pressed down on my diseased lungs and poured bitterness into every small bite of food. He was angry when I spoke American English to the other newspaper delivery guys. He particularly disliked my easy banter with our delivery manager, the delightfully humorous Aaron Liebowitz, who smiled and joked and rubbed the top of my head in the manner of a kind American dad.

I would think, See, this how you can do it! You don't have to hate me! My father desperately wanted to be American, but the majority population rejected him, less for the color of his skin, over which he had no control, and more because of his intimidating hostility, over which he possessed full dominion.

Later, I'd realize that it was natural for him to resent a son who'd been spared the horrors of wartime and revolutionary China, and thought he was miserable merely because he wasn't liked or loved and suffered periodic abuses. My father's father, my *gung-gung*, was the offspring of a nameless, lower-order concubine, and he had taught my father that all humans are unloved. I had never met my grandfather, who had died in faraway China from an opium overdose, but I was his true descendant.

Facing the reality that my father detested me, in this moment in an officer's quarters, I felt as if I'd taken a knock-out blow to the head, feeling a lightheadedness that invited me to buckle and kiss the canvas as if it were my absent mother.

The major had patiently waited while I had fallen into the rabbit hole of my past to find the unwanted truth of the Red Queen.

"My father," he said, "served the Army without ego. He was very successful, really a great man. He didn't measure himself by rank. He just loved to teach us what was right. You know what? It was always about values." Later, he'd tell me about his "Pop," who had taught his son the West Point rule to never lie, to deeply and permanently own the inflexible integrity of selflessness.

Attracted to character guidance, I curiously refused it when offered. "But sir, what we do is about getting ahead, hyper-competitive. We reward winning and individuality, not selflessness."

"That's part of it. And you're good at some of it. For what *purpose?*"

"Sir, to excel."

"Wrong! To *serve*. Mr. Lee, are you trying to be the best for the right reasons? I can see your brains whirling. What are you thinking?"

I took a breath. "Sir, the truth is, I just try to get by, to survive. To not be noticed. Everyone here was a star in high school, so it's okay to just be average."

"Well, let's agree right now that that's bull. Someone pounded Little Man thinking into you. To lead, do the right thing. I fought next to the bravest guys in the world. They weren't trying to survive or just get by. They had guts to do the job right and to care for their men. I saw courage to make the songs of Homer pale. I lost men, praying that my strength could be given to them." His voice suddenly caught; he blinked away tears, his emotions, his penetrating, ineffable grief for men he had lost, uncomfortably reaching me like vapors of a tear gas grenade. He said things that I've now forgotten. He leaned forward. Drawn by a greater gravity, I leaned closer to him.

"It's about doing right and doing it right. Don't go through all this stuff," waving out his small window in his small quarters, "unconsciously, just being a nice guy, trying to be liked. Use your moral backbone to correct your laziness, or you'll be useless to the men you lead. They'll need you to have it when they're in the soup." He stood, stretched a sore back and moved. "It's a beautiful day out there."

He was leaving. I put on my cover, my hat, adjusting it. We stepped outside. As the junior, I walked to his left, traditionally, to free the sword arm of the superior. He was a leftie and I wondered if I should change sides, but we weren't wearing sabers. He had a long stride hiccupped with back and leg pains. He ignored them. I have a long back and short legs, like a rice farmer, and I lengthened my stride, taking two steps to his one. We traced the river to Trophy Point.

"Pop said I was coming here before I knew what West Point was. Then I saw a picture of Trophy Point." We gazed outward. "I turned down other scholarships. The telegram saying I was in came a week before Beast Barracks began.

"A few months ago, in Southeast Asia, facing hard decisions, I thought of two rivers. The Aufidus, now the Ofanto, in the south of Italy, near the Adriatic."

Cannae, I thought. I'd studied the Battle of Cannae and knew it better than I could distinguish a calculus equation from the portion of my anatomy I employed for sitting. His knowing that ancient battle made me think we were similar.

He had read the "Hannibal Against Rome" chapter in the third volume of *The Story of Civilization*, Will Durant's 10,000 page, four-million-word work. The words describing the classic Battle of Cannae became imagined actions in his head. For 2,200 years, Cannae had been studied by all generals in all armies, and by all would-be generals in the Western world. For him, history informed his future.

"The Battle of Cannae, where Hannibal taught all soldiers ever since how to boldly maneuver. And the Hudson, here, where I prepared to soldier. Here, at the river, we made the promise to serve, boys taking the oath of men."

I'd stood here at the end of every semester, each time I thought I might flunk out, trying to imprint the breathtaking and almost hypnotic image into deep memory, in case it was my last.

Cannae—the ancient, classic battle of annihilation. I knew that battle fought by Hannibal by the Aufidus, and felt closer to this intriguing engineering prof who spoke lyrically not of bridges, but of the hard rivers they crossed.

I'd lost some of his words. He was talking about Benedict Arnold. "He commanded Fortress West Point, key to the Revolution. Arnold was our best field commander, brave in combat, oft-wounded, lived big, ate fabulously, married and chased rich Tory women, became a damn war profiteer. And he went totally nuts when he didn't get promoted. Hating Congress, he stood here and saw West Point as something he could sell to the enemy. Right there," he said, pointing to Constitution Island, "is where Arnold ran away to the enemy when his plot to betray West Point was uncovered. Arnold saw neither truth nor the essence nor the right."

So far, the story didn't indict me.

Major S continued, "Washington—George—faced the same view and saw his war strategy: Ally with France, use Fabian tactics, and maneuver constantly until the French neutralized England's navy. Keep the Brits off-balance, but hold the key to prohibiting the British from dividing the colonies, east west and north south—West Point. His quarters were here, on the river, just below us to the south."

I felt the force of his words inside my chest. "Washington wouldn't return to Mount Vernon and his wife until he beat the British Empire or Lord North hanged him for being a traitor. If he could train leaders who could train other leaders, America could win. That was the beginning of America. It was the beginning of this Academy. It started with leadership and it's still about leadership, and it'll always be about leadership and that'll never change. General Washington didn't see his wife for nine years and never considered quitting or making a profit or a name for himself or chasing a pretty woman." He turned from the river. I did, too. "What do you see?"

I quickly ignored the great gray eminence of the Cadet Chapel, which dominated the rocky landscape, and the gray masonry of the main academic building, Thayer Hall. I smiled at the gray mass of the Mess Hall, the new sparkling gray granite Cadet Library, and nodded at the lighter-gray gym. "I like food, the books, and the weight room, and I'd like to get out of here to see the outside world more than once a semester."

"You have the eyes of Benedict Arnold, of ego. Think you can outrun me, Mr. Lee?"

"Yes, sir."

"Don't kid yourself." My heart jumped. I liked his attention, was mesmerized by his will, worried by his raw moral authority, and scared by the threat. What would happen if he caught me?

The major would prove to resemble Ulysses S. Grant, who pursued another Mr. Lee through the Overland Campaign to Vicksburg, Petersburg, and Richmond, across half the continent, taking three years and costing half a million deaths. Teddy Roosevelt said that Grant owned "tenacity, a stubborn fixity of purpose, an iron determination." This was the guy I tried to make light with.

I knew that I admired Schwarzkopf the way all males with father wounds look to wiser men. I wanted to be a man of fiber, able to do the right thing despite, as ethicist Stephen L. Carter said, the "risks to self-interest." I also wanted to defy the major, to not need him, to chart my own course regardless of harm to others, to not need anyone who'd later betray me. I didn't want to risk striving to be better in case I failed for lack of ability.

"See truth, the moral spine," he said. He looked at me as if I were someone from his memory, in a place that held meaning that informed his present thoughts. His mouth grew stern; the meeting was over. I presented arms. He returned it and he strode back to quarters with a unique gait of strength and wounds.

When he was in his 70s, the wounds on a once-athletic body accentuated the limp. His shoulders narrowed, his back ached, and his great arms thinned, and I slowed to keep pace with him. Now, the sun was low and maple leaves danced on empty playing fields. Trophy Point's commanding vista held me. I reviewed what he had said in that hard, male, irresistible voice, my wobbly conscience regretting numbnuts responses to him. I thought of my past and the miracles that had brought me to a new life of promise. I suddenly loved West Point because it was speaking to my better self, and not to the part of my *anima* that had fed cynicism and fear. I loved it because it fed me and gave me friends and kept me from my past. I loved West Point because it gave me a noble purpose, to train so I could be of use to others, to be an American. It was easy to admire the purpose of West Point, and it was easy to resent the effort it demanded.

Tourists took photographs of Trophy Point and Battle Monument's soaring central marble column, of the commanding vista of the river, and of a lone Chinese cadet. A child asked his mother if I was an American; she shushed him. I was light of heart. I'd met an accomplished person; it didn't matter that he was drawn to my weaknesses—that was, in my life, customary. At the YMCA, Coach Gallo had focused on my inability to box, and in high school, Mrs. Marshall had zeroed in on my lack of confidence in writing. I looked upriver, through the dappled, failing sunlight that blinked through arching trees, to the distant Adirondacks from which the Hudson flowed, as if an answer was waiting there for all of us.

I already knew that he was the man I had wanted to become. He was inviting me to employ moral vision in lieu of my deeply held self-interest, my Augustine *incurvatus in se.* Maybe this was the reason I was here, but something told me I was kidding myself: This guy Schwarzkopf could be the most remarkable person here in a community of remarkable men; he's not really interested in you. You drew his attention by being stupid. You idiot. This won't last. If you know anything, you know that.

I headed back to the Company for footballs to throw, baseballs to catch, guys to run with to the Post Movie, cherry cokes to drink in the Weapons Room, weights to lift, and poker and Hearts games to win. We were an assembly of men bonded by stark commitments, the felicities of unified manhood and of shared pain, and afflicted with juvenile cruelties borne by the absence of women. The cool of the shimmering blue river penetrated my light gray uniform and I was surprisingly warm. I loved to play with the guys and had never been happier. I thought that was why I felt light-hearted and strangely optimistic, but I was wrong.

Make Me Look Good

The Master said, "Can you really love the people without urging them on?"
Kong Fuzi

I had probably been looking for a man like Major Schwarzkopf since I was six years old. I imagined what this mythic man would look like: He'd be big, like my boxing coach Tony Gallo, smile like the actor Burt Lancaster, and be courageous, strong, and able to face the tyrants of the world.

Two years before meeting the major—in cadet time, what seemed to be about 50 months—I had been generically preparing to meet Schwarzkopf, the toughest leader I would ever know. I was a lowly and abused Plebe bean-head as West Point prepared us to breach the walls of Troy, burn the towers of Ilium, blind the Cyclops, survive the anger of Poseidon, and best those horrible children of Ares: Fear, Terror, and Discord.

We achieved this by screaming, shouting, bracing, starving, suffering, and by reporting to the fearsome Mr. Albrecht.

"SIR! MR. LEE REPORTS TO HIS SQUAD LEADER AS ORDERED TO STATE THAT HE HAS BRUSHED HIS TEETH AND HAS MOVED HIS BOWELS IN THE LAST TWENTY-FOUR HOURS!" Sputnik could've heard me. Mr. Riley, a very large football player, had resigned in the morning and was probably already home in Philadelphia eating food and hearing my howling. Fourteen incredibly long hours after he quit, eight survivors were repeating our teeth-to-intestines medical mantra to Mr. Albrecht. Given that we wouldn't be allowed to eat more than the equivalent of a light meal a day for 11 months, West Point's focus on dental hygiene and constipation were new mysteries.

We sweated through our fatigues. More accurately, I perspired while the armpits and backs of my Anglo squad mates were being darkly drenched. We were given little water. Were our organs liquefying? Another West Point mystery. It didn't matter; when my squad leader saw my poorly-shined—more accurately, criminally mis-shined—shoes, I'd be out-processed by morning, and Mr. Riley and I could drink all the water in the world and laugh and eat on impulse while trying to decode what had happened to us at West Point

Tall, large, and light-haired, Warren Harry Rudolph Albrecht, Jr., our squad leader, was a Cow and magnificent Cadet Corporal. He was a real-life, flesh-and-blood copy of Sergeant Markoff, the archetypal French Foreign Legionnaire from *Beau Geste* who tried to kill half of each recruiting class to harden the survivors. A squad leader could easily force us out of Beast Barracks back into civilian life. I missed water and food and disliked screaming, but I desperately didn't want to get kicked out. A good Chinese soldier was *ren-che*, the ninja-like one who endures.

He began inspecting us, marching down our line, humming the music of military correction, fortunately finding only minor infractions to be logically remedied by torture. After four days, we were learning to dress and present ourselves as New Cadets and accept that the march of progress had been reversed. On demand, we bellowed the Definition of Leather, Schofield's Definition of Discipline (inspiration, not harshness), the number of lights in Cullum Hall, and other essential data in our strange new world. Our squad leader stopped and looked down, doing a violent double-take, as if he'd seen water, food, or an escape tunnel—my three big hopes. He was studying my shoes the way a sommelier might regard the appearance of yak dung on a French tablecloth. West Point was the world capital of polished shoes.

"MISTER! I SAID use Kiwi polish, soft rag, and a touch as light as God on Adam's finger! NOT BRASSO, A BRICK, AND A HAMMER! Remove your right shoe." I did so. He faced the sweating squad as it vibrated in the rigid Fourth Class position of attention. New York's thick, soupy, cheap imitation of air and its 99% humidity made breathing like sucking steam through a straw. Air-conditioning was unthinkable because it suggested comfort. Hence, the wind never blew from the Hudson; it sucked, and the weather was usually an enemy. Holding a shoe, I quivered at 5,000 isometric micro-vibrations a second in the herniated posture of a New Cadet partaking the late evening and early morning pleasures of Beast Barracks. These pastimes included "Swimming to Newburgh," in which we mounted the room-divider half-wall to simulate the Australian crawl stroke; Shower Formations, in which we wore paper-thin bathrobes and perspired hard enough via screaming Plebe Knowledge under hazing to advance from the ground floor to the fifth including the final test—sweating a nickel to the wall, a feat I never accomplished; Clothing Formations; laundry details, etc.

"Everyone look at Mr. Lee's shoe as an example of what NOT to do."

All did, contorting from the waist with rigid awkwardness while remaining braced—muscularly forcing the throat into the back of the neck. Bracing made us look like lunatics with fence posts nailed to our spines, victims of a train wreck in which we'd all suffered similar orthopedic injuries. We tried to nail our chins to the wall behind us. I studied my remaining shoe, the latest cause of crisis in a life that Cassandra, who could foretell doom, would've recognized. Through fogged glasses, it looked like a pink slip out of the Academy.

"Mr. Lee, stand fast. Squad dismissed!"

"SIR!" we cried. "ALL THAT WE ARE AND ALL WE EVER HOPE TO BE WE OWE TO MR. ALBRECHT, OUR FIRST DETAIL BEAST BARRACKS SQUAD LEADER!" It was a shameless derivation of President Lincoln's famous tribute to his mother and an affectionate way of saying good night to Mr. Albrecht, a sentiment that would not keep him from rousting us at 0300 hours to determine if we were tired. My squad mates quickly exited, relieved they hadn't been singled out to stay in the dark chamber of Torquemada's miseries.

Failure to master the summer skills of marching, manual of arms, spit-shining, uniform alignment, Plebe knowledge, marksmanship, bayonet practice, hand-to-hand combat, or the precise geometric division of an apple pie we would never taste could mean separation. All of my young life, I'd worn scuffed, unshined, cast-off hobo shoes with flapping soles. Incredible. My *yeh*, fate, was that I was going to be kicked out because of them.

Mr. Albrecht looked at me. "What am I going to do with you, Mr. Lee?" he mused.

All questions must be answered. "SIR, I DO NOT KNOW!"

"Ah, Jeez, lower your damn voice! It's 0200, three hours to Reveille, and I'm very tired of listening to 900 stupid little amoebic Dumbcrots screaming at the top of your puny little lungs." He kicked back in his chair, scraping the linoleum floor. He drummed fingers on the desk. He was a shade more than two years my senior, and looked like a fully grown man. My glasses cleared; he looked at his roomie, who shrugged.

"We gotta know," he said. "How come you're not sweating or stinking?"

I stopped myself before shouting the required response. "No excuse, sir," I said.

"No, no, you Smackhead-Crotbean! It's a real question. Answer it."

"Sir, Asians perspire, but not as much as Caucasians and Negroids."

"How the hell would you know that?"

"Sir, may I make a statement?" He nodded.

"Sir, I the hell know that . . ."

"Don't repeat my curses."

"Yes, sir. Sir, I know that because I did sports in an inner-city YMCA for 10 years with white guys and black guys and they perspired more than I did and more than the Chinese guys at the Chinatown Y that we competed against. Sir, may I make a correction?" He nodded again.

"Sir, I meant, Caucasians and people of the Negro persuasion, and the Asians of the Chinatown Y, against whom we competed. Sir, I apologize for the idiom and the dangling preposition." We were to use only proper English. My voice croaked like a frog's.

"No shit?" he asked.

"Yes, sir. No shit, sir." I gulped for repeating the profanity.

They thought for a while. "And you're an Oriental mathematical genius."

"No, sir."

"Don't get modest on me."

"Sir, I am terrible at mathematics. Sir, I am better at English."

"English?"

"Yes, sir."

Mr. Albrecht looked at his watch, sighed, opened his Kiwi polish, poured water into the lid from his canteen, moistened a well-used soft spit shine rag in the lid's water, softly applied a sheen of water to the shoe tip and lightly applied polish atop the water in slow circles. I considered slurping the water in the tin lid, my eyeballs pulled between memorizing his process and gazing at the beckoning water drops atop the open canteen. He explained the technique in workmanlike terms. His roommate finished setting out his freshly-starched khaki uniform for the next day, took a last look at the training schedule, collapsed on his cot, and began snoring.

Now, two years later and hours after encountering Major Schwarzkopf, I lined up the 10 sweating and bracing Fourth Class Plebes of my squad, necks pressed toward spines to produce waves of youthful wrinkles, eyes rigidly fixed forward, chests puffed outward, hips rolled under, hands cupped with thumbs aligned at the seams of their trousers, muscles vibrating in isometric tension, emanating worry and fear. Some did it properly; others, spastically. They had survived the hot wet summer of Beast Barracks and weren't soaking their fatigues; it was September and they were in gray class uniforms with black ties. But the weather was seldom kind at West Point, and they were meeting their academic year squad leader for the first time. They were scared because none were from the West Coast, and he turned out to be a big Chinese man, of an ethnic tribe beyond their experience, and they sweated as if it were July. I was later told that some thought of me as "a terrifying Chinese devil."

They were like the characters from a World War II movie, with an entertaining array of regional accents, body types, big city and small town origins, and contrasting personalities beneath the drenching and difficult Plebe position of attention. Lou Descioli was a guy from Philadelphia who loved sports. Larry Henderson, a fast-twitch kid from Mitchell, Indiana, would become one of West Point's toughest boxers. Bill Malkemes was a sharp, perfectly squared-away Army brat who would captain the tennis and squash teams. Dick Martin was a tall, athletic track man from Springfield, South Dakota. Paul McDowell was a bruiser without a discernible neck from Levittown in eastern Pennsylvania who would become an Army linebacker. Tall and cherubic Tom Page, son of a West Pointer, came from Raleigh, North Carolina, and, like Malkemes, had lived around the world. Tom Rozman was a Connecticut kid who'd had a year of college and exuded an edge that announced he was ready to take on the world. Tim Sauter, also from Levittown, looked like a brainiac. Bill Spracher of Bluefield, West Virginia, had a classic accent in a voice that could sing the nails from the nave of Notre Dame. Last was Steve Wilson, a wrestler from Davenport, Iowa, with shoulders so big they appeared artificial. Underneath the bracing of the 10 new cadets I sensed fear, confidence, anxiety, hunger, sarcasm, humor, and hope.

I inspected them, humming the music of correction, which increased their quivering. "Chin up, mister. Level shoulders. Eyes forward, Beanhead.

Check your alignment. Look down; feet at 45 degrees. Buck up that shine. Press that neck inward. Straighten up; you're canted." I didn't ask them to recite Plebe Poop. I remembered Bue, Ogles, Vikesland, Sepsas, DeMattio, and Tackett, our company mates who'd survived Beast only to be ejected by math, English, or physical education. Dave Bue had the makings of a great captain. I'd tried to tutor him in English, but he was gone after finals. I'd experienced his separation as my fault. Other guys had been understandably undone by focused hazing and had been bounced for excess demerits.

"Knobheads, I'm Mr. Lee, your squad leader. Hard to believe, but two years ago, I was in your shoes, except mine were not as spoony (super-neat and squared-away) as yours. You knew in the Acceptance Parade when the upper classes jumped into your socks that you're in one of the toughest companies in the Corps. That's the bad news. Good news is I won't haze you just to haze you. If you have a real problem, you can bring it to me." I sensed soundless sighs and improved breathing.

"Tonight, I'll teach you Smackheads your academic year duties of Minute Calling, Laundry Detail, Mail Carrier, Sinks Detail, formation responsibilities, and the system standards in A-3. You have to grow up fast and I'll teach everyone twice. After that, you're on your own."

I explained the duties of each and didn't ask if they understood. I could see their brains exploding with the immense load of details. Three of them looked like they might cry. I was already being more than compassionate, but dialed it up even further with endearments.

"Listen, little Dumbsmacks, you can handle all that and I'll repeat the brief tomorrow night. Don't make me look bad. I got enough to carry without having a damn Beanhead problem. You can avoid becoming a Plebe catastrophe. What are your questions?"

The Plebes were too terrified to make a sound. They flinched at an explosion of noise. In the hallway, upperclassmen began celebrating the end of summer leave, military training, and the reunion of the company by beating each other up and drenching each other in water, shaving cream, and toxic deodorant sprays. When I'd heard that ruckus for the first time as a Plebe, I thought people were being murdered.

"Dismissed." The Plebes saluted. I returned the salute. They deepened their intense braces, took breaths, and exited into the upper class maelstrom of the hallway.

"Hey guys!" cried a Yearling, a sophomore. "Look! Gus's Plebes! Fresh meat!"

I thought I was a pretty hot squad leader. I hadn't tortured my Knobheads. I thought I was loyal, helpful, friendly, courteous, kind, and cheerful, not unlike a good Boy Scout. I thought of Major S's lessons and regretted releasing the Knobs into the waiting arms of the upperclassmen.

I opened the door. "Let 'em go, guys," I said. "They got work to do."

I had been crummy in math as a Plebe and almost flunked out. Now, the scary Major H. Norman Schwarzkopf had tried to help me. In like manner, I could help these knobs help each other. I could assign Malkemes to coach the Poop Magnets, the ones who drew hazing. Sauter looked like a Hive, a brain, so I could buddy him up with the ones who shared my lousy math skills. We gave lip service to the concept of helping classmates, but left it to individual initiative.

"Ping Childers," I said to my William Holden—today, Brad Pitt—like roomie, "what do you think of my matching Plebe Goats to Plebe Hives, brains-to-stragglers, the spoony to the gross, right from the jump, instead of waiting for them to get in trouble at mid-terms or demerits?" "Ping" meant drive hard to get it right. In Chinese, *ping* meant soldier.

He thought it was a good idea. I left the room and quickly re-gathered my Plebes. I'd sipped from Major S's magic potion and was trying to help others advance in character through what I would end up calling the Buddy Check. I also thought it would make me look good.

First, Fix Yourself

Failure to cultivate moral power, incapacity to stand by what I know to be right, incapacity to reform what is not good—these are my worries.
Kong Fuzi, Confucius

My Solids professor directed me to return every Saturday either after parade or after the home football game at Michie Stadium, where the Corps stood for the entirety of the contest and screamed until we all sounded like Jimmy Durante. Major S would drill me with mechanics problems, staying with me as I tried to evade his lessons as they became progressively more difficult.

"Man, sit still!" he ordered. "You squirm around like a Vaselined pig."

"Sir, I wish! You are tough to get away from."

Just as I had gone to the library to read what I wanted, I willingly returned to Quarters 39 not for the engineering, but for our talks.

"You know, out there," he said, "the country's changing. In some ways, the change began with the assassination of John F. Kennedy. And not for the better." That had been three years earlier.

"I was at USC," he said, "in a missile engineering class, when we heard President Kennedy had been shot. If I'd chosen astronaut training, I'd have been at launch pad LC 1-1 at Point Arguello. Those guys were locked down in a capsule in a space simulation and didn't find out until three days later that the Soviets were suspected of murdering our president."

"Wow, sir, weren't you like, too large for a space capsule?"

He shrugged. "Lost an inch of height jumping out of airplanes and some body parts in Vietnam, where cockroaches the size of your hand think you're a biscuit. To go into space, I'd have lost another inch." He stood, I stood. "Sit," he said. "Just getting hot dogs. Where were you that day?"

We were high school juniors, listening to a Spanish radio station in language class. Karin Carlson, the bright, lovely, blonde, Grace Kelly-like girl of my dreams, was next to me as we passed notes; it was my apex of happiness in those days. The announcer spoke very rapidly.

"Interrumpimos este programa de noticias: El Presidente John F. Kennedy ha sido asesinado en Dallas, Tejas. . . ." The school buzzer rang: 10:50 am on the coast, Friday, November 22, 1963. Karin and I looked at each other. I said it couldn't be; the words were not to be believed. I asked Mr. Biggi to get an American station. The news was the same. President Kennedy, our charismatic and hugely patriotic movie star president, was dead. He'd inspired the youth of America to serve their country. A decorated combat veteran, he'd visited West Point. His death had triggered a sense of tragedy that continued to cast a pall over bright days. I felt as if the world had ended. Three years after the assassination, the feeling persisted.

"It was an awful, terrible day," said the major. "Had the same feeling twice before—during the Cuba Missile Crisis and when I was a kid and thought Hitler was going to win. Then my Pop went back into the Army and into the war. It gave me hope. I was sure he'd win it for us."

"Sir, you really thought your dad could win World War II?"

He quickly turned at me. I showed a startle reflex and he softened his face. I had the gift of pissing off elders.

Cooking franks and warming sauerkraut enhanced the scents of autumn. Underfed as a kid, I had still loathed Edith's German food. To erase my insensitive question, I tried, "Sir, I used to hate sauerkraut. How come I don't now?"

"Am a chef or a chef? Made the whole pack." He opened the oven. "How many?"

"How many you willing to requisition, sir?"

"Eight each. Then I'm out and we call for pizza." A tremendous idea, beyond the rights of cadets.

"Eight's a good round number, sir."

"It's a damn *big* round number. Works?" I nodded. He cooked the others while dressing the dogs, heavy on the mustard and relish, serving me the first four on an old Melmac plate with a pungent pile of warm sauerkraut.

"Pig heaven," I said. "Good deal, woof-woof! Thank you, sir." I inhaled the first dog.

"Want me to say grace?"

"Umph surekrinashnapayin." I gulped most of the dog. "I mean, Sir, I'm kind of a pagan."

He said grace and I stopped chewing, the uncomfortable words tumbling from my resistant ears. The franks were more digestible than his thanksgiving or his questions.

"Why don't you study?"

I was the rare Asian with a mental block in math and the rarer Chinese from a black 'hood who learned African-American English, ditched Mandarin, and tried surviving with an abusive German mother. I didn't say any of that. I said I had a math block, and held court on its depth and breadth. I also marveled at my easy consumption of once-hated sauerkraut.

"Mr. Lee, that's pretty boring. At least you didn't make me throw up. Barf-bag excuses are boring. A mental block is just a nice term for fear. Working at what you fear builds character. Rationalizations do nothing but make you look puny. Engineering problems aren't the problem. The problem's in your spine."

"Sir, how'd you know I have scoliosis?"

He put down his food. "I didn't. I don't mean that. Talking about you having backbone instead of a *wishbone*. Character, Mr. Lee. Draw the last Warren Truss problem."

Profs would say, "Take boards," and we would rise from seats to scrawl solutions on chalkboards, writing "QED," *Quod Erat Demonstrandum*, Thus Is It Proved, at the bottom when we were done. I'd written thousands of QEDs for hordes of fouled-up problems, with few justifications for the great Latin declarative expression. I redrew the truss problem.

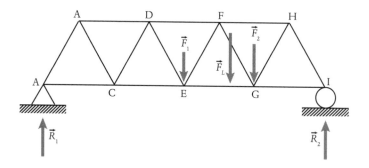

"Struts and beams have zero torsion," he said, "loads on diagonals alternate between compression and tension. Where?"

This was like being with my father as he jammed bad-math juju into my unyielding and superstitious brain and demanded answers, which were uniformly gibberish.

"The center?" I asked. He nodded, drew in loads of 100 pounds at hinge A, 300 at E, and 200 at G. "Now calculate forces at the nodes. Outward or inward? Your guess is inward. It's *outward*. Now, first step in Methods of Sections?"

My face was red hot with fear. I couldn't think and almost panted as vision lost focus.

"Solving three unknowns takes three equations. Make an imaginary cut to isolate the three members for load calculations." He showed me why and where to make the isolating cut.

Sucking in a deep breath, I managed, "Sir, you're showing me how to do the problem."

"Very good, Mr. Lee, a very sharp observation."

"Sir, are you supposed to do this?" Profs gave problems; they didn't bring cadets into their quarters to explain the course and help them learn.

"Okay, squad leader. You got a Plebe that can't write or do a military task. Action?"

"I help him. But we're cadets and that's my job."

"We're leaders and that's *why* it's our job. Leaders help others cure weaknesses so they can succeed. You don't do it to look good. But first, you have to fix yourself. Profs are officers first. We ought to help cadets solve problems because it models leadership. I admit this isn't an opinion shared by many. Now, remove one section. Why?"

"Sir, can you get in trouble for doing this?" I was rattled that one as gifted as Major S was in the minority. I'd gone too far and tightened my neck, anticipating the blow that would knock me from my small chair to tremble on the cold kitchen floor. My father's voice: "SO STUPID! I SHOW YOU MATH BUT YOU NOT DO! I SHOW YOU—YOU NOT LISTEN!"

Major Schwarzkopf surveyed me. His authority resembled my father's, but his nonviolent presence was bright and new and tremendously inviting. He walked me back through the problem. "Why do we remove one section?"

"Because it has bad breath? Sir, I don't know." He looked hard at me. "Sir, I figure I should be driving you pretty crazy by now."

"I've faced worse. I see you drove someone else nuts." He ran his tongue inside his mouth. "To calculate force at the hinge at E-D, we use what function?"

"Sir, Duh." I was sweating.

"Don't mouse-out on me, Mr. Lee. Stay with it." Slowly, with a kindness that came from a different kingdom, he used different words, showing me a method. "Look: carefully. Now get it right."

I peered and I saw it—an undetectable shadow of a black cat frozen in an unlit coal cellar—*nothing*. I wanted him to stop. "Sir, really . . ."

"What's the angle? That's a hint, Mr. Lee." He pointed at the struts with a thick digit, and the mists thinned: an equilateral triangle. Was this just cosine? It couldn't be that simple: adjacent over hypotenuse, angle—60 degrees?

"Cosine. The x part of E to D, the new F2, would be, uh, F2 times cosine of 60 degrees?"

"And the y component?" That strut element was opposite over hypotenuse.

"I think it's F2 times the sine of 60 degrees."

"Good." He drew a new problem. My emotions a jumble, tip of tongue testing the air for predators, I followed what he had just showed, and did it. He clapped me on the back. I was almost knocked from my chair. I was Daedalus in flight, luminous clouds beneath me, the solar orb warming my wings. I remembered that first successful street tussle against Lucky Jerome Washington and pitching a fourth-grade talk in functional English that didn't draw hatred and derision. It was the moment that I shot the game-winning jumper from the key against Poly High, five seconds before the buzzer. I emptied a bottle of Tab, breathing easily without the basal crackle of scarred lungs. It wasn't the soda that cleared my airway; it was his huge left hand hitting me sharply on my back.

"Thank you, sir. But I don't think I could do that again."

"You like to mouse-out, to quit on me."

"Sir, our section, do we really tick you off that much? That first day, you were pretty angry and kept looking at me. I thought it was my fault. Was it?"

He started to speak and stopped. I was going to ask him what he was going to say, but chickened out when he hit his left palm on the desk, and stood. Time to go.

"You're goddamned lucky to get me. Stay close. Learn to get out of your own way. I just might make something out of you."

6

Beware the Past

*The initial trauma of a young child may go
underground, but it will return to haunt us.*
James Garbarino

Major Schwarzkopf was brilliant. He flashed anger at injustice, could scare the socks from 12 cadets with a glance, and made hot dogs like Nathan's, the world-famous Coney Island establishment. He also had a 1965 Pontiac GTO convertible with four-on-the floor and a 389-cubic-inch V-8 with high-rise intake manifolds. Arturo and I eagerly watched muscle car ads on one of the Academy's four recreational TV sets:

"Some sporting cars are only pussy cats; the Pontiac GTO is all tiger. Agile, nimble, with plenty of growl. All wide-track, quick handling, heavy-duty suspension, bucket seats, full carpeting, and even a real walnut dash. Go price one, (sticker price, $3,643) one of the wide-track Tigers from Pontiac, GTO."

Schwarzkopf was the "ideal" man, so, in the manner of the media, I sought his flaws. I tried to blame him for ending our study sessions so he could meet a date in the city, work out, play tennis with officer pals, or study. When he thought of something he couldn't do, such as illegally jump a military flight back to Vietnam, he'd nervously shake his left wrist, rattling the second watch, a black-faced waterproof Rolex, which told the time in old Indochina, 11 hours away on the far side of the international date line, where the Asian moon of long history watched over a tropical land of perpetual war.

"Perimeter security's up and they're starting to un-laager," he'd say. "Sergeant Hung's bitching about something that's not in good military order. I hope they have no casualties."

But if Schwarzkopf were truly an ideal man among men, why would he spend his time with stragglers and academic nincompoops like me?

"Sir, you ever fail at anything?"

He had just asked me an engineering question. He said, "Have you?"

"Sir, more times than I can count. Failure doesn't hurt so much when you get used to it."

He made a face. "I've failed. It's the human condition. Not Malraux's version; more like in the Bible. When I was young, I kind of mucked up things in my family. I was supposed to do things that I just didn't get done. I have a relative I still can't really connect with."

He jangled his wrist. "It was a long time ago." He thought about saying more and decided to save it. Much later I learned about the "It" in *It Doesn't Take a Hero*, the book he wrote after retirement in which he reveals how his mother's alcoholism affected him and that his childhood had been a severe trial.

"Listen, Sport. You can fail in your career and there's not a thing you can do about it. Many of our best colonels never make general. You can be right and get canned *because* you were right. But you don't want to fail when you have to take moral action. The results don't matter. All that matters is that you do the right thing."

Two of my roomies, Steve "Ping" Childers and Jim "Pastor" Adams, were high-character young men who actually honored all persons, including females, with the courage, courtesy, and gallantry conventionally ascribed to an earlier age. They sang in choirs, taught Sunday school to little children, avoided the common temptations of youth, and shrugged off the rebuke of classmates that disliked and distrusted their full array of virtues. Ping and Pastor's high crimes would be uttering a sharp "Darn!" at the point of absorbing a cry-inducing physical injury.

I, on the other hand, had caused my mother's death. My *true* mother, as I referred to Edith Swinehart in those days, had indicted me in such articulate English that I had to be guilty. I'd been plagued by a bully who could hit like Rocky Marciano, was chronically ill and short of breath, but Edith was my torment, my undefeatable Goliath, my irresistible Typhon of the underworld, my negative shadow, my nemesis.

Shielding me from Edith's fury was 12-year old Mary, youngest of my older sisters. Mary had been my surrogate mother for a year while our ailing birth mother, mah-mee, was very sick. Then the Cancer God took our mah-mee and Mary's role became official. Immediately, Edith Swinehart landed as the new Lee *taitai*, Mrs. Lee. My sister hoped for Mary Poppins, but we got Medea, the scary lady who killed her own children. Edith took over our Chinese Christian home with the sentimentality with which the Goths rearranged Rome. Against Edith, Mary had developed a feral stubbornness of spirit that I would later copy. On Christmas Eve, only a few months into her regime, Edith histrionically ordered Mary to leave our apartment for not being complimentary about an unfair teacher. Mary refused to back down on this, or on the real issue, which was her belief in God. Edith wasn't prescribing a Go-to-your-room time-out; Mary was being banished from her father, brother, and home for the rest of her life.

Mary turned to our adult sisters. Seeing now their first hint of the reality of Edith, they viewed Mary's eviction as a boon. They forgot that mah-mee, on her deathbed, had made Mary promise that she'd care for me and raise me to be a good Christian boy, and that Mary was a girl who kept her promises. As Edith pushed her to the door without a coat or a suitcase, Mary turned to our father. He shook his head and left the apartment. I saw very little in the years before glasses, but I later knew that Mary's heart was broken in a way that resisted repair. She looked to her last good hope, me.

Even as a tot, I knew China's *Iliad, Sanguozhi Pinghua*, The Romance of the Three Kingdoms, and the heroism of brave and valiant *ping*, soldiers. I was the six-year old son of a veteran Chinese Army infantry officer and fighter pilot. I stepped up like Guan Yu with his red face and big spear, whose miniature image appears in Chinese restaurants around the world. Edith put her face into mine with a look of such wild malice that I was seized in paralyzing fear, a child inside the mouth of the mythical tiger. My heart and feet stopped. Mary and I looked at each other. Mary had lost her mother and was losing her family. I was supposed to act. I looked down.

When I looked up, she was gone. We wouldn't see each other again until we were adults.

I've been told that six-year-olds can't take moral stands, but they can. My child's conscience clearly knew the right from the cowardly and I grasped with the certainty of pain and the consequences of loss that I had chickened out. Now, I was at West Point, the school founded for people of courage and valor, professionally committed to act rightly in the face of incalculable fears.

★ ★ ★

Norman Schwarzkopf's father was, in no small way, the source of my professor's courage. He had been an American army officer with deep German roots who'd been gassed by the German army in World War I. He married and had two daughters and a son, Herbert Norman, Jr., who later changed his name to H. Norman. The "H" stood for nothing; Norman Schwarzkopf would stand for principles. The father had a refreshing respect for all people of the world and a disarmingly warm smile. Famous for founding the New Jersey State Police and for the arrest of the Lindbergh baby kidnapper, in what was called "The Crime of the Century," he also hosted a popular true crime radio program, "Gang Busters." Like a good part of pre-TV America, Norman and his sisters listened avidly to their father's voice every Saturday night. He hated discrimination and taught his children to surrender bus seats to any adult, regardless of color, and to remember that fate, not merit, had made them Protestant Caucasians, the most popular ethnic flavor in America. "You have advantages," he said. "Never look down on those without them." It was a message warmly repeated by their mother and deeply absorbed by their children. Asians were rare in the Corps of Cadets and Major S was color-blind. Later, he and his boss, a radical general named "Mad Max" Thurman, would make the service more accessible to women.

Norman's father was recalled to active duty for World War II and sent to Iran to build a police force to defeat an ancient culture of banditry, guard the flow of oil to the Allies, and deny that oil to Hitler's marauding Panzer forces. He gave his West Point saber to his young son in a gesture that resembled the accolade, the dubbing, of knights.

World War II would take a hundred million lives; Norman's mother feared for her husband's survival and missed him so profoundly that she self-medicated her depression with alcohol. Emotional terrorism and despair followed, requiring the keeping of secrets and the engineering of sturdy imaginary bridges to a land of pretense. These were moral challenges that required tactics and powers that couldn't be summoned by a child with a commemorative sword.

Norman's dad had commissioned him to be the man who protected the family against all odds. It was an impossible assignment for an eight-year-old. Alcohol soothed, troubled, and then took dominion over his mother and converted a happy home into one of long misery, and left a lonely boy to contemplate the pains of failure.

* * *

I'd bought hot dogs and potato chips but neither of us was eating.

"Sir, the worst thing about West Point? No Chinese food."

He plunked his big feet on his desk. "You live in San Francisco's Chinatown?"

I said I went to a Chinatown evening school after public school for a couple years until I got a food-buying job at the Y. I grew up in a black slum, in today's argot, a ghetto or the 'hood. Becoming a successful black male youth was an honorable goal for which I was poorly equipped. His best friend when he was a kid in Iran was a Palestinian Jew; his best friends in a Swiss boarding school were a French Jew, an Italian-East Indian, and a Czech; his first girlfriend was French.

"So how does a Chinese ghetto kid get sauerkraut?"

I said my mother was German. When she cooked, she cooked German.

"A German mother. You look Eurasian, and you're big for an Oriental."

"Sir, I'm actually full Chinese, with a pinch of Mongol and Manchu from their invasions. No European blood as far as I know." (Much later, my father would reveal that I'd been mistaken, for, to the disgrace of the clan, one of our ancestors had married a French woman) "My German mother's technically a stepmother, but she's my real mother, who raised me, taught me English, and gave me rules, really, better than the other one. The other one was superstitious and ignorant and corrupt and Christian and not very smart." This small passage about my biological mother had become a mantra.

He studied me as if I'd thrown chicken *chow fun* noodles on his desk. He asked a lot of questions.

"Sir, I really don't remember my birth mother. No, my sisters, don't really like my real mother." I was on a roll, speaking about the *verboten und geheimnis*, secrets. "My youngest sister, Mary, really hates my real mother, which makes sense, cause she got booted for being defiant. Now, she refuses to call our father her father, which is crazy."

"Let me understand this. Your youngest sister denies that her father is her father? If you don't mind telling me, *is* he her father?"

I nodded. "He's her father. It's just that when she needed him to act, you know, to be—" I was gesturing, looking for the words—"to do the actions of a father, you know, the duties of a father, he didn't. He ditched her. Just like I did. I was her last, best hope to stand by her."

"And you call your stepmother your 'real mother'?"

I'd made a secret deal with Edith. I thought she was so powerful that God didn't know about it. If I called her "my real mother" and never used those words for the woman who'd given me birth, Edith wouldn't hit me in the face. I promised to not reveal the bargain and to keep other, worse secrets.

I realized I hadn't said anything.

"Right, sir, I call her my 'real mother.'"

"That's a pretty tough family situation. You still speak Chinese?"

"No, sir. I lost it, along with that religion claptrap."

"So you're not Christian, or Buddhist?"

"Sort of Confucian, because of my Uncle Shen. Old Gung Fu-tzu would find a lot to like in the Academy. One of his big things was *Ke ji fu li*, Subdue the self and do that which is right. Kind of like Duty, Honor, Country."

"But you're not a fan of mandatory chapel, which is a form of submission."

"Sir, other than hating it with all my heart, it's okay. Marching to church sucks."

"That's too bad. Chapel helps me organize my thoughts. Whenever I'm in Dutch, I find it very useful."

I made a face; the idea was almost repellent. So he wasn't perfect, and I had found his fault. Strangely, I felt no pleasure in the discovery.

He said he had two older sisters. When he was young, they picked on him mercilessly; they'd rather see the dentist than treat him like a human being.

"Really, sir?" I laughed. "My sisters were the same! They complained about Chinese mothers wanting sons. I can see their point, because male children were favored in China, but it wasn't like it was my fault." I was making excuses. We shared five sisters across Eastern and Western cultures and none had wanted a brother.

"Sir, what was your mother like?"

He took a breath. "Your father pretty tough, strict?" he asked.

I nodded.

"Quick with the belt, was he?"

"Sir, faster with his fists. My stepmother was no slouch. She could punch."

"Well, by God, you did grow up in a German family!"
We both gave small laughs.

Pathfinding neuropsychologist Donald Olding Hebb theorizes that humans are drawn to each other by early childhood patterns of relating. The patterns are powerful and invisible and can be irresistible. Thus can people of similar backgrounds, be they helpful or harmful, magically find each other in a crowded room. Certainly, this occurred with Diane, my beloved spouse, and it informs how I would have natively raised our children had I not undergone a character reformation. That reformation, despite my deep resistance to change, began in Major Schwarzkopf's quarters.

I wonder if early family failures linked the major and me at a level that the radar of the soul understood, creating pings that suggested a connection. He at eight, and I at six, had been given responsibility for dealing with the father's struggling wife. Each of us had failed, and failure had created lasting effects, at least, for me.

I've wondered if my professor's unhealthy childhood lesson made it easier to unleash his volcanic temper at any senior person who might seem to approach the error he had made as a child —the failure to obsessively care for those under one's responsibility.

7

Serve Your People

You can't help someone up the hill without getting closer to the top yourself.
H. Norman Schwarzkopf

Major Schwarzkopf admired Alexander's tactics of ferocity against the enemy more than Napoleon's strategies of world domination. Napoleon, a foot shorter than Schwarzkopf, went to war in Egypt with an academy of 143 scientists, scholars, and savants to lend a scholastic air to invasion and with the adage, *Toute la gloire vient de l'Orient, comme le soleil*: All glory to the East as goes the sun. When Schwarzkopf went to help the South Vietnamese defend themselves in the East, he abandoned the academy to happily sing, *L'audace, Toujours l'audace*, to Alice Cooper's "School's Out": No more pencils, no more books, no more department head's dirty looks.

His one-year captain's tour of duty in Vietnam moved at light speed. He begged Military Assistance Command Vietnam (MACV) to extend his tour, to let him finish the job. The Vietnamese paratroopers he advised were *his* guys. The Vietnamese Airborne was the country's tactical reserve, its rapid deployment force, and they had spent the year moving from one desperate battle to the next. Together, Schwarzkopf and his men had experienced the rare pleasure of continuously landing hooks and uppercuts to a very difficult and elusive enemy who was now on the run; they had created an ideal coalescing of classic, rapid South Vietnamese tactical maneuvering and modern American communications and air support. The relationship he'd formed with his men and with Colonel Kha and Colonel Truong would be very difficult for a new U.S. advisor to replicate, and discontinuity jeopardized the men. In football terms, this was replacing the position coaches for the second half of the contest. But his MACV boss in the backwaters of Saigon wasn't going to confront West Point's prestigious brass, and hadn't Schwarzkopf promised to return? He was told, Get on the damn chopper, now!

If we were inattentive, Major S whacked his unsuspecting desk with a pointer, striking it with such force that it shattered, introducing us to the theory of ballistic shrapnel. A dozing cadet would get a mark from a thrown chalk fragment hurled by the major's formidable left arm.

"WAKE UP, NUMBNUTS!"

We wondered why he was so angry and if he took everything this seriously.

In front of his desk on the display table sat a three-dimensional figure of a pyramid with internal ribbing and struts, a symbol of engineering stability. It was about two feet high. The importance of bridges was incontestable. The relevance of tombs for pharaohs and Amen-ra was less clear. I unsheathed my Decilon slide rule and visualized cuts and moment-arm calculations on struts, ready for Lord Carnarvon's curse and a formation of marching mummies.

Major S pointed at the pyramid's apex with his new shiny pointer. "There are PAVN, North Vietnamese regulars, with Soviet automatic weapons, dug in at the top of this hill. Numbers unknown. You are the rifle company commander. Your mission: Take the hill. What do you do?"

I couldn't help melting a little inside. I'd long groused that since only the top 5 percent of each graduating class was eligible to join the Corps of Engineers, obviously the other 95 percent of us would never use our engineering degrees. But we'd all have to solve tactical problems, and Major S was serving us, teaching us some of the essentials we'd later require. To do this for us, he was willing to welcome hell or damnation—the two natural choices—from his superiors. For the truly slow, such as myself, he was also actually teaching us engineering. It was a breathtaking revelation.

Ross "Wrinkles" Irvin was an agile athlete who would miraculously avoid death in Vietnam, survive catastrophic aviation crashes, and emerge unscathed from other statistically hazardous situations. He suggested that we use the new rage and vogue, an airmobile operation, and we agreed to land in fast helicopters and set a base of fire while attack elements made the assault. We had a number of good plans with variations in details consistent with the fire and maneuver tactics we'd learned and practiced in the wet heat of Camp Buckner, our hyper-intense, two-month field training sequence north of West Point, during the previous summer.

Major S heard our solutions. "They're good and would take the hill," he said. Chests swelled in pride. "But they produce an inevitability of casualties, do they not?" He looked grave.

We nodded. The reality of risks in combat was unavoidable; we'd already attended burials of nine young graduates who'd been our First Classmen. Bob Arvin, our former First Captain, was now, with many of his classmates, in Vietnam, and would join the honored dead before the end of the year. West Point life invited a sense of Chinese fate. So go the fortunes of war. In the Teflon texture of youth, the casualties were never ours and the fear would come later.

"Remember, your soldiers trust you. Their lives are in your hands. They're the most precious asset you possess. Never waste lives if there is anything you can do to prevent it. It doesn't matter if you get in trouble for doing it."

We didn't have pregnant pauses; we employed a wooden male immobility. He was patient. One cadet finally said, "Sir, how do you avoid casualties? What would you have done?"

He smiled, like Burt Lancaster flashing a bright gallery of ivories in "Elmer Gantry." When he smiled, I smiled. "Artillery loves to shoot. I'd call in the big guns to take the top 10 meters off that hill. If I had air support, I'd call in a strike. The rifleman's worst enemy is a lieutenant who sends him frontally against a fixed position. The glory of the Infantry is saving your own people."

Back in his Q, we did Solids problems as I remembered his dazzling smile and gathered fragments of his interesting life. "Sir, we're already scared blind and s---less. Half of us having heart attacks the moment you enter the section room. I don't think you have to throw things and bang things and break pointers."

"In 'The Magnificent Seven,'" he said, "Steve McQueen tells the bandits, 'We deal in lead.' Mr. Lee, be glad it's chalk. And don't use any frigging damned profanity in my Q."

"Sir, I am damn sorry." I asked if he learned to cuss in the Swiss boarding school he'd attended.

It turned out he'd learned creative profanity playing Army football. "Coach (Vince) Lombardi's curses were colorful, inventive, and memorable. I played offensive line and was too slow. He motivated me to get out of the way of our running backs. How do you tell *Coach Lombardi* not to cuss? You don't."

"So sir, maybe I *could* outrun you."

A crocodile grin. "Want to bet? I hope you're not one of those guys who calls Plebes 'smackhead' and 'beanhead' and all that. There're already under genuine pressure. It's not respectful to call anyone names."

I thought I was unnaturally kind to Plebes, and didn't admit that I used those names, but resolved to quit using them. Nor did I tell Major S I was failing Juice, Nukes, Fluids, and Thermo—Electrical Engineering, Nuclear Engineering, Fluid Mechanics, and Thermodynamics—lest he think I was lazy or stupid. Larry Rapisarda and Tony Cerne were tutoring me in Juice, but I was having trouble understanding them. Their mathematical intellects idled at 8,000 rpm while mine red-lined at 500 revs. I couldn't keep up but was too chicken to say "I don't get it" more than 20 times a session. I figured that one of them would knock me out of my chair.

Major S's brain also ran at very high speed, but his father had taught him to be patient with the disadvantaged. The major was the rare genius who understood the pseudo-thinking of the befuddled. He was serving me, helping me think in a way that might change how I behaved. If enough of that occurred, I could become a lieutenant who could save lives that I'd otherwise lose.

I helped others and my Plebes in humanities, in which only a few struggled. Physical conditioning for Plebes was compromised by undernourishment and sleep deprivation. I prepped the Crap Magnets—the Plebes who drew heavy hazing and quill, or demerits—by helping them with spit-shining (mastery per squad leader Albrecht), rifle cleaning (something I learned quickly), Plebe knowledge (memorization—something built into every kid who went to evening Chinese school), and calmness under pressure (not my strength, but practice makes perfect).

To my thinking, the best way I could serve Plebes was to feed them. I had hated Plebe year's deprivation of food which, for me, was the perfect expression of your-worst-phobia Room 101 from Orwell's *1984*. As Plebes, we'd be required to cut our meals into small bite-sized portions, fit them into empty milk cartons, and then pass them down to the end of the table to be discarded as garbage. Most Plebes in First Regiment lost 20–25 pounds while those in the easier Second Regiment lost less. I'd been saved by a few weeks on the gymnastics team training table, where eating was permitted, but after Coach confirmed I could only do lousy minimums on the high bar, I was back on the involuntary weight-loss program of company tables. A gigantic, broad-shouldered, soft-voiced Firstie ex-football player with pre-dictably bad knees named Bill McCreary was consistently compassionate to the hungriest and weakest of us. On Sundays, when he, as a Firstie, could've left Post to party in the city, he attended his non-mandatory breakfast and lunch to create a safe table at which nine hungry Plebes could eat. It had kept me spiritually alive.

Now, on Sundays' optional meals, in the absence of the Firsties, Ping, Arturo, More Beer, and I commandeered a couple of tables and fed the hungriest Plebes to satiation. This did not go unnoticed by the Tactical Department, which figured that if pain was good, torture was better, and that we were acting like a Sons of Liberty humanitarian relief organization. Our tactical officer, the Tac, had corrected me for laxity with the disciplining of Plebes. Arturo had suggested caution, as I was a ranking junior and acting table commandant.

"There are other guys feeding Plebes," I said defensively.

"*Sí, hermano*," said Arturo, "but those guys, let us remember, they are all Anglo."

"I'm Anglo and I'm being watched," said Ping.

"We're just serving some guys," I said.

"Literally," added More Beer, passing more cold cuts to the ravenous Fourth Classmen.

"Men," I said to the food-stuffing Plebes, "what do you love most about Woo Poo Tech, Hudson High, Army School for Boys?" It was in all-male days and we thought we were witty.

They hurriedly swallowed. "Sir," said Steve Wilson, a big, scholarly, gruff-voiced Iowan and champion wrestler with the squarest shoulders in the Corps of Cadets, "I love the general party atmosphere and the friendliness of the upper classes!"

"A cheery thought, Mr. Wilson. Next."

"Sir," said Mike "Poo Bear" Bain, a pleasant and frighteningly brilliant Army brat, wrestler, and linebacker who resembled Clark Gable, had lived around the world, and had a tendency to smirk when it was most danger-ous, "I admire the deep intellectual freedoms, the wide variety of academic majors, and the ability to study pre-med so I can become a physician!"

Involuntary laughter—a capital crime for Plebes—rippled across the table. But the idea of a West Point graduate becoming a doctor was a knee-slapper.

"Good one, Mr. Bain!" I said.

"Mr. Bain," said Ping, "I believe you're confused. We don't heal—I think we're at the other end of the business."

"However, gentlemen," I added, "Mr. Bain's humor was sufficient to earn you a fall-out."

The Plebes sighed, relaxed from the stiff position of attention, and released their necks from bracing. Their happy smiles stretched flesh and could've lit the moonless night.

Mr. Bain was seriously committed to the study of medicine. He bought the textbooks of a pre-med curriculum and studied them independently while maintaining near-perfect marks in West Point academics.

While Mr. Bain studied organic chemistry, we did athletics and parades while avoiding the Inquisitions of the Tactical Department. I kept read-ing recreationally, playing cards and sports, and reveling in the sweet, deep, oxygen-rich distance from my past.

Outside the Academy, miniskirts became popular; Ronald Reagan was elected governor of California; Simon and Garfunkel released "The Sounds of Silence;" cigarette packs had to carry health warnings; protests against the war in Vietnam grew while support for the war was plummeting; and a young Ba'athist former chief of security named Saddam Hussein, sentenced for attempting to assassinate the president of Iraq, began to recruit his new security apparatus from the prison population.

Love the Ones You Lead

*The skillful general conducts his army as if he were
leading a single man by the hand.*
Sun Tzu

Lindbergh's solo flight across the Atlantic, his marriage to the glamorous and much envied Anne Morrow, and the birth, kidnapping, and murder of their only child had become worldwide headline items. My parents had read the tragic news of Baby Lindbergh's death in Shanghai. The elder Schwarzkopf's solving of "The Crime of the Century" placed him in the public mind above Sherlock Holmes, Lord Peter Wimsey, and Hercule Poirot as the world's most eminent criminal detective. Although absent during the Second World War, he must have easily deduced that young Norman was barely surviving their emotionally troubled home in which his gender was proving to be a disadvantage. He thus allowed his son to leave the majestic trees and ivy-covered Lawrenceville stone house to attend Bordentown Military School in Trenton, New Jersey. Trenton! Where Washington's barefoot farm lads had crossed the icy Delaware and whipped the Hessians. Bordentown, a school for young men, had been Spring Villa Female Seminary until 1881, when Reverend William Bowen turned it into a more profitable military school. It operated with great success until the Vietnam War made military education unpopular.

It was late Saturday afternoon and I expected Major S to stand, stretch his back, and say, "Sport, time to go." We had done the engineering. I was torn between wanting to know more about Vietnam and asking him for food.

He stood. I stood. "Relax," he said. I sat again in the hard chair by his desk. He looked out his window, six or seven feet from me, his mind far away. He began to share fragments from his tour as an advisor to the Vietnamese Airborne.

After Captain Schwarzkopf had been in the bush for a few weeks, he discovered that he no longer stank like an American, a westerner.

He'd eaten green leafy *cai lan, com,* and *nuoc mam*—amber sauce of fermented anchovies and sea salt—and exuded a kinder, neo-Asian sweat. In triple canopy jungle, scent from French Gauloises cigarettes, American Old Spice, or wet Caucasians could broadcast position. His mind was adrift.

Schwarzkopf, he said to himself, snap to! You're the only American in this line of march and you're slipping in this damn mud like Porky Pig in slop. Show off your flashy education and do something impressive—get your candy ass up this muddy hill.

They'd ambushed the enemy and he'd lost one of his soldiers. He winced when he thought of the young trooper's wife. He didn't like body counts for the rear-area Saigon mafia, but he couldn't disobey all his orders. He and his counterpart, Lieutenant Colonel Kha, a devout Catholic and superior tactician, saw that the enemy weren't VC, Viet Cong. They were People's Army of Vietnam, or in U.S. lingo, NVA, for North Vietnamese Army regulars. In the major's mind, they were invaders, no less so than North Korean *Inmingun* when they infiltrated into South Korea or East German *Nationale Volksarmee* troops entering West Berlin. Although the government of South Vietnam had garnered no recognition as an exemplary democracy, they had needed U.S. intervention to survive and had invited the American presence in their country. (Later, U.S. forces would enter Cambodia, but would withdraw after their incursion without seeking to overthrow its government.) They were matching, from Hanoi in the north, every American soldier coming across the Pacific, which, because they were seasoned fighters, tended to neutralize the American buildup. U.S. advisors were reporting this but Schwarzkopf wondered if anyone was really getting the picture in the Pentagon.

"*Nuoc,*" said Sergeant Hung, offering a full canteen to the major.

"I almost leaped at it. I liked being called *Trau Nuoc,* Water Buffalo, which was my nickname because I could empty a canteen in one long swig."

A "water buffalo" was also the affectionate term U.S. soldiers used for water point tanks and Lister bags. "I was drenched in sweat. Two hundred Vietnamese eyes were on me to see what I would do. Well, I was their advisor and they were my soldiers and we were now very short on water. I declined the canteen."

Stopping, they set a perimeter that he checked as officers and non-commissioned officers (NCOs) cared for the wounded, cleaned weapons, repaired feet, and shared pickled *cai lan* broccoli and *rau mong* water spinach in fish sauce made more dense by evaporation. Rice from canvas bandoleers went in a common pot as they ate cross-legged by squads. He and Kha walked the perimeter, joking with the men about the quality of the communal rice. He and Kha were last to eat. He later worked on his rotting infantryman's feet.

"I loved everything about it. There are two types of soldiers. Those that want to be in the action and the rear area types. (They were called REMFs, Rear Echelon Blankety-Blanks.) In the bush with Kha and Truong and the guys, I was miles from the rear area brass who were more interested in career advancement than in getting it right with the fighting.

"We knew warfare out there. We'd studied Sun Tzu and Clausewitz and Jomini. My guys out there, Colonel Kha and Colonel Truong, had read Napoleon in French and knew more Latin than I did. We knew that you gotta be decisive and win fast. The enemy wants to drag things out until we run out of political gas and the rear area was supporting the drag-out. Everything the brass said to me triggered my anger and my disapproval and made me question my ability to be a career officer. To them, I was a rebellious officer, ungrateful for being offered a position of safety in the rear. You know, William Tecumseh Sherman would've booted them out of the army."

Demosthenes orated that soldiers who maintain discipline while under enemy fire become *homothumadon*—of one mind and heart. *Homothumadon* is a spiritual furnace in which individuals can be fused together by a life commitment to a true higher moral purpose. Without knowing that word, all effective leaders seek to create *homothumadon*.

Major S said that he looked at the tough, tired, but upbeat Vietnamese paratroopers and admired the hell out of them. They'd volunteered to protect their country, eaten from common pots, fought shoulder to shoulder, bled together, and lost brothers against an enemy who was assassinating and beheading their village leaders and families. They died for each other and they were his men, patriots who leaned on him. He spoke few of their words; most dialog was in French. They'd committed all to the fight: sacred honor, lives, and families. Because of shared combat, he felt a pride in them he'd not experienced in the company of American troops.

He would later say that he was bonded to them like no others. He felt he couldn't leave them and wouldn't leave them. He thought that his boss would see that keeping him there, with what he'd learned, with the relationships he'd formed, would save lives. He'd earned Vietnamese Master Parachute wings and had been wounded, both events wrecking his already questionable back. He knew from the beginning that he could soldier. But the question was: Could he keep his damn mouth shut with rear-area types who never got muddied or bloodied and never lost a man? Could he take orders from an ignoramus careerist who won't listen or learn? What job could he do that doesn't require honesty?

American soldiers were taking over the war while criticizing the Vietnamese, who had been in the soup since the French invaded in 1884. In between, they had fought and stalemated the Japanese army that had defeated the Koreans, Chinese, British, Australians, New Zealanders, Americans, Filipinos, Malays, Singaporeans, Hong Kongese, and the islanders of the Western Pacific. The Vietnamese knew war the way Moses knew the law, but many American officers that Major S encountered scorned their skills and called them "gooks."

He'd snap, "Don't say that! They're our allies. They've been fighting for a hundred years and their enemy's being supplied by Russia." This generated neither agreement nor affirmation. The more the United States assumed responsibility for the war, the more Americans disenfranchised and discounted the Vietnamese for not carrying more of the fight. It was a puzzling American dynamic. How could a nation composed of immigrants look down their noses at people of another land?

Even after the Army of South Vietnam, the ARVN, proved unable to match the North Vietnamese forces, with units being overrun, fighting poorly or fleeing battle, Schwarzkopf maintained that U.S. policy, by assuming control of the war, had unintentionally doomed South Vietnam to become fatally dependent upon the U.S. Army formations and our artillery and air power.

"It's always about leadership, political and military. You need both."

He said that studying a muddy stream, he thought of the Hudson, where the great bosom of American military experience had been planted. He thought of the Aufidus River and of Hannibal's historical battle.

Major S would later say that he wondered if in the nuclear age of guerilla warfare he could ever lead a coalition army and pull off an envelopment against a tyrannical force. It did not seem likely.

"Cannae" with a question mark added sounds like "Can I?"

Major S turned from the window. "Vietnam was the best year of my life. I ate fish in fish sauce, slept with *serpent en boue*, fought for weeks *sans eau, nourriture ou renforts*. (He told me that the French meant he slept with snakes in the grass, was continuously without bath water, reinforcements, and effective resupply.)

"I smelled bad—German Euro-stink. But after a bout of malaria, a good heavy dose of jungle rot and dysentery, and a rice-and-fish-balls *nuoc nam* diet, I *became* Asian. Hell, I even almost smelled Asian.

"I was closer to those guys than anyone in my life." His eyes were wet. "I loved them. I refused to leave them to come back just to teach a bunch of cadets. No offense, but lots of officers want this kind of duty. I didn't. MACV ordered me out. I don't do well with rear-area types. Well, I did give my word to West Point."

He paced, ferocious, caged. "I hate being here!" He glared, then calmed himself.

"Sorry, sir," I said. "I wish I could go with you. I'd rather be there with you than studying engineering here. Sir, we're together 'cause I kind of remind you of your men."

He shook his head. "You're here because your study habits are stupid as shark poop, so dumb it settles to the bottom of the sea. You're closer to Gomer Pyle than to one my paratroopers." He smiled and I laughed. "No, all I'm doing with you is matching strength to weakness."

"So, sir, I guess I can't put a QED on my deduction," I said.

"Enough lessons. Time to go, Gus."

I went down the stairs of Lincoln Hall. He had called me by my first name.

Do the Right Thing—
Regardless of Risk to Self

*Make us to choose the harder right instead of the easier wrong, and
never to be content with a half-truth when the whole can be won.*
Colonel C. Wheat, West Point Chaplain, 1918

Struggling with his alphabetically demanding name, Major S became for us The Bear, the towering ursine carnivore who could jolt the most indifferent cadet into deep caring, the Calvinist who'd declared war on the sin of sloth, and the spear-carrier who could tackle a rhino and cook it for lunch.

The section took seats in the windowless classroom, ready for him to examine us, explain the universe, or make flames suddenly leap from our heads. The common hope was that we'd survive the writ and he'd reward us with answers to the mysteries of life.

He sat on the edge of his desk; we flashed fast smiles and looked at each other in micro-glances. A life lesson instead of the exam. He's not going to give us the daily writ!

"Listen up. We do engineering proofs. Today, we're going to do leadership truths to pack meat on the idea that we lead by example."

Leadership truths. We perked up. He wrote on the board:

**FIRST PRINCIPLE (we'd learn it was the only one):
IT'S ALWAYS ABOUT LEADERSHIP**

"This is the first principle. It's *always* about leadership. Now, leaders need two things: character and competence. Which is most important? Who says competence?"

Most raised hands. Those who knew I'd been holed up in his Q watched me.

"Who says the most important is character?" The rest of us raised hands.

"That's right. Character means you have to do the right thing *all* of the time. Character guarantees competence because to do the right thing, you must acquire and develop your competence.

"But it doesn't cut both ways: having competence does *not* guarantee character. I know officers who use intelligence and proficiency to lie, steal credit, slack off, gossip, cheat on their wives, and blame others. Officers without character are a real threat to their troops and to the mission; it doesn't matter how brainy and hard-working they are. Their lack of character will eventually break them. I'd rather have a dumbass who has the character to learn than a self-centered genius. It's always about leadership, and leadership is always about character."

He let that sink into our still-developing male crania, which we would later learn do not achieve full growth until 25. My few available and youthful neurons were at attention. I didn't like it, but my conscience said he was right. I reluctantly wrote: Character First.

"Without character, you're bound to become self-loving show-offs or officer blowhards." He glanced at one of us who liked boasting. "Care so much about your soldiers that you get yourself right. They see you stop your worst habit, they'll be inspired to stop theirs and to do their jobs better just to please you. If you have high character, that means they'll in time do the right things on their own.

"Here's a trick: You have to cure yourself really fast, but be patient enough to let your example of doing right slowly permeate into the minds of your soldiers. You have to be faster than they are in self-repair. So be patient as hell." He smiled. "Like me, with you."

I knew he was right because I felt instantaneous guilt about card games, horseplay, recreational reading, mooning about lost love, and about becoming a professional in feeling sorry for myself.

"You know what doing the harder right is instead of the easier wrong." A line from the Cadet Prayer, which we'd memorized as Plebes. Part of it said,

Strengthen and increase our admiration for honest dealing and clean thinking, and suffer not our hatred of hypocrisy and presence ever to diminish. Encourage us in our endeavor to live above the common level of life. Make us to choose the harder right instead of the easier wrong, and never to be content with a half-truth when the whole can be won.

"You need fine judgment to know the harder right. You get that judgment by practicing and by learning from errors. Character comes from practicing good judgment until you get so good at it you can teach it to others. Right, Mr. Lee?"

"Yes, sir," I said, stiffening. Section seats were hard; mine was becoming painful.

"Fact is, we intuitively know the right thing, but we need judgment to see the harder right thing and then build up the guts, the moral musculature, to do it.

"The first principle is, *it's always about leadership*. Here's Schwarzkopf's Two Laws of Leadership. The First Law is, use your fine judgment to do the harder right thing. Doesn't matter what it costs. Do it *whatever* it costs. For a leader, it means taking care of your people." His mouth was set hard; his lips disappeared. He wrote on the board:

FIRST LEADERSHIP LAW: DO THE HARDER RIGHT WHATEVER IT COSTS

Later, I saw that "judgment" meant moral reasoning, and would replace it with the verb, "discern." "You *will* follow the First Law, no matter how hard it is on you." He nodded at Dave "Snake" Sackett, who nodded back. He faced each of us in the U-shaped configuration of desks. Each of us nodded. We had gone from the high pleasure of no daily writ to a deep solemnity about becoming leaders. The Bear's fierce commitment to make us advance our character was seeping into our chests.

It's always about leadership.

"You're not here to have a fat college experience and drain kegs and endanger girls who come in range. You're here to kill your egos—*ergo* Beast Barracks and the Honor Code and Buckner and the Cadet Prayer and Cadet Chapel and the Tactical Department and all the discipline and the hard regs and the rest of it.

"Schwarzkopf's Second Law: Leaders *take responsibility*. Can't lead if your people distrust you because you're there for yourself. Give all credit, take all blame, and take all the heat. If there's bleeding to be done, don't make them do it— you do it." He wrote:

SECOND LEADERSHIP LAW: TAKE NO CREDIT. TAKE RESPONSIBILITY.

"Will you do the Second Law and take responsibility, no matter how much you want to avoid it, no matter how much it hurts?"

We nodded. I wrote down the two laws. I neatly underlined them, boxed them, and drew a light bulb next to each. I remembered to write: It's always about leadership.

"Leadership is *do the right thing* and *take responsibility*. I don't care what anyone else says. We have a lot of psychological mumbo-jumbo taking up the leadership space. I'm not giving you claptrap and I'm not giving you suggestions. I'm giving you *laws*. Leadership isn't a style. *Styles* change.

"What are your questions?"

"Sir," asked "Snake" Sackett, our fearless leader, in his careful and methodical West Virginia voice, "if the first principle of leadership is that's it's always about leadership, what's the second principle?"

Major S grinned. "There is no second principle. Just the first." He saw our confusion. "If it helps you, the second principle is Do the right thing and take responsibility."

"Sir, what's the difference between a truth and a principle. You sort of used them interchangeably, there."

"Principles are based on everlasting truth. The rightly lived life—getting it right—is based on principles. Principles don't change like styles do. Laws uphold principles.

"Stagger desks for writ. Men, it will be a bastard."

It was.

Later, in his Q, he pitched a hard problem. I figured the solution without his help. I felt so good that I whooped around his Q, dodging his lamp, and doing a victory lap around his furniture as if I'd taken the checkered flag at the Monaco Grand Prix, with the laurels, prize money, champagne, and press releases to come. If I had a voice, I would've serenaded him with Roger Miller's "King of the Road."

He laughed, "Easy, Sport." I liked amusing him and considered doing one of my three magic card tricks. "Why'd I teach you how to do these problems?"

"Sir, to help me climb out of Section 8 and save me from an ejection seat so I can become secretary of state and inspire the peoples of the planet to ditch communism and adopt world peace."

"What's Schwarzkopf's First Law of leadership?"

"Sir, Schwarzkopf's First Law is do the right thing and care for your troops, regardless of risk to self."

"Right! And Schwarzkopf's Second Law is take responsibility. You learn skills to teach them to others. Today, it's Solids for bottom-section classmates. Two years from now, it'll be caring for your troops and their health and welfare. Character takes practice. Practice brings change. No practice, zero change."

"Sir, so I've just been a tool to get more cadets to know this stuff? You've been bribing me with hot dogs to make me into a hive tutor?" Hives were hard-studying cadets, busy as bees at perpetual work.

"Sport, you've just decoded my Laws. If you're ready to practice teaching it to others, have a potato chip."

His work with me was not for me alone. I was but a conduit to others. I liked it while not liking it; a good part of me wanted this remarkable officer just for me. But it was a great potato chip, full of taste, loud and crunchy, and very salty. As I returned to barracks, the saltiness dominated.

10

Love Them No Matter How Hard

He who is not content with what he has would not be content with what he wants.
Socrates

Ping Childers and Jim Adams held fast to what they called blessings. I should've focused on needs—curtailing recreation and improving grades—but I focused on what I missed, Chinese food and suffering for the girl of my dreams.

The great task of life is choosing the behaviors by which we should live. This is easy in America and a breeze at West Point, where unlimited servings of honor and ethics are in the water supply in Rusk Reservoir and in very air that one inhales while catching one's breath from a state of continuous effort. But in what the Bear's father had called the battle of life, I meandered as a sun-seeking beachcomber armed with flip-flops. I did each day without toughening my virtues and, apart from divine osmosis, without a plan to acquire them. I well knew the concept of the self-disciplined heroic ideal, and was at West Point, the cosmic fitness center for character, but I lacked intentionality to develop it on my own motion.

My true core values were Food, Avoidance of Pain, and Play. I liked tossing footballs and baseballs, unaware that habits are moral boomerangs. While moral discipline requires constant tending, character indifference knows no bounds.

In the decisive measures of life, character and personal values, H. Norman Schwarzkopf and I were opposites. But we shared key family features and an interest in history, which we began exploring as the academic year progressed.

He rubbed a healing shoulder wound. "In Vietnam, patriarchs run families and villages. A Vietnamese woman, a remarkable, very well educated young woman, told me that Chinese culture influences Vietnam. Are Chinese families the same as the Vietnamese?"

So, he had a Vietnamese girlfriend. I stopped myself from asking to see a picture of her. I had no photos of my other mother or my sisters.

"Sir, like I said, my family's probably more German than Chinese."

He laughed. "Your German stepmother."

"I was a kid when we stopped being Chinese. My real mother doesn't speak Chinese, so I no longer speak Chinese. What I know about real Chinese families comes from reading and an uncle who drilled Confucius into my head."

"So do you think that Chinese are mostly Confucian?"

"With Buddhist and Taoist strains. China absorbs invaders and turns them into Chinese, like, to use a scientific example, *The Invasion of the Body Snatchers*. So I have Mongol and Manchurian blood. The Goths gutted Rome and its culture; China's invaders just took over the government and social system and the best land and ran everything as if they were Chinese."

"Genghis Khan didn't destroy the Chinese Empire?" He leaned forward.

"Right, sir, he didn't. His grandson, Kublai Khan, became the new emperor of China, naming his dynasty the Yuan. Chinese culture was considered the center of cool back then; Japan and Korea are variant copies of traditional Chinese culture."

"And Chinese and Vietnamese families are similar."

"Although they hate each other. A big difference is Chinese families are based on *jia*, the clan, a bundling of extended families. A girl marries a son of a *jia* and is bolted on as a laborer. *Jia* raises the children and organizes labor. I think Vietnamese families are based on the village and they raise their kids that way, which is radically different. Makes it harder for them to emigrate."

"Do traditional Chinese clans believe in romantic love?" He was always serious; now he looked unusually serious.

I shook my head. "It's in the poetry, sir, but it's not lived out. A matchmaker, *chih huo*, finds the spouse the clan needs, like an herbalist or a scholar—and always, it's about money and beauty. Matchmakers get big commissions for those matches. Confucius had Three Followings: A female

Chapter 10 · 61

follows her father in childhood, husband in life, and firstborn son as a widow because men die first.

"A woman's big emotional relationship isn't with her husband or son and definitely not her daughter, who gets married off. Her big relationship is with her mother-in-law, who's kind of like her First Sergeant for the rest of her life. They'll work together until one dies."

He recoiled. "The mother-in-law! Sure about that?"

"Sir, it's normal. Some Chinese girls I knew wouldn't marry a guy unless they liked the mother."

"You mean, in China," he said.

"Sir, right here in the USA. Well, in Chinatown, San Francisco, USA."

"Your parents, were they in an arranged marriage, and who married up?"

"Sir, I have no idea. It's weird, but I really don't know much about my family." Such questions had not been allowed.

Major S was the only son and last-born child of a combat veteran. He had a disabled mother and older sisters who disliked having a brother and a painful political conflict with an older sister. I was the only son and last-born child of a combat veteran with a long-dead mother and older sisters who resented having a brother and I had painful political relationships with older sisters. My *Gung-gung*, paternal grandfather, had lost the family fortune and his own life at a young age to opium addiction and his family was under the shadow of alcohol. We were bachelors with German mothers and bad backs, he from being a wounded paratrooper that would soon land him in surgery and I from scoliosis, which had assigned me to the Posture Correction Program. We lived in small spaces, woke every morning to the same big booming cannon and happy little military band, and knew something about history, Asia, and family conflicts.

Mah-mee and my sisters had survived China's long civil war and Japan's genocidal invasion. As young girls fleeing bombings, death, and rape, they had seen that which no adult should witness and had lost what no child should surrender. Our father, a professional soldier and fighter pilot in Chiang Kai-shek's weakened Nationalist Army, had abandoned our family to try to kill Mao Tse-tung by bombing his position in the Jinggang mountains of Hunan, then to travel the world on secret diplomatic and military missions, working with American soldiers in the war, as well as to consider other women, with a preference for Hollywood actresses.

My sisters hated war, disliked our father, and logically feared soldiers. Believing that Heaven had failed to live up to its promises after our devout Christian mother's death, one had lost faith while the other two had never taken to the concept of a caring God. Each was unusually smart, uncommonly beautiful, oriented to liberal politics, and as fixed in her opinions as Sisyphus was to his rock.

I like to think that if our father had been kind, they'd have emulated him and joined the Army or the Marines. But when he added intense disdain for family to his deep love for the military during the worst war in history, my sisters became passionate pacifists, a commitment that would deprive both the Army and the Marines of three enviable fighters.

When the woman I called "my other mother" fell ill with cancer, she asked 12-year old Mary to raise me, making her a child missionary in a black 'hood to care for a crying, legally blind, and lung-sick Chinese baby brother.

When the Bear's father left for the war, he tasked his eight-year-old son to care for the family, making him a parent over three females superior to him in age, height, experience, education, and strength. One was his mother. After the fragmented family failed to thrive, he was providentially given the opportunity to live in boarding schools and to join his dad in Iran.

Mary was exiled to Minnesota, where our 23-year old firstborn sibling, Elinor, gave her sanctuary. Because my new mother didn't like children, I was six when I was tossed daily into the all-African American streets of the Panhandle of San Francisco to become bully bait. After a nasty pounding, I was befriended by a smart and tough ball player named Toussaint Streat. "Too" was my first friend. He taught me to walk, strut, talk, play ball, and deal with verbal violence, but I couldn't street fight. When I was seven, a garage mechanic named Hector Villanueva pressured my father to send me to the downtown YMCA for deliverance. Three coaches taught me to box six days a week, and a lovely YMCA café manager named Lola fed me. By 15, I no longer was a toothpick in a tutu and looked pseudo-athletic. With a miraculous late telegram from West Point, I packed a suitcase and left with the jubilation of the Hebrews departing the brickyards.

My older two sisters were distant in geography and in politics and disliked my going to West Point for every reason they could find. Elinor had little confidence in our father's judgment and had learned in China to fear and distrust soldiers. Middle sister Ying, an admired school teacher, was married to a brilliant, left-leaning Berkeley mathematics professor. She later became a leader in the anti-war movement, a political activist for women's rights and the anti-nuclear movement, and became a city councilwoman. In lieu of my becoming a soldier, I think she would've preferred that I'd enrolled at San Quentin to study Karl Marx in the relative safety of the prison library.

I returned to San Francisco on periodic leave to learn from Ying how wrong I was. Ying had generously become my dearest sister, and disagreeing with her was very painful. With my sisters, it became easier to avoid politics.

While high school buddies who didn't go to a four-year college remained patriotic, I disliked the hostility of university peers who celebrated a growing hatred of America. But the deeper hurt of the anti-war movement centered on Karin Christine Carlson. I wanted her approval. During high school, I'd often walked by her house to sit on the sidewalk and hyperventilate. I failed to win her romantically, so I settled with being her close friend. Her boyfriends inevitably were basketball teammates and buddies, and abiding those relationships required Oscar-level acting to present what I thought was an adult attitude.

She accelerated graduation and was at Cal Berkeley, leaving me behind in high school. My love of high school was dimmed by her absence. She should've been next to me in Social Studies when the telegram arrived informing me that I'd received a congressional appointment to the United States Military Academy at West Point. Congressman William Maillard's message announced more than a college scholarship: It was my entry into the American middle class, the group that celebrated Christmas, supported Boy Scouts, gave free food to poor families, and saved China from the Imperial Japanese Army. They were healthy and ate regularly without relying on child labor. They were the ones with good lives. Instead of enlisting in the Army, for there were no funds for college, I could go to a school intentionally designed for *Táoyě qingcāo*, to forge character, repay America, and become, in turn, fully American.

I was going to the modern Lyceum of Aristotle, the Confucian *Wen-lin*, the Forest of Pens of China's greatest scholars, and the Spartan *agoge* warrior's training forge, in which individuality and selfish will would be nobly exchanged for public service. Our school celebrated, the faculty applauded, I got flirty looks from pretty girls who before had ignored me, and experienced more handshakes than Willie Mays. The appointment honored Lincoln High, and I was excused to make phone calls I couldn't make from home. My counselor, the kind Mr. O'Keefe, beamed, shook my hand, patted my shoulder, and gave me his office. At his work-piled desk, I dialed, my heart pounding as if I'd swum the length of Flieishhacker Pool while toting an anvil.

"Karin, it's Gus. Great, how are you? Listen, I have news: I got into West Point!"

"No-no-no!! No Gus! *Tell me you're not going!* It's, it's incomprehensible that you'd go! You're going to go to college! You're coming to Cal, aren't you?!" There was a flood of words about my losing the freedom to learn and grow and experience. I was going into a straightjacket of repression where I wasn't to think but to obey; to be brainwashed into justifying war and killing and to put my own life at risk for what? I was being trained to add to the misery of the world and to willingly submit to it and believe it. She said Eric Hoffer's *The True Believer* showed her that people can't see beyond the fixed idea that was nailed into their heads.

I picked up the pieces of myself. "Like the fixed idea that *you* can't see beyond?"

"Oh you have it so wrong! My poor beloved Gus! How can I save you and make you see the path you'd miss? It'd be so far out if you came to Cal now! Let me lead you to safety and open your eyes to the infinite beauty of the real world that I'm discovering, and you'll love and you can love it with me and you'll live! You have a special purpose in the world and it's not *there!*"

After one quarter at Cal, she'd become politically passionate, as if she'd met a Svengali (Eric Hoffer) who shot horrible drugs into her precious, beautiful, perfect arm and nailed anti-American ideas into her head. Didn't she know me, that America had saved my family and that I owed her my service, that I'd been raised to be a soldier, and that communism was dangerous to life and liberty and true tyranny wasn't going to go away because of books by temporary mystics?

"But, but you knew I wanted to go there!"

"I didn't think you'd get in! You're legally blind and you have breathing problems. You said it would probably keep you out. I've learned all about the draft and how to get out of it. You're 4F—undraftable! It's probably *illegal* for you to go to West Point! Come to Cal *now* and I'll introduce you to really cool guys who'll make up stuff so you can get out of West Point!"

"God, you're not happy for me. At all."

She, a princess, emitted a porcine snort. "You're damned right I'm not happy! God, tell me you're not going to go!"

"When are you coming back to the city?"

"I'd come right now if you said no to West Point. Edith won't let you see me, but I'd ring your door bell until either you or I got past her nasty presence."

"I graduate soon. I might be sort of breaking away. Can I see you?"

"I'd do anything to talk you out of this horrible, horrible thing!"

"I don't want to talk about West Point anymore."

"Okay. You know where I'm coming from. When you're ready to talk about, about, you-know-what, call me. I'll come to you. Don't go, Gus. PLEASE don't go!"

Norman Schwarzkopf had two older sisters; one, Ruth, was his political opposite. Their father, detective and war hero, passed away in 1958. He was a young lieutenant in the 187th Airborne Infantry, 101st Airborne Division, at Fort Campbell, Kentucky. Norm, Sally, and Ruth met at the funeral, but he wouldn't communicate with Ruth again for 15 years. The separation had been long in building.

When he was a cadet, Ruth married Raymond Jean, a brilliant, leftist French Marxist who taught at Brown. Ruth became active in the feminist, civil rights, and anti-nuclear movements. Her friends were French communists who detested the American military, the army that had liberated France from the Nazis. Raymond had been part of French colonial society in Vietnam, the ruling class that had exploited the Vietnamese and triggered America's war in Vietnam. Raymond Jean said it was a tragedy that Norm had been in war.

He held his tongue about French Army leadership in World War II, which had fumbled into a 30-day defeat to the German Army, surrendered two million men, collaborated with Hitler, to whom they donated their warships, killed American troops in North Africa, and gave their Jews to the ovens of the Third Reich. He could not find an instance in history in which genocidal tyrants had been deterred by well-meaning diplomacy. I remembered that China had tried to negotiate with the Mongols and the Manchus and were forced to huddle behind the Great Wall. From the sack of Troy to Panmunjom, non-combatants with good will had become dead, missing, or captive.

Ruth did not agree. Norman Schwarzkopf actively supported civil rights and was pro-feminist, but with one of his sisters, it was best to avoid politics.

"Gus, why'd you come here? And don't say, 'My dad made me.' What are *your* reasons?"

I looked at my shined shoes. "I always wanted to be a soldier. My mother and sisters trekked out of Japanese-occupied China through bandits, war-lord troops, deserters, and law-breakers, with no man to help them. The Japanese Army raped, tortured, and murdered women and girls, and killed more in China than the Nazis killed in Europe. I always regretted missing the war. At night, trying to sleep, I imagined I was there, armed, protecting them against enemy soldiers and *dufei*, bandits. I was getting the crap beaten out of me on the street, but I had this Walter Mitty imaginary life in which I won great gun battles that saved my sisters and my mah-mee in China."

"Gus, I'm sorry you lost your mother. It had to be hard. Hard to want to protect your mother and find yourself damned helpless."

I moistened my lips, and said nothing.

"What?" he asked.

"Sir, I haven't told anybody this before, but I, I just want to tell you. My Uncle Shen—a relative by Chinese *gang*, relationship—said that my father, who was a *Kuomintang*, Nationalist, fighter pilot, took on a personal mission to kill Mao Tse-tung for a couple years from the air. He might've done it if he hadn't been fired for continuing to pursue Mao in violation of orders."

"When was that?" asked Major S.

"I think it was before the Long March, so it would've been the early 1930s."

"You know," he said, "I saw myself as Hannibal at Cannae, and as Norm Cota, Class of '17, leading pinned-down regiments and the 'Bastard Brigade' of the 29th Infantry off the shingle at Omaha Beach. But to actually be in combat at a point of decision that could change world history—your father was close. How'd your family come to America?"

I said I didn't know much about our family history; my father never spoke of it. Uncle Shen had told me that my father's closest friend was his roommate from St. John's University in Shanghai—the "Harvard of China." This friend was T. A. Soong, the financier-president of the Bank of Canton, whose sisters by marriage became Madame Sun Yat-sen, Madame Chiang

Kai-shek, and Madame H. H. Kung. Mr. Kung was the president of the Bank of China and a descendant of Confucius. Sun Yat-sen was the revolutionary leader who became the first president of the Republic of China and the "George Washington" of his nation. Chiang Kai-shek was a soldier who became Generalissimo and the second president of China. T.A.'s older brother was T. V. Soong, China's Minister of Foreign Affairs. The Soongs were the Kennedy-Roosevelts of China; no family in Asia was more powerful or prosperous, and I knew more about them than I did about my own parents.

"T.A. Soong was my father's best friend in China and his buddy and employer in San Francisco. That is, until Mrs. Soong suspected that my real mother—Edith Swinehart—married my father to get at the Soong's fortune. My uncle said that T.A. Soong gave my father a check for $50,000 for Edith to leave my father, who went nuts and angrily ripped up the check. I don't know if any of that's true, but my father suddenly lost his job at the Bank of Canton and we never saw the Soongs again. I used to kowtow to Mr. Soong when he visited. My father couldn't find work in Chinatown or anywhere else, so we became really poor. I think that's when my father became even angrier at life, and started focusing on his losses." This had happened soon after he had married Edith, when I was six years old.

The major sat back in his hard chair. "Your father went from living with princes and power to losing his country and becoming an unemployed immigrant with a new wife. In our profession, we can lose the best of us and then die hard ourselves."

I nodded. We'd been attending funerals for guys with whom we'd eaten meals, played sports, marched in parades, and cheered on at home games.

"Listen," he said. "Bad things happen to everyone. Details change, but everyone gets hammered. Don't think you're exceptional.

"You have to forgive relatives and people who put the thorn in you. You have to move on. Hell, I'm not proficient at this, but I believe it. The people who mess you up are usually in worse jams than you are. The trooper who'll drive you nuts is the one you have to show a deeper understanding because he's living in the Ouch Pouch, the Bruise Bag. If it hurts your feelings or makes you unpopular, or even hated, it doesn't matter. Understand?"

I was confused enough to shake my head. He stood and stretched. I tried to sit straighter.

"You're a good squad leader, so you know a commander's got to love them through his own discomfort. Doesn't matter what they do to you. Consider yourself bulletproof to criticism or unpopularity. It doesn't matter really if they hate you if you inspired them to do the right thing and they take responsibility for their duties. You must always love your troops regardless of how you feel or what pressure you're under. But it doesn't have to be reciprocal. Ultimately, they have to trust you but not necessarily like you. Trust is the result of doing the right thing. That's what it means to get it right."

"Sir, I don't know how to do that. Where'd you learn to do that?"

"Oh, man." He started to speak and stopped. "I learned it," he said slowly, "in spades, in Tehran. I was a kid of 12. I was dealing with my family. You got to love them through the pain. If you can do that with family, you can do it with your men."

He faced away. He stood and looked out at the river. He spoke quietly.

"I got away from this subject when I was in Vietnam. Now it's here. In my quarters. I want you to un-ass my AO, now." AO meant area of operation. He was kicking me out.

I gathered my gear, took a few steps, and was at his door. I turned and tried smiling at him. I saw his profile and the angry jut of his huge jaw. Breathing strained.

"Mr. Lee, you have classmates who need my time more. You got your Saturdays back. I've given you what you needed. Dismissed."

Learn to Discern

Let him who would move the earth first move himself.
Socrates

Un-ass my AO. The words ached like a bad tooth.

"Hey, what's up?" asked Ping Childers. "Not seeing the Bear?"

"The man might have some other responsibilities besides you," said More Beer.

"Welcome back, amigo," said Arturo Torres. "We have been a man short and I have had to catch my own passes. This makes me tired."

I'd missed Saturday afternoon recreation, and returned to dating, playing catch, vying for five-buck poker pots, playing Hearts, and reading Michener's *The Source*, Greene's *The Comedians*, and Clavell's *Tai-pan*. I left our top floor digs in the Cadet Hilton to Company E-3 to keep Dave "Snake" Sackett and others up to speed with what the Bear had been cramming into my engineering knowledge. I kept my Plebes out of trouble with upperclassmen and in better academic condition than I enjoyed. I'd miss them when I flunked out or graduated. I had long talks with Plebe Mike Bain, with whom I shared a mystical radar-ping linkage. I practiced external cheerfulness, a feeling worsened by my 3,000-mile separation from Karin, distanced by our galactic divide in politics, and by the astronomically minute chance of ever being her boyfriend.

On top of that, I missed Major S. My improved grades had reduced the acuity of our connection and my nature had somehow removed me from his life lessons.

I appreciated solitude, so it made sense that I'd lived with people who'd ditch me. Coach Tony, the ex-Marine who'd served *in loco parentis* with me for a decade, had quit the Y after I left for West Point without leaving a forwarding address. That had happened over a year ago, before the beginning of Yearling year, when I returned to San Francisco to see him.

Un-ass my AO.

I was nine when I'd mentioned Coach's missing wife and kid, and he went into a rage, throwing things, cursing, wrecking his room—a human tornado. It scared the living daylights out of me and it literally scared the crap out of his dog, Semper. I'd asked the Bear a question. He thought about Tehran and a family problem, and had brought the unwanted into the sanctity of his Q.

I'd dealt the cards but was too distracted to neatly stack my chips. "Arturo, I asked the guy about his past. I shouldn't have, and it pissed him off royally."

"Let it go, man," said Arturo. "What I hear, it takes very little to tee-off that man. Maybe it is more about him than it is about you."

"He scared the crap out of us, but one-on-one he never got angry. He coached me and a bunch of us out of trouble in Section 8. I went too far, talking to him like he was a buddy. So stupid!"

"Be *real* stupid and raise on my raise," said our dark prince, Michael Anthony Dibenedetto, a quick-witted, sweet-tempered fencer with a piercing gaze who wore a patina of the pessimist.

Arturo shook his head. "Say, *pendejo* and not *stupid*. It is way more literate."

Later, I'd cruise to Second Regiment and play pool with Beast Barracks buddies "Big Ace" Bill Reichert and Rich Carlson and learn running tips from trackmen Chris Iaconis and Warren Bowland. We'd been fused by surviving Beast. Now, two years later, we struggled to remember the names of the classmates who, in that torrid, mind-warping summer heat, had found the 20,000th logical reason to turn in their rifles and leave the madness for college.

I was not at peace; Major S remained stuck in my oxygen-depleted chest. I thought I was missing his hot dogs, sauerkraut, Tab, and chips, but I preferred burgers, fries, and Cherry Cokes. Doggone it, I knew he'd ditch me. But I had to see him to apologize.

I also understood something about Vietnam that I sensed no one else understood, and I needed to tell him about that and learn what he thought of that understanding.

WABC's DJ, Cousin Brucie, was playing the Temptations on Arturo's radio. "Man, *muy loco*. He told you to stay away." His fine handwriting performed DeLorentz Nuclear Physics equations, which described time and space dilations—the bending of unseen dimensions that were frighteningly distinct from the simpler physics of Sir Isaac Newton. He could talk, complete his homework, and tap feet to "My Girl" while looking like Caesar Romero dining on *menudo* at poolside. Later, after serving in Vietnam and retiring from the Army, he'd grow a mustache, teach college, and complete the look. He had a casual elegance, a fine sense of humor, and an incessant cool.

"The Bear, *El Oso*, he doesn't give an order and let a cadet rescind it, even if it's you."

"Well, it's my fault. Gotta see him to apologize, to make it right."

"You blame yourself for everything. We had the power failure that blacked out New York City and we and the whole world went dark? You actually thought you caused that in lab."

I smiled. "I thought I did. So did Colonel Saunders and half the Physics department."

Psychologists tell us that we naturally seek control over others and our environment. Facing an uncontrollable situation, blaming ourselves lends us a comforting sense of control. People don't hurt or leave us without good cause or for a reason beyond our control, and we curiously might feel more powerful if we view a sad outcome as being our fault.

Arturo said, *"No siempre es culpa tuya."* It is not always your fault. He turned down the radio. "It is not good for you to take instant blame. Maybe first-born sons do this in Chinese families. In Chicano culture, men get slack. *Ahogarse en un vaso de agua!"* Don't drown in a glass of water. In other words, No mountains from mole hills.

"Yo siempre digo algo estúpido." I always say something stupid.

"Gustavo, then say something smart to the man. You must tell the Bear you're D in Juice and Nukes. He's a great teacher and he cares for you. Tell him you're in trouble and, I swear, he will roll a spare cot into his Q and get you proficient by Christmas, and you can stop scaring your buddies that you're going to get found."

He put down his pencil. "If you don't do this, it *is* your fault. Go do the right thing."

I had trouble discerning the true right thing. "Good ideas. But he's given too much to me already. He said that there are other classmates who need help more."

"Whoa, *compadre*! That is because you haven't told him how much trouble you're in. Not telling him you're in trouble is almost like being cool on Honor."

"Cool on Honor" meant to cut corners on the Honor Code, to take ethical shortcuts instead of the harder right and to tell "half-truths when the whole could be won." Cool on Honor acts weren't formally Honor Code violations, but they were in the "quibble" zone where a cadet played in the gray area instead of in the bright, full light of virtue and integrity. It was the moral Numbnuts Zone.

I knew Arturo was right because my conscience was troubled.

"Further, *amigo*, leave high strategy discussions about Vietnam alone; it's not going to be on the exams. But you don't tell him about Juice, he will kill you later for not telling him, and you will still be in trouble in Juice."

Know Your Fears

To him who is in fear everything rustles.
Sophocles

After Sunday chapel, I did what Coach Tony had instilled in me when I was a fragile seven-year-old. It was a beautifully brilliant Hudson Valley autumn afternoon and I went to the dark weight room.

Maybe Major S had un-assed his AO and would be there.

It was an old, wide, and often quiet space with high, ancient, clouded windows in the days before banging iron became a national pastime. There were signs on the walls that were then quite original: "The more you sweat in practice, the less you bleed in battle. Losers quit when they're tired. Winners quit when they win. A West Pointer never quits. When the going gets tough, the tough get going. Pain is good and feels better than losing."

There was a sprinkling of solo lifters and only one person at the bench presses. It was Major S. He wore a sweatshirt with sleeves that might have been removed by a blunt machete. He was benching the big-man-standard, four-plates, 225 pounds, with his bad back, doing eight reps a set. He looked like a guy who could straighten a horseshoe like it was taffy.

I set up on the bench farthest from him and matched him, straining my left rotator cuff because I hadn't first stretched with the bare Olympic bar and then logically warmed up at 135. I could've herniated my pancreas and dropped the bar on my throat, but the Teflon god of resilient youth was in the gym. I stretched the damaged shoulder at a nearby station, jumped up, and impulsively did 25 pull-ups in an L-bar position with my legs held at the horizontal, an easy performance for a light-boned Asian who'd been on the Plebe gym team. I was showing off; Major S could out-bench and out-squat me, but he was too big to take on the Academy record in pull-ups, which I'd challenged but had not bested. I should've stopped but didn't.

Removing the towel I wore Jack Kennedy-style around my neck and tying it around my ankles ala Houdini, I then set a 45-pound dumbbell across the towel and did 20 parallel bar dips, vainly swallowing my desperate grunts. In Chinese terms, I was waving my little toy hammer at Lu Ban, the great father of all carpenters who had built the universe.

"Want to work on your weakness?" he asked.

"Yes, sir," I said, and started to add 25-pound plates to the bench's Olympic bar.

"Talking about your character," he said. "Being showy, trying to be liked, to get along instead of get it *right*. Don't kid yourself about the power of fear over your actions."

"What am I afraid of, sir?"

"Figure it out and tell me. If you can't name your fear, you can't face it or overcome it. C'mere," he said. "Spot each other." I stripped my bench and we used his, lowering weights to increase reps, increasing them for heavy lifts, moving plates in unison as iron-mongers do.

What did I fear? I was afraid of flunking out of the best society I'd ever known, of the humiliating move to Boarders Ward, where cots became ejection seats and arcane auguries were performed to separate you from the Corps, never to be seen again. I was more afraid to tell him I was afraid of flunking Juice and Nukes, classes in which he could easily help me. I wanted his momentary approval and that of others, not wanting to lose *guanxi*, face, with him. Deep down, I was afraid of being alone and unloved. None of those were honorable fears worthy of a Cadet Corporal Squad Leader of men and a builder of character in others.

My turn to bench 300. I lowered it to my chest, started to move it up, inch by inch, my face turning red, my muscles straining, and my left side stronger because of my circular back as I started to tilt the bar and hit failure. It was no longer moving. I shook my head. The Bear pulled it up and helped me re-rack it.

"Good try. What do you weigh, about 170?"

"Yes, sir," I gasped, totally out of air.

"How can you be gassed after trying one rep?"

"Sir, I sort of have short lungs."

"Draw in your air. I don't want you dropping the bar on my face."

I could see my father's reaction of shame to my flunking out and Edith descending into a lifelong cataclysmic rage for the damage done to her self-esteem. Those images should bother me but they didn't. Other guys seem to care what their parents thought of them. Why didn't I?

The Bear did 300 without my help.

West Point was an escape from the world of my past. It had a noble gravity and a selfless ethic for which I hungered. That which was intrinsically clear and cherished to me was somehow untranslatable to my sisters, to many of my collegiate peers, and, most tragically, to Karin, the one person I wanted to understand my inner self. I'd never taken serious aim at the engineering, but the honor concept and the promise of character had penetrated my conscience even if it couldn't reach my tongue.

When I was honest with myself, I thought, Man, I'm really not going to make it.

I spotted his bench presses as we worked back down to 225, doing 8–10 reps with lighter weights instead of 3–5 with the heavier. My turn; I lay on the bench. I looked up at him. I was going to tell him I knew a key historical fact about Vietnam and wanted his opinion.

"Flunking out of West Point," he said, "would be about the worst thing that could happen to you. But it's not the absolute worst. Can you figure out what that is?"

"Sir, what do you think made your father so friendly to you?" Stupid, I thought. That's where you got in trouble! It was as if someone else had asked the question; I almost looked around the cavernous room for the person who had spoken.

I was upside down looking up, but I could tell he made a face. He looked around the near-empty gym. "He was the completely decent man," he said softly, giving me a gift from his inner life. "A truly selfless public servant. He really believed in Duty, Honor, Country. It's why I wanted to come here. I was a cute roly-poly kid who followed him around like a puppy. He truly loved me. Every time I needed him, he was there. Sometimes, I'm kind of an emotional person. I think it tracks back to how I feel about my father, and that tracks back to how he treated me. I miss him more than I can say.

"It's a good question, because the way a father loves his kids resembles how a commander loves his soldiers. My mother was the same way.

A very organized nurse who taught us compassion for others. You're delaying. Lift."

I lifted. We took a break, drank water, and wiped our foreheads.

"I'll tell you two stories," he said, "about fear. When I was a kid, I was most afraid of disappointing my dad. In Vietnam, it was letting down my troops."

He pursed his lips. "I'm 12 years old and new to Iran and I'm with my Pop in a Baluchi tribal leader's brown tent with the hot wind blowing and I'm pretty hungry. I smell food and animal waste and desert dust on everything, in your hair, eyes, down your shirt."

He was talking 90 miles an hour. He wasn't in the USMA gym; he had piloted a Persian rug to the land of the Medes, of Cyrus the Great, Xerxes, and the conquering Achaemenids.

"Outside, donkeys and camels are all over the place being run by kids with sticks. Pop's in a long tribal robe and I'm in one that I kept tripping on, and we're in the chieftain's tent with 20 of his main guys. They're robed and wearing curved daggers and holding bolt-action Lebels, Mausers, Lee-Enfields, and Krag Jorgensens from World War I—guns I'd later shoot. We're sitting on colorful tribal rugs and leaning on rough pillows that take your skin off. You'd have loved this: We're facing mountains of rice of every imaginable kind. When we eat there's talk, and these tough, bearded, leather-faced guys are showing their teeth in laughter. Well, they decide it's time to honor me so they give me a sheep eyeball to eat. Everyone's watching me with great anticipation and I whisper to Pop, 'No way I'm eating this.' He hisses, just like a table commandant telling Plebes to eat mayonnaise, mustard, A-1, and hot sauce by the spoonful, 'Eat it!'

"I assure you I had no interest. Honestly, my gut wanted to jump out of my throat. I gulped it down and all these hard guys are cheering and clapping. My Pop said I'd helped international relations, that he'd have lost face if I hadn't gulped down that eyeball. He said he was proud of me."

The Bear smiled as if he'd hit the walk-off homer in the bottom of the ninth in Game 7 of the World Series.

"Vietnam was the best year of my military service. But the happiest time was with my Pop in Tehran. We had late night talks, really about anything. Hunted tough game carrying green melons that we drank from like canteens. I explored the Shemran foothills on bikes with my best pal Michael Lieberman, a Palestinian Jew. Saw the Shah in a parade with hill folk sacrificing live animals to him. Heard muezzins make their five calls to daily prayer from minarets, that eerie, spine-tingling music that said I wasn't in New Jersey anymore."

I tried to put myself in his place. I couldn't imagine talking with my father. I'd tried hundreds of times to get him to say something to me from behind his *Chronicle* and *Chinese World* newspapers, his shield against seeing my face. I spoke hopefully about history as I made him rice porridge *tseuh*, known as *congee* and *baicho,* with *chu t'sai* coriander, and packed his peanut butter sandwich lunches, which he carried on his job searches and his short-time employments. The more I pressed, the more he'd stretch the paper until he told me to be quiet, or he threw it down and stomped out.

The Bear and I were now working shoulders and back.

"Second story. Vietnam, Central Highlands, a two-day sweep along the Cambodian border with lots of contact with VC. We lost three dead." He stopped. "We evaded the last ambushes and returned to camp after dusk to learn that part of our battalion was lost and still somewhere out there. Our troopers were preparing sandbags and NDPs (night defensive positions), preparing to shoot the hell out of anything that moved. I asked the battalion commander, not my normal guy, if he had anyone to send out to bring in the rest of his unit. He said no.

"I said I'd go. Wasn't as scared as, say, the first time I was caught by mortar rounds dropping in. But I could see getting myself killed by our own guys as well as by the enemy. I'd have to go alone to reduce noise, and find the lost troopers with radio and flares when the last thing you want to do in Indian country at night is to talk while lighting yourself up. Something said that I wouldn't be able to find them, but I shut that off or I'd just be listening to my own noise.

"I kind of became two people, a big, stupid American named Schwarzkopf who was going to tromp into the dark sounding like a herd of elephants and walk into the waiting VC, and another guy who was wisely going to stay in the perimeter and rest his beat-up body and his torn-up feet. But the first guy went out, drew fire, found them, and guided them in without a loss and without catching friendly fire."

"Sir, how'd you actually find them out there?"

"Picked a key terrain feature and navigated off that. Made radio contact with Mike Trinkle, the other American advisor, and started quartering azimuths. It was absolutely dark. Only way to link up was to shoot flares, but if I did I'd become a pop-up target for the enemy. When I thought we were close, I found the best cover I could find and fired a flare. I was afraid I was near a VC, but I guess I was close to all of them, 'cause I was getting fire from an entire front and now they knew where I was. Mike made it to a small clearing, but couldn't see anything. I kept moving and dodging bullets with their little sonic cracks as they blew apart the brush. I kept whispering into the radio and firing those red flares until Mike saw one.

"Fear's a very powerful emotion. You know what it's there for? To keep us from doing something utterly stupid and to remind us to use courage to do the right thing, to do it right. Without fear, you don't need courage. But without courage, you're a coward, and, therefore, a danger to others."

"Schwarzkopf's First Law," I said. "Do the harder right."

"That's right, Sport. First Law. Courage in your gut and bravery in the field—the same thing. It's knowing how hard and risky the job is, and feeling all the fear of getting killed or having your limbs blown off and no one finding your body to tell your folks what happened to you. It's knowing that and going ahead and doing it anyway, not only regardless of the fear, but sort of because of it. You can't let fear rule your decisions or conduct."

I wondered if my parents would care if no one found my body.

"Good thing is, the more you practice bravery and courage, the easier it gets. That first time, my heart was going faster than a bat out of hell. Why, sometime after my third firefight, I stopped checking all my body parts and worrying if I needed to change underwear. That's the advantage of practicing doing the harder right. It goes from being an out-of-body experience to being a habit. The fear never goes away. It's there to remind you to keep bashing on. That sour feeling in your stomach is actually a bright green 'Go' light."

Assess Need

*Leadership should be born out of understanding the needs
of those who would be affected by it.*
Marian Anderson

The Bear decided it was easier to meet me in the weight room than in his Q. I was getting stronger. His back was worsening and he could no longer do squats, military presses, or clean and jerks. We were down to bench-pressing and occasional rotations on the lat machine. We had a steady pace on lats. He stopped just as I got my arms into that good, deep, swollen pump.

He lowered himself to the floor as if he were old, and lay flat on his back.

"Sir, can I get some meds for you from your Q or the hospital?"

"You asked if I ever failed." He was looking at the ceiling lights, or at heaven. "Last summer, we did an operation in pretty bad country on the Cambodian border. Headquarters' paper plan—the estimate of enemy strength and disposition, fires, air support, coordination with neighboring units and reserves—all were three-oh excellent." In those days, West Point used a system in which 3.0 was the perfect maximum.

I sat near him.

"But the actual details hadn't been done. The failure to plan was like undone homework. We walked into ambushes and lost 40 dead. A damn mess, terrible. *That* is failure."

"That's why you want us to do our homework, especially the stuff we don't like to do."

He nodded. "I hadn't drilled lead units to face serial ambushes. Didn't matter that we didn't have enough time. Just five sentences about interlocking ambushes before we jumped in might've helped." He rubbed his face. "I used imaginary thinking. You know: 'If I thought of it, surely others must have thought about it, too.'

"Another favorite is: 'I thought someone else was handling that.'"

I gulped. That sounded like me.

"Imaginary thinking, by my imaginary friend," I added. The Bear laughed.

Dr. Jim "Sully" Sullivan, a West Point brother, calls this "magical thinking." Magical thinking is Schwarzkopf's imaginary thinking plus wishful thinking: If a thing ought to be have been done, it probably was done and therefore requires no action on my part. Its corollary is, "I'll do it later."

"You must . . ." The Bear's voice cracked. He closed his eyes. In the absence of his voice, I heard West Point. Guys shouted on playing fields. A chopper flew low over Post. A fellow in the squat rack room cursed and jettisoned about 400 pounds of iron, vibrating the building with the familiar crash of big York plates on an ancient wooden floor. The Bear was doing steady breathing as he tried to relieve the pressure in his back.

"Sir, since the prep was so bad, should you have refused to do a poorly planned op?"

He gave a bitter grin as he shook his big head. "It wasn't an illegal order and Vietnam's not our country. The Vietnamese Airborne Brigade—my parent organization—isn't American. It sounds like a mouse-out, but I wasn't in command. I couldn't do the Second Law: I had no decision-making authority and couldn't take command or responsibility. All I could do was refuse to go, and then my guys would be going in without me and my radio for air support. A typical 'cluster,' which is what war brings and therefore requires so much of us.

"War, like fear, brings out the best from the best of us and the worst from the unprepared. War made some of my guys want to torture VC prisoners to get intel." He shook his big head. "I couldn't let that happen. It caused a stir: I was just an advisor. But I'm an American advisor." He cleared his throat. "*Was* an American advisor.

"Back to your point, I recommended against the op, but when the best commander and tactician I ever knew said his paratroopers had to try to relieve the folks at Duc Co with a lousy plan and without support despite the cost, I knew my duty and saddled up.

"So I'm at Duc Co. We'd relieved the trapped guys and paid hell to get there. Forty dead paratroopers, 80 wounded, and I'm in a blue funk, trying not to curse myself for oversights. Colonel Truong's my good example, taking care of his guys and doing it better than I am 'cause he's doing the right thing while I'm using my boots to kick my own ass. Really, I was too deep in grief. We have Huey's in and out and I'm enjoying rotor wash 'cause it blasts dirt and body parts from my fatigues. I'm helping medics, carrying canteens, and holding plasma. After action, my only job is looking in the eyes of my guys to let them know they're okay and that it's going to get better than it is right now.

"A chopper descends right on top of us. We got to move some of our wounded and I'm about to tell the pilot he'd better have brought the morphine, water, ammo, grenades, and food I've been yelling into the radio for or I'm going to roll him and his damn Huey into the bush.

"Out steps a senior officer and his court. They're in starched fatigues, spit-shined boots, Brasso'd belt buckles, and acting serious around a TV film crew that came in with them. Sergeant Hung helps me strip off my LBE (load-bearing equipment) and my bloody ripped-up blouse (fatigue shirt) and helps me throw on the filthy, less-ripped version I'd worn into a state of disgust a month ago. I looked like the Creature from the Black Lagoon. I stank of my dead and fish sauce and spoiled rice, and I see there are no supplies in his command chopper—just radios and briefcases and cameras. I'm still worried about PAVN in the perimeter and now I'm fighting my anger.

"The officer presents himself. I salute; he returns it like we're in parade formation at West Point. I smell British Sterling aftershave. Know what stank worse?" He looked at me.

I shook my head; I couldn't imagine.

"The rear area types around him. They reeked from eating way too much Kiss-Ass.

"He asks me, 'You getting mail?' I blink, like he said he'd like to change into an evening gown and chase butterflies in the moonlight. He asked me if I was *getting my mail*.

"I said, 'Negative, sir, and that mail was a little off my Go-do list.'

"Then he says, 'How's your chow?' How's my chow? I knew this guy; everyone knew this guy. He'd been a hero in the Battle of the Bulge and he'd been a high-ranking cadet, had held high positions and did well, and he'd been in the soup and had done the right thing. It was incredibly hot; I wondered if he had heat stroke, but he was cool. I was the one who was dripping sweat and was livid with him for being notably absent on this desperate, last-minute allied operation. He hadn't expressed any concern for the best fighting men in Asia and was interfering with my caring for our wounded and was using aviation for PR instead of for medevac and resupply. I had to beg him for the gear we needed to make it for the next 10 hours, and I pissed him off. A staffer said he'd get me everything we needed if I'd smile while the photo guy took pictures for the press. Let me tell you, Sport, I smiled like a ring-tailed sonovabitch!

"He assumed he had the right questions. He didn't use eyes or nose. He didn't do an assessment. Man, it was so basic! He didn't look to the needs of others; he was concerned about looking good for the damn camera man. All he had to do to help, man-to-man, was to ask what my guys needed. Don't ask about my mail or chow. Don't ask about *me*. ASK ME ABOUT MY MEN!"

His voice echoed like the crashing of iron. A big officer that had been doing squats peered around the corner.

"If he'd done that, he'd instantly have formed a relationship with me and my troops. Crap, I would've followed him on a PR mission if he wanted. What frosts my ass is that if the 40 dead had been American, he'd have asked better questions. But they were Vietnamese, and we had guys with that attitude. Senior guys. Guys with stars. He didn't care about my human men. I knew we were in trouble. Generals like Sherman and Grant, Ridgway and Cota, they would've encouraged me to watch out for my people. That's when I saw that shift in values from my Pop's generation."

The Bear rolled over and inched himself off the floor. "I lost all respect for that guy, right there and then. Do you see it? Leadership is doing the right thing with people so they'll do the right thing. To do that, you have to relate to your people. You have to fight to create a relationship because for whatever reasons, it's not natural for most of us. What's natural is to wear your rank and use authority to just tell and coerce people into doing what you want."

"You mean, like West Point."

"Yes. Like West Point. And not like West Point. Just don't be an elite careerist."

The Bear said leadership consists of two laws. First, do the right thing and care for your men. Second, take command and responsibility by equipping and preparing them. I remembered Confucius: Knowledge is easy; action is difficult.

Later, I'd wonder how, at Duc Co, at that improvised landing pad, the Bear might've given the effective leader's feedback to the senior officer so he wouldn't continue landing on top of his people and asking unintentionally wrong questions. I could see the bad results of a leader no longer respecting another.

Was disrespecting an ineffective leader the "right thing" response to someone else's disrespect?

It was easier for me to think about how the Bear, man among men, could improve himself than it was for me to look at me.

I, a far more common person, would require dramatic failures to galvanize me to change my behaviors to form those relationships, and to learn how to deal rightly with disrespect.

Major S would answer these questions, and more.

His answers would become my life's work.

14

Solve Problems at Root Cause

Don't find fault. Find a remedy.
Henry Ford

I stood with the Bear as we awaited our dates. I was dating a bright, attractive, and sweet young woman I'd been seeing for more than a year. She was a school teacher and grad student, and owned a car, which in our culture represented an apex in status. She would arrive in an hour, and was my first girlfriend since childhood.

I was nine when Mr. Lew, my fourth grade teacher, told Edith I needed glasses. "He can't see cars," he said. "Without glasses, Gus will be staying home with you." I donned my first pair of glasses and saw the world, got good grades, and understood boxing and why people went to movies. I saw Phyllis Green, the loveliest girl on the block with the biggest eyes. She took my hand in her white-gloved grip and squeezed it as we left church, announcing to all that live-long world that the little China boy was all hers.

Now, Major S and I were in the Gothic Revival Hotel Thayer, which looms like the dark Bastille inside the main gate to Post. The afternoon bus had unloaded platoons of young women in Wendy Ward outfits, well-coifed hair in Alberto VO5 hair-sprayed flips and beehives, and carrying cute overnight cases. They were met by their neatly scrubbed uniformed cadet dates in Dress Gray who took their cases from white-gloved and well-manicured hands. The touching was regulated; public displays of affection tended to be remedied by the Academy with death, torture, and revocation of citizenship. The young women would be housed in the Thayer's economical, six-girls-to-a-room quarters. The dark wood-paneled lobby was lined with flags, branch shields, and military art, and was packed with a boisterous crowd of officers, wives, cadets, and escorts. Cadet girlfriends were familiarly amused by the formal pomp and uniforms. First-time dates looked about with expanding eyes, prepared to see the White Rabbit and the hookah-smoking Caterpillar.

Cadets were on parade-ground conduct: attentive, restrained, and exhibiting perfectly straight backs. I straightened mine as I was standing next to West Point's Achilles, the warrior-athlete whose presence seemed to out-shine all others. The Thayer wasn't just a Hudson Valley guest house; it was high theater where actors were in costume and controlled by threat of pen-alties. I imagined Karin, the unattainable dream girl, in an Audrey Hepburn small black dress, a pillbox hat, and white heels, greeting me with opened arms. The ludicrous idea—she was at Cal and probably wore cut-offs, tee shirt, and sandals, and had almost hugged me once for 0.1 microseconds—evaporated in the reality of crowd noise.

I said that this might resemble the Duchess of Richmond's Ball at her Brussels residence the night before Waterloo. The crowd coyly observed the tall, broad-shouldered, heavily be-medaled Major Schwarzkopf as they might've spied upon Arthur Wellesley, the Duke of Wellington, on that chandelier-lit historic June 1815 evening on the Rue de la Blanchisserie.

"Waterloo," said the Bear, "is a pretty worthless lesson in the military art. They fought in a confined box on muddy ground, which prohibited maneu-ver and produced terrible casualties. That's why we study Cannae. There, Hannibal could use principles of war: vision, maneuver, economy of force, deception, surprise, and unity of command and mass at the point of decision."

"Sir, I don't remember vision as a principle." Whenever the Bear refer-enced Cannae, which was often, I learned something new about a battle I'd studied since childhood.

He looked toward the entrance. "Vision and strategy are unnamed axioms to help us think big. They get us outside the enclosed space of tactical thinking. Small thinking and chasing short-term results is an American disease, a com-mon malady of young lieutenants." He looked at his local-time watch.

"Is your person late?" I asked.

"I'm 30 minutes early." It was the old Army saw: "On-time" is late and "10 minutes early" is almost on-time. *Ergo*, report 30 minutes early for the unpredictable, and you're "on-time."

"I meant to ask," he said. "How'd you do with Sergeant Rock at Buckner?" Camp Buckner was two months of field training following Plebe year.

I frowned. "Gee, sir, that's ancient history. I don't think I met Sergeant Rock."

He said "Sergeant Rock" was his term for Army sergeants who trained us in field problems. Buckner was the training camp north of West Point where we learned tactics not in the classroom, but in the field. Named for Lieutenant General Simon Bolivar Buckner, the Okinawa ground commander who was killed during the battle, Buckner's Sergeant Rocks gave us tactics problems, assigned classmates as squad members, and graded our performance as we practiced small-unit leadership to take assigned objectives.

I'd drawn a bad one, a bigot. The first task he gave was to write an operation order to solve the tactical problem. His second task was to pick on me.

The sergeant was a tough, wiry, bantam rooster with a prideful stride. I hadn't liked his appearance at first glance and disliked him more when I heard his Southern accent.

"Mr. Lee, you're the squad leader for this problem." I thought he looked and sounded remotely hostile.

Disliking prejudice, I upped my own bias against people I thought were bigots.

The sergeant said, "Mister Lee, do us paragraph three 'n give your boys your genius execution order." I told the guys to take a knee and detailed my concept of the operation, the scheme of maneuver. Formation. Route. Individual assignments. I'd devised a Cannae solution for one machine gun in a bunker. As I briefed the plan, I knew it was way too complicated. Frank Nader, a quiet football player from Minnesota, was my trusty and reliable Buckner buddy. It was like having Ajax the Greater as your foxhole pal. He nodded, his face saying, No sweat. We'll make it work.

The sergeant stood over me. "Ya know, ah didn' think ya'll could do this."

God, I hated him. I turned away and tersely described the route to the objective.

"Man, oh man. Where you learn tactics, boy? Ah'll say this, ya'll sure know how to wipe out yo' own people. Well, go ahead, then. Git 'em all kilt. Ah'll git me some cold water."

The wet heat was oppressive and my face turned redder. I wanted to punch him out. My classmates were uncomfortable. This wasn't going well and I didn't know the way out. We took out the machine gun but at a cost of three of my guys who the sergeant declared dead or wounded in the exercise. Frank admitted it was too complicated. I asked him what he thought of the NCO responsible for grading our "lane," the rocky playing field upon which we were learning the art of war.

Frank, his fatigues soaked, shrugged massive shoulders. "Seems he kind of hated everyone, like he had a bad day and was taking it out on us."

"He had you focus on the Op Order?" asked the Bear, referring to a detailed plan of action on the objective. I came out of my memory.

I nodded. "Yes, sir. Task one. But that sergeant kept questioning my decisions."

"What if he was doing that to train you?"

"Sir, if he was, he did it the hard way. He was pretty blunt. I don't think he liked me."

"How important is that?"

"Pretty important, sir." *Everyone* knew that.

"Who knew more about that problem and about soldiering, you or him?"

"He did, but he put me in charge and then kept contradicting me in front of my guys."

"What can you do about that?"

"Sir. How can you lead if the guy makes you look bad and he doesn't respect you?"

"Well, your job is to make good from bad. Got to link-up with the Sergeant Rocks. What if you're supposed to respect him, regardless of how he treats you?"

I remembered that day at Buckner. I said I'd tried connecting with that guy at least three times.

The Bear's moral look burned into my exposed retinas. "That's a pretty puny number. The Rock had to make it tough for you, Sport, just like real life. To fix conflicts and to build professional links, try *seven times seventy*."

"Uh, that's how many times you expect me to try to build a relationship? How'd you come up with that?"

"Yes, that's what I expect. The number comes from the Bible. So what can you do about that now?"

"Sir, that was almost two years ago. Other than 'Sergeant,' I don't remember his name. I'm not sure I registered it back then. I'm pretty sure he was just an E-6." A staff sergeant.

The Bear looked down at me. Steam didn't shoot from nostrils, but a brow darkened and the mouth tightened. Luminous eyes seemed to send a message: Square yourself away, cadet! He's either still with 1st Battle Group here at West Point or he's somewhere. It's the Army. You can find him.

What if it was my bias rather than the sergeant's? Thinking I was clever in blaming the prejudice of others, I'd practiced that disease with the ease of a bigot on a biscuit. Uncle Shen would have reminded me with the words, *wǔ shì bù xiào bǎi bù,* the soldier who runs away jeers the soldier who retreats a few paces more.

"I guess I could find the sergeant," I said.

A lieutenant colonel squeezed through the dense Thayer lobby crowd to greet the Bear. They exchanged words and Major S smiled so powerfully that the lights brightened. He laughed with a roar that was so unlike the serious, contained, and rather introverted man in Quarters 39 and the fiercely temperamental prof in the classroom. Here, unguarded, he was a man I hadn't met. He could laugh like Danny Kaye and smile like Louis Armstrong. Something unseen that was beautiful and caring and bright beamed from within him. "We'll talk, sir," said the Bear to the light colonel. "Why look up Sergeant Rock?" he asked me.

"Sir, seeing how he was supposed to make it tough, maybe I should apologize to a guy who was just trying to do his job." I liked the rather adult sound of that.

"Listen, Sport, he's not a 'guy.' He's a highly competent NCO, the backbone of the Army, the spine of the profession of arms, and ideal for saving stupid cadets like you from tying up." Tying up was West Point lingo for committing a gross error, or blundering badly, bound up in unsolvable Gordian knots.

"Sir, that's what I meant. He's a highly competent NCO, the backbone of the Army, the spine of our profession of arms, and ideal for saving stupid cadets like me from tying up."

He smiled and my chemistry changed. "Why else contact him?"

"Jeez, sir, isn't apologizing enough?"

"Think about it. Have a good night with your date." He clapped me on the shoulder, making the sound of an artillery round simulator. Folks nearby jumped.

I met my date and we took the quiet walk along the river back to main post and the Weapons Room, where we could grab a meal and dance to "Cherish" and "California Dreamin'" and later catch the movie "Tarzan and the Valley of Gold." I told her I wanted to get her ideas about something that my prof had said before she arrived. She knew I was still orbiting around a distant California girl.

The sergeant had been trying to tell me my plan for the exercise was too complicated. The Bear said that leadership was why we were at West Point. Leadership, he said, is about two things, character and competence. Do the right thing. Honor all persons and know your stuff. It was hard to remember and harder to do.

I told her that Sergeant Rock had an attitude and I had paid him back. Was I supposed to honor him, even if he wasn't respecting me? If I forgive him, isn't that rolling over, like Neville Chamberlain kowtowing to Adolf Hitler? Didn't the Bear disrespect that senior officer who couldn't assess the needs of his surviving men?

"You have a remarkable professor," she said. "He makes you ask deep questions. I think he's very fond of you."

"He wants me to respect all persons without conditions. He got that from his parents." I said that as if it were a revelation.

"Well," she said, "his advice is even getting to me. As a teacher, I naturally favor my smart students, and the slower ones have to know that. And I'm not focused on their character."

I'd learned from the Bear that disliking a principle or failing to do it well doesn't disprove it. If I don't like a high principle, my dislike might say more about my own shortcomings and what's wrong with me than it does about the principle. Or, the other guy.

I could hear Major S: "That's the nature of character lessons; we natively resist and dislike them. Human nature intellectually likes the harder right but natively prefers the easier wrong. The root cause is probably in us."

I'd also lacked the technical competence to see Sergeant Rock's warnings about my over-complicated Op Order. I could've shown the guys that I could hear a contrarian opinion without pouting and trying to pay back, as if every unfair person in the world were one of my parents.

She took my arm and snuggled closer as small house lights began twinkling on the far side of the river. She knew that the Officer in Charge would be haunting barracks and facilities and not trolling Thayer Road for PDA.

According to the Bear, apologizing to Sergeant Rock was only one of two reasons to contact him. What was the second? The answer was an elfin spirit that disappeared around corners a moment after I sensed its presence.

I never called and never apologized. It was inevitable that my Sergeant Rock served multiple tours of duty in Vietnam, risking his skin to teach dumb, arrogant, college-educated lieutenants to open their little ears to wisdom. I've wondered since if he returned alive.

Later, I learned there are answers that live neither in the world of the intellect nor in the world of feelings. This is the moral realm, and it was in this space that Major S pressed me. I learned that if we practice the behaviors of character, we form habits of character.

I was morally bound to courageously respect a person who didn't honor me. That would mark a person seeking to align with the self-imposed heroic ideal.

My primary shortcoming was moral. And the root cause solution with Sergeant Rock, and with all of my genuine challenges, resided not in the faults of others, but inside my own chest. I thought other people were the problem, but the root cause of my leadership struggles were my own moral faults, in my own imperfect heart.

The beauty of this unspoken lesson from Norman Schwarzkopf is that while I have scant power over my environment, I own total dominion over my emotions, the valuation I place on my past, and all my moral decisions. Others might disrespect my feelings, but my job was not to respond to others on the reactive emotional plane, but to try to help others solve problems at root cause, a condition that tends to live inside our own chests.

Kong Fuzi had instructed that when we see an upright person, we should emulate that person. When we see an un-right person, we should look at ourselves.

Later, I would believe it.

15

Inspire Change

If you do not change direction, you may end up where you are heading.
Lao Tzu

In Victor Hugo's *Les Miserables*, Bishop Myriel, a simple country priest, meets Jean Valjean, a hungry, raggedy, and brutish ex-convict, rejected by the world and abused by the powerful. But Valjean has saved lives and has preserved the unpopular habit of aiding the weak.

Bishop Myriel greets, feeds, and houses him. In the morning, Valjean repays the generosity by stealing most of the church's silver. Arrested by gendarmes and hauled before the priest in the forbidding priory, he awaits a final sentence. Valjean feels fear, but the stronger emotion is shame.

Bishop Myriel says the prisoner forgot to take two silver candlesticks, which he deposits in Valjean's bag. The prisoner is released. Valjean reflects on this, and is changed for life.

Cadet Jimmy Patrick Michael Sullivan, formally Seamus Padraig Michal Ui Suilleabhain Beare, aka Sully, was stout and fit enough for the cover of *Ring* magazine. Physically he was our broad-shouldered Jean Valjean, with a penchant for attracting institutional punishments while standing up for the underdog. He'd validated Plebe boxing by being fearless, tough, and unbeatable in the ring. He closed with his opponent until his welcoming of pain and his delivery of misery eroded the heart of the stoutest opponent, and all knew the victor who had landed the blows. He could take a punch, demerits, and bad grades with the resolve of the bare-knuckle boxers on the scratch lines of yore while graciously pulling his punches against the less skilled.

Sully lived in barracks known as the Lost Fifties, which were furthest from Central Area, the heart of the priory of West Point. Beast Barracks once operated in Central Area's massive, crenelated, black granite, neo-Gothic fortress before the wrecking ball did what Benedict Arnold and the British Army could not. Regiments once marched in Band Box parades across its great concrete apron. Medieval sally ports admitted marching formations of cadets to the tunes of playful fifes and gut-thumping drums. West Point looked like a movie set for films featuring knights and warhorses; its occupants often felt like overworked and underpaid extras.

Within this cinematic and imposing Central Area lived Cadets Thayer, Grant, Lee, Sherman, Jackson, Custer, Goethals, Pershing, MacArthur, Eisenhower, Bradley, Patton, Arnold, Groves, Taylor, Stilwell, Ridgway, Gavin, Franks, Schwarzkopf, and Christman. In the coldest winters they were heated largely by dormant fireplaces and good intentions; cadets to this day remain strangers to air conditioning, although there are rumors of coming changes.

The Lost Fifties loosened standards with every footstep from the Central Guard Room. The Fifties were on the far side, nearer the river and notions of freedom. Its denizens were regarded by stricter companies as a tribe of untamed outliers who barely wore the uniform.

Although he was a top athlete who watched out for classmates and became our Mark Twain, turning prosaic events into humorous Homerian tales, Sully lived in what was universally accepted as the grossest cadet room in the long history of lousy, disreputable West Point quarters.

Larry "Whitey" White, Jr., roomed with Sully in the Pigpen. Whitey's father, a colonel and West Pointer, had achieved in World War II a record of stark bravery that remains the stuff of legend. Later, his son, Whitey Junior would be decorated for fighting in three wars, would bypass promotion to general to instead serve where he was most needed, and would later retire as a highly-decorated full colonel. But in preparation for war and trying decisions, young Cadet Whitey first had to live in the Pigpen.

The E-4 Company Tactical Officer, a Quasimodo with a cattle prod, would enter cadet rooms like bold Caesar crossing the Rubicon. But he approached the Pigpen with the moral defeat borne by a broken survivor of Napoleon's winter retreat from Moscow.

The Tac, a major, knew Sullivan and White had hidden a forbidden coffee pot and evil popcorn popper in "The worst of all cadet rooms in the storied history of lousy, rat-infested, disreputable West Point quarters." The Tac sadly viewed the room. "I know they're here." He pounded on Whitey's desk, his big fist radiating outward shock waves. A duct-taped side panel on Sully's desk popped out to clatter on the floor, followed by the massive popcorn popper. It broke into its constituent parts, each of which bounced loudly on ancient floor boards.

"Ah-ha!" cried the Tac. In the ecstasy of scientific discovery, he slammed a happy hand on the desk. A second panel clanged on the floor. Whitey scrunched his face. Sully, a seasoned con who'd experienced worse encounters with the Tactical Department's armed guards, remained stoic.

The coffee pot relied on the second panel for security. It achieved Newtonian disequilibrium, obeyed gravity, and struck the floor at the standard acceleration of 32 feet per second. The fall ejected the small percolator cap from the mother canister; it bounced and warped on the floor, making a magical, endless Motown-styled backup chorus of *wha-wha-wha-wha-wha-wha* as Sully and Whitey now bared teeth in painful rictus smiles.

The Tac's face was a painter's palette of red, vermillion, purple, heliotrope, and puce as he considered rage, violence, grace, and final defeat. Through clenched teeth, he managed, "You have so many demerits, Mr. Sullivan, that if I put you on report for everything that is wrong in this room, you'd be a civilian by morning reveille. I don't have enough ink to write up these violations. I have little hope for you, Mr. Sullivan, because you are impervious to correction. You almost celebrate every punishment I can give you."

The saddened Tac looked at the popcorn popper, his Golden Fleece, and departed. It wasn't a replay of Bishop Myriel, but it was close, and a harbinger of events to follow.

On Saturday nights, cadets played and watched sports and endured a B-grade Post movie. Fortunate high-achieving cadets with charm, East Coast linkages, and the favor of the Cadet Hostesses dated women who drove or bussed to West Point for unnaturally formal encounters. Men like Sully, who owned the secret sauce of bad grades and excess demerits, were confined to quarters and lived on the edge of expulsion for multiple causes. One Saturday eve, Sully and 11 of his closest prank-certified bandits filled trashcans with water and dumped them on unsuspecting cadets four floors below.

The prank was in keeping with the cycle of pain, and was so unbearably funny in their highly restricted and monastic lives that it caused fits of unstoppable laughter.

Sully and his buddies were in hysteria, shrieking, howling, pointing, and laughing, clapping Sully on his strong back for his Davidian accuracy after he'd drenched another cadet.

There was a change in atmosphere, a deepening of density. It was the aura of Grendel, the original terrifying monster of *Beowulf,* before heavy footfalls and horrified screaming and terrible dying. A classmate who faced the door froze; he appeared to have swallowed his face. Sully turned.

The Bear was in the room. He stood one foot from Sully's face.

"Room, Ten-HUT!" cried Sully, his big voice echoing across the Lost Fifties toward Vassar and Nova Scotia. Cadets snapped to attention. Some vibrated like tuning forks.

Major Schwarzkopf exuded displeasure. Hearts stopped. Breathing was arrested. Faces turned red for lack of oxygen. Twelve chins pulled inward; 24 testicles retracted. Some of those with the greatest number of demerits almost fainted.

The Bear's presence meant Slugs, heavy penalties, and consecutive life terms in Gulag. A Slug was a major cadet penalty that imposed marching punishment tours back and forth with a rifle in Central Area, many hours of confinement to one's room during free time, and many demerits. For those with the worst rap sheets, it meant expulsion.

Bishop Myriel could now destroy the life of the prisoner or inspire him to be a better man.

"Let me tell you something," said the Bear. "The mothers of America are about to give their sons to you to lead in battle. Don't kid yourself; that's a sacred responsibility. This place is hard because the job that awaits you is harder than going to the office, harder than nine-to-five, harder than getting a paper cut or a harsh word or losing your paycheck. You men will have to make life-and-death decisions about those sons who will be your soldiers and your mission. That's your sacred duty."

He scanned the wet, dripping, stupidly-garbed cadets. He looked at Sully, who'd grounded the empty trashcan. The young men glanced at themselves, and saw fools.

"At ease," said the Bear. Some breathed. Some remained rigidly at attention.

"Those young soldiers in your care will expect you to be real smart and to know your job and be in top physical condition and to be real serious about your work. You must not waste their lives. You should not waste your time, not here. You should be getting ready.

"Fortune, gentlemen, favors the prepared." He took a deep breath, his huge barrel chest expanding, as if he were a great fire storm on the Plain, consuming their oxygen.

"Some soldiers are smarter than you. Sergeants have forgotten more than you'll ever learn about war and dying and holding people together when panic punches you in the face.

"But there's only *one thing* you have to be truly great at. That's your *character*."

He waved dismissively at the dripping cadets. "This stupid grab-ass activity pisses me off. It's bull. Every time you do it, you degrade yourselves. This isn't worthy of you or of what you want to become. I never want to hear about you doing anything like this again."

Sully was shamed. He later said that he remembered the words of tough Sergeant Major Sobalowski, an old Screaming Eagle of the 101st Airborne with whom he had earlier crossed paths at the Academy. "Here, we fix many t'ings. But one t'ing we can't fix, is *stupid*."

The Bear's earnest voice filled their ears. "Accept this reprimand as men accept it. Accept it as a way to change. Take this and learn to inspire others to be better men. I've shown you how to use mercy. Now mop up this area and get back to your rooms and straighten up your lives."

The Bear fixed each man with his gaze. Sully, who'd been punched by some of the hardest fists in the Corps, internally blanched with the moral force of the man's gaze. He'd just been given two silver candle holders in a reprieve that would echo across the span of his life.

Take this and learn how to inspire others to be better men.

For almost 20 years, Sully and I have been mainstays in West Point's National Conference on Ethics in America. While most West Point classes generously fund buildings, monuments, activities, and academic chairs, the Class of 1970, whose motto is "Serve with Integrity," endowed an annual ethics conference. A group of 20 members of the class perform the necessary planning, design, liaison, and execution of that conference.

A decade ago, I asked Sully why he donated his time and treasure, year in and year out to the Conference. He walked me out to where the ancient barracks of the Lost Fifties once lurked.

"When he caught us with the water," said Sully, "I was ashamed, then grateful, then uplifted by the beauty of what his speech meant. He reached into my chest and changed my entire life. I had a kind of savagery in me. Came out in my belligerence, my fighting, my quick temper. It showed itself in the underlying cruelty behind my seemingly innocent cadet pranks.

"So that night, I changed. That merciful correction Schwarzkopf gave me governed the way I served as an officer. It was the best ass-chewing I ever got. I'm still grateful.

"I owe him and the Academy and God a great deal for the repair of my heart."

16

What You Ignore You Endorse

He who loses wealth loses much; he who loses a friend loses more;
But he that loses his courage loses all.
Miguel de Cervantes

He was a picture-perfect male, academically sharp, classically handsome, and could display charming urbanity. He had earned great renown as a womanizer, a notorious and insatiable backseat swordsman. I will call him "Big Diff" Courtland Difford. He was a ranking senior, a Firstie Cadet Captain six-striper, a year ahead of us Cows. He commanded his own table in the Mess Hall, where he held forth over eleven other cadets representing all four classes.

"Get the right volume in the glass and the right number of cubes in my drink, Mister," he said coldly to the huddled Plebes at the foot of the table as they busily prepped hot and cold beverages and food and dessert servings for the upperclassmen. The glass was passed forward according to a strict protocol to avoid elbow bumps and spillage. After measuring volume and counting cubes, Big Diff fired opinions on complex topics faster than *Time* magazine could print them.

"Berlin Wall? Hell, tear it down," he said. "Right in frigging front of them. If they bitch, blow 'em away. And the SDS, Students for a Democratic Society? Send them to Red China."

"What should we do about Red China?" someone asked.

"Nuke 'em!" he said.

The table fell silent.

I didn't want to be the one to speak up, but curiosity got me. "You mean that?" I asked.

"Wouldn't have said it if I didn't."

"Wow, Diff." I grounded my fork, an unusual act. "Why study Humanities and world history and Toynbee and Durant when we can just use your solutions?"

"Exactly," he said, swirling ice cubes in his afternoon tea. "I understand. You don't agree because you're Oriental." He smiled.

"I don't agree because hitting Red China would leave us uncovered to the Soviets, who'd have their full inventory to nuke us back. And wiping out China would put us in the same league with the Japanese Empire when they attacked Pearl Harbor, only a lot worse."

"Wrong, Gus. The Russians are terrified of us and we have cause to attack China."

"The Big Diff is kidding," said one of his senior classmates.

"Like hell I am," he said. His voice declared: I rank everyone at this table. He didn't like me breaking the bonhomie of the meal. He gazed at me the way butterfly collectors consider slow *Lepidoptera*. But I was a Second Classman with rank and felt bulletproof.

"Gus," he said, smiling again. "I've never had an Oriental. Got a sister for me?"

Got a sister for me. Although I hardly knew my siblings, his question burned and insulted at too many levels for my math skills. I simply couldn't count the ways that he'd violated everything West Point stood for and sullied all that we were supposed to be as men of moral rectitude, as *jun tzu*. I hadn't gotten much sun, so clearly I blushed as blood rushed from my brain to muscles and fast-twitch tissues. My mouth was dry, hands moist with the adhesives that would allow me to hold onto an enemy while I hurt him.

"Sorry, Diff," I said. "My sister has something you wouldn't like: She has good taste."

Big Diff frowned, then laughed, his gleaming ivories bright. "Har-har-har! That's good! *Touché!* Let me know when she changes her mind. She'll regret the time she lost with the best deal she'll ever know. She'll be all over you to . . ."

"She's already over you."

He was happily bantering; I was in a mud sling.

"Look at you, Lee, a little puffed-up pullet! Who'd the hell want your ugly sister, anyway?"

"I would've sworn it was you."

"Well, little buddy, you just misunderstood what I wanted her for."

"Enough you guys!" said Arturo. "Diff, you are talking family here."

I nodded at Arturo, grateful, empty, out of ammo. All I could do now was ignore Difford. And stew over his words. To chase dames was natural. But there was something unnatural about Big Diff's method of pursuit. He looked like magnetic Jack Armstrong, All American boy, but dishonorably and rabidly chased women for momentary usage. What was wrong with him? How could I express that? What should I have said? Being in an all-male organization had plusses—it prevented preening. But our hormones had met the hedonism of the Sixties, and the results stank. If Big Diff could exploit women like a snorting pig and be admired, we were in real trouble.

Saturday afternoon found the Bear doing heavy, floor-warping squats. I thought his back had magically healed, but when I saw his face I realized he was instead testing his capacity for unmitigated pain. I began doing human-sized versions of his monster repetitions while grunting like an anguished hog.

"You're making more noise than those weights require," he observed.

I nodded. "Sir, I got a question. Back at Buckner, I disrespected Sergeant Rock. At lunch this week, a Firstie six-striper, famous for being a crazy skirt hound, asked in front of the table if I'd introduce my sister to him, you know, like feeding chum to a shark. My sister. But I'm, like supposed to respect him, right?"

"You straighten things out with Sergeant Rock?"

"No, sir."

"Okay, Sport. In this new situation, thank you for not naming the Firstie. That'd be gossip. Now, how can you do the right thing and also respect him?"

"I dunno, sir. It's why I'm asking you. This time, the guy outranks me."

"*Sans rapport*, irrelevant. Mr. Lee, it takes guts to speak truth to a superior, to higher authority." He stretched. That reminded me to do the same. I hated stretching, muscles or soul.

"You know, when I got to Vietnam they gave me a desk job. Luckily, I ran into Leroy Sudduth, my West Point roommate, a honcho in the Green Berets. Leroy helped get me into the field. Guess what? There were officers jostling each other trying to get *out of the field* for safe rear-area assignments! That frosted my ass! I told them to wake up and march to the sound of the guns, to remember why they got commissioned and accepted monthly pay. They looked at me like I was smoking marijuana. I told a superior we shouldn't have *anyone* hanging out in clubs and swimming pools and buying souvenirs and being paid to avoid combat. We should all be out there alongside our South Vietnamese allies who are doing the fighting and dying so we can get the damn job done in a decisive, military manner and go home and not try to turn Vietnam into a damn PX! It's like leadership wasn't really doing the job. He didn't listen so I told him I'd take it upstairs. He wished me good luck but he didn't mean it. I went to higher authority. Two weeks in, I had two colonels trying to fire me.

"Listen, when you have to speak truth, *rank* doesn't matter. Only thing that matters is the *harder right.*"

"So the harder right is to tell the Firstie to go forget himself . . ."

He made a Bear face, a wince, a scrunch with bared teeth. "No, no, don't get me wrong. I'm giving you a summary of what I said. I'm sure I was very respectful in saying it."

I made a quizzical face, and he laughed.

"Okay," he said, "maybe I wasn't as subtle as I should've been. Just tell the Firstie you don't appreciate him disrespecting your sister. Respectfully. That so hard?"

I thought about it. "I just wanted to punch him out. I also considered calling him names and then calling him out. Really couldn't do either one, which kind of left me out of options."

"Yeah, it's a big playing field between going Fist City and cowardly silence, with lots of better options for truly effective leaders. Gus, leaders confront bad behavior; an officer corrects wrongs and prevents injustice. Bad officers look the other way and make excuses for superiors and for buddies. But officers who actually do that right thing and speak truth to authority, are the minority. They fight the weaknesses of human nature.

"But what you ignore, you support, encourage, endorse, and cheerlead. You want this Firstie to keep victimizing females? I don't think so. Talk to him. You don't have the authority to order him to change, but you have the duty to give him feedback so he doesn't interpret your silence as consent."

"Diff, I don't appreciate your disrespecting my sister." I practiced that 20 times. Big Diff Difford lived in command country, away from company barracks, but I was assigned to his table for another month. Sometimes I sat next to him, my internal voice saying, It's not the right time. Wait until we're one-on-one. I was making excuses.

"Arturo," I said, "you spoke right up at the table at Big Diff, remember? Was that real hard for you? I'll see the raise."

"No. Would've been hard to be quiet. I'm in," he said, throwing chips.

"I heard about that," said More Beer Lorbeer. "You know, even in the Berlin Brigade, which was an elite unit, it was real hard to correct a superior. I'll see you and raise five." The Berlin Brigade was a top U.S. Army unit of two battle groups and two highly fit infantry regiments. Surrounded by the USSR's Red Army, they were at the tip of the spear and constantly prepared to fight to the death when the Reds invaded.

"Guys, it's real hard in Asian culture to argue with an elder."

"It's not that easy in the US of A," said Ping Childers. "See the five and bump five."

My planned correction grew stale and then I moved to another table. Speaking then would reveal I'd been paralyzed earlier. With 50 excuses, I'd justified my silence.

In June, Big Diff graduated to great fanfare and reported to his first unit.

Thirty years later, an Army wife told authorities that her husband's commanding officer had given her a choice: have sex with him or he would give her husband a disastrous Efficiency Report and ruin her husband's career. The commanding officer's abuse of this woman had lasted a long time. It was discovered that for years this commander had used his authority and threats to induce a number of Army wives into coerced sex. That commanding officer was General Big Diff Difford. The Army court-martialed him; he was found guilty of charges and specifications and sentenced to punishment, which, in my opinion as a JAG and prosecutor, was unjustly light.

My silence had been an act of disrespect to Big Diff. More importantly, it dishonored the women he victimized, the husbands he cheated, the families he destroyed, and the children whose spirits he had broken. Instead, I'd paid homage to my fear of conflict and my desire for social acceptance.

When I was 20, Major Schwarzkopf had equipped me to remedy my fear of conflict. I should've found Sergeant Rock and apologized to him.

That would've been my warm-up for telling Difford that I didn't appreciate his disrespecting my sister and that I was disappointed in his womanizing, a practice that was beneath him and not worthy of a West Pointer.

Difford probably would have brushed me off, and I might have lost a chevron of cadet rank, but I believe that conscience is stirred in the worst of us, and can be triggered by simple words from the least of us. I knew that then, because the Bear had taught me rightly.

17

Learn from History

We learn from history that we learn nothing from history.
George Bernard Shaw

The war in Vietnam was in its second year and it was not going well. Thousands of American soldiers had been killed, the North was increasing its operations, and the South Vietnamese Army appeared to be unready to take responsibility for the war while the United States was acting as if it were an American conflict. Massive anti-war protests, covered in detail by the media, were spreading on the nation's college campuses.

"You want to talk about Vietnam," said the Bear. Driven by hunger and generosity, he'd invited me back to his quarters after the exciting victory over Penn State. He began to make food. Being back in his Q was like coming home.

"Sir, there's something I know about China and Vietnam and I think our faculty doesn't know it. That's what I wanted to talk to you about. I've been holding it in like for years."

"Go ahead."

"Sir, did you know that Vietnam's greatest traditional arch-enemy is China?"

"China? But China and North Vietnam are allies."

"Sir, I think only in name because we're near China's border again. I think China would actually fight North Vietnam long before it'd genuinely help it. Chinese will go through the motions of helping the Vietnamese, but the hatred's real and it's deep and down to the bone. Hanoi's real ally is

Moscow, not Beijing. When Russia helps North Vietnam, they get to gore China at the same time."

He stopped his work. "So Vietnam's arch enemy is China, and they're both Red, but they're not allies. Russia's hated China since the Mongol invasions. With what evidence do you support that wild conclusion about China and Vietnam?"

"Sir, the Chinese Empire triggered the hate when they invaded Vietnam in the first century A.D. They set up a full military occupation and a Chinese imperial government. But the Vietnamese never stopped fighting and resisting with guerilla warfare. China had to keep sending more troops to beat down the rebels."

The Bear looked up. "Like we are, now."

I nodded. "Sir, Vietnamese peasants fought China's army—the biggest professional army in the world—much bigger than Rome's. But the Vietnamese, using China's own homegrown, Sun Tzu-based guerrilla tactics, defeated them in a protracted conflict that culminated at the Battle of Bach Đằng River in 938 A.D. It was the longest war in world history. Made the Hundred Years War look like a skirmish. And the border between them is still armed and they still hate each other. Beijing has to love us fighting the Vietnamese for them."

He looked at his bookcases. "Rome and Parthia. Arab invasions. Spanish Moorish War—that lasted 781 years. Vietnam fought China longer than 800 years?"

"Yes, sir, the Vietnamese fought the Chinese Empire for *a thousand years,* and not only that, they *defeated* China. Then, the Mongols invaded Vietnam three times, and, also failed." I accepted the warm plastic plate.

Major Schwarzkopf thought while I ate a steaming hot dog with all the fixings. Not eating, he nodded. "If true, these two Oriental peoples have hated each other for 2,000 years, up to the present. History in the Far East uses a different clock . . ."

"A slower clock, sir."

"Also true in the Middle East, where it's also much slower than the West. They expect little change in centuries. We expect change *tomorrow.*"

"Sir, the Vietnamese then beat the next invaders, like I said—the Mongols, the French, and the Japanese. Technically, we're fighting the Fifth Indochinese War. What we have to remember is that they've always outlasted stronger armies."

The Bear gave a quick grace, thanking God for the food. I stopped chewing.

"And your point?"

"Sir, our government's saying that we're in Vietnam to stop Red China. But China is Vietnam's arch enemy. Ironically, fighting in Vietnam *helps* Red China more than *deters* it. Plus, the Vietnamese are world champs at fighting foreigners. The Chinese army, a thousand years ago, said it was like fighting locusts. The Vietnamese couldn't destroy the Chinese army, but the Chinese army couldn't defeat the Vietnamese. And, they killed lots of Vietnamese civilians, which added to the arch-enemy relationship."

"Classic protracted warfare," said the Bear. "On a slow Asian clock."

"Sir, does this info help you? You know, like you learning from the least of these?"

"You mean, other than depressing the hell out of me?" He laughed and so did I. "I'm surprised you're quoting the Bible."

"Geez, I didn't know I was."

"You're an interesting guy, Gus Lee. I don't think it's about learning or teaching so much as it's about leadership. It's the part about feeding the hungry, clothing the unclothed, caring for the sick and visiting the prisoner, the least of these. I didn't know that Vietnam really hates China. That could mean China won't send half a million troops into Vietnam to fight us like they did in Korea. If they did, it'd be to conquer North Vietnam more than to stop us. That bears some thinking.

"Second, the Vietnamese are uniquely conditioned to fight until the end of time. That means we absolutely must equip the South Vietnamese to defend themselves. Set a thief to catch a thief; set a guerilla fighter to stop another. It can't be an American war, which is what's happening. Okay, Sport. You helped me. I don't know exactly how, but I'll think about it." He smiled. "A 20-year-old kid gives his old, wise professor, a man who's lived around the planet and gone into the bush to see the elephant, a history lesson."

From the least of these.

It seemed his thoughts were far away. He looked at the watch that told him the time on the other side of the date line and frowned from an unknown thought.

"Want my hot dogs?" he asked. He'd lost his appetite.

General Matthew B. Ridgway was a 1917 Academy graduate and a fearless combat commander who led airborne drops against the Nazis and reversed the chaotic American retreat in the Korean War. Ridgway was the Army Chief of Staff in 1954 as France was losing in Vietnam, so he sent a survey team to Indochina to assess what it would take for the U.S. to defeat the communist guerillas. He was radical; most U.S. generals and admirals believed airpower, not superior soldiers on the ground, would win wars. The team foresaw an American nightmare; Ridgway spoke truth to authority and delivered the report, and President Eisenhower chose to not intervene in Vietnam.

Behind the scenes, French President Charles de Gaulle said that if America did not support his war to reconquer Indochina, France would quit NATO and join the Soviet bloc. Reluctantly, America began funding France's renewed imperialism.

In 1966, as we began the academic year at West Point, the United States was deeply committed in Vietnam. France abruptly withdrew from NATO, ordered NATO headquarters out of Paris, made diplomatic overtures to Moscow, and openly criticized the United States for its military intervention in Vietnam.

18

Be an Honorable Man in All Things

There's always one to turn and walk away
And one who just wants to stay
But who said that love is always fair?
And why should I care?
Diana Krall

"Free next Saturday?" he asked. Major Schwarzkopf was in gray slacks and a heavily starched white dress shirt with gold cuff links and shined black shoes. We seldom wore civvies. When we did, we tended to wear Academy colors: black, gray, and gold with unstylishly short hair.

"Yes, sir." He'd been canceling our meetings and going to New York, and was now packing. I never cared about clothes but I studied how he dressed.

"How come," he asked, "you're always available? Break up with your girlfriend?"

I said I was dating a couple of people while still being in love with a girl in California.

"You date girls but hang out with a hard-ass officer who pushes you around. And you're chasing a girl 3,000 miles away who's not interested in you."

"Sir, sounds like a winning formula to me. I thought everyone did that."

"Not in my world they don't." I noted that he folded shirts with great care.

"Sir, no offense, but you've been seen dating several different, kind of spectacular, women. Unless it's the same person and she changes identities."

"You guys talk about my dates? And the talk is I'm some sort of socialite?"

"Sir, you're the talk of the town. Or, maybe your dates are; they look like they're from *Playboy* magazine. Not that anyone here reads it, or, looks at those pictures."

"Watch your Honor Code, Mister," he said.

"Sir, you're admired for lots of things, to include dating great looking women. You know that we cheered you a couple weeks ago when you brought your date into the Post Theater. You were like a rock star." Cadets had whistled and applauded.

Later, he brought another woman whose more quiet beauty and warmth stilled us with somber envy.

The Bear evaluated ties and picked two that were wider than the ones we wore in the early 1960s. "All that hullabaloo for a truly disgusting movie. We left after 10 minutes." He became serious. "Dating is about finding your mate. I know after a few dates if she's the right one. It's a serious search mission. It's finding the person you're going to spend the rest of your life with and have children with and trust your life to. I want a wife who'll inspire her kids to get to heaven. And me too. But there's no way I'd lead someone on without a real future, regardless how good she looks."

That was a sobering statement. "Woof! Well, sir, let's talk about history instead."

He laughed. "This topic makes you bark like a dog? Think about this. It's the biggest decision you'll make."

"Sir, what if you end up being crazy about a date, but it's not reciprocated?"

"I'd not waste her time or mine."

"But, sir, if she's the OAO?" The One And Only. "Wouldn't she be worth the chase?"

"Gus, what would happen if I courted her like Don Juan and convinced her to marry me when she didn't really want to? She'd be marrying me to be an Army wife. You said we were in for a long war; I'd be gone a lot and she'd have to sweat my not coming back or coming back with missing pieces. She'd have to raise kids with a dad who'd routinely come home at 9 or 10 at night. You may have noticed: We're not civilians.

"I guess if I met the exact right person, and she'd be broken by Army life, I'd have to make a career decision. But the girl I have in mind? She'd be okay with traveling around the world and being part of a tight-knit community that serves the nation."

I paused. "I never thought about that. The girl in California, she's real anti-military."

The Bear shook his head. "That's four things you're stupid about."

"Four? I thought it was just math and chasing my dream girl. How'd I get four?"

"You're weak in math because you choose to not study and you think avoiding conflict is smart—that's two issues of character."

"Oh. Those four."

"What's your reasoning behind chasing the unavailable girl?"

"Sir, I'm an optimist. She dates these guys who are just fluff. I'm not fluff."

"Listen, 'optimism' is a nice word for making excuses. 'Things will turn out well' is imaginary thinking and that's a lousy strategy in war and it's worse in life. So what's doing the right thing with her?"

"Sir, I just can't see any alternative to pursuing her."

"Not too long ago, you pounded on me about leaders at the top who just can't see any alternative to what they're doing. You know, the Vietnam-China situation."

"Jeez, sir, it's not that bad, not as bad as not understanding history!"

"I love history, but I think choosing the wrong wife would be a little worse than not grasping the significance of the Industrial Revolution."

"Sir, I guess this is going to sound stupid, but I've invited her to New York during Spring Leave. I think she's coming."

He sighed and closed his suitcase and zipped up the garment bag. "She paying her way or are you footing the bill 'cause she's without funds?"

"She has funds, I think, but I'm paying."

"Well, Sport, that sounds like reinforcing a lousy original plan by sending more troops to execute the original lousy plan."

"Sir, I'm just trying to date her. It's not like international diplomacy."

"As previously referenced, international diplomacy may prove easier than what you're trying. An individual's policy can be as disastrous as a national one, *pourrait-il ne pas être,* no? Could it not be?"

"Sir, what would you do in my shoes?"

"I'd tell her to fly out if she's really interested in me. If she's not, if she's coming as a tourist for a free trip to New York City, then stay home with the Fluff Boys."

I thought about that. It sounded right, but felt awful, undoable. It struck me that I was as stuck on her, like a death march, with the same fixity of purpose I had about avoiding Edith, my stepmother. I missed one so much that it hurt, while the other was painful to think about. I didn't like the similarity, so I chose to not think about it anymore.

"You listening, Sport?" He was tying his tie, the second-to-last act of a free man about to take a weekend.

"Sorry, sir. I sort of checked out there."

"Gus, you asked my advice. When have I been wrong?"

I tried to think of a humorous remark I could make. There wasn't one.

"Sir, how do you tell a date you don't want to see her anymore?"

"Ah ha! Thinking of how to tell your California gal?"

"No, sir. Thinking about the ones I'm seeing here."

"Well, that's a good start. How do I do it? Pleasantly, I say I'm going to be busy. Polite code. What do you tell the girls you're dating but aren't serious about?"

"Sir, I was up front. I told them about the girl in California. I discussed this with our Honor Rep. (Each company had an Honor Code Representative who was the resident expert on the Code and on regs.) It's not an honor violation to see a girl you're not going to marry." I smiled smugly.

"What's your plan to not break the heart of the girls you're dating?"

"Sir, I can't break their hearts. I'm not doing anything with them that their dads would kill me for. We don't go that far."

"Well, good for you. What's your plan with them so everyone's clear about what the future is so there isn't emotional disappointment and hurt?"

"Sir, I don't have one. One's a college grad and the other's from a rich family and is pretty worldly. They're both older and wiser than me. I just see them occasionally."

"Holy crap! That's cheesy! Listen, Sport, if you date and she has any hopes for the future, and you keep seeing her? Maybe it's not an Honor violation, but it's not honorable. There's a famous saying: 'The man who lies to a woman pierces her very heart.' You should remember that."

I frowned with the truth of it. "Who said that?"

He shook his head. "Not important. A commander reveals his intent through a crystal-clear window to his troops. An honorable man reveals his intent to the people in his life with the same clarity. You have to be an honorable man, Gus, in everything you do. That's a double-down with your soldiers and with the women in your life.

"I wouldn't bring out your California girl unless she's crazy about you. Otherwise, you're nuts. Don't date anyone more than twice unless you're looking to pursue her, whether she's close or far. Otherwise, you're just using them to avoid loneliness."

"Those are pretty harsh rules, sir. I doubt if many in the Corps (of Cadets) do that."

"Gus, don't let social culture dictate actions. Don't be common. Be honorable. You know the line: 'Live above the common level of life.'"

He did the final act and put on his Rogers Peet gray sport coat. He picked up his suitcase, I took his garment bag, and we went out the door to his Pontiac GTO. Fall was sliding all too quickly toward winter snows and the sleet of Gloom Period.

Becoming a man Major H. Norman Schwarzkopf might admire wasn't going to be easy. I wondered if I should aim lower.

Years later, when I saw a photo of Brenda Holsinger Schwarzkopf, the ideal woman that he married, I realized that she was the reason that the Corps envied the Bear in the Post Theater. No one remembered the movie; we all remembered her.

19

Cross the River of Fear

As a general of his forces, there are certain commands of his Majesty which, as his general, I am unable to accept.
Sun Tzu

Using updated grades, the Academic Department re-sectioned our classes. The Bear, perhaps now more favored by his department, was moved up to Section 5. So was I.

Early in the new section, after doing well on the daily mechanical engineering writ, he rewarded us by giving us a military tactical problem as a hypothetical. On an ancient and well-used chalkboard, he drew a small section map with terrain features and the international border between South Vietnam and Cambodia. He wrote with such speed that he kept breaking the chalk. The fragments that couldn't keep pace with his fearsome velocity fell to the floor. His voice was sharp and hard.

"You're a captain with a company-sized infantry unit. Your mission: Stop enemy infiltration into South Vietnam from Cambodia. Your AO is at a major incursion point in heavy jungle on the Cambodian border. This is the specific border the president of the United States has ordered you to not cross. PAVN (the NVA) has invaded Cambodia, put Kampuchean villages to the torch, wiped out the inhabitants, beheaded the village chiefs, and now uses that area to laager their forces for routine, platoon-sized strikes on your unit and allied units on your side of the border in Vietnam. After hitting you and causing casualties, they flee back across the border to sanctuary. It would take a brigade-sized force to secure the border against their penetrations, and your company represents two percent of the strength of a brigade. You can't set a static Maginot Line defense. Presume further that you're isolated with limited air and artillery support.

"In a nutshell, if you pursue the enemy across the border, you violate a direct order from highest national command authority, with all that such an act entails.

"If you don't pursue, you're going to keep losing your men. What are your questions?"

We looked at each other; we looked somber. Questions began flowing.

"Sir, are we leading Americans or South Vietnamese?"

The Bear said, "Good catch, but let's presume it's irrelevant. Either type will serve equally. Just keep in mind that if it's American troops, you'll need five times as much in resupply volume than with ARVN, with all the exposure that comes with it."

"Sir, are we being effective in stopping infiltrations?"

"Forty percent effective and dropping, where 60 percent effective is failure."

"Sir, what'll happen to mission effectiveness if we successfully hit the NVA on the Cambodian side of the border with our riflemen, before they hit us?"

"I'd expect 80 percent effective. In this difficult area, that'd be unqualified success."

"Sir, have we reconnoitered across the border, so if we crossed, we have good intelligence on terrain and likely enemy resistance?"

"Recon shows the enemy hasn't fortified its positions on the other side of the border."

"Sir, would a company-sized strike across the border likely stop the attacks on us?"

"Yes."

There were no more questions.

"Okay, Captain," he said to us, "what do you do?"

I knew the answer. This wasn't college; it was West Point. We honor our promises.

"Those who'd disobey the president and would cross the border to take out the enemy, raise your hands."

Three guys raised their hands.

The Bear regarded them in silence. "Lower your hands.

"Those who would obey orders and therefore devise a plan to deal with our losses in other, less disobedient ways, raise your hands." It was a given that when the Bear asked questions, there could be no abstention or neu-trality. You had to commit to a solution. He'd told me that Eisenhower, the builder of the greatest coalition force in modern history, required every team member to commit to a position.

I firmly raised my hand with the majority of the section.

The Bear studied our faces, the lawful and obedient. "I don't agree with you. You've taken the first step to becoming *careerists*." His tone with the last word equated careerism to his opinion about his being a TOAD instead of being an actively committed infantry officer in a time of war. He regarded career protection as naked selfishness.

"I think you're wrong. No, keep your hands raised so you can feel it. You must not be stinking *careerists*. Guys, you're not paid to protect your career. You're paid to protect your men and accomplish the mission. You're not paid to 'get ahead.' You promised to serve. *Serving* doesn't mean getting your guys killed to look good to higher HQ. Choosing between saving the lives of your men and ending your career. Come on, guys; that's an easy choice.

"Hands down." His tropical tan had faded. The color in his cheeks returned.

"YOU HIT THE ENEMY!" He slammed his big left fist on his desk. The lamp fell, the pencil holder sailed outward, and dust particles atomized. "Hit them in their soft spot, destroy their weapons, and use an excellent egress plan to get your guys and key enemy prisoners back to base camp. Then tell your boss you violated the order, you crossed the border that you weren't supposed to cross, and you happily take the consequences."

I thought of George Washington reporting that he'd cut down the fabled cherry tree. It was consistent with a man who refused to question a fickle Congress that wouldn't pay his troops, actively entertained replac-ing him with political, careerist officers, and who declined the kingship of America. I was about to say, "Sir, like Washington and the . . ."

"In the style," said the Bear, "of your classmate last year. He turned himself in for an Honor violation for not reporting classmates who were cheating in Physics and Chemistry. I think he should've turned his buddies in because he raised his right hand at the river and took the oath and promised to follow the Honor Code, regardless of the emotional pain. We love our classmates, but you must love honor more. A man who puts friends in front of principles will screw it up. 'The officer on duty has no friends.' You see me mess up, you'd better challenge me! That's what leaders are expected to do. You do the right thing and you welcome the pain that comes from doing the right thing. You don't give a damn for the pain. You can even welcome it."

I remembered that beloved classmate. We still missed him, and always will. I'd romanticized his turning himself in for having tolerated cheating. The Bear was saying that if you promise to do something honorable, you'd better do it, particularly if it involves buddies. I assumed I could do it. I took a deep breath. This was all so hard.

I looked hard at the Bear. He's saying, "Because I can do it, so can you. Because we have to do it, we must do it, so must you."

We were lifting in the gym. I said, "Sir, that border problem wasn't really a hypothetical, was it?"

He smirked as he mongered the heavy iron. "I look," he grunted, "like an . . . independent SOB . . . who'd go out of his way . . . Unnggghh! To protect his men?" He dropped his 80-pound dumbbells with a loud, echoing crash.

"Sir, you look exactly like that kind of officer. Sir, what happened to you after you reported that you'd violated a presidential order? I mean, I'd think you'd end up on a remote radar station in Korea or counting polar bears up in Fort Richardson."

"Hey, don't knock polar bears." He grinned. "I kind of like bears and I'd love that kind of duty." He racked weights and stretched. "That was a sweet mission across the border, but we got no prisoners. I called in the results of the sortie and gave them the coordinates of our strike. I was waiting for someone to say that I was relieved and that they weren't going to send a chopper for me so I'd have to walk out across half of Vietnam with my knapsack and a bandoleer of rice.

"A superior says, 'Is that where I think it is?' I say, 'Roger that, sir. Deep in Indian Country on the other side of the bright yellow demarcation line.'"

"He says back, 'On my map, it was a good mission. Out.'"

I was dumbfounded. "That's it, sir? Higher (higher HQ) just ended the transmission? They didn't write you up, give you a Slug, put you on the Area with punishment tours, break your saber, or whatever they do to you in the Regular Army?"

"Well, they didn't do nothing. I got more ammo and medical supplies."

"And those two colonels who wanted to fire you? They weren't part of this?"

"If they were, I didn't hear from them."

"Wow, sir. So God really loves you."

"Whoa, I thought you didn't believe in God."

"Sir, I don't. Heck, I don't even know why I said that. Must've been like a druggie flashback or something, except, I don't take drugs. Sir, I'm sorry I blew the answer on your crossing-the-border hypothetical. I hope I'm not a real *bad* careerist."

"Relax. You'll get it right. I said you guys were *on your way* to becoming careerists. You feed Plebes on weekends, buff up your boys' abilities, and use persuasion instead of screaming. This wins no points with the Tactical Department. That's not the pattern of a careerist."

"Well, that's good to hear. Sir, don't you think that problem you gave us in class was kind of a trick question?"

He huffed as he finished a set of 85-pound dumbbell presses and dropped the weights on the old, complaining floor. I sympathized. I did my next set using 55 pounders.

"Listen, Sport. Every real question in life comes off as a trick ethics question. And the answer's always the same to tough questions: Do the right thing."

"Regardless of what the heck happens to you."

"Exactly."

"Sir, are there always guys around like those two colonels who wanted to fire you?"

He sadly nodded. "Officers who take stands for the right appear via addition. Rear-area types who pontificate about combat while avoiding it, and the ones who dish down on Vietnamese soldiers without having been in action, and general officers who won't risk their stars to say a policy won't work—they seem to multiply."

"So there are Courtney Massengales in the Army," I said. Massengale was the dangerously egotistical antagonist in Anton Myrer's popular Army novel, *Once an Eagle*.

He nodded.

"And you've been taking them on since you got commissioned."

He shrugged his big shoulders.

"Sir, it's sad you'll never be a general. I really think we need generals like you."

He laughed. "You're probably right about the first part. Don't know about the second. I haven't made all my mistakes yet. I hate injustice so much I could spit. Instead, I yell at people. We'll see how I turn out." We racked his dumbbells as we both upped the weights.

He asked me about the Battle of Crécy. I knew it was in the Hundred Years War, but little else. Liking the Battle of Agincourt and Henry V's stirring Band of Brothers speech before battle had led to my ignoring Crécy, a similar engagement that had also been won by English archers.

"It was the summer of 1346," he began. "Kings ruled by divine right, chosen by God, so before battle, kings normally drank and ate with their closest nobles and prayed for deliverance. The night before Crécy, the English king, Edward III, walked the lines of his longbow men, the divinely ordained regent touching the shoulders of poor, unwashed commoners that stank of marching across France. Edward blessed their arms, thanking them, encouraging them, for the next day these unarmored men would face 10,000 French knights on war horses, the equivalent of today's heavy tanks, while being outnumbered more than three to one; Edward had less than 2,500 knights. In those days, as you know, knights determined victory.

"On the other side of the field, France's King Phillip VI was drinking with his nobles while calculating the next day's ransoms from capturing England's outnumbered horsemen." He rubbed more chalk on his hands for the next lift. "You know what happened. The English had prepared defenses. The French knights attacked pell-mell, racing each other to capture the enemy like it was a game. They trampled their own Genoese crossbowmen. The English longbow men stood their ground and mowed down the French with their new, ballistic-like Bodkin arrowheads, killing them by the thousands. It was a total rout. Edward III and Philip VI were like Sam Damon and Courtney Massengale, the characters from *Once an Eagle*. Both had smarts, but Damon selflessly loved his men. Massengale loved rank and promotion."

"We have to be Sam Damons," he said.

I kept in my mind the image of crossing the Cambodian border. I was afraid of crossing borders, with or without presidential restrictions. I later envisioned that border as my river of fear. Brash officers would cross it regardless of risk to their men; fearful officers wouldn't cross regardless of risk to the mission; and courageous officers would always confront their fears to protect their men and advance mission, willingly giving up private hopes for recognition or advancement. The harder right.

The Bear wanted us to be river-crossers regardless of risk to self. To be this, we'd have to be virtuous men who'd routinely sacrifice self-interest for principles and for others. *He* could do that. I knew he was right. I'd have to think about doing that myself.

I remained in dire difficulty with Juice and Nukes. I hadn't told him about that. I now wondered if that was my river of fear.

20

Respect All Persons

I pray thee, O God, that I may be beautiful within.
Socrates

I whistled "Winter Wonderland" on the long uphill ice-covered walk from the Commissary. Out of breath, I realized my tootling sounded like the peeps of a frozen baby chickadee. It didn't suggest music but captured by the spirit of Christmas, and warming to my third New York winter, I persisted. I tried to blink away pelting snow. Between my zero vision and the world sat frost-covered glasses that now could only detect traffic by a collision. In heavy rain, I used to joke that I needed windshield wipers. In snow, I needed a guide dog and a flare gun. In the drifts, unable to tell sidewalk from street, I stopped, tugged my glasses from the skin of my face to clean them, and had the psychedelic sensation of global disorientation and skin-hurting cold. I smiled at a French impressionist world of blurred shapes and weeping colors. Some became a car with a loud horn. It was a bonus West Point preview of coming Manchurian weather attractions on the Korean DMZ.

When I was a nine-year-old kid with new glasses, I saw piles of fake snow in San Francisco's Christmas-decorated department store display windows. I thought back then that real snow was only in Siberia and the North Pole, and otherwise was a Hollywood fiction to season Christmas movies.

Encountering real snow was another West Point shock. It was cold, heavy, and chilling, whipped by cruel, biting, and horizontal cyclonic winds that vacuumed icy air from the frozen Hudson and shot it through Long Johns and wool uniforms to set up housekeeping inside our bones. The worst part was that it returned every year.

I now stood inside the relative warmth of the building to shiver and shake the amazing snow from my heavy caped, Sherlock Holmesian long winter overcoat and to pound thick snow and hard ice from frozen shoes and feet. I ascended the stairs as my half-functioning, paralyzed lungs sought air. East Coast and Korean winters always occluded my vision, shut down my airways, and made my back and my flat feet ache more quickly.

Major Schwarzkopf, in gray Army sweats, put down a big book in his small quarters to find plastic cups as I ungloved. His radio was loyally set to Cadet Radio Station KDET, which would play Christmas carols with its muscular broadcast radius of one mile while his ancient room heater clanked its own happy tune. The carols never failed to fill me with nostalgia for warm family Christmases I'd never known and a wonderful hope that I'd actually experience them. Yet, there was a sadness to this moment, as if this moment in a BOQ was not how people should celebrate the holiday.

"Merry Christmas and Beat Navy, sir," I said, raising the egg nog. It was a familiar Dickensian, YMCA Noel that I'd known since I was seven: lost boys separated from families, wanting loving parents, and yearning for a heartwarming Norman Rockwell Noel while raiding the cafeteria for sandwiches and leftovers. The Bear casually waved at my toast and sipped. I guzzled mine and quickly refilled.

We'd beaten Navy, 20-7. Nothing like wiping out one's enemy to warm the heart with good will toward men. In front of a national television audience with President Johnson and 100,000 in the stands, we marched onto the Philadelphia field only recently renamed for the late John F. Kennedy. The brigades of cadet and midshipmen stood at attention, excited for the game, praying for victory, and missing our recently assassinated president.

Christmas leave was coming; I asked what he would do.

The Bear didn't answer. Later, I learned that the growing anti-war movement that was splitting the country was impacting his family as it had hit mine.

He said my parents would be excited to see me. There are true confessions and faked ones. I gave half-hearted ones to the Bear.

"Sure, sir." I paused. "But, not really. I just try to avoid them. When I can't, I try to be polite." I smiled for levity and the Christmas spirit. "But I think I grind my teeth a lot."

"Let me ask you this: Is your father hard on everyone or just you?"

"Sir, he's pretty generous with his anger, not just me. It's . . . it's hard to explain." I took a deep breath, which caused some chest rattles. "Thing is, he's embarrassed by me."

"Even with you here at West Point?"

"Sir, he parades me around to his friends when I'm home on leave. But they're really not his friends; he really doesn't have any. But he's disgusted with my low engineering grades. He's hated my dislike of geometry and trig since the third or fourth grade."

"You had trigonometry in the third grade?"

"Sir, that's when he started trying to teach me geometry and trig and began throwing calculus at me. I really didn't understand his Chinese *or* his English. Or his math. I, uh, sorta went crazy." I'd said too much. I couldn't look at the Bear. He'd become very still.

"How did you go crazy?"

I bared my teeth, unable to hold back from him. "I . . . laughed. I'd start laughing at his lessons. Hysterical laughing when nothing was funny. You don't laugh at a Chinese father but I couldn't stop. He'd hit me, and I'd cry, which just made him hit me more. One time, I think he was afraid, or worried, but I didn't have glasses so I couldn't have seen that. But it was like I was above the table, above us, watching myself do it. I was panicked by his anger and really scared that I couldn't stop. Like I'd become someone else, a person I didn't know, and he'd have to kill me. I was weak and blind and unathletic and the undesired member of the apartment. I was kind of insane. Edith told people I had a gear loose."

"How long would these episodes go on?"

"Couple years, I think. Third and fourth grade."

"How long would each episode of unstoppable laughter last?"

"Sir, I have no idea. I'd come to on the kitchen floor, alone. My stomach muscles would be sore for days, but I was also getting pounded on the street and was getting crushed in boxing every day, so it's hard to say. Always seemed like a long time. But then, the lessons stopped for a few years."

"Going crazy wasn't so crazy. It got your father to leave you alone."

"Sir, I didn't mean to do it."

"Not saying you did. When I stepped outside the wire to retrieve the lost elements of our patrol, I watched myself do it, too, like I was someone other than Norman Schwarzkopf. And let me tell you, Sport: I was being crazy, too."

"Little difference, sir. When I was kind of crazy, I wanted to avoid pain. You were rescuing your men."

"Yeah, but both of us were in a pickle. Look, Christmas is a real special time. I loved it every year when you let bygones be bygones, sweep out the old, and sweep in the new. You know, heal wounds."

The Chinese say that as well, except for the forgiveness part, but I said, "Sir, you sound like Ben Franklin."

"Well, Old Ben said a good conscience is like a year-long Christmas. There's a special bond between fathers and sons. Crucial in developing manhood. See the truth of it in the people around us. Guys with good dads solve problems just like their dads. I think guys who didn't have good fathers blame themselves for not being better. Look, if it's not there between you and your father, I've seen it built from scratch. The son can do it."

Ancestors watched from Chinese graves. I shook my head, tiny genetic tremors running laps on my spine. My father was remote, shrouded by Confucian formality, and bristling with rage. Sons had no authority and girls were chattel. To confront the father was to commit mortal and social first-degree suicide.

The Bear looked at my inner silence.

"Not liking your father isn't good," he said. "Listen, if he's hard and distant, which is typical of a lot of fathers, you need even more to be patient and attentive. Last year, living as a Vietnamese, I figured out that idea is like that *yin-yang* opposites thing."

"Sir, our *yin-yang* is that our father does the opposite of what we'd like."

"Sport, don't pack that into the Army or try to lead others with that because it's not about like or dislike. Real leadership is far above how we feel about things; it's about doing the right thing irrespective of how we *feel* or where we came from. Courage isn't an emotion; it's a decision. Emotions are easy, so we have cowards.

"Gus, don't return disrespect for disrespect. You got to respect *all* human beings—even your worst enemy in the middle of the biggest damn firefight of your life. Disrespecting the enemy gets you into hate and then you'll make emotional decisions that'll endanger your guys.

"I say, forgive your father. Heck, forgive all the people that pounded little-man thinking into you when you were a defenseless little sprout. Look,

I confess that I'm not a champ at doing this, but my problems don't make what I'm saying less true."

Advancing into his 60s, my father had studied for and obtained an engineering license. He'd just gotten his first true paying American job with a major engineering firm in San Francisco and was reportedly delirious. I was happy for him. I wrote him a congratulatory letter, a missive framed in respect, untainted by my emotional reactivity, unadulterated by my lifelong fear of him and my old fixation on like or dislike. I could sense my sisters' criticism, that I was forgiving a person who didn't merit forgiveness.

It was Christmas, a time, regardless of faith, for goodness and light. I'd always wanted to be in a family like Karin Carlson's, whose wonderful mom and dad had warmly welcomed me into their home. When carols played, I imagined flying like a small Chinese spirit into their front room to watch Karin and her brother open presents, and Mrs. Carlson would say, "How I wish Gus were here. He'd love being part of us." If I could learn how to be part of an Anglo middle-class family. I'd have to learn more to ignore history and respect my father.

On Radio KDET, company mate and disc jockey DJ "Moose" Altemose said, "Songwriters Nöel Regney and Gloria Shayne saw a young mother pushing a baby carriage. It was the Cuban Missile Crisis, back when you Firsties were high school seniors fearing impending nuclear holocaust that would end the world. They wrote 'Do You Hear What I Hear' as a call to peace. They were so emotionally ripped they couldn't sing the lyrics. Here's the beautiful Diahann Carroll covering this song, with a special dedication to the Avengers in A-3." Moose spun the platter, the drums rolled, and for an instant, as I often did in those days, I imagined it was Karin singing to me.

Said the king to the people everywhere
Listen to what I say
Pray for peace, people everywhere!
Listen to what I say

The Bear sang along with the words, "pray for peace, people everywhere." I remained silent; whenever I sang along with the radio, roomies would bare their teeth in agony and remind me that the performer didn't need my help. My jaw dropped; the Bear had a stunningly beautiful voice.

I wanted to ignore the Bear's truths about how I should live, not just as an Army officer and a leader of men under stress, but as a human being in an imperfect world. I wanted to pretend to merely agree with him and move on to any subject not involving my father. But I was decked by the sentimental punch of Christmas and its carols, and knew that I needed to listen to what he said, that I should lead the way to peace with my angry father. Beyond writing a letter, I just didn't know how.

"How do I do that, sir? How do I respect him when he's being a . . . you know."

"How do you treat me? Listen to me, even when you don't like what I say?"

"But sir, you feed me."

He grinned. "Listen, Sport. If you think you were hurting because you didn't have enough to eat as a kid, you haven't a clue what pain it caused your father that he didn't have a job and struggled to buy food for an immigrant family in a new land. Officers don't make it about their own hardships. They know someone else is always hurting more. When you're with him, just treat him the way you treat me."

Do you hear what I hear
Ringing through the sky, shepherd boy,
Do you hear what I hear
A song, a song, high above the trees
With a voice as big as the sea
With a voice as big as the sea

21

You Need Reliable Friends

Think not on those faithful who praise all thy words and actions, but on those who kindly reprove thy faults.
Socrates

We were talking about family again when he said he was lucky; his father was warm and funny. I sat forward.

"Pop had a great infectious laugh and made *me* laugh. He loved teaching me to do right. He was a hero to me. He was a great soldier who got gassed in the trenches of World War I, and a great detective—a crime stopper. We did real adventures, driving across Persian deserts at dawn to meet tribal leaders in their tents, firing old military rifles on police shooting ranges that he'd built for the Iranians."

"That sounds great, sir. A little like Lawrence of Arabia."

"There was some of that," he said. "In Iran I figured out there's a universal standard of leadership, and it's simply based on the leader doing the right thing. Pop encouraged me to study all people. If I saw a great role model, he said I should copy him. If I saw a lousy example, he said to not do what that guy was doing. Some of that he told me in Farsi."

"That's Confucius! 'See a superior person, emulate him. See an inferior person, look to correct yourself.' My uncle recited that to me in Mandarin last year. I could only recognize two of the words."

"If you're around Chinese speakers, I bet it'll come back to you. I forgot French until I had to use it in Vietnam, and I became almost fluent again." He drank his egg nog. "Science marches on but the best-tasting stuff makes you fat."

"Nothing you have to worry about, sir."

"You kidding! I'm not like you and my Vietnamese paratroopers, born without big guts and 28-inch waists. Remember how much you ate as a Yearling after being starved as a Plebe? Of course you do. You still eat like each meal is your last. You eat more than a pack of hungry wolves. Well, Yearling year, I packed it in and had to diet to make Corps Squad," intercollegiate athletics. "I work out to make sure I don't re-gain."

We were talking about what cadets discussed—sports and girls—without the normal other topics of movies, cars, and complaints about academics, demerits, bad weather, and restrictive Academy life. Some prayed, others drank, few slept enough, no one used drugs, there was no online pornography, football players got knee surgeries like the rest of us took aspirin, and our penal colony members walked punishment tours on the Area. Major Schwarzkopf and I discussed history. It was Christmas, I was sentimental, and felt the Bear was like family; I wanted to talk about Christmas and hope. I started to speak.

"Did you know," he said, "that Hannibal, much more than Caesar, Adolphus, and Napoleon, uniquely showed us, the United States Army, at Cannae how to fight modern war?" In 216 B.C. at Cannae on the Italian peninsula, Hannibal the Carthaginian enveloped and destroyed a superior Roman army in a stunning execution of the military art. For 22 centuries, soldiers and would-be generals had studied it.

"Sir, I didn't know that."

"Gus, what was *the key* to America's success in World War II?"

I thought: so many choices. We were truly unique in industrial strength. We beat the world with it. "Industrial capacity. We were the 'Arsenal of Democracy.'"

"Wrong! It was leadership, which produced our Allied coalition. Without our Allies, all the industrial capacity in the world wouldn't have mattered. First principle: It's always about leadership, and always will be. Without it, we'd have lost. What was our Allied coalition premised on?"

"Mutual need, sir."

"No. It was premised on leadership's ability to respect all persons. No respect, no leadership. No leadership, no allies. Our respecting England, Canada, Scotland, Wales, and the Commonwealth states, and the Chinese, French, and Poles produced reliable allies, without which we couldn't have landed at Normandy and gone on to defeat Hitler. George C. Marshall knew that back in 1919, that'd we need a coalition of democratic states to defeat Germany in a second world war. Most people thought he was nuts: They thought there'd be no need for coalitions because Germany would never rise from the ashes of defeat, and there wouldn't be any more wars. Of course, he was right and they were unbelievably wrong.

"Hannibal taught Marshall that lesson at Cannae, and he's still teaching it to us today. Without a unified coalition of free peoples, we can't beat the great tyrannical states. Hannibal won with a free army of Iberians, North Africans, Gauls, Celts, Italianates, and Africans."

"Even though," I said slowly, "tyrannical states, like the USSR, raise bigger armies."

"Right. Tyrants like Hitler and Stalin create empires and build slave armies that can overwhelm the smaller forces that the democracies can muster, just like Darius and Cyrus and the Ottomans. That's why democracies must band together. They have to do it in peacetime to practice together so the tyrants know it'd be suicidal to take on the coalition of the democracies. And if they do cross the border, then the coalition can whip them. It's the Tolkien myths: elves, dwarves, trees, and men overcoming their individual weaknesses to produce synergistic strength against evil tyrants."

"Sir, you read Tolkien?"

"Stay on course. Listen, Carthage was a center of world trade, putting Hannibal in an ideal nexus to form relationships with foreign tribes to resist Rome. The U.S. economy is the center of world trade and we're riding a decade-long economic boom in jobs and income. Everyone needs our high-quality steel, cars, planes, and manufactured goods. We're the Carthage *and* Rome of this century. And all we have to do is . . ."

"Build coalitions like NATO and SEATO."

"That's right. Democracies need reliable friends and then practice at war so hard, so strenuously, that no one would dare fight us or our independently sufficient allies."

I said quietly, "Like we should do in Vietnam."

"Like I hope we're *starting* to do in Vietnam," he said.

"Sir, we study engineering instead of how to make coalitions." I beamed at him. "I rest my case that West Point ought to let us have non-engineering majors."

He shook his head. "Be realistic. West Point's not going to change its engineering essence anytime soon, or ever. We're talking coalitions as key to the military art; stay in this lane. You can study that without making Sylvanus Thayer, the father of the Military Academy, rotate in his grave. Here's the irony: We study Cannae for Hannibal's maneuver decisions when we should be learning how Hannibal formed a winning coalition of very diverse peoples. With the end of colonialism, that's now of premium import. We should be studying him more and Napoleon less."

I rubbed my face, a nervous gesture when my brain was about to explode. "Agreed, sir."

"What does this have to do with you, right now?" he asked.

"I should be forming a coalition of reliable, democratic friends."

"What does that mean in real terms?"

"No Republicans, sir?" I made a Gallic, Maurice Chevalier smile, the smug and humorous boulevardier who knew the world.

"Very funny, but no cigar," he said without humor. "Drop and give me 50 pushups. Stop, I was just kidding. Gus, you need to pick friends who'll make you a better man. Not just guys to pal around and play cards and do RF's in barracks."

I thought about Rap, Ping, Arturo, More Beer, Pastor Jim, Tony, Moose, Tree, Meatball, Moon, Tommy, and the others. "Sir, I think my friends try to make me a better man. They really do. I think I drive them crazy 'cause I'm not more, you know, responsible."

"Gus, you're very lucky. Having honorable friends is everything. Given that, what's your next job?"

"Sir, to be that kind of friend to others."

It took me a moment to understand my unease. It wasn't about me; it was about him. I knew he was angry that he had to be here instead of with his beloved Vietnamese paratroopers. He resented his department head for ranking academics above fighting at the front, and thought poorly of officers who were avoiding combat. He played tennis with friends but he seemed in many ways to be almost monk-like in serving his academic penitence while awaiting a return to the Army outside the Academy. I imagined asking him if he truly respected all persons, but I was afraid to disturb the incredible connection I had with him.

The Bear wanted to lead an allied force of varied free peoples to rid the world of dictators. He'd bled red, white, and blue and had a great respect for other cultures, but in truth was a citizen of the world.

He wanted to command an ideal coalition army not to kill the enemy, but to outwit him and undo his capacity to fight, to decisively defeat an enslaving army with minimal allied, civilian, and enemy casualties.

He'd envisioned his Cannae when he was a kid in Lawrenceville reading descriptions of Hannibal and the coalition war of ragtag tribes against mighty Rome, and spoke to me about that iconic battle as if it were an American story and precursor to our Revolution, making Hannibal an early George Washington.

I bet Major Schwarzkopf haunted the library for data on Cannae when he was a Plebe, as I had.

I looked at this big, serious man and felt sadness for him. He ought to be a world leader, and wouldn't be. He could lead that great campaign to stun the enemy with minimal casualties on both sides. It was clear he'd never get the chance. The Army would punt him for his unrelenting hatred of injustice, his habit of confronting superiors with forthright speech, his spending time with the weak, and that scarifying temper and hurled sticks of chalk.

The next big war would be a nuclear push-button exchange executed from underground bunkers. Vietnam was becoming big for us, but I had to admit it wasn't being done by a large, unified coalition of democracies. We were violating one of Marshall's key axioms of an army of a democratic state.

I stepped from his Q into the unnatural calm produced by the tail of a great storm. The snow-covered Academy was luminously beautiful. The great bronze statues had become ghostly white pillars. I thought of Lot's poor wife, wondering if we were violating more than Marshall's axioms by breaching the greater principles of war in Vietnam. We weren't fighting decisively. We didn't understand China's role. We were using Imaginary Thinking in trying to plant a democracy in a land without topsoil.

The wind-whipped snow from black mountain tops, the klieg lights on the mount of the great Cadet Chapel, the ranked lights from the Library, barracks, and the shipping on the ice-frozen Hudson described something not of this Earth.

The air was so still that the near-zero temperature seemed Mediterranean. My shoes were still frozen, my glasses quickly fogged from my thin breath, and the world beyond was losing the clarity that it once had, but it was alright. I was warmed by having in my life a reliably moral mentor, whose lessons, I sensed, could be applied in all circumstances.

22

See Your Limitations

We have left undone that which we ought to have done and we have done those things which we ought not to have done.
The Book of Common Prayer, 1549

The harsh winter of 1966 seemed to abruptly turn to spring; I like to think that it was shortened by the moral heat wave generated by a great bear of a man who feared no season. One of my Plebes was failing boxing, so we were in the boxing room to sharpen his skills. Another Plebe in the squad, Larry Henderson, was one of the better fighters in the Corps, but his combination of speed, power, and ferocity didn't add up to a profile that our failing Plebe could emulate in time to pass the class. I'd pulled the Plebe out of afternoon intramural ("Intermurder") athletics and got gloves, mouthpieces, and headgear to review footwork, defenses, and punches. He was country, I was city; he was South, I was West; he was great at math. After the lesson, he showered and I joined a fast-paced pick-up basketball game with our intramural roundball team. I took a break to wheeze in air, head down, slouched with a fatigue-curved back, sweating heavily for an Asian. God, did I love this gym. I removed my badly fogged-up glasses and wiped my face. When I looked up, I enjoyed the distant splashy world of Manet and Renoir that my natural vision produced. The gym looked like Monet's garden of diffused colors. A buddy plopped down on my right, breathing hard.

"Hey," I said.

"I believe it's, 'Hey, sir,' isn't it?" It was the Bear.

I quickly sat up. "Aw, jeez, sir, sorry. Didn't know it was you." I put my glasses on, but they were opaque and of no utility.

"Give me your glasses." I was about to say that he didn't have to clean them, but he was a leader who fed, clothed, and bandaged his men, made sure their needs were met, and prayed over them when they were wounded. I handed them off in the general direction of his voice.

"A little closer, Gus," he said. I leaned outward until I felt him take them from my hand.

I went back to listening to the movement of the game.

"What the hell?" he said. I'd heard that same tone of disbelief when he assessed my first attempts at engineering problems.

"Sir, that happens. The lens is so heavy that it sometimes just comes free of the frame."

I couldn't see his facial expression since I couldn't see his face.

"The lens didn't come out. I'm observing that these lenses are thicker than my neck! They *are* like bottoms of Coke bottles. I'm getting dizzy looking at them! Gus. Why wear them when they're fogged up?"

"Sir, better to have seen with fogged glasses than never to have had any glasses at all." I smiled into blank space. "Think Tennyson would like my little tribute?"

"I doubt it. What's your vision?"

I said it was 20 over 900.

He repeated the numbers. "Really. What's the Army standard for legal blindness?"

"Sir, it's 20-400 if not correctable to 20-20. Sir, I'm not correctable to 20-20, but I had glasses specially made for marksmanship and I qualified Expert with them, so they put me in the neighborhood of full correction. But I can't wear them for more than an hour or I go blind."

He didn't laugh.

"Sir, I'm just kidding. I wouldn't go blind. At least, I don't think so. But my eyes blur up and I can't see for a couple hours and I get pretty noticeable headaches."

"How'd you get in here with legal blindness?"

"Sir, I got four medical waivers from the Surgeon General of the Army. For my eyes, for asthma, scoliosis, and fallen arches, or flat feet."

"Jesus," said the Bear. I heard him scratch his buzz-cut head. "What kind of night vision do you have?"

"Sir, uh, I really can't see at night. Sir, can I have my glasses back?" I wiped them off on my tee shirt and saw Mike "Tree" Peters motioning me back to the game. I pointed at Major Schwarzkopf and his huge, weight room-swollen arms and waved, No Can Do.

"You earned your Recondo badge. You must've passed night land nav," land navigation.

I said that even with moonlight on a night patrol, I'd missed an obvious crevasse and fell for quite a while, with time to wonder at which ring of hell I'd land. I crashed into bushes and rock. The patrol almost lost me because I was lights-out. Later, stumbling blindly in the dark and navigating by the music of the spheres which only the poorly-sighted can hear, I miraculously passed the course.

I'd said too much, and I'd never said any of this aloud. It was *ji hui*, inauspicious talk, to speak of bad outcomes. As a kid, I knew that talking about the chance that mah-mee would die contributed to her death. Sitting in Arvin Gym, renamed for our former First Captain from the great class of 1965, who had been killed in Vietnam, I got the otherworldly sense of superstitions coming true. I wish the Bear hadn't asked me, for now it had been said, in the open, and another had heard it. And that person was Major S.

"What were you going to do about this?"

"Sir, the docs say my waivers are good for Airborne, Ranger, and Infantry Officer Basic." I was employing Imaginary Thinking; something always saved me. Science was coming up with new stuff, and infrared Starlight scopes would soon be miniaturized. By this time next year, I figured, they'll have glasses that will help me see at night. I preferred to think about that and didn't want to see the risks my legal blindness would create for my men.

He shook his big head. "You're kidding yourself. Can't jump with glasses in Airborne. You have to navigate at night in Ranger. Infantry officers, to lead, logically have to see better than their men. You'll endanger people around you in both schools and be a hazard in the field. How the heck did you do the Slide for Life at Buckner? You can't wear glasses for that."

"Sir, you know they wave a little red flag when you're supposed to drop so you don't smack into the cliffs. The sergeant yells, 'Recondo! Do you see the red flag?!' After they took my glasses, I'd felt my way up to the slide station by feel and by buddies guiding me. Who they were, I'll never know. But I had to say, 'No, sergeant, I do not.'

"They got a bullhorn and waved a huge American flag which I could see. 'Recondo! When you sees that big-ass American flag wave an' you hears that bullhorn say DROP, Recondo, you drops yo' blind ass in that lake. DO YOU HEAR ME?!' Funny thing is, I actually saw the flag, so I dropped."

"Real funny. In Vietnam, you have to see at night or you'll get your guys killed. You got to accept your limitations in this. Are you listening? I can't believe you'd put yourself on an azimuth you know won't work and just keep marching on. Jesus!" Agitated, he stood. So did I.

"Listen to me. Don't go Infantry. I know you want to follow me and all that rot. Forget it. I forbid it, and I order you not to, and if you do I promise you I'll kick your ass out. You're high enough in overall class standing to go Artillery or Signal Corps where you're not going to lead a platoon of ground pounders into the soup without even knowing you're doing it!"

Some of the guys in the gym had stopped playing. Admiring the ferocity of the Bear reaming out a Cow was like watching a particularly intriguing Road Runner cartoon.

"See that your limitation endangers others, so don't deny it and accept it as a man accepts it. Jesus Christ, Gus, sometimes you're as dumb as those fish with lights! Now you make sure you graduate so you can go fire cannons or lay out communication wire instead of lead night patrols!"

The Bear was the Poster Man for the glory of the Infantry. I wasn't a natural warrior like so many in the Corps but I wanted to imitate him.

As Whufers, WFRs, or Written Final Reviews—final exams—approached, the Bear and I agreed that I was ready in Solid Mechanics and it was time to stop meeting so he could help others while I prepped for the other courses. I experienced pleasure in realizing that next year was the easiest in academics. Firstie classes were a breeze compared to Cow year. I was going to make it.

There was a grander reason for our not meeting than the approach of finals. I didn't know then that his bachelor habits of isolated study, preparing solitary meals, spending Saturday afternoons with academically challenged cadets, and assessing the appropriateness of women were approaching their terminus; Major Schwarzkopf had found his soul mate.

The exams fell like the hammers of Thor. But all of my Plebes passed their finals; they'd all made it through the hardest and most doubt-incurring year of their young lives.

I passed my mechanical engineering WFRs and received the Bear's congratulations via a phone call to the orderly room.

23

Pay the Price

We have 40,000,000 reasons for failure but not a single excuse.
Rudyard Kipling

We approached the glory of June Week. First Classmen prepared to toss their white dress caps high in the air to celebrate graduation and to form arches of sabers for Chapel weddings, Plebes neared their long-awaited freedom, and we Cows were going to be the seniors, prepared to enjoy the glorious First Class Trip across the nation to tour the Army installations where we'd later take our officer basic courses. On two beautiful days in May, I flunked the WFRs for second semester Electrical Engineering and Nuclear Physics.

Larry "Rap" Rapisarda had given us Goats a series of basic solution templates with which we were to attack the likely problems in the WFRs. Unable to use mathematical reason to grok the algorithms, I "spec'd," or memorized, them, drawing them again and again on reams of blank paper and taping them to the walls. Now it was test day. I stretched as if I were about to fight an opponent several weight classes above me.

We entered our Juice section rooms, staggered desks, and received the thick WFR. I followed Rap's advice: I began by first sketching out the templates on scratch paper so I could use them to match template solutions to questions. I was nervously sketching when I slowed and suddenly stopped. I blinked, shook my head. I silently moved lips: C'mon, you know this; you've done this a hundred times. Just write it down. A boxer can get staggered by a great punch to the jaw and be quickly reanimated by a following punch to temple. I slapped my forehead, trying to free those 15 tiny little frozen neurons that knew the code to electrical engineering.

Instead of ignition, a thick, heavy, almost humid cloud swept over me, gently bent my back, and slowed my rapid breathing. In the midst of the greatest examination of my life, I almost nodded off in a cumulative mental fatigue. I snapped out of it. Good God, stay awake!

What would the Bear do? He'd bear down. He'd fearlessly figure out the solution. He'd remember the template. Be the Bear. I smiled with the thought of him, his certainty, his strength. I magically thought if I invoked the idea of him, his brains would suddenly pour into my cranial vault. The other thought invaded the moment: I should've told him I was in trouble. He'd have happily helped me. I'm an idiot.

In the Advanced Nuclear Physics WFR, I was more prepared for the mental brick wall. I got halfway through the memorized solution templates before I collided with ignorance. After the exams, the Corps gaggled into the sally ports to see our posted grades. I'd gotten top grades in the Humanities, easily passed Solids and Thermodynamics, and failed Juice by a mile and Nukes by a couple of yards.

I'd known the possibility while denying probability. My roomies found it hard to speak. Ping Childers looked at me as if we'd never see each other again. Arturo Torres thoughtfully avoided saying, "You should've told the Bear you needed help."

Another A-3 Cow, whom I'll call Griff, had also flunked Juice. We sat together as the company filed in to wish us luck, to convey academic encouragement by shaking hands, slapping the back, punching shoulders, squeezing arms, thumping the chest, and giving the cheer of athletic teammates. "Go get 'em!" "Knock them dead!" "Grab some tenths for me!" "Kill those blankety-blank re-exams!" We were all thinking of "Gwigs," the much-beloved company mate who'd been found in Juice in the last term.

Plebe Mike Bain and I had spent hours talking about the world. He seemed to understand that these courses were for me a mystical Chimera. Realistically, he said that if I didn't pass, I was to visit his parents at Fort Sam Houston, San Antonio. His dad was a colonel. On several levels, this did not sound inviting.

My Plebes seemed the most stricken and surprised. I realized that I'd somehow misled them into thinking I was a universal brain. A few of them put on a brief musical skit reminiscent of "A Funny Thing Happened on the Way to the Forum." It inspired such powerful emotions of comradeship and loss that my throat closed. I could barely thank them.

Apparently I hadn't fooled the profs. Rap Rapisarda, who should've been enjoying well-earned free time with his beloved Barbara, planned my cram recovery program in both subjects.

I found the gumption to call the Bear with the bad news and to say that Rap had produced an action plan for the re-exams. His phone rang without an answer.

The class of 1967 marched up to Michie Stadium and graduated with a great tossing of white caps and loud bellows not heard since the defeat of Og at the Battle of Edrei. As new second lieutenants, they led the Recognition Ceremony in which every upperclassman shook the hands of every Plebe in his company. Cows then followed Firsties to execute the pleasant task of bashing in each of the Plebes' brilliantly polished brass breastplates with the steel butts of our heavy M-14 rifles. Their momentary pain was the prelude to the happy handshake and the end of the longest year of their lives. The Firsties packed up, sentimental and ecstatic about truly leaving the Point. They left for the war in Vietnam, and the world seemed so much quieter.

The Academy was in our annual post-graduation manic hootenanny as we played musical chairs with our housing. I'd prepped the Plebes for Buckner and the challenges of Sergeant Rock. I shook their hands and wished them luck as they returned the sentiment and boarded the familiar smoke-billowing truck convoy to summer training. The smell of exhaust, hot metal, burning oil, and simmering canvas was a bouquet known to every American soldier.

Every year a fourth of the faculty and staff rotated out of the Academy for new assignments. A year ago, the Bear was one of the few officers on faculty and staff who had been to Vietnam and, within that minority, the first to be in combat and to have been wounded. Now, with nearly half a million troops in Vietnam, and in the days when over 90% of our faculty were officers, many professors were bound for hard duty in Southeast Asia. The BOQ was like barracks: awash in men moving gun boxes, book crates, suitcases, uniforms, barracks bags, and athletic gear. Weaving between movers, I walked up the familiar staircase to learn, with relief, that Major S was on leave. Telling him that I'd failed would mar his incredible dedication to me. It would also trigger his considerable anger, a thing I'd just as soon not enjoy.

Rap began tutoring me. We were at cross purposes. I was capable in Humanities, and he couldn't believe my engineering learning curve was not only flat, but negative in the Y-axis, and plummeting. I found Rap's patience inconceivable while my brain's capacity, under pressure, to learn the new and retain the old began to evaporate. I sat facing piles of incomprehensible Juice and Nukes problem solutions, feebly sparking as my once useful brain shut down like a New York brownout.

The only occupants of barracks who hadn't packed up their rooms were 14 Cows who'd also flunked Juice, Nukes, or English, including Griff and me; 100 Yearlings who were facing re-exams in Physics, Chemistry, and English; perhaps 200 Plebes who were facing execution by Mathematics and English; and our brave and loyal classmate tutors. Rap was of course helping others who'd flunked and had the pleasure of working with fellows who were demonstrating greater mental alacrity than I. That could be said of anyone who could add two numbers and produce the correct answer. There were also two Firsties who'd exceeded the limits of decorum and sobriety who were serving confinement to rooms while the Tactical Department decided to commission them with diplomas or separate them with neither. I was the only Cow facing two course re-exams.

The Class of 1968, dressed in Army summer khakis and well-shined combat boots and carrying B-4 bags, was falling into massed ranks to depart Post. Not being part of them allowed me to see how adult and manly we now seemed. During our Beast Barracks, we were disappearing by thousands of combined pounds; now, we were muscularly filled out. I said "See ya" to classmates as they left for the First Class Trip, in which we, as the new Firsties, flew to the installations that housed the five combat arms branches into which we'd be commissioned next June. Each branch would wine and dine us and set us up with blind dates in cotillion dances and hops in a naked effort to induce us to elect their branch at graduation.

"You'll join us on the Trip after you pass," our classmates said, shaking hands, looking at me and Griff for longer spaces of time than were normal. We said goodbye to everyone in the company, to our best buddies. I had trouble looking at them.

Now, I stood at the concrete apron to the Plain. I was in the cadet summer uniform to say goodbye to my classmates, who were dressed in the uniform of soldiers and streaming to the awaiting buses. I wanted to be a rock but had all the makings of becoming a rolling stone as they streamed past Griff and me.

"Man," said Griff, "this sucks."

"Our first stop is Fort Belvoir, Virginia, home of the Engineers," said Ping Childers. "They saw your engineering grades and I don't think they want you. Gus, skip Belvoir and pass those re-exams. We'll see you at the second stop, Benning, home of the Infantry, and I'll buy the beers."

"See ya there, Buddy," said More Beer Lorbeer. "I came within a tenth of being found in both of those darn courses. I would've given you those tenths if I could've. Kinda wish I'd got found so I could stick here with you and we could both do the turnout exams." Pastor Adams repeated an ardent and rather uncomfortable prayer and Tree Peters was of the same heart. "Just play Buck Owens and the Buckaroos," advised Moon Beahm, "and you'll be good." Arturo shook my hand in both of his, then put his hand behind my head, shaking me. "Work at it, man. Work hard. See you in Georgia. *Carnale, que vayas con Dios*. Do not disappoint us."

"Good luck you guys!" bellowed our company. They, Griff, and I gave the thumbs-up.

I thanked Rap. He'd offered to stay behind and I insisted that he go on the trip. The Engineers really did want him. We both knew what was going to happen.

"I think the first thing," said Rap, "is try to sleep. Recover strength. Then just burn-in the solution structure. You're going to see the same problems in the re-exams." It was good advice. Ever vigilant, I had never been a sound sleeper. Every year during finals, I accepted insomnia.

"Gus, you willing to do Cow year again?"

One remote possibility, usually exercised for football players, was the turn-back option. If you couldn't pass the re-exam, you could repeat the last year. George Patton had done that.

I shook my head. Repeat Juice, Nukes, Solids, Fluids, Thermodynamics? What was passing for my version of a brain fizzled with the thought.

"I thought you really loved West Point," he said sadly.

"I do. But I think I hate my stupidity in engineering, and I probably hate the stupidity of having to take it, more. I know it's immature." It was ironic; after having trouble with sergeants, I was on my way to becoming one. Instead of being last in engineering, I would be the first to report to Vietnam.

"Thank you, Larry," I said, and we shook hands. When classmates meet now, as old men, we hug. Back then, we'd rather shoot ourselves.

The failed cadets were organized into a provisional company. As the last ranking upperclassman, I became company commander, responsible for the good order of a tribe of once outstanding high school graduates who now bore the academic mark of Cain. We looked like gulag prisoners and felt a guilt that should only be experienced by people who harm pets.

The re-exams were administered. A minority passed and sprinted in happy exfiltrations with their gear to join their companies at Camp Buckner or to go home on leave. The majority out-processed to become ex-cadets, and as the ranking cadet, I shook hands with them and wished them well. It was an incredibly depressing exercise.

I went to the gym for a quick workout, hoping it would cure the fatigue and clear the cobwebs from my pea-sized mathematical mind. I hoped the Bear would be at the bench-press station. I could osmotically absorb a hint of his intellectual acuity like a starving *yaofan* want-rice beggar steals the aromas of a Chinese kitchen. The Bear wasn't there. I lifted weights with great intent but my muscles almost instantly hit exhaustion. I walked down the great gym steps which had carried the weight of great Army athletes.

Griff passed the Juice re-exam. I failed both of mine. I helped Griff pack as he donned khakis and boots. We shook hands and using his incredible foot speed, he sprinted for the connections to link-up with our classmates at the Fort Benning gala. He sat in the back of the southbound bus and waved through the window. I waved back and we both flashed thumbs-up.

I never learned the fates of the two Firsties in confinement, but they were also gone. As a ranking Corporal, I should've been out-processed before the others, but I was now the last cadet at West Point.

I went to Thayer Hall and spoke to some of my Humanities profs who were remaining to teach another year. Lieutenant Colonel Pennell Hickey, deputy department head in Military Psychology and Leadership, had been a wonderful teacher and friend. He and his wife had housed my visiting dates with uncommon cheer and warmth.

"I had no idea you were struggling in engineering," he said. "I'd be happy to tutor you should you wish." He smiled. "I still get the willies when I think about those WFRs."

"Sir, that's not the best thing you could've told me."

After reveille, I shaved under the subdued lighting of the worst barracks on Post and was forced to look in the mirror to avoid cutting myself. I saw someone grimacing back at me, as if he'd found the key to wisdom but had lost it in a pocket of one of his trousers.

24

Learn Your Lesson

How does it feel to be on your own, with no direction home,
Like a complete unknown, like a rolling stone.
Bob Dylan

I was standing in his Q.

"Did I get the straight poop?" asked Major Schwarzkopf. He seemed taller than when I last saw him. He was definitely angrier.

"Sir, I flunked both re-exams. They gave me more re-exams, which got easier and shorter, but I flunked them. My brain kind of imploded, stopped working. I mean, I guess I stopped being able to think. In the last Juice re-exam, I couldn't even remember my section number. You write your name and your section number. I couldn't remember it."

"Goddamnit! Why in the name of good God hell didn't you tell me?!" In that moment, I saw with clarity his counsel about respect. I hadn't honored the Bear with candor, with genuineness. I'd chosen instead to follow the path of least emotional resistance, what we at West Point universally knew from our common prayer as the easier wrong. Of course he was angry. I saw that his inward reaction was attributable to my lack of action. But how he expressed that inward reaction to the outer world was his choice.

He scanned me as a commander checks his troops. "By the way, you look like hell."

"Well, thanks, sir, and here I shaved real close and shined my shoes. Sir, truth is I didn't want you to think badly of me. I didn't want to ask you for more favors. It was more important to keep up the appearance that I was doing better than for you to see that I was so stupid. You'd already given me so much . . ."

"Sport, you're not *stupid*. You're *unnaturally cosmically dumb and stupid!* Damn, do you lack judgment! Judgment's more important to a lieutenant than brains and brilliance! Well, damn it, I am very sorry to hear this." He paced, fulminating, huffing like a great Jurassic thunder beast driven by primitive hungers, his cheeks turning colors. I saw him restraining curses and rejecting recriminations, gathering himself to remember to act calmly in the rages of disappointment.

"Don't do anything really stupid, now."

"Sir, I'm not going to harm myself."

"Yeah, you already did that. I mean, don't throw away your textbooks and notes." He rummaged in his tiny bathroom. "Here," he said, giving it to me.

It was a small Army cardboard pillbox. I'd gotten a number of these last year for pain mitigation after being hospitalized with a busted leg from doing a hand-to-hand combat demonstration for Secretary of the Army Stanley Resor.

I read the label on this pillbox: "U.S. Army Nha Trang Field Hospital. Follow physician instructions. Do not exceed recommended dosage."

"They're stay-awake LRRP (Long Range Reconnaissance Patrol) pills," he said. "You're bushed from staying up late cramming. Now it's too late for sleep. Study tonight as if you were going to get *another* re-exam in each course in the morning. When you get drowsy, take one pill. If you want my help, come by. Or, I'll come to Boarders Ward. But you have to ask."

He took a deep breath that expanded his huge chest. He closed his eyes. I thought he was using Jefferson's "count to ten" method of restraining his temper, but his cheeks weren't red, and he said, "Amen" and opened his eyes.

"Now go get it right."

The pill worked better than strong Army coffee. I stayed up all night, ruffling through well-worn notes. I was glad Rap wasn't there to see my useless milling of dead paper. The fellow who found the Rosetta Stone was a Lieutenant Bouchard, one of Napoleon's savants, a technical expert in the expedition to Egypt. Bouchard held the stone, recognized its potential import, but could not decipher it. I splashed water in my face. Looking at a sad Bouchard in the mirror, I knew that there was no way I'd ruin the Bear's rest to witness my futility. Not after all he'd given me.

No damned way.

The next morning I checked the message center in the Central Guard Room after reveille. I was to report to the Department of Electrical Engineering at 0900 in Class uniform. I was to bring pencils. I took yet another exam on Thevenins and Nortons and fearsome circuits of unknown origins. Again, I'd left the section number blank, accompanied by several essentially empty problem solutions. Dazed, I was directed to the Physics Department where I took the final-final-final exam on DeLorentz Transformations and time and space dilation equations and the thrills of quantum thinking. It resembled a long and endless dream of falling when one's innards seek to relocate in one's throat and there is suddenly a universal absence of handholds. I knew with the deadly certainty of gravity that I'd flunked.

That afternoon I met a major from the Dean's Office. He said he was sorry to inform me that I was being separated for academic deficiencies. I asked the useless question: Had I failed both re-exams? I appreciated his kindness as he continued to provide information.

"Mr. Lee, the graders may never fully understand the reasoning for your answers, but rest assured, with few exceptions, they were incorrect." A hint of a smile.

Feeling the reality of losing West Point, and against all good judgment, which the Bear would like to see me exhibit, and my earlier intent, which I quickly abandoned in the panic of leaving, I asked if there was a turn-back option to repeat Cow year.

"Mr. Lee, truly? You'd have to pass engineering again and tighten up on the Plebe System. Major Noll, your Tac, declared you to be the best squad leader he's ever seen and made a big play for your retention. That had a big impact on the Academic Board. But his boss, the Third Regimental Commander said you're lax with Plebe discipline, so you lost points. In the final analysis, your medical profile is the worst in the Corps. Docs gave up on the issues of scoliosis and pes planus, although your fallen arches will keep you out of combat arms. You have to notice that your natural stride makes you slower than anyone else so that you're always running at the end of a 25-mile march. But your vision and pulmonary function are not acceptable even in the Army, much less for a cadet at West Point or a combat arms officer.

"We were wondering. Did you have a political patron that got you your rather unbelievable number of medical waivers?"

I said, no, that I'd never met my congressman.

"Well, then," he said, "it must've been fate."

I was at Trophy Point, gazing at the world through the lenses of Erinyes, the obnoxious Fury of incessant negativity. I tried to memorize the vista of the river and its valley with the eyes of Washington, to carry it with me into my darkened future, sensing I would never stand in this place again. The British were beating the brains out of his barefooted boys of the Continental Army; Congress had fled Philadelphia and wasn't supporting him; the not-lean but very hungry and ambitious Horatio Gates was back-stabbing him; and his best combat commander, Benedict Arnold, had gone over to the enemy with his knowledge of the fortification plans of West Point. Despite this and more, Washington became better, stronger, and clearer against terrible odds.

Bright sunlight danced on the calm waterway as it made its sharp turn around this western point. The Hudson had changed its dark-brown late-winter uniform to one of shimmering and beguiling blue with a brilliance of its buttons and epaulets that hurt the eyes. Birds chirped and sang five-note calls in the maples, Black Ash, White Spruce, and Eastern Hemlocks. The valley was a deep green and the sky was a poetic Chinese heaven. Without the Corps, Firstie cars and moving vans, or great crowds, the Academy was eerily silent. It was an achingly beautiful day.

I heard his fast, hard footfalls. I saluted and the Bear returned it. Then he performed a quick perimeter 360: We were alone.

"Sir, thanks for getting me those additional re-exams . . ."

"Goddammit, Gus! I could've saved you!" hissed the Bear. "If you'd told me about Juice and Nukes I'd have gotten you through them if I had to tie you to your chair and bolt the material to your damn glasses! What made you think I'd think less of you if you were honest! Don't you get it that I'd *love* that?! Yeah, sure, I'd yell at you, and then that'd be over and we could hit the problems, and you'd pass and be schmoozing on the First Class Trip, eating your way across the States, and then you'd have the easiest year at West Point, get your ring, and graduate and get to throw your cap in the air."

I nodded. "Yes, sir."

"This way, you didn't tell me, and you REALLY get yelled at, and you lose out and Sport, you didn't call me last night!"

I nodded.

"What are you thinking right now?"

I took a deep breath, surprised that there was some left after his correction of me. "Sir, I tied up about every way I could. I'm going to miss this place more than I can describe. I was walking out of Thayer Hall and looking at the coat hooks. I stopped and looked at one of them. I, I realized, I'll never see that damn coat hook again. Weird, huh? But it's like I've been cored out. It's such a loss. An inconsolable loss, unmatchable, but it's also familiar, like I've been in this space before. Anyway, sir, the big point is I'll always appreciate the time I had with you."

"You seem pretty damn calm about having taken a gut-shot."

"Sir, I'm kind of tired. Like I'm a fugitive, running my ass off from half of the Academic Department who's been after me with hatchets for three years. I almost made it."

"Listen, Sport, there's no 'almost' in Army leadership. Focus on what you've learned from this. Focus on whether you learned your lesson or not. I want you to learn from this God-awful pain as a man learns from error. Have you gotten your orders?"

I said I was to report to the regimental sergeant major at 1400 hours.

"I'm about to leave. You *will* write me to tell me where you're assigned. Keep me posted about your future plans." He looked at his local-time watch. "In two hours, you'll go from being a Cadet Corporal to a United States Army corporal. You won't get any choices like a West Point grad, but don't do Infantry. Direct order, understand?"

"Understood, sir."

"I'm so pissed I may not shake your hand."

"I understand that, too, sir. Thank you, sir, for all that time, the tutoring, the hot dogs. The talks. The advice. I'm going to miss . . ."

He shook my hand hard, his incandescent eyes burning into me. He spoke to me, but I'd failed him and angered him, and my brain was working with the efficiency of melted butter and my eyes no longer saw and my ears no longer heard. His last words wafted into the warm air over the river. I would never see him again. I had become *kuei*, a ghost.

I packed up and moved out of Boarders Ward, the Academy's somber ejection seat. I left my cadet uniforms for the A-3 guys to divvy up. I kept one black Class shirt, stuffed my Army uniforms into the B-4 bag, and grunted my book boxes in my unnaturally short, flat-footed stride to the transportation drop point for shipment to my next post.

I went to Regiment, Building 720, the nondescript beige Army structure atop a granite mound behind our barracks in which the Honor Committee met to hear honor violations cases. The all-cadet committee had the obligation to separate a cadet for an honor violation. Scores of our classmates had been found on honor for creating a cheating ring in sophomore Physics and Chemistry. One of them had been a great friend and roommate. Building 720 was where lives came to an end. I inhaled its gravitas.

I reported to Major Noll, our likable A-3 Tac. He gave me his personal quarters address and asked me to write to him. He thanked me for being a responsible and engaged squad leader and assured me that I had a bright future. He said that the sergeant major had my orders and offered his help in any future matter.

Regimental Command Sergeant Major T. L. Dolonitz was the Army's first Command Sergeant Major. Highly intelligent and competent, he was short, broad-shouldered, and was blessed with the most painful, bone-crushing handshake on the planet. He had killed men with his bare hands and had inspired terrified men to fiercely do battle as an interdependent and trusting team. It was said he'd have been selected to be the Sergeant Major of the Army, the top NCO in the world, but the position required public speaking, which he did with an unintentionally humorous, Eastern European polyglot, Danny Kaye-like panache textured with random German expression afterthoughts. Rumor was that the sergeant major's name had lost 15 syllables when U.S. Immigration could neither comprehend his speech nor read the tattered and blood-stained birth certificate that had somehow emerged from Nazi-occupied territory. The other rumor was that as a kid, he'd taken the birth certificate from a Nazi collaborator that he'd killed without a weapon.

What was true is that he spoke Polish, French, and German, He'd been in the 26th Infantry of the Big Red One and landed against enemy fire in North Africa, Sicily, and Normandy, where he was wounded grievously, received his fourth Purple Heart, and was recommended for the Medal of Honor. By war's end he'd been awarded four Silver Stars, two Bronze Stars for valor, eight campaign stars for combat in Africa, southern, western, and central Europe, the French Croix de Guerre with Gold Star, the USSR Medal for Outstanding Service, the French and Belgian Fourragere, many other decorations, and the thanks of the nation.

"No, didn't get Medal of Honor," he said. "Admin mess-up, no problem. I was alive and with my soldiers."

I accepted his mélange of linguistics; my father spoke 28 Chinese dialects and had learned functional English from German Army officers, rendering Father's speech a guttural puzzle to all who dared to listen.

With a fearsome frown that drew most of his face into the epicenter of his significant nose, Sergeant Major Dolonitz wiped his spotless desk with an OD, olive drab, Army towel. Without looking up, he waved a massive, square hand at a tinfoil package.

"For you," he said, nodding, "yes, from wife and daughter. Say hello. Yeah, yeah, so to stop already the t'anking me." He put down the towel and rubbed an old facial wound. A couple times, the sergeant major had asked me to babysit his daughter. I refused payment but happily accepted his wife's sugar cookies, which enriched the famous larder of our cadet room.

"Major Noll, he vill miss you."

"And I him. And you, Sergeant Major."

"Hush the mouth. I too old for anyone to miss. You ast me last week for Airborne and the Ranger School and 82nd Airborne, ya? But I have de file, right here." He opened his desk drawer and threw my 201 file down to whack on his desk. He thrust a thick digit onto the jacket with the decisiveness of delivering a bayonet to the throat. "This file, I check, is right. Says you are smart in some and also at same time, very stupid. Says hearing lousy. But is okay," he said, holding up a palm while keeping his finger on my file, as if it might otherwise fly out his window. "Everyone in Army have the hearing all blown to hell. The big guns, ya? Your eyes? Vorse zan blind grandmosser." He crossed himself. "Gott rest her soul. You breathing all mess up so you can' bring in ze air. The back crooked an' the feet, they very bad feet. I say to Major Noll, dis man pushing on me for schools he can' do. Not with his bod. I say, Major, maybe we all downside-up, ya? Maybe this man not be soldier."

"Sergeant Major," I said firmly, "I *have* to be a soldier. *Must be.* And, it's *my* bod."

"Ho! Sergeant Major see why you get 'F' so easy! You very, very wrong in the t'inking part of the head. Is not your bod. Is Uncle Samuel bod. Now, t'ink: You should be college, no?"

"Sergeant Major, I told Major Schwarzkopf I'd do ROTC after two years of enlisted service."

"Goose, listen to me. You lose glasses, helpless, ya? Moonless night, no lights, you blind, I come out of chair an' kill you dead before you say 'Jack the Robinson.' Even it better, I come at you from bush or drop on you from tree. You not see Sergeant Major."

"Sergeant Major, you could probably kill me if I saw you were coming."

He nodded. "Vell, ya, is true." He removed his finger from my file and I breathed again. His finger was free and he pointed it at me. "You don' argue wis me?"

"Sergeant Major, you could kill most of us, and then we wouldn't have any lieutenants. I've kind of lowered my sights. I'm now fighting to be an enlisted man. Nothing else I can do."

"Goose, not everyone be soldier. You have brain and t'ree years of West Point. Good jobs for smart boy like you." He rubbed fingers together, making the sound of number one sandpaper. "Make more buckaroos than sergeant major, ya?" He pulled my orders, started to hand them to me. He stopped to study me. I wasn't breathing. I kept my hands in my lap, not wanting to accept a total separation from the American Army.

"Vait." He took my orders and left, his footfalls passing the offices of the Third Regiment's Tactical Officers. Major Noll, Company A, was at the beginning of the hallway while the sergeant major and the colonel of our regiment operated in the center. Time passed.

An hour later, I heard the sergeant major returning. I looked at my watch; he'd been gone 10 minutes. He held the orders and a new, sealed envelope.

"This," handing me the new envelope, "you not like. Take, take!" "Original orders"—he held them up—"vas discharge you from Army for always, no two-year obligation to Uncle Samuel. All done. Wash hands, like you never been in Army." He dropped those original orders in the trash can. "No, don't open new envelope. Later. Goose, you not like t'ose orders but they keep you in the Army and this sergeant major, he like them lots." He smiled.

"You listen to an old man. In Old World, east, west, all same. Dey hang someone like you an' me from the trees. You, cuz blind. Me, cuz dangerous. Here, we have new life, ya? I vish you all the luck in the vorld, Goose Lee. Don' forget. Is always good, be young an' alive in America!"

Act like a Man

Man looks at the outward appearance
but the Lord looks at the heart.
1 Samuel 16:7

I accepted Mike Bain's invitation to visit him and his family in Texas on my leave. Mike had grossly exaggerated my strengths, and his family was accordingly unnaturally warm and welcoming. Although swamped in the feelings of epic failure, I discovered the emotional and material luxuries of a family whose members liked each other and produced wonderful food with the regularity of a mess hall. I concluded that everyone who flunks out of West Point should end up in such a home to be fortified for whatever follows. It was like camping out in the Bear's Q if he lived in a big house with a grand kitchen and an attentive mother who cooked without ceasing and did your laundry despite protests. The only problem was that I didn't want to leave and I far exceeded the norms of a polite stay. I thought Mike's act of comradeship could never be exceeded, but he would prove me wrong by later introducing me to my wife.

Fort Ord was an early Army outpost in the coastal dunes of the California desert. It later became 2,000 acres of an Army artillery range that was expanded in World War II to become a training center for the wars against Japan, North Korea, China, and now, Vietnam. When he was a cadet, Edward Otho Cresap Ord had been deemed a mathematical genius. William T. Sherman, who would later lead the incendiary march through Georgia and South Carolina, was Ord's roommate. Later, in the Civil War, Major General Ord's relentless drive on Appomattox Courthouse, while former roommate Sherman marched to the sea, compelled Robert E. Lee to sue for peace and end the Civil War. Ord's son Jules led the charge up Cuba's San Juan Hill that Teddy Roosevelt famously completed; Jules was killed at the peak. The fort was named for his father.

Fort Ord sat in bleak sands that reminded me of *Beau Geste*'s legendary Fort Zinderneuf in the vast Algerian desert. Not far away, because of systematic irrigation, lay picturesque Carmel and Monterey and the rich agricultural and artichoke fields of Salinas.

I reported to Ord to do penance for my sins as an acting drill sergeant and to complete my military obligation as an American citizen-soldier that had begun at West Point.

I was humbled by the nature of my peers. They were in their late 20s and 30s and emanated the tough seasoning that men develop by creating order from armed, dangerous, and disorderly males. Each was a Sergeant Rock, a hard-core professional who knew the craft of soldiering in the deepest pores of their tough and field-roughened hands. Unhappy draftees called them "lifers," a name that scorned their commitment to serve in the hardest profession. I resolved to sit in preparatory classes as if the Bear were by my side, watching how I respected and understood. On long forced marches in which we called the cadence and the spirit songs, I imagined Norm Schwarzkopf and his long stride next to me, fortifying me when my lungs, back, feet, and legs began to fade. The California clime, free of high-temperature humidity and sleet, suited my glasses. I worked out industriously and increased my strength.

The sounds of West Point included cannon shots, buzzers, Plebe screams, and the best martial music in the world. Fort Ord echoed with the musical arias of 500 drill sergeants bellowing at 50,000 men as they double-timed (ran) from firing ranges to hand-to-hand-combat training pits to hushed assemblies for eye-popping fright lectures on the consequences of venereal disease and meningitis.

My new boss was Field First Sergeant Kalei Solomon, senior drill sergeant, top sergeant, and master of the planet. He hailed from Hawai'i and either had strong Samoan bloodlines, which meant he was very large, or was a descendant of Epimetheus the Titan, which meant his girth was of divine dictation. His biceps were like shoulders and each shoulder was the size of my head. He knew everything about the Army, had calibrated eyeballs that could measure deviation from standard at 200 meters, could simultaneously destroy any three men whether armed or not, and could probably kill a small mammal with a hard look.

When trainees entered the tear gas tent during chemical warfare response training, drill sergeants got a work break. The Field First, with a hint of head motion atop a thick neck that had been modeled on a Giant Sequoia beckoned me to him. I learned he was a man of few words, most of which were unintelligible.

"Wassamattayou, Sergeant Pake?" He looked concerned, like I had polio.

"I'm fine, Field First. What's 'Pake' mean?"

"Hey! You *serious* with me? *Ay-yaa*! *Pake* mean 'Chinese.'"

Ay-yaa! was standard vernacular Cantonese for "no way!" or "I was way wrong!"

He raised his massive brow. "Hey, Pake, so you *katonk,* right?"

"Katonked? No, Top Sergeant, I'm cool. Strong, today. I look katonked?"

"Holy shit, man. *Katonk* mean mainlander Asian, all out. *Katonk* not from Hawai'i. Is funny. First, I think you FBI, From Big Island. Da Big Island of Hawai'i, sometime less language, dig?" He did a quick 360 to ensure no eavesdroppers. "But you fool me, an' I tell you straight to face, dat not happen much.

"But Sergeant Pake, I look at you, see you tan good, like islander. Got da big guns, good arms. Balance out da thick glasses. You spend da money for your troop. But, never island talk, you. Most pake they burn and got da skinny arm an' they stink they so stingy. Sergeant, you look Hawai'i but you not. But I think you *akamai*. Very smart. West Point."

"Not that smart. I didn't finish."

"Hey, man. You get in there! Push three years. Hell, brah, dat *akamai*. I get jam up there in two minute they kick my Dole pineapple public education butt in da street. You okay. You baby NCO, but you *akamai* and I use your book brains for good shit."

I learned that what I'd lived at West Point for three years translated into being able to train 50 basic combat trainees in nine-week cycles. We lived with a familiar schedule that began with predawn reveille and ended long after lights out when the next day's training schedule was reviewed, and hot-washed clean. I relished each day's freedom from electronic circuits and nuclear physics problems. I loved being back in California, but I ached for my old company and the Academy as if it were a missing limb.

Basic Combat Training was a rigorous compression of Beast Barracks without the hazing and Camp Buckner without the strenuous land navigation course. I lived in private quarters at the end of a two-story barracks filled with ordered bunk beds. Most of the trainees had been drafted and exhibited various forms of Baby Boomer discontent. They were humorous, challenging, confused, natively resistant to authority, and on occasion, hostile to the point of lethality. Some arrived with graduate degrees; many came with an interest in killing the cadre or themselves.

Regardless of their intent, they knew drill sergeants were there to prepare them to soldier so they could survive on a battlefield, a physical space I had yet to see. Each trainee had a different set of challenges, and it was like having my Plebes back. Instead of 10, there were 50, with resumes that were far more mundane. Race relations were tense in those days, and reception started bunching the street gangsters of East L.A. into special training platoons. The challenges of applying the Bear's difficult leadership principles with 50 hard cases armed with rifles, bayonets, and, occasionally, grenades, ranged from the perpetually amusing to the sphincter-tightening amusements of being in the Twilight Zone.

Against the raw hatred of some draftees, I consistently applied the Bear's secret sauce of respect all persons. The angriest Compton street gangster couldn't sustain rage against me when I kept counterpunching with unconditional respect. My job was to create harmony from conflict and skills from ignorance. The results were almost supernatural. The work proved to be the most consistently wholesome labor of my life.

In 1964, when I left for West Point, California seemed highly unified in spirit. Now, in 1967 America, my generation and I had changed.

When I deplaned at Travis Air Base near Sacramento, ground personnel recommended that we not travel in uniform lest we draw violent protesters.

"What they protestin'?" asked a soldier from the South.

"The war," said an Air Force specialist. "They want peace and attack people in uniform."

Despite the Bear's recipe, I still lost a steady stream of trainees to gang fights, drug use, AWOLs to commit violent crimes in neighboring towns, desertions for the familiarity of old streets, and imprisonment in our detention cells. The recipe promised dramatically improved leadership effectiveness, but, as all right things, it wasn't guaranteed to work for everyone.

During reveille runs we looked west across the Pacific toward Vietnam, where we all expected to ship and where the Bear could soon expect to return.

I wrote to him to say I loved training troops and that I was becoming a useful NCO. I thanked him for his lessons. I said my mind was beginning to heal and was emerging from the state of stunned stasis in which I'd been since spring leave. I had a partially blue and heavily dented 1955 Chevy I'd bought for $300 from a Vietnam-bound E-7, and said I was willing to trade it straight across for his GTO. I asked how he was and if he was still coaching slow cadets, banging iron, and killing tennis balls.

His first letter was very brief. It resembled paragraph 3 of a standard Op Order. It said nothing about himself, and had 15 admonitions about my doing nothing but the right thing. The second letter reminded me of his voice. During rare free moments, I liked to read it aloud at the usually cold and windy beach. If I lowered my voice to match the timbre of the surf, and pretended the water was the river instead of the ocean, it seemed to recreate his presence.

> West Point develops character by getting you to do a thousand things you don't want to do until they become habit. Habit is the certain proof of competence. It's similar to learning the 10 distinct skills required of an offensive lineman. You practice again and again until a 230-pound slab of bovine beef becomes a tackle.

You did 900 of those 1,000 things you didn't want to do at West Point. You're 20 years old. Sergeant, your mission is to now go do the missing 100 tasks. Some of it you've begun by being a serious student and by respecting people you might not like.

But how to do this now, you might ask. Simple. Every time, do the harder right.

You're not in school anymore. It means you must now act like a man. Get it right, Gus.

On a soft Saturday night, a group of drill sergeants from our battalion invited me to join a poker game. I assessed the table and guessed there was only one true player.

"I'm trying to quit," I said.

"Listen, Buck Sergeant, don't try tonight. Siddown, Lee."

I felt the tug of camaraderie. I also felt the impulse to take their money.

"I can't afford you sharks. Thanks, but I'm quitting tonight."

I looked forward to his letters. His next had numbered lessons.

Gus, I've been thinking more about some of the things you said. Here are some of your Imaginary Thinking products:

1. I'm smart so I don't have to study and so stupid that studying doesn't help.
2. I'm so smart that I don't really need a backbone.
3. I need a college degree but I won't fill out applications to get into college.
4. I don't stand a chance with Dream Girl so I'll pursue her, knowing it's hopeless.
5. I dislike misery and misery is my best friend.

I didn't like his accuracy, and scrunched my nose as I continued to read. It was like listening to him. Still, I didn't agree with all of his points. I could tell he was still angry at me. Then I remembered the depth of my blue funk the last time we were together. I had embraced misery and made it my flag.

He'd want me to write the "harder right" outcome after each numbered item.

I later dug out the Bear's letter, and gritted my teeth to reread it. I began filling in the *harder right* discernments after each item.

It was an iterative process.

1. I'm smart so I don't have to study; studying doesn't help.
   ~~Play fewer cards. Study more~~. NO POKER. IF IN COLLEGE, I WILL STUDY.
2. I'm so smart that I don't really need a backbone. Have a fair one. Better than many. I WILL TRY THE HARDER RIGHT. WASH, RINSE, REPEAT
3. I need a college degree, but won't apply.
   ~~Plenty of time. I'll do it. I'll do it soon.~~ I'VE APPLIED TO CAL.
4. I don't stand a chance with Dream Girl so I'll pursue her, knowing it's hopeless.
   ~~I will never quit. I ought to quit. She's not interested.~~ I STOPPED CHASING HER.
5. I dislike misery. Misery is my best friend.
   ~~Misery's underrated~~. HOPE NOT. BUT AM STILL HURTING ABOUT WEST POINT.

The Field First called me to his office. I removed my Smokey the Bear campaign hat and he bade me sit.

"You baby sergeant E-5 but you pretty trippy. Got big *kahuna* back you up to da max." He winked. "You know who, right, brah?"

I sighed. "Yes. Major H. Norman Schwarzkopf."

He curled a lip. "No, man, not no *officer*. Command Sergeant Major T.L. Dolonitz, he got your six. Not bad, Sergeant *Pake*! He biggest hero in this man's Army! You go ROTC, get commission." He said other things in Hawai'ian vernacular that ultimately meant my military obligation had been satisfied.

While slowly beginning to out-process, I received the long-awaited letter from Admissions of the University of California at Berkeley. I'd asked the Dean's Office at West Point for assistance. They had sent a very helpful letter of recommendation to Cal with a copy to me:

> The U.S. Military Academy requires each Cadet to pass all courses. Mr. Lee was in the upper academic third of his class but was separated because of failing grades in electrical engineering and nuclear physics. With these failures, his overall grade average was a B+. We use a letter grade because

West Point utilizes a 3.0 grading system that does not translate well into the 4.0 grading system of civilian institutions.

I opened the letter from Berkeley. I was refused admission without explanation. I didn't want to leave my training platoon or the battalion or the Army. I'd miss my trainees and the socially distant cadre. I still intended to get an ROTC commission so I kept my uniforms in case I found a college that would take me. I said my goodbyes, wished all good luck, and drove away with the windows down so I could hear the familiar music of big-chested drill sergeants leading massed cadenced singing of trainees. It sounded like deep Gregorian chants, the songs of soldiers offered to heaven.

> Cee-one-thirty movin' down the strip (repeated by the trainees)
> Airborne daddy gonna take a little trip (repeated)
> Stand up hook up shuffle to the door (repeated)
> Jump right out 'n count ta four (repeated)

I was a total civilian. I felt unearthly, disconnected, my anchor chains cut. I'd broken the law of gravity and was *gung hsu*, a free-floating Chinese spirit. I'd left my *jia*, my clan. The world was full of new possibilities I didn't want. I drove my dented chariot up the Pacific Coast Highway, listening to Motown and the Beatles, and more Beatles.

It was 1968, a year after my last visit with Karin in Berkeley. She was in grad school in Madison, Wisconsin. She was going to marry an older guy. I imagined driving to the church and voicing my objection—I'd seen Dustin Hoffman do that successfully in "The Graduate"—but I knew I wasn't supposed to mar her happiness and was convinced she wouldn't run away with me. I was her friend and friends didn't do that. The Berkeley campus was now more congested, the political activity at Sather Gate and Sproul Hall more dramatic, the students seedier, and my short haircut more unusual. The scent of marijuana, popular in some of the lower enlisted ranks, spiced an *a capella* group singing, "Hey, Jude." Every radio station had played that Beatles song on my pleasant 125 mile drive up the California coast.

The admissions officer dressed formally, looking ready for television, but not for looking at my military buzz-cut.

"Frankly," she said, "we don't think your background is entirely appropriate here. We are seeking to close our ROTC programs."

I remembered the Bear's teaching. "Thank you. I can understand my background raises concerns. Could you please tell me if I would've qualified academically for admission?"

"Given what I've said, it really doesn't matter, does it?"

"Can you take a sad song and make it better?"

She looked blankly at me.

"It's from, 'Hey, Jude.' I think everyone's listening to it."

"I think you are wasting my time." I felt like a leper.

"Ma'am, I apologize." She could've simply said, "Na na na na, na na na na."

Randy Reed, a high school buddy with exceptional brains, recommended I apply to UC Davis. It was originally an agricultural college situated in the broad Sacramento plain and was more conservative and traditional than the other UC campuses. It had the largest ROTC program in the state, and Randy thought that Davis Aggies would find a short haircut and military background less controversial. I thanked him and applied.

Classmates said that the beautiful young lady that the Bear had courted at the Academy had said yes and that they were at Command and General Staff College at Fort Leavenworth in Kansas. I wrote him there, congratulated him on finding his wife, and asked him for a letter of recommendation to UC Davis. He said he would give me one.

UCD accepted me conditionally, requiring that I maintain a 3.0 GPA to remain for more than one academic quarter. The UC system required 180 quarter units for a bachelor's degree.

UCD evaluated my transcript for equivalency. It eliminated 12 units of PE (unacceptable for a non-PE major), 15 units of military art (no equivalent UCD courses), Plebe year's 6 units of Earth, Space, and Graphic Sciences (ES&GS was a platypus class that had no equal in our solar system), and 8 units of law (no undergrad equivalent). After eliminating 41 units, UCD recognized 177.25 quarter units from my three West Point years. I realized that a West Point cadet took enough coursework in two and a half years to earn a four-year degree, while also carrying military, leadership, and athletic loads, marching in parades and punishment tours, and working 11 months of the year.

I technically only required 2.75 units—a light gym class—to get a B.A. But residency for graduation required three full quarters. I found Davis to be the collegiate version of Mike Bain's hospitable home. I was 21 years old, had failed in engineering, and had no clue how college worked. There was no cannon and reveille music to start my day, no uniform flag at the central guard room to tell me what to wear, and no marching to meals. How did the Bear perform in a civilian college? He'd gotten his masters at USC, on this very coast. He would have simply employed his natural cool while not sweating the small stuff. He'd try to fit in without causing the normal stir that his large body and larger presence precipitated.

When Professor Larry Peterman entered my first university class, Political Science 148, Political Theory, I stood as if the Bear had entered. Everyone else remained seated.

"We're more formal in the East," I said quietly to those around me, and sat. Some looked at my white pressed dress shirt, black slacks, spit-shined shoes, and military buzz cut with an alarm that I failed to understand. They actually looked afraid of me.

"China, Japan, or Korea?" asked a student. "You know, what part of the East?"

"New York," I said. This was before Asians began to populate Western colleges.

I was asked if I was a narc. (Did a narc seek drugs or arrest users?) I was neither, so I shook my head.

When the ROTC professor of Military Science discovered that I was a former drill sergeant with three years of West Point, he instantly promoted me to be the ROTC brigade commander. This was tough news for ROTC scholarship men who'd been bucking for the top spot, but Lieutenant Colonel Adamski pleasantly instructed me to accept my fate. In the space of one year I'd gone from Cadet Corporal to Army drill sergeant to Cadet Colonel, a rank that didn't exist at West Point. I was in the company of super patriots who'd joined up during the Vietnam War. Another ex-USMA cadet, Jim Tirey, a fellow victim of the

Academic Department, and I teamed up to fully prepare the brigade for Advanced Camp (now Leadership Development Advanced Camp, LDAC), which was their version of Buckner. I made formal requests for Airborne and Ranger Schools, and Tirey and I reminisced about our days by the Hudson.

To use the West Point expression, I was puffing out my puny bird-like chest about my suddenly exalted rank when I heard news about the Bear. He was now Lieutenant Colonel H. Norman Schwarzkopf, a battalion commander who was fiercely shaping up his troops.

He'd made lieutenant colonel below the zone, an early promotion in advance of other majors in his year group. How the heck did the Bear get promoted and promoted early? He thought his military career had been ended because of overly direct speech to superiors in Vietnam. His resentment of being a TOAD during a time of war must have led the Department of Engineering to torpedo the Bear's remaining hopes of a military career. That was definitely his last promotion.

By Christmas, he was commanding 1st Battalion of the 6th Infantry at Chu Lai in I Corps. He'd later say he found the unit Disorganized, Dispirited, Demoralized from hostility at home, and suffering from Disciplinary problems and Drug use—"the Five D's." Not surprisingly, Colonel Schwarzkopf sternly brought them into shape and got his troops out of their holes to aggressively patrol in a replay of the aggressive tactics of Generals William Tecumseh Sherman against the Confederacy and Matthew Bunker Ridgway against the People's Liberation Army of China. Casualties from combat, drugs, and criminal behavior dropped.

Others noted that he displayed anger when helicopters tried to avoid landing during a firefight to pick up his wounded.

"There's only one style of leadership," the Bear used to say. "That's leading from the front while avoiding the cesspool of the rear area. Besides, leadership isn't a 'style.' Styles come and go and suggest it's about personality. Leadership's a discipline based on unchanging principles, and it's about character. It's always about leadership."

Before long, he was wounded again after he jumped from his chopper to rescue men from a minefield. He'd later be wounded again while my classmates completed Airborne and Ranger schools and the Officer Basic Course to join him in the war. We were losing hundreds of soldiers a month, and sometimes hundreds of soldiers a week. Our class president Bill Ericson and the last man in our class, cheerful Rick Hawley, were among the first to be killed. Inspirational "More Beer" Lorbeer, smiling Mike Murphy, "Country Moon" Beahm, jovial Tim Balliet, brainy Barry Hittner, and courtly George Williams, all of Company A-3, had thus far survived their wounds.

I got a bachelor's degree, a commission in the Infantry, and a quick pass into graduate school. While the Army again questioned the utility of my body in combat, I was on my way to a Ph.D. that would return me to West Point to teach. But I was anxious to be with my classmates, and could drop out of grad school and request orders for Vietnam. My graduate advisor said that it would be unlikely, after having abandoned my slot and my advisor, that I'd be readmitted to grad school. I'd disobeyed the Bear's directive to avoid the Infantry and night-seeing spectacles were yet to be invented. I didn't want to ship out until I had Airborne and Ranger schools behind me.

"Your eyes," said my ROTC commander, "and Ranger School are natural enemies."

The 1960s were the beginning of an overproduction of Ph.D.s, so the department upped requirements to increase the chance that its doctoral candidates would get teaching positions. This meant a longer tenure as students. I reported this to Infantry Branch.

"Negative, Lieutenant. You got three years to get a degree. That is, if you pass physically. Your profiles, physical incapacities, have to resolve before I give you a slot at the Infantry Basic Course. Look, you got an education billet, so get your degree. You'll have plenty of time to get to Vietnam. This war's never going to end."

Larry Peterman said there was no way to get a Ph.D. in three years. A masters, yes.

He said that a law degree took only three years. It was also a teaching degree that should work at West Point. UCD King Hall School of Law accepted me and Infantry approved. I was also asked to become a half-time university assistant dean to assist minority undergrads cope with college. I didn't play cards or horse around, and I worked on school and counseling in a soft life. Mike Bain, the Class of 1970, and all of my Plebes graduated and threw their caps in the air. Mike was accepted by two major medical schools, so the Army kept its promise and funded his education in return for an extended military obligation. His wonderful girlfriend Linda was at UCD, so Mike enrolled in med school there. I was in law and grad school, and Mike and I roomed together. It was a delightful time.

While I was studying, the Bear heard that one of his companies had mistakenly entered a minefield. Two officers were down and two soldiers were trapped. Medevacs were inbound and the Bear ordered his helicopter pilot to land and evacuate the wounded. As the Bear studied the minefield, a soldier triggered a mine that fractured his leg. In pain, the soldier thrashed. Knowing this could detonate other mines, the Bear crossed the minefield and pinned the wounded soldier to the ground while another soldier splinted the broken leg. Another mine detonated, killing three and wounding another officer. Lieutenant Colonel Schwarzkopf received his third Silver Star, a Purple Heart with oak leaf cluster, three Bronze Stars, and a Legion of Merit in recognition of being the division's most outstanding combat commander.

Years later, after he retired from the Army, he said that the war made him question whether he should stay in. He questioned the justification for war, a thing he had studied and hated at the same time. Generals have to tell the government the truth about what victory requires and what the aftermath will look like.

"We saw the lack of real communication happen in slow motion in Vietnam. Now we have a volunteer army, and you saw how powerful and effective they can be in the Gulf War when the generals are honest about what victory requires. But if soldiers question the why of war, it could be Game Over."

I graduated from law school in 1976, the same year the Bear took command of the 1st Brigade of the 9th Infantry Division at Fort Lewis, Washington. He was a full colonel, disproving my notions about his promotions, and had children, which was the final exclamation mark that ended our shared bachelorhood. I thought of writing him, and he was but a two-day drive north, but I wanted to wait until I got the Ranger tab and became a TOAD at West Point. I was so close to it, I could taste it.

Thus redeemed, I'd fly to his command in full fig, present arms, and say, "Sir, Captain Lee, West Point TOAD, reports that he owes all that he is and all that he can ever hope to be to his Professor of Solid Mechanics, Colonel Schwarzkopf!"

The Bear would rise to full height with that sun-warming smile, return the salute and shake my hand, clapping me on my back with his trademark thunderous blows.

That would indeed be a very happy day.

26

Base Decisions on Good Character

Being deeply loved gives you strength,
while loving someone deeply gives you courage.
Lao Tzu

In the Army, I tried to follow H. Norman Schwarzkopf's brain-knocking, heart-thumping, adrenaline-shooting, and chest-expanding life lessons. I kept notes on his messages in my mental cargo pocket. When encountering a difficult conversation, an eventful decision or a crisis, I'd ask myself, "How would the Bear handle this?"

The problem was that he'd base his decisions on good character, which, I was learning, was both the hardest quality to assess and the hardest condition to develop in one's self and in others.

Rap and I were deployed in Korea. He was a primary thinker for the Defense Communications Agency in U.S. Army Garrison Yongsan and tested strategic low-noise microwave backbone lines, pre-digital voice channel multiplex equipment, and assured strategic communication systems for United Nations and U.S military commands and the Pentagon. Yongsan was near the center of the national capital of Seoul, a bursting metropolis of 12 million closely compacted citizens with some of the most dangerous traffic intersections in the world.

I was a JAG (Judge Advocate General, or legal) officer with the 2nd Infantry Division at Camp Casey on the outskirts of the quiet agricultural village of Dongducheon on the barren and deforested Demilitarized Zone (DMZ), its featureless face graced by beautiful white egrets and the memories of golden ginkos, screw pines, and spruces. Korea is mostly mountains, but in spring, flowers bloom throughout the Bando, the peninsula, while the DMZ remains relatively bleak. In summer, the humidity is inescapable; in winter, the weather, driven by high winds from Manchuria, becomes punishment.

Rap and his wife Barbara had a growing family that they expanded by adopting children in-country. Besides protecting liberty and making the world safe for electronics, they were also doing missional work at the Little Sisters of the Poor's Orphanage. They invited me to help serve there on occasional weekends. I didn't want to.

How would the Bear respond? Base your decisions on good character. I accepted doing basic handyman work at the orphanage.

One of the Bear's truisms is that one can do almost anything difficult with a reliable friend. I therefore bypassed hanging with several officers of interesting but questionable repute and focused on Don Meinhold, a bright, hard-working, steady JAG captain who was married with kids and advocated neither booze nor infidelity. He was Class of '70, a peer of Mike Bain, Sully, Whitey, and my Plebes. He preferred to observe and listen rather than boast, to reason instead of react, and to correct wrongs rather than avoid. He was tall, big, and tough, a menace if provoked, and had some of the Bear's anger in the presence of gross injustices.

He'd figured out that West Point was not a party school, a conclusion I hadn't reached until I got booted out. He played rugby and feared no one. While I saw Korea as an adventure, Don was as pleased to be on a Korean hardship tour as Achilles was warmed by the death of Patroclus. After expending years of eligibility and readiness for a deployment to the Korean DMZ, Don and his wife had been relying on the Army's assurance that they were no longer in the zone for a levy to Korea. Accordingly, Don got one week to report to the DMZ for a year and was placed on the 18-hour flight to Asia two days before Christmas. I was happy to see Don at the 2nd Infantry, but Don did not share the sentiment.

We did a great deal of criminal law in the busiest court-martial jurisdiction in the Army. We were also the next-door neighbor to a million North Korean *Inmingun* troops who intended harm upon us and all of South Korea. The 2nd Infantry ran three to five miles every morning at reveille, regardless of cardiacs in summer and hip-shattering falls on the Manchurian winter's slick ice.

North Korean troops were killing our patrol members on the Imjin River. They captured the USS *Pueblo* and its crew and tunneled under the

DMZ to assassinate South Korea's first lady while missing the president. We later learned that the USSR's Leonid Brezhnev had told Kim Il-sung, the Beloved Leader of North Korea, that Russia would help them fight the Americans only if the United States first attacked North Korea. Kim could not initiate the conflict, and therefore actively sought to provoke a U.S. response that would trigger his war.

Camp Casey was strategically located in the narrow valley that was the center of the attack corridor that North Korea's *Inmingun* would take in an invasion of the South. We were 17,000 soldiers with a single armored battalion's 56 tanks against 1,000,000 North Koreans, 3,000 tanks, and 7,000 cannon. Obviously, we were here primarily to show the flag and symbolically stand by our South Korean allies. We were to slow the advance of the Soviet-styled northern army. It was here that the expression, "We're speed bumps for the enemy," was first coined.

"If they cross, it'll be hell even delaying them," said Don.

The Bear would seek to reduce casualties on both sides.

"We'll have to use nukes," I said, with a nagging sense that Schwarzkopf might give me a failing grade for that answer.

"Messy in close-quarters combat," he concluded.

Whatever might occur, our division commander, the inspirational Lieutenant General David E. Grange Jr., had ensured that we'd neither be surprised nor unfit to fight. ("Second to None, Fit to Fight.") When we weren't running every morning, we were marching with full combat gear in hot humidity or punishing sleet. The Bear would be running his battalion the way Grange was running the 2nd U.S. Infantry. It'd been 11 years since I'd last contacted him, and as I ran and lifted weights, I imagined him ahead of me and out-lifting me. We were soldiers together and I wasn't running from his lessons.

I became a fan of Korean cuisine with the exception of *kimchi*, pungent fermented and pickled garlic cabbage, a national dish that inspired heartburn of the I'm-dying-of-a-heart-attack variety.

I learned a lot of trial practice wisdom from Meinhold, toured the Far East with a focus on Kyoto, Nara, and Osaka in Japan (American soldiers weren't allowed into China), practiced *taekwondo*, had a wonderful Korean girlfriend who I knew I'd not marry—in clear contravention of the Bear's counsel—pumped iron, and, like everyone else on the Z, participated in over-work. Don was the ideal battle buddy. We were walking through Casey on a subfreezing winter night when a woman screamed. Don, a father and husband, ran to help the victim. I, a bachelor by practice, chased the fugitive. I think the Bear would've managed to have done both, but I was only human, and a blind one at that.

We passed a building security light and he looked over his shoulder. In the height of the Bruce Lee era, he concluded that having an Asian guy on his heels was not happiness. He hit slick ice and he went down and I fell on him. He swung a woman's purse at me and I blocked it. He kicked himself free to fight for balance and now we were both skating in boots. He was scared, and the position of his feet announced that he could tussle, but wasn't a fighter.

Respect all persons.

He telegraphed an overhand right. Flat-footed, which I am by nature, I parried it. Boxing takes short punches and hand speed. Street fighting calls for busting hands. I landed a quick right cross on his hard jaw, as if my hands were wrapped, and blocked his next amateurish but spirited swing. I delivered a short left hook to his temple. It wasn't the best hook I'd ever thrown, and it lacked energy on the ice and accuracy in the dark, but it was workable. He sat down, his breath bellowing from his chest.

"I'm a captain," I said, my breath thinly punctuating frigid air. "You're under arrest." I stripped off his belt and bound his hands behind his back. I tried to say, "Don't run," but I had no more air to speak. I found the handbag and lifted it gingerly to protect latents (fingerprints). We both huffed and puffed back to the scene of the crime.

The next morning I was processing handcuffed in-custody defendants. They were brought in one by one by MPs into my semi-frozen ramshackle office. Outside, helicopters pulled pitch and rattled the thin excuse for windows and the thinner pretense at walls. One of the in-custody customers was my quarry.

"NO, NOT HIM!" Cuffed, he tried to push his beefy MP escort out the door so he might follow; the MP quickly discouraged him. He jumped up and down like a kid in need of a bathroom. "Dat's da Bruce Lee karate cat hit me upside the head! He my frickin' lawyer?! No @#$! way, man! He pounded the crap outa me 'n stole mah belt 'n set me up wif a purse I ain't never seen!"

"Perhaps," I said, "you'd prefer another attorney?"

The Bear's lessons in unconditional respect had guided me to honor a bad-acting soldier. In my earlier manner of thought, honed by my early

Code of the Street, a person who kicked me deserved to be punched into mush. Honoring a man who violently assaulted women and intended me harm was a lesson for life.

Don had requested a "Christmas Drop," a reduction of a few days from his full 12-month hardship tour in Korea to rejoin his family for Christmas at Fort Carson. Having no family, I made no request. Due to divine intervention, I got the Drop and because of bad juju, Don didn't. I flew out early, he flew late, and we returned Stateside on opposite sides of Christmas after 20-hour flights to the Land of the Big PX.

On the long flight, joined by exhausted grunts making a chorus of thunderous snoring, and tired of causing and experiencing pain by leaving girlfriends, I resolved to cease my relationships with women. The Bear would've endorsed this. Over the Pacific, I created an admirable vision for my life: Fight injustice, honor all persons, improve my basketball game, make 300-pound bench presses routine, and read the classics. I looked forward to being an unencumbered and guiltless monk.

I was assigned to the Presidio of San Francisco, where Mike Bain and his wife Linda were stationed. In the Presidio BOQ, dropped my bags, and fell on the cot. Moments later, a messenger said that Captain Bain had invited me to a Christmas Eve party at his quarters and to come stag. I'd been asleep for 17 hours and had 30 minutes to shower and dress. The shower was glorious—unlimited hot water. I didn't miss the howls of 20 unfortunate-smelling men trying to soap off the sweat produced by a three-mile run in 20 seconds of ice water before the tank ran out, or the scents of open sewage, and fertilized rice paddies. I sang like a froggy Mario Lanza at the top of my one good lung and may have induced wolves to howl in Siberia.

At the bottom of a barracks bag that I'd packed two years ago, my best civilian clothes were as wrinkled as the face of a bulldog pup and reeked of decayed moth balls. I found boots that were stylistically banned on the West Coast. I got dressed, proud to have shoes on the correct foot. Nothing fit. For four days a week during a long year's deployment, I'd banged iron in Camp Casey's small space that had been generously advertised as a weight room; I'd outgrown my civilian wardrobe. I doused the clothing with stored aftershave to combat the scent of two years with camphor balls. I sported a Republic of Korea buzzcut and rubbed in vintage hair gel to subdue the spikes. The chemical combination of decomposed aftershave, calcified hair goop, and extract of camphor and turpentine could have instigated an Environmental Protection Agency investigation.

I resembled a dangerous escaped convict who'd stolen clothes from innocent children, cut his hair with a chain saw, and covered the evidence by smearing himself in radiated mercury. All that was missing was a dull glow.

Linda Bain was in the waiting area and we hugged as long-lost siblings. She saw my outfit, detected its curious blend of aromas, and kindly remained silent. She tried to iron out the wrinkles in my shirt with her palms. We stood in the ease of a California Christmas.

"Good," she said. "A light wind is airing out the *eau de mothballs*."

Quarters were dressed for Christmas for Mike's background (Jewish), for Linda's (Jewish-Mormon), and for me (Atheist). Deep dialogs competed with carols, and I felt Christmas' wishful sentimentality. I was back in America with potable water, showers, flush toilets, refrigerators, supermarkets, non-suicidal traffic, reliable electricity, non-Arctic climes, a thoroughly democratic republic, an ocean between us, and a million bad guys. I'd come home to a nation with the world-shaking habit of sending its sons, daughters, and riches to far-off lands to help beleaguered strangers. A sitting area led to a great room where a crowd of young military healthcare couples enjoyed each other's company.

On the sofa sat a gloriously beautiful woman playing a guitar. She was singing like Sarah Vaughan and was luminous for reasons I couldn't name. She considered me with a penetrating insight I'd have preferred to avoid. She was looking past apparel—evidence of a yard sale gone bad—to see if I had an operational soul.

"Diane," said Linda, "this is Gus. Gus, Diane Elliott. Diane's a masters-prepared clinical nurse specialist on the UC San Francisco clinical faculty. She works with Mike, and you are each other's company tonight." Linda smiled innocently. I'd been set up on a blind date. In my myopia, I hadn't seen it coming. I hadn't told the Bains that I was now committed to the austere life of a studious, professional, all-respecting, basketball-playing atheist missionary.

Diane smiled and my breathing deepened. She looked into my eyes and I felt the invitation to a positive addiction. She fascinated me, and I hung on her words. I forgot to tell her about my life plan. She had an inner allure I'd never felt. She asked what I did and I said I did a lot of flying around, seeing interesting sights, and retaining my freedoms.

"You must have loved *Peter Pan*," she said, laughing.

We spoke, her words opening doors and vistas. Things I feared in a relationship seemed irrelevant.

I got it; I found the name for her allure. She was a woman of character, of ethical substance, and my brand new life plan didn't matter. I asked her for a date.

"I'm sorry, but I don't date," she said.

I was stunned. Was she engaged? Had I been speaking to the wrong woman?

"Dating," she said, "is what men do to have fun with women, and I don't do that. I choose only to see men who are looking for a committed relationship."

Even though that aligned with how Norman Schwarzkopf had defined dating, these were tough words for the delicate ears of a baked-in bachelor.

"But how would you know if you wanted such a, a relationship, if you didn't date?"

"I think," she said, "it once was called *courtship*. And that's something that actually leads somewhere." She smiled wonderfully. "It's kind of the opposite of flying around."

I shivered. She was speaking in code about the unmentionables: Children. Responsibility. Mortgages. Debts. Diapers. Unknown consequences to my military career. The things my father never figured out and I resolved I'd never do lest I become him. I really didn't want that Darth Vader moment, the one that says with the music at dramatic minor key: Luke, you ARE your father.

Asking her for dinner and a movie would mean more than linguine and "Superman." It would mean facing everything I'd spent my life seeking to avoid. I still wanted to see her.

Six months later, at the Fort Mason Officers Club, I asked Mike Bain for the ring. It took a while, as he was one of 19 Best Men, many of them officer classmates, and no one wanted to drop it as it traversed half the room. A radiant and gorgeous Diane said yes to me in front of witnesses as Linda Bain, Matron of Honor, stood by her. I, of a long and ancient line of wandering men with abandoned wives, exiled children, multiple concubines, secret affairs, rejected love children, addictions, deep debts, financial bankruptcies, and irresponsibility, vowed to be her husband forever and to stand by her even if we lost everything. It was a replay of the oath at the river that I and other West Point classes had made to defend the Republic against all enemies foreign and domestic, and, like the officer's commission that followed, it was for life. I knew the Bear would be proud of me, regretting for a small moment that Diane and I hadn't arranged a military wedding in Full Dress Blues in which we would process under an arch of sabers held aloft by fellow officers.

By gum, it was great, as Sergeant Major Dolonitz would say, to be young and alive in America!

27

No Right Way to Do the Wrong Thing

*A great many people think they are thinking
when they are merely rearranging their prejudices.*
William James

Lieutenant General David Grange's 2nd Infantry Division on Korea's DMZ was a sharply skilled, physically fit, militarily proficient, high-morale, combat-ready organization. I learned it was not the norm.

President Nixon had successfully ended the anti-war protest movement by terminating the draft. The Vietnam War would grind on for two more deadly years, but with the end of the draft, the morally incensed movement for peace had stopped its protests.

The American draft had contributed states' militia to the Revolutionary War, filled the ranks of the Union Army that stopped slavery in the Civil War, and had won two world wars to free the planet. The draft was continued after World War II and provided much of the force that saved South Korea from annihilation in the 1950s and from subsequent eradication thereafter. West Point's faculty and staff were of the World War II and Korean War generations, and until the mid-1960s it was a spit-and-polish, Yes-Sir culture in which senior NCOs were gods. By being at the Academy in the 1960s, I was trained in the version of the United States Army of those generations when Americans joined hands to accept the risks of national security. Today, that responsibility and liability are borne by less than half a percent of the population.

When student protests peaked, the draft Army of the Vietnam era presented a different cultural profile plagued by rampant drug use, in-barracks violence, racial conflict, lawlessness, attacks on superiors, and nearly a thousand assassination attempts—"fraggings"—of officers. It now seems impossible that conditions were that lamentable and that the leadership of that time was both deeply challenged and frequently dysfunctional. I was also in this version of the Army.

The Bear had said it's always about leadership, and it was likely that we lacked a sufficient number of effective leaders. When draftees were well-led, they reflected the Army culture of earlier generations that defeated formidable foes in World Wars I and II.

Ending the draft at the end of the Vietnam War accelerated the American withdrawal and Vietnamization of the war, transferring combat to the South Vietnamese. Ten years before, this was the condition that the Bear believed to be the highest-right basis for helping the South resist the violence of the North.

It could be said that now, without the draft, young men had been excused from national service. The Army's ability to blend men of different colors and backgrounds into the famous American melting pot was forgotten. No longer would the average young American male learn iron self-discipline, selfless teamwork, the tough mastery of new skills in conditions of privation, and the patient endurance of hardship.

It was 1978 when I completed my tour in Korea and returned to America. The draft was gone, and the Army was broken by failed national and military leadership, demoralized by 58,000 fatalities, 153,000 wounded in action, and three million Asian deaths. It was spiritually dismasted by public disavowal. The government had neither truly committed the nation to, nor articulated a moral imperative in support of the war, and no senior general had pulled a Matt Ridgway by speaking truth to authority about the costs and consequences of a decisive victory.

Now, without the draft, the Army couldn't find volunteers.

I'd gotten a top rating out of Korea and was assigned to Army Recruiting Command, USAREC. The Army Chief of Staff, General Bernie Rogers, a Rhodes Scholar and former West Point Commandant, was moving what he thought were his best people into recruiting before the Army died of anemia. With new leadership, USAREC led the Army's effort to reform and rebuild itself after the war in Vietnam. I was assigned to USAREC's 6th Brigade, covering 11 western states and commanded by Colonel D. Hamilton Willoughby, a dynamic, hard-working, results-pounding officer who was proud of the platoon sergeants, drill sergeants, and top sergeants who'd been decorated for valor. They were now his recruiters, charged with another mission impossible.

Diane appreciated my near-civilian-like office job that allowed me to be home for most dinners. She was athletic, healthy, and a dancer, but her job was demanding and she was frequently ill. I was very worried. My birth mother had died young.

"Honey, I'm not sick," she said. "We're pregnant."

I hugged my wife in a moment of shock, disbelief, joy, and pleasure. I reminded myself to write to the Bear to let him know of the wonders that had come to Cadet Lee.

I met Colonel Willoughby, a West Point graduate to whom I attributed the best qualities of the Academy.

Army Intelligence, he said, believed that some of our Army recruiters had erroneously enlisted foreign agents into our ranks. "Worse, we may have sensitive matter in classified overseas sites." This was code for tactical nuclear weapons. "These secret agent recruits could be going after them.

"Gus, you enjoy your tour in Korea?"

On the civilian flight back to ROK, I studied the printouts of hundreds of suspect Army recruits who were assigned to classified positions.

I was joined by a ROK Army liaison and chilly, black-suited gentlemen from the Korean CIA. Sergeant First Class Billy "Rainbow" Fua was a tough and brilliant Green Beret linguist who was detailed as my interpreter. We were in Yongsan Garrison's Criminal Investigation wing, enjoying a third week of questioning ethnic Korean prisoners who wore the uniform of the United States Army with documents that did not match their appearances.

Our key person of interest, according to his 201 military personnel file, was a 25-year-old Army Specialist Fourth Class from Los Angeles with perfect ASVAB (Armed Services Vocational Aptitude Battery) qualification scores who stood five feet nine inches and weighed 165 pounds. But the man in front of me was in his 40s, barely spoke English, was five feet six inches, weighed 190, and couldn't tell L.A. from New Delhi. Army Intelligence had checked his dental work and inoculation scars and concluded he was an *Inmingun*, North Korean Army officer. The Korean CIA listened to him speak and said he spoke the Pyongyang dialect of North Korea. The pressure to know if he was in fact an enemy agent and to discern his mission was almost excruciating.

He spoke in guttural Korean, offering a tale about being born with the appearance of a grown man. His scorn of us while withholding possible information about our nukes was taxing the Bear's axiom of respect all persons. Billy wanted to take the guy out for some beef *bulgogi* to loosen his tongue. Our stern brothers from the KCIA had expended all of their Asian patience. They wanted to take the subject for a short visit to KCIA HQ at Namsan.

"Rainbow" Fua was from Hawai'i. Without turning his head, he whispered, "To put electrodes on his goods." Goods were one's private parts.

I liked the idea of dispelling this man's arrogant mocking to get needed answers. The Bear had faced this dilemma in Vietnam. He'd say, "Respect all persons."

I called a break. In the hallway I said, "The U.S. Army doesn't sanction torture."

The KCIA said they lived under a constant threat of annihilation from men identical to the hard case on the other side of the security door. The senior man pulled me aside.

"I understand," he said in perfect English. "I promise we will not coerce him."

"Sir, I can't release him for the same reason I can't allow you to question him. He's an American soldier and you're here as a formal courtesy to a valued and loyal ally."

"He is *not* an American soldier! He is Korean and belongs to us. Captain Lee, loan him to us and no nukes get dropped on America or us."

There wasn't an American there who wouldn't have given up his life to stop that. Some of us would be unforgivably slow to stop torture by others, but Americans should never order it, sanction it or allow it. I learned that from the Bear.

"I can't do that, sir. I'm sorry."

"Big mistake," said the senior KCIA representative. "Rethink this."

The subject never gave a statement. We prosecuted him and other illegal aliens to ensure they could never become citizens or enter the country on visas and removed the enlistees with false identifications, fabricated backgrounds, and improbable test scores from the U.S. Army. Many were ethnic Koreans, and their names went to the FBI. The KCIA asked me for their identities.

The Green Beret said, "So they can put electrodes on their goods."

We didn't share their identities. I gave bottles of Johnny Walker Red Label whiskey to our KCIA colleagues, but received no smiles in return. I sympathized.

Sergeant Fua and I had a hundred soldiers to interview, but it was the Army, it was Korea, and scheduling their interrogations was painfully slow, even with our authority from UN/Combined Forces Command. The Bear was an Airborne Ranger and I was still trying to emulate him. In contravention of his instructions, I'd served and then been commissioned in Infantry and, unable to get orders, had talked my way into Airborne School to earn my basic wings. Using permissive leave, I showed up at Ranger School, but they'd been warned about a blind, sweet-talking JAG captain without orders. I was met with abrupt rudeness.

"Men," I said, grinning. "Cut slack for a former EM (Enlisted Member). There's nothing personal in this."

"I look stupid to you?" asked a grizzled first sergeant, his frown sprouting more frowns. "I let a blind Army lawyer in here without orders, 'n he gets dead 'n now I got CID (Criminal Investigation Command) up my back door 'n' 60 pages a paperwork 'n I got four years to 20 (retirement). Believe you me, it's *damn* personal! Now, sir, *didi-mau* (move in Vietnamese) 'n un-ass this AO!"

The Bear, like Rainbow, had earned Vietnamese Master Parachute wings. During a long delay in enlistee interviews, the ROK liaison, Captain Kim, arranged for me to jump with the ROK Airborne. Two theoretically simple jumps simulated "Twilight Zone" episodes with near-death outcomes, but I'd earned foreign national airborne wings in a continuing salute to my mentor.

On the flight back to the States, I reviewed the sad case files of soldiers who had broken the code. We were investigating 3,777 allegations against 749 recruiters and a handful of senior officers. I was by nature weak in every dimension, a person dependent upon the kindnesses of strangers, so I could've been a cheater, but angels had kept parachuting into my life in a consistent conspiracy of grace. So thinking, I returned to Diane, whose maternity wardrobe reflected an expanding midsection, a happily expectant wife, and a newly decorated baby room. She had missed me, looked deeply into my eyes as we spoke, laughed easily, and life was good.

"I want the baby to come out to play," she said with the brightest smile. "Tell me what happened over there. Tell me everything."

I did. When we spoke, my mind improved in clarity as I separated essence from fluff. I appreciated her wise insights. They always improved my work. So *this* is marriage.

"Does torture actually work?" she asked.

"We know that people can break, but torture also disorganizes the mind and can garble facts. But I had a mentor at West Point who basically said there's no right way to do the wrong thing. American soldiers can't do or condone torture, whether it provides accurate answers or not, or we're not George Washington's army."

I was sent on other investigations. We learned that more than half the volunteer Army's recruits were Category IVs, which was the lowest possible mental classification. Cat IVs could not legally exceed 15 percent of the force. Recruiters, to meet quotas, had accessed a deep entrepreneurial spirit by enlisting ex-felons, drug addicts, prisoners, and even the dead; they were not going to fail. Many of the recruiters were in our brigade. I reported back to Colonel Willoughby, proud of the investigation's hard but necessary work.

"Cool your jets, Captain," said Colonel Willoughby. "You've just help gut my organization, rip out its heart, and bring great discredit on the United States Army."

"Sir, how did I bring discredit?"

"We're losing our best producers. Do this right," he said.

"Sir, it sounds like you're asking me to be cool on Honor."

"I'm telling you to live in my command without playing Sherlock Holmes and being my enemy. Listen, you don't want to be my enemy."

Formal, large-scale Army investigations follow criminal law protocols. Individual responsibility is set by naming an investigation for its senior officer. The Peers Investigation, under tough Major General William Peers, had delved into My Lai. USAREC's worldwide fraudulent recruitments were given to the deputy commanding general, Brigadier General Douglas Connelly, and my work was folded into it. The recruitment problem threatened national security, and the Connelly Investigation made bi-weekly reports to Senator Sam Nunn and the U.S. Senate.

My boss in my unit, 6th Brigade, was Colonel Willoughby. My technical chain of command boss was the top lawyer at USAREC HQ, Lieutenant

Colonel Charles A. Murray. He was a legendary and humorous Airborne Ranger Infantry officer, West Point Class of 1962, who became a JAG after being wounded in his second combat tour in Vietnam. He was also General Connelly's chief counsel, and he named me to the team.

In the end, we would relieve 393 recruiters for falsifying official documents, committing mass fraudulent enlistments, and bribing processing personnel. Like the Bear when he was a captain, I was on my way to having my boss regard me as his enemy.

28

Stand Tall in the Storm

In a time of universal deceit, telling the truth is a revolutionary act.
George Orwell

Diane weathered a long labor with courage and grace, and we greeted baby Jessica Michelle Lee on a fine San Francisco Friday morning to the cheers of her parents and the admiration of the birthing staff. At Diane's invitation, we sang "Happy Birthday" to her. Jessica was beautiful with a small porcelain face and tiny, perfect features. She was a wonder. Diane cared for our little daughter with an ease that came from the great love in her heart and reflected her intense study on the care of infants. In my arms, Jessica's warmth and trust produced sensations that exceeded the range of known feelings. My sisters were happy for us. They called her *Bohbooie,* Little Precious. Informing my father was a formality, as he had never liked children, but he seemed pleased. Diane was from Kansas City and new to the Bay Area, Mike and Linda Bain were in Germany, and the vast majority of my Best Men were at Davis, out of state, or on distant Army posts. In many ways, we were on our own.

A physician asked us into a quiet office. He said Jessica had heart issues and that surgery was needed to repair a patent ductus areteriosus, an infantile complication of blood flow. The surgery was deemed low risk and she emerged intact, in pain, and weakened. A pediatric cardiologist told us that there could be other problems.

In Recruiting Command, an explosion of ethical violations had become full-time work. I pressured Colonel Willoughby for briefings so he could act on them. I briefed the 10 cases in which recruiters had confessed to systematic fraud and had broken criminal statutes to enlist unqualified recruits; 20 more files were merely grave.

"When I told you," said the colonel, "that your job was keeping me out of jail, that didn't mean threatening my guys with the clink on flimsy evidence."

"Sir, these recruiters admitted the knowing enlistment of unqualified applicants. They confessed to fabricating the supporting documentation and then bribing Military Enlistment Processing folks to look . . ."

"You're killing my day. No actions on these cases."

"Sir, no action will look like a cover-up and USAREC HQ will do the reliefs."

"Gus! The Army's screaming at us to put bodies in boots. Think I'm worried about what my decisions might 'look like'?"

"Sir, I'm asking you to worry about doing the harder right."

He waved at my files. "You got 'cases.' I have 10 of my top-producing NCOs who are making mission. Every day I delay, the hangman lets those guys put up numbers that I—and not you—have to report up to Major General 'Mad Max' Thurman at HQ. We're in California, the biggest state in the Union and I'm expected to find those recruits. I don't care how many are Cat IV. I wasn't put in command to mess around. Dismissed."

I stood. "Sir, I got to tell Command Legal at USAREC about our nonalignment."

"Go tell the Easter Bunny. Look, I know others think you're pretty. I don't. Get out of here, Gus, I have work to do."

How would the Bear deal with this? He was up the road a ways, commanding an infantry brigade at Fort Richardson, Alaska.

In combat, the Bear had disagreed with his boss, did the highest right action regardless of risk to self, and then reported his disobedience of orders. I called Colonel Charles A. Murray, the top JAG at USAREC HQ outside Chicago, the top lawyer in the command.

Colonel "Cam" Murray had a razor-sharp mind, an inviting laugh, a fiery commitment to justice, and had left the Infantry to become one of the sharpest constitutional lawyers in the land. He'd been a few classes behind the Bear at West Point, was married with a young son, attended Mass, and swore like a sailor.

"So," said Murray after I related my situation, "you enjoy being tortured by your boss." He laughed infectiously and so did I. The men who served with him realized that his laughter was more engaging than his jokes, making us love him all the more.

He told me to send him the 10 action files with my findings and recommendations.

"I'll review them to General Thurman for action."

He said we had major wildfires in the global recruitment system. He assigned me to Investigative Team Bell, a "Tiger" team, a sharp, quick-action strike force headed by the USAREC Inspector General, Colonel Lawrence A. Bell. Team Bell's job was to go to the worst fires in the system.

"You have a sick baby, just did a hardship deployment on the DMZ, and we sent you back to Korea for a half tour. I'd spare you if I could but I need all the boots on the ground. You're to meet Colonel Bell 0800 tomorrow at District Recruiting Command Montgomery, Alabama. You knew the Army was more than a job, it's an adventure. Tell Diane that our parish is praying for baby Jessica's health. Sorry you have to fly."

Colonel Bell was a straightforward combat veteran aviator from the Citadel with a keen investigative mind. We found that recruiters had opened their stations at night to give the test answers to people off the street so they could pass and be enlisted. We worked without sleep and closed the cases in time for Murray to call in his JAGs to HQ for a briefing. We landed in a howling winter storm at O'Hare and drove in a blizzard to USAREC HQ in Fort Sheridan, Illinois. It was midnight, which gave us six work hours until sunrise. I greeted the HQ JAGs as we unfolded new cases. Winds howled like the gusts of Manchuria. Captain Rob van Hooser mumbled that desk-sized computers would someday cut data processing time in half. We ridiculed his techno-thinking. Little computers? Laughable.

The phone rang at 0200. The CG, commanding general, wanted Murray and me.

Lieutenant General Maxwell "Mad Max" Reid Thurman was a rail-thin, Oxford-aesthetic, eccentric bachelor who worked 20 hours a day, regarded sleep as a habit of the weak, shook the grand temples of the status quo to make sweeping reforms, and was a fire-spouting, officer-eating terror when he encountered incompetence, lack of drive, or weakness of will. He actually inspired USAREC's motto of "Be All You Can Be." In three years, he'd become the Army's Deputy Chief of Staff for Personnel and would name a young one-star general, an officer I "knew" would never again be promoted named H. Norman Schwarzkopf, to be his Director of Personnel.

Thurman motioned us in and propped his feet, ice-encrusted rubber galoshes, on the corner of a busy desk that included the 10 action files that Colonel Willoughby had disregarded. He'd returned in an ice storm for this meeting. We stood at attention. Huge-lensed aviator glasses slid down his narrow nose. My legal memo was on his lap.

"Have a seat, Charlie," he said.

"You got my man here at attention," said Murray. "If he can do it, I can, too."

"Seats, by all means," said the general. We sat. "Lee, I don't support reliefs in these 10 malpractice cases, much less judicial action."

That got my attention. "Sir, I'd like to know why."

"You don't need to know why! I need memos that help accomplish mission. This memo doesn't do that. What the hell did you base your findings on?"

"The facts, sir."

"Well, son, there are never enough of those. Reverse your recommendations."

My heart raced. Adrenaline didn't impede seeing reality. My battle buddies in the 2nd Infantry on the DMZ had worked through hard days with stout hearts. Now I had Korean CIA spooks with electrodes hanging out of their coat pockets and two-star generals monkeying with ethics. General Grange would never talk like this. Thurman was like a guy out of "The Godfather." Disheartened, I said, "I can't do that, sir . . ."

"Murray," Thurman interrupted, "told you to play hardball. So you antagonize your commanding officer, Colonel Willoughby, a future general. Murray's a banged-up guy who's just a JAG *advisor*. Willoughby's your boss. You're mucking up my system and ticking me off!"

The Bear, were he in the room, would throw the yellow B.S. flag, sprinkle a colorful profanity on it, and do something in the name of the harder right to abruptly end his career.

"Sir," I said. "Colonel Murray's given me no guidance on my findings."

"Then why is Murray backing you up? What's so special about you?"

"Sir, I know he gives you his best legal judgment. Nothing special about me."

He dropped his boots on the floor with two loud impacts. He sat up. His green desk lamp threw shadows of old Dutch paintings on his lean face, his glasses glittering. His chair squeaked as he rolled closer. I heard Colonel Murray grumble.

"Captain Lee, this is you and me, here. Reverse your findings. Now." His clear radio voice vibrated my dental cavities; I was learning why he was called "Mad Max" and "The Maxatollah." His aggression and penetrating gaze were physical realities. I wasn't going to back down; I just hoped I wouldn't lose continence or faint.

I licked dry lips. "Sir, I have no legal basis for reversal."

"On the contrary, Captain. I'm telling you to," his words like machine gun fire, the cerebral authority of an incisive intelligence slapping me around like a beginning boxer. My heart was doing calisthenics inside my chest cavity as he came closer. He was rather small and thin, but he was General DePuy's acolyte and a guy not to make mistakes. DePuy was one of the chief architects in the post-Vietnam rebuilding of the Army. "Sir, I got to advise you that your ordering me to reverse judgment is not appropriate."

"Jiminy Christmas, Charlie," said Thurman as he thumped his desk and turned his head, "where do you get these iron-butt JAGs? Remember those kids out of law school who'd waffle and fold?" He smiled and opened the first file.

"Captain Lee, I concur with your memo. We got some good men who forgot their oaths." He adjusted his glasses and looked at me. "I needed to confirm you knew what the hell you were doing. You did good. Way to stand in Colonel Willoughby's storming."

And yours, I thought as my breathing returned to normal.

"Let's get down to cases, Charlie." He moved faster than I could think. We got three hours sleep before the next work day. He ordered the immediate relief of the 10 malpracticing recruiters and ordered security repairs at the processing centers to find the bribe-takers. He awakened his six brigade commanders, including Colonel Willoughby, and instructed them to immediately convene conferences to hear his message. It would be delivered by the JAGs, and the directive was that malpractice was to end with immediate effect, whatever the cost in good people. He gave his ethics bullet points to each of us six USAREC JAGs who were responsible for individual brigades. We'd then join overseas teams, in a replay of my sortie to Korea, to relieve malpracticing recruiters. I was to go to the Federal Republic of Germany. I repaired to a desk to review the bullet points to deliver at my brigade's conference when I received an urgent message.

It was Diane. She was crying. I took notes. Jessica has mitral valve insufficiency. Diane's research and consults with top cardiologists: the earliest intervention can't be tried until Jessica turns three, but not a single mitral valve infant had survived to one year of age. Our Jessica probably had only months to live.

I began to experience numbness, a retreat of the soul.

Diane detailed what she was doing for next steps and indicated where I could help. Her background as a clinical nurse specialist and clinical faculty, and her heart of a lioness, would help Jessica face coming tests. Diane cried, very hard. She was back on the phone.

"Can you come home?" she asked.

I felt a familiar, bachelor tug of independence, of being John Wayne, a guy with a Winchester, a loyal dog and a fungible horse. No family, no dying child, no responsibilities beyond protecting families on the range that were not yours. But I wasn't a cinema actor; I was an acolyte of the Bear, a student of H. Norman Schwarzkopf, a fraction of a West Pointer, and a man who'd made a promise to a wonderful wife and a precious daughter. My investigation team beckoned and Germany awaited. There were bad guys out there and I thought I had special skills to get them.

I covered the mouthpiece. "Sir, I have to go home."

"Go," said Murray. "Tell her you're on your way. Forget Germany." We gathered my luggage. In a record snow storm, he drove me to O'Hare to put me on a flight.

Jessica was in acute discomfort and painfully thin. Diane was stalwart, reducing her work hours to care for our baby, who had trouble breathing, eating, digesting, thriving, growing, living. I employed the Bear's teachings at work and chose magical thinking and Chinese superstition at home: Science will find a new cure to save Jessica. Thinking or speaking about her possible death was *ji hui*, inauspicious language in which speaking of a terrible outcome would invite its occurrence. I thought I was cursed with a malign fate, bad *yuing chi*, bad karma. I felt death's pursuit of our daughter. I knew it was crazy, but I sat, armed and vigilant, outside her door at night to protect her.

29

Do the Hardest Right

David came running toward Goliath, powered by courage and faith.
Goliath was blind to his approach – and then he was down, too big and
slow and blurry-eyed to comprehend the way the tables had been turned.
Malcolm Gladwell

Colonel Willoughby assembled our brigade conference in Las Vegas. I reminded him of Army regulations that prohibited our personnel from holding meetings in Vegas. He directed me to not attend the conference, as he would deliver the ethics bullet points in my stead.

I remained behind in our HQ when I received a call.

"Do you know who this is?" A whispering voice, one of our battalion commanders.

I said I did.

"Willoughby," he said, "assembled the battalion commanders and instructed us how to make sales calls on casinos and car dealers and stuff like that. We're supposed to get these business people to give free rooms and cars to our recruiters to increase production. I taped it so I didn't have to take notes. Didn't know it'd record a violation of ethics. You'll have that tape to you in about two hours.

"Listen carefully: I never called you. Your secretary never heard my voice. This conversation never happened. There's no tape and it's clean of prints. Captain, no way can you reveal my name to anyone, especially the Boss. I don't need that hassle."

I told him he was protected by Army Regulation 600-50 and by the attorney-client privilege. "I'll never reveal your identity. Sir, who saw you make the tape?"

"No one," he said. So he taped the boss covertly, wiped prints from the cassette, and was calling anonymously because things were that bad. My guts dropped just as they had when I realized that a soldier in Yongsan Garrison was probably an enemy officer who was close to getting his hands on our tactical nuclear devices.

"Sir," I said, "you are now appointed a USAREC Investigating Officer. You are to take notes on what happens and get them to me. Thank you for the call." He hung up.

The boss has really crossed the line, but he was past listening to me and this is not the time for me to lose my job. Talking about this new problem would only make it worse. He's making his own crisis and won't listen. I was making excuses to avoid what I didn't want to do. It had taken my YMCA boxing coach 10 years to teach me that if I hated being a coward, I had to go directly at my biggest source of anxiety.

I was facing the Bear's river of fear and I didn't even want to get wet much less drown. I was racing on the hamster wheel of hopelessness. If I acted for the right, no good would come of it and I could be unemployed. If I didn't act, I was a coward.

If the Bear left the protection of the camp to find the lost guys, he'd die. Almost as if he were someone else watching his actions, the Bear picked up his weapon and stepped into the dark jungle. At the Cambodian border he couldn't legally cross, he'd crossed it to protect his men and reported himself as a violator. At Duc Co, he lamented the rows of his dead Vietnamese paratroopers that no number of enemy dead could redeem. The Bear asked a U.S. chopper crew to transport his dead to base. Seeing that the corpses were merely Vietnamese, the pilot said he didn't want their blood and guts in his chopper. Incensed, the Bear ordered and the pilot refused; the Bear jumped on the Huey's skids.

He told me that he said, "You don't get my dead to base, I'll hang on 'til I fall off. The paper work alone will kill you." I imagine that the pilot looked at this exceptionally big and scary American officer, his uniform torn and bloody, grenades on his LBE, a loaded CAR-15 on his shoulder, and a .45-caliber Colt 1911 in its sidearm holster, glaring the fiercest gaze since

Medusa lost her head. The crew loaded the dead onto the deck of the Huey and the pilot delivered them.

The Bear said that it was my job to not sweat my career and to do the harder right despite risks. Thanks a lot, Norman Schwarzkopf.

The Bear would laugh at my making a small situation appear serious. I could hear him say, "Gus, you're pole-vaulting over mouse turds. Go do the hardest right, which is easier than you think 'cause you're braver than you know. Fight injustice with your own skin. No other way. Don't repeat your cop-out with that womanizing Firstie."

The tape arrived; I played it and took notes. Colonel Willoughby had instructed the commanders to persuade car dealers, casino owners, travel agencies—a huge list—to provide free vehicles, gambling weekends with free chips and meals, plus flights and massages for our top-quota recruiters. He told our guys to appeal to the business owners' patriotism and to "guilt them" into giving gifts. Since regulations said gifts couldn't be solicited, they were to "un-solicit" them.

The problem was that in the Army, soliciting and receiving gifts are strictly prohibited. Guardians of the republic do not work for bonuses, perks, favors, or gifts.

The boss instructed them to conceal these actions from USAREC HQ and "that damn JAG." They were to deny that they heard these instructions. The orders to cover up were more grievous than the plan to bribe soldiers; he was suborning perjury—directing people to lie under oath.

In crisis, discern with wise and reliable friends. I had found the best one of my life.

Diane listened to the tape. She said that a nurse manager couldn't do in a for-profit hospital what this commander was trying to do in the Army of George Washington, Abraham Lincoln, Matthew Ridgway, and Dwight Eisenhower.

"I'd make copies of that tape," she said. "I'd also tape a mirror at the end of a broomstick to check under your car for explosives every morning. Then, 'Book 'em, Dano.'"

I had Tech Services make five copies of the tape and logged three of them into the Provost's evidence room. I called Colonel Murray and gave him the brief.

"Let me get this straight," said Murray. "A promotable colonel tells his 11 battalion commanders to break the law and conceal truth from investigators, and not one of those chicken-hearted lily-livered SOBs stood up to question him? What the @#! is going on here?! What do you think I'd do if I were one of his subordinates?"

"Sir, you'd probably commit first-degree career suicide and ask him if he'd lost his mind. I had a mentor at West Point who made that his specialty."

"Ah, Gus, you speak as an officer of the King and the voice of reason. I'd say, 'Sir, promise you'll never again take hallucinogenic drugs before giving a briefing. There's no damn bloody way I'll break the law for you or for any man. Get this: Any officer here who follows those illegal stinking orders will have to answer to me, personally, right here in this room or out in the street, and if you have a sidearm I'll take you down with my teeth. Now, boss, for the sake of all that's holy and right, please revoke those illegal orders which we cannot by law or by oath obey, or I'll bust you like Eliot Ness.'"

"Jeez, sir, that sounds just like the Bear, uh, Colonel H. Norman Schwarzkopf."

"Don't know him," said Murray. "But that makes at least three of us that can tell a hot rock from a hot rock." I closed my eyes. God, I loved West Pointers. Willoughby had graduated from the Academy and wore the ring, but he'd adopted a results-at-any-cost set of standards. It broke my heart when any officer used his position for self-gain; it was particularly bitter when it was an Academy graduate who had been required to walk a narrow path for those four long years.

Charlie Murray liked to put me on airplanes. I was on the next flight to Vegas to enter the Strip's gaudiest casino. It was late afternoon and I was disheartened to see our officers and NCOs at gaming tables and slot machines attired in shorts and aloha shirts surrounded by people imprisoned by their weaknesses. If a citizen had a flaw, Las Vegas would pull him in with neon lights and free alcohol and create an addiction.

Colonel Willoughby opened the door. He wore a polo shirt and slacks.

"Standing out a bit in uniform, Gus?"

"Sir, I come bearing good news. May I come in?"

He occupied an expansive suite. I played the tape recorder. He frowned as we listened to his instructions to his commanders, then he turned it off.

"Sir, don't ask me where I got it."

"Who gave you the tape?"

"Sir, I can't tell you that. But I have good news that'll keep you out of jail."

"You're not listening," he said. "Give me his name or I fire your ass."

"Sir, I can't tell you that under pain of death. The source isn't the issue. The good news is that our battalion commanders await you in a third floor conference room where you can revoke your illegal orders. You can un-ring the bell. You get to use a legal time machine, ride back to last night's meeting with the guys, and make it disappear. Then I'll make you happy by getting out of your AO and return to Post."

He liked the last idea so much that he paused. He stepped into my face.

"Who gave you the damn tape?" He was close; I knew what he had for breakfast, yesterday.

"Sir," I said, matching his intensity, "it came to me in an unmarked envelope; end of story. My job is keeping you out of jail. Revoke your earlier orders, and General Thurman will kiss you on both cheeks and I'll extol your virtues in every ethics briefing I give for the rest of my life. But if you leave our battalion commanders dangling in the wind on your illegal orders, I'll report your violations of Standards of Conduct to Higher per para 3-dash-10 delta." I smiled like Cary Grant. "Just reviewed the reg."

"Listen," he snarled. "I'll relieve you for disobedience, drop an Efficiency Report that'll choke you right out of the Army, and sue you for malpractice and disbarment."

His anger washed over me. "Sir, this is more about your career than my puny one. Sir, please listen to the best legal advice, ever. I'm trying to help you . . ."

"We are motivated by incentives, rewards, bonuses, influence. I'll do whatever it takes with whatever rewards it takes so our guys meet mission. I will get this done despite you. Who gave you the tape!?"

"Sir, I think motivation and influence can be misused. What really motivates us is someone doing the right thing."

"*Stop!* Stop being the wise-ass sergeant who thinks only *he* holds the wisdom of the Army and walks around with a big attitude about officers."

I took a breath, unsure of the words. "I'm an ex-cadet. I flunked academics end of Cow year 'cause I couldn't figure out the essential. I'm ashamed, deeply ashamed, that I didn't graduate. But I still get to live the Honor Code, the rest of my life. What's essential, Sir, is our doing the harder right, every time, despite risks. We learned that together."

He pointed at my chest, his finger like a knife. "*Who gave you the tape?*"

"Sir, my Solids prof taught me to do the harder right but I let him down by flunking out. There's no threat you can make that'll make me disappoint him again."

He nodded and stepped back, thinking. He smiled. "Super, that's super, Gus. Great story. You of course will do what you think is best, but you're too smart to cause a ruckus over a puny misunderstanding that is NOT 'essential.' USAREC's tied up with bigger fish than a free weekend in Las Vegas. You're about to cash in your life for a bag of casino chips. Okay, you have hang-ups about the Academy because you flunked out. Want to push your head-case problems on the real world by pretending we're back at the Point. Well, Gus, you help yourself and good luck to you. You'll need it, and more."

My former self would've found agreement; my complaint suddenly sounded trivial and I was causing a ruckus for a puny cause.

The Bear's face appeared before me. He wasn't smiling. I woke up.

"Sir, I assure you, in accordance with the regulation, I will send this to Higher."

"I assure you that if you think on it, you won't, and you're a pure idiot if you do. Now who gave you the tape!?"

Following Colonel Charlie Murray's earlier instructions, I went to the conference room to find 10 of the 11 battalion commanders. I asked for their attention.

"Per directions from Command Legal Counsel, USAREC, who speaks for the commanding general, I'm taking statements from each of you, one by one." I gave them the order of interviews, pulled out a legal pad, and began asking questions of my first witness.

"Cease work!" cried our chief of staff, a full colonel who out-ranked us all. He was tall, thin, and shaking in anger. "Stand down, Captain," he said, pointing at me. "Rest of you, elbows and assholes to the door. Un-ass this AO." They started to move. I took a deep breath.

"Sir," I boomed with the baritone of a first sergeant in the field, "I'm act-ing under the authority of the Command Legal Counsel, USAREC's voice of law. This is now a 600-50 formal investigation and no one, including the CG, can impede it."

"That's it! By God you won't do this! OUT!" he screamed at the commanders.

"Sirs," I said, "stand fast. I need you here. We're under the ethics regulation."

"Out!" shouted the chief. They hesitated. A few trickled away; the others slowly followed. The chief, who was 6 feet 3 inches, put his body on me. I turned to leave and he grabbed me and I snapped my arm free to pursue those who had agreed to give statements.

I reported my findings on Colonel Willoughby and the chief of staff to Colonel Willoughby and sent a copy to USAREC. Colonel Willoughby immediately relieved me from my duties, wrote an Efficiency Report that focused on my lack of competence and lack of loyalty to mission. He sent a formal complaint to the State Bar of California demanding my disbarment.

I was still a member of the Connelly Investigation into recruiter malpractice, and was back on an airplane with my team. But at 6th Brigade, my home station, I became persona non grata.

In my few visits home, I held and tried to feed an amazingly cheerful but very thin Jessica. Her smile and giggles when I entered the apartment lifted up and then tore open my heart. I marveled at Diane, who soldiered on through multiple medical appointments, feeding options, and desperate care protocols without hesitation.

Months later, after traveling across the country advising General Connelly's investigative Tiger teams, I was ordered to return to 6th Brigade. Expecting a ruckus with Colonel Willoughby, I found Colonel Lawrence Bell, now the USAREC Inspector General, working at my former desk.

"Sir, either you got seriously demoted or I'm in the wrong office."

Colonel Bell motioned me to sit.

"Gus, we found lots of problems here. Effective tomorrow, your brigade's command group of four senior colonels, notably D. Hamilton Willoughby and the chief of staff, will be relieved to be retired or prosecuted. You are now the Command Judge Advocate, the senior legal officer, for the brigade. You will be detailed to give ethics lectures at various Army schools and General Thurman has approved you for an award.

"Your new brigade commander here is Brigadier General Caleb Archer. You may not know this, but he was the author of 600-50, our Standards of Conduct ethics reg." In other words, I'd gone from reporting to Captain Bligh to working for Sir Thomas More.

Serving with General Archer was an honor as he reasserted the principles by which soldiers had pledged to live. He inspired a return to the behaviors that defined honorable service. After I'd reported Colonel Willoughby for ethics violations, most of my fellow officers had avoided me. I was now greeted as if nothing had happened. Knowing how hard it is for me to demonstrate principled conduct in the face of pressure, I had learned to cheerfully forgive. Yet, in a small way, I'd imitated the Bear by aligning my decision and actions on what I had discerned to be the hardest right.

The Army family, led by Colonel Murray and Rob van Hooser and the other HQ JAGs, offered encouragement, support, and prayers for Jessica's health.

Jessica and Diane needed me at home. My heart's desire was to stay in the Army where I could serve the country for pay that was so low I could feel nobly free of greed. Diane asked me to leave the Army for my higher duty to my family. I felt the vibrations of Norman Schwarzkopf's presence; his essence and Diane's inner being clearly resonated.

My father had abandoned our family to preserve his military career. With great difficulty, I resigned. H. Norman Schwarzkopf's wisdom had seen me through my military service. I'd put off contacting him until I had sufficient achievements to warrant his care for me. Now, I was out of uniform, and would be unable to report to him as I'd wished.

30

Recover from Loss

Our prayers should be for blessings,
for God alone knows what is best for us.
Socrates

Diane was with Jessica at the hospital for lab tests. One day I was an Army officer, and a week later I was a deputy district attorney for Sacramento County, living in my old college town of Davis and nearing Christmas. I was selecting a jury when Jessica's small and over-laboring heart arrested. Diane and I were outside the Pediatric ICU, PICU, our arms around each other, when she died. The hospital chaplain offered to pray for her and us. Numbly, I refused. I felt a loss, a sucking vacuum that would not stop. I'd never grieved for my mother's death and separation from my sister Mary, and I think that Jessica's passing had triggered a grieving for all three. I was drowning in guilt over her death. Unable to rest, I found that alcohol tasted like rocket fuel but served as sleeping pill and painkiller. I'd looked down at friends of the grape and I now became dependent upon it. I was a dark walking nightmare of self-pity. Kind friends dropped off meals and condolences arrived while I regressed to a younger self, allowing a sorrowful and disabled persona to enter our marriage and our life. The District Attorney and my trial team told me to take as much time as I needed. I thought I'd been in the bottle for months, but Diane just reminded me that after two weeks, I shaved, donned a three-piece suit, and drove across the Yolo Causeway to the office. It seemed every day was December the ninth, and I would always be racing death from the courthouse to the PICU, and never reach the tape in time to save her.

In the office, the staff had taken down photos of their children. I gathered the staff by sections and thanked them for their kindnesses, cards, the flowers. Law enforcement and the military tend towards formal faith lives, so I manfully thanked them for their prayers. I asked them to bring back pictures of their kids. I said that Diane and I needed to see those photos, now more than ever.

My bureau chief distributed files so I got no cases involving child victims. But I inherited one nonetheless, and justice prevailed. The victim was somewhat resurrected and Diane and I tried to take her into our family, without success. But we now had a mindset with which we'd later bring two other children into our family.

I was a wreck, the kind of male that would've made the Bear sick to his stomach. Providence intervened as Diane resolved to stay with me and my broken self. I gave up the bottle. Work with dedicated and humorous colleagues was a tonic, but Jessica's absence filled our days. I missed the Army and its rigorous camaraderie, and I was in my 15th year of dreaming every night of being reinstated as a cadet and rejoining my company. In those dreams, everyone else had also aged, and we were reunited in Company A-3 for that missing year. Around our 10th year of marriage, Diane acknowledged that I'd probably have those dreams until I died. Getting a cute and loyal puppy from the animal shelter didn't fill the greater vacuums of the heart. I knew the puppy would someday die.

We were soon blessed with a healthy and wonderful Jena Marie and Eric Michael. Diane worked part-time, then chose to be a full-time parent. I was an acting deputy attorney general and director of training for California's 3,000 prosecutors. Jena was 7 and Eric was 5 when I lost my job. I'd declined an offer from one of Sacramento's largest law firms; the time requirements would replicate military service. I applied and interviewed for less stressful non-supervisory government legal positions.

"You," said a hiring manager, holding my resume, "don't want a lowly staff job."

"Oh, I really do," I said. "I'm done with higher-level positions."

"You're an ambitious ladder climber. Arrived in the DA's Office from the Army, never even saw a civilian courtroom. In three months you're leading the municipal court trial team. Second year, you're a supervising deputy.

Then you become the deputy director at CDAA getting the big bucks. Gus, you can't help it; you'll try to replace me."

"I was just lucky. In the Army, the worst thing is a careerist. I'm not a careerist."

He thanked me for coming in and wished me good luck in securing a judgeship, partnership, or director's position. The scenario, usually with less candor, repeated itself. All I wanted was a staff position that required little of me.

Diane got a full-time job. I became Mr. Mom, the first male room mother at West Davis Elementary School. I shopped, cooked, cleaned, and did part-time legal work. I bonded with our kids, but I was haunted by memories of my father's unemployment throughout my childhood.

I was a full-time dad when a packet arrived from Shanghai. A man named Lee Lon-lon introduced himself as the only son of my father's only brother—this Lon-lon was my first cousin. He and his two sisters, Jane and Lulu, had survived civil war, invasion, world war, revolution, the Great Leap Forward, and the Cultural Revolution. He sent greetings to my sisters. With the letter were pictures of "beautiful, gracious, and devout Auntie." He was referring to my mother. Jena thoughtfully asked me, "Where's my missing granny, your mommy?"

I said she died a long time ago.

Jena, who'd never known a bad mother or granny, asked, "Was she nice?"

I said the hard truth was that my mother and I didn't like each other very much.

"Gus," said Diane softly, "I think she's asking about your real mom, not Edith."

"Oh, her. Jena Roo, she died when I was five, and I never really knew her."

That night, after singing Jena her bedtime songs, she said, "Daddy, nothing would ever happen to Mommy. But if something did, Eric wouldn't forget her and he's five, just like you were when your mommy died. How come you forgot your mommy?"

Her question could've come from the Bear. "Sweetie, I don't know. I spoke baby Chinese to her and after she died, we stopped speaking Chinese. Maybe I lost the words to even think about her. But I'm going to ask Auntie Elinor, Auntie Ying, and Auntie Mary about their mother so I can tell you what she was like."

I interviewed my sisters in the legal manner, as if our mother had been a homicide victim, and as a deputy DA, I needed to know her backstory so I could bring her to life in the courtroom. Tell me about her friends, her habits, what she read, was she nice?

I took notes as if the Bear were holding forth in our Solid Mechanics section room when he explained leadership, character, and competence. I started a journal for Jena. Every night after we tucked the kids to bed, I, who'd never written a journal, read a new chapter to Diane, who'd never edited. She provided sage guidance on what to add, what to change, and what to cut. I followed all of her advice. My father, a Nationalist Chinese army officer, had worked with the U.S. Army with Captain Ed Schenck at Fort Benning and in China during World War II, so I placed "Major H. Norman Schwarzhedd" into the story in lieu of Captain Schenk.

The Schwarzhedd character was a larger-than-life Army officer who loved the people of the world and was fearless in war, dedicated to helping those in need and fiercely fought evil and injustice. He entered combat while magically avoiding damage to the soul. As all the characters in a journal that was later converted into fiction, it was based on a person I knew.

The story seemed to write itself. In three months, I had over 300 pages. Writing had reminded me of the values taught to me and other street urchins by the Central YMCA of San Francisco, and of the YMCA Mind, Body, Spirit that had prepared me for West Point's Duty, Honor, Country. I remembered sermons and the kindnesses of Christian men and women who respected all children, regardless of background and lack of grace. I remembered Christian talks at the Y and sermons in the all-black Zion African Methodist Episcopal church in which I was the only minority. I remembered the generosity of my first friend, Toussaint Streat, and found myself crying as I wrote. I had scorned Christians, the people who had saved my life.

Later, Diane found Toussaint, and we reunited after a 33-year separation. I'd wanted to be a paratrooper, knowing, with my body, it would be impossible. Dr. Toussaint Streat, M.D., Chief of Family Practice, Kaiser Permanente, had always wanted to be a physician, knowing, as an African-American slum kid, it was Fat Chance

"Diane," I said, "could I excerpt a section from the journal and submit it to *The New Yorker?*"

"Gus, I don't think it's an article! It's a *book!*"

Our book was sold for a late 1989 release. My fine editors asked if I knew Amy Tan. You know, personally. I said I didn't.

A grad school roommate and the best natural athlete I ever knew, David Kai Tu, whose family is also from Shanghai, ran a Silicon Valley engineering firm. He asked if I'd like to talk to his cousin, who was a writer. What's his name, I asked.

"Amy Tan," he said.

Amy generously gave an author quote to *China Boy* and became a wonderful friend. She offered terrific advice about how to handle being an author, got me into Molly Giles's writing group, and now supports our daughter Jena, who is a better writer than her dad.

Once Amy and I were on a local San Francisco TV program. In the audience was Amy's mother, Daisy, and my father, T.C. Lee. Daisy was a small and delicate woman with a lovely face, the spirit of a survivor, and the history of Chinese laments writ upon her stout heart. During a commercial break, Amy leaned over and said, "Your dad's pretty cute. We ought to get him together with my mom."

I grimaced. "I wouldn't do that," I said. "Does the name, Wen Fu, mean anything to you?" Wen Fu was the monstrously abusive husband in Amy's second novel, *The Kitchen God's Wife*. Wen Fu was a fictional representation of Daisy's very dangerous first husband. "My father looks cute, but he's terrible to women. My sisters would take to the streets to protest introducing him to any woman, much less your sweet mother. You know that line from the cartoon, Hagar the Horrible? He's 'Hagar' to his friends, but 'Horrible' to his family?"

But Daisy liked T.C.'s looks. After several meals at fine San Francisco Chinese restaurants with Amy, her husband Lou and her mother, Diane, my father, our kids, and me, against all rational prayers, Daisy and T.C. became an item. Amy and I became putative siblings when her mother and my father became a live-in couple in the East Bay. They later traveled together to China with Amy and Lou for the filming of *The Joy Luck Club*. Director Wayne Wang wrote my colorful father into the script, and he appears, with Daisy, in a number of scenes.

While they were there, my cousin Lon-lon phoned me from Shanghai.

"Cousin!" he said. "We send congratulations! Such big news. So happy for Uncle! You have a new mah-mee!" "Uncle" was my father.

"New mah-mee?" I said.

"Yes, Cousin! I'm sure Uncle told you, yes? No? Oh, oh. I am so sorry. Dear cousin, Jian-sun"—my Chinese name—"your father married Amy Tan's mother, here in China! Such great news!"

The news floored me. I thanked Lon-lon for his courtesy. I was worried sick for Daisy.

I was at the airport when the party returned from China. Daisy, who was very lovely and very short, exited Customs by herself.

I presented her with a large bouquet of roses. "Welcome back," I said. "With all our best wishes for true happiness."

"What you mean, 'True happiness'!?"

"For your wedding, your marriage."

Daisy Tan looked at me as if I had lit my hair on fire.

My father thankfully appeared. I gave him the flowers. "Congratulations," I said.

"For what?" he barked.

"Your wedding and marriage."

"Ah, so stupid!" He took the flowers. "We not married! Had to say we married to China communist! Not let you sleep together not married! Then, had to tell everyone we married. We NOT married!" He smelled the flowers and gave them to Daisy. Daisy gave them back to him. I took the flowers.

They went on to share the kind of adventures not normally associated with people in their 70s and 80s. When Daisy realized how T.C. treated her after the first few months of dating, she stopped eating and developed acute hypertension in a frightening "Gaslight" imitation of what had befallen his first two wives. Fortunately, they separated, and her health and weight returned.

The advance royalties for *China Boy* were the equivalent of several years of salary, but I knew that had been the equivalent of manna from heaven. I couldn't support the family on wild good fortune (speculative writing), and persisted in looking for less demanding (non-managerial) government staff positions. I could've returned to the DA's office, but I was burned out from dealing with tragic victims, paroled recidivists, and criminal defendants, one of whom had issued a particularly intense death threat to me that put my family in danger.

I'd been unemployed for almost a year when the State Bar of California called and asked if I'd accept the newly-created position of Senior Executive for Legal Education for the state.

Instead of training 3,000 prosecutors as I had at CDAA, would I be willing to manage a staff in three cities, coordinate the state's certified law schools, and design content and launch and implement mandatory continuing legal education for California's 140,000 attorneys? My new boss would be Herb Rosenthal, an inspirational and dedicated leader who was an Army Reserve JAG colonel whose wise decisions created resonances with the Bear and Colonel Murray. I found myself employed by the institution that had received Colonel Willoughby's demand that I be disbarred.

I began to meet with law school deans, independent bar associations, and the heads of government agencies to create an interlocking continuing professional education network. Almost every time I encountered a hiring manager who'd turned me down, he or she would say, "See, I said you were looking for a higher position!"

I sent a copy of *China Boy* to General Schwarzkopf. It wasn't the same as reporting to him as a TOAD Airborne Ranger officer at West Point, but I thought it was better than flunking out of the Academy.

31

Learn from History

Pray for peace, people everywhere.
General H. Norman Schwarzkopf's nightly prayer,
hoping that Saddam would peacefully leave Kuwait before
he was ordered to start Operation Desert Storm

Norm Schwarzkopf was named the Commander-in-Chief (CINC) of U.S. Central Command (CENTCOM) on Thanksgiving Day, 1988. It was when "Rainman" was the number one movie, Michael Jackson's "Man in the Mirror" topped the charts, and I looked at myself and saw the need to change in deeper ways than I already had. That year, the Soviets withdrew their broken army from the hard mountains of Afghanistan, where one of my USMA classmates had been serving with the *mujahadeen* against the Soviets. Being CINC meant a fourth star for the Bear and a family move for Brenda and their three children to CENTCOM HQ at MacDill Air Force Base in Florida. I think he viewed the assignment as he'd viewed combat survival—with surprise that the bad guys hadn't gotten him and that his outspokenness and temper hadn't ended his career. Four stars remain the highest permissible rank, and he therefore wouldn't be promoted again. I was finally right about his chances for promotion.

CENTCOM was a paper mélange of disparate elements that would have to be hastily glued together to meet a security crisis in the Middle East, North Africa, the Persian Gulf, or the mysterious reaches of Central Asia. This was a region where foreign misunderstandings and misadventures had been both comical and tragic. It was a place of traditional Western defeats.

I was very happy for him; he held a great and abiding affection for the people of the Middle East. Far from experiencing culture shock in the Levant, he had long ago embraced its customs, courtesies, deserts, minarets, and muezzins. He regarded Islam's complexities with a sympathetic under-standing that was uncommon at the time. It was in the Middle East that he had relished companionship with his father. It was in the fabled Levant that he had learned to honor all people, from xenophobic tribal warriors to arrogant embassy school bullies. With his father's love for all people, Iran was for the Bear a classic preparatory school that would equip him to honor Palestinian Jews, French-speaking Vietnamese paratroopers, indolent West Point cadets, sullen Viet Cong prisoners, anti-American Europeans, and the soldiers and warriors of the Middle East.

Iran and Arabia were to him the romantic and beckoning lands in which he learned that leaders need strong moral backbones whether they speak Farsi, Arabic, Hebrew, or German. He'd been a boy when he had eaten the eye of a sheep and stood tall in tribal desert meetings in which his father had treated him as a grown and trustworthy man. It was the land of a thousand and one nights where he'd imagined repeating the feats of Alexander the Great the Macedonian and Hannibal Barca the Tunisian, of imitating the utterly tenacious and shabbily dressed Ulysses S. Grant.

But CENTCOM was a joint command of contentious and viciously competitive U.S. military branches. Inter-service rivalry traced to the con-flicting Pacific war strategies of General Douglas MacArthur and Admiral Chester Nimitz, the failed Desert One rescue of the Tehran hostages in which the abstract commitment to have all the services share based on right to participate instead of on the requirements for success produced disaster, and the harsh realizations from the Grenada and Panama operations that the services, when compelled to work together, instead of being "joint," could be as contentious with each other as they were with the foe.

The CINC, like Hannibal, Marshall, and Eisenhower, was a believer in coalition warfare, committed to creating an unprecedented level of "joint-ness" between both allies and the different services and to doing it decisively.

He told me in later years that he saw Gorbachev's USSR moving from global saber-rattling to open discussions of *glasnost* not as a political moment but as an historic game-changer. The Bear sat in the front of an intensive For-eign Service Institute course on the Middle East and took prodigious notes.

After taking that program, he said he looked at the map of the Middle East and radically concluded that the great present threat in the Arab world was not the USSR's Kremlin or Iran's Ayatollah, but Iraq's Saddam Hussein. Iraq's air force had, without provocation, attacked the missile frigate, USS *Stark* in neutral waters, killing 37 American sailors at a time while the United States wanted to regard Hussein and Iraq as a pragmatic ally against Iran and the ayatollah.

The Bear received little affirmation for his theory, but as CINC, he was expected to carry the responsibilities of his command, which included his independent assessment of threats and possible capabilities by all foreign powers in the vast region for which he was responsible. The USSR was undeniably morphing from global aggression into something less confrontational at the same time that Iraq was building up its military and preparing for further hostilities. Soon after reporting, he accordingly directed the CENTCOM staff to candidly reassess the preeminent threats in the Middle East. The research produced a surprising conclusion: The likeliest hostile action in the region was the Iraqi army invading Saudi Arabia through Kuwait.

In March 1990, the CINC assembled 500 CENTCOM staff to write Operation Plan (OP) 1002-90, the comprehensive strategic response to a possible Iraqi invasion in the Arabian Peninsula. Long a disciple of the Battle of Cannae, Schwarzkopf insisted that the plan reflect the Army's new Air-Land Battle Doctrine: Disrupt the enemy's thinking; deceive the enemy to focus forces and energy away from the point of decision; and maneuver lightning-fast to flank the enemy with pincers.

OP 1002-90 was smart, logical, and would stop an Iraqi advance from conquering Saudi Arabia. But the Bear disliked the absence of a counter-offensive to force the Iraqi army back to its own borders, so he conceived a four-stage follow-on plan to liberate Kuwait, which would be Saddam's stepping-stone into the Saudi kingdom. It amplified the disruption of the enemy through three stages of an air campaign, increased the deception in the enemy commander's mind, involved a sharp, short, and decisive ground war, but did not involve a taking of Iraq's capital. Yet, it was designed to be a war-ending battle; the equivalent of a walk-off grand slam.

The CINC began commuting on the 30-hour flight to the Middle East to build relationships with political and military leaders in Saudi Arabia, Egypt, Pakistan, Kuwait, Jordan, United Arab Emirates, Bahrain, and Qatar. This was one of his great gifts. He listened carefully and spoke graciously, in the Arab form. He honored his hosts by dressing as they dressed, wearing the white cotton *thaub*, black outer *bisht* cloak, white *ghutrah* head covering, and black *iqal* cord.

Later, in discussing his early relationship building in the Middle East, he told me that he "kind of looked like Lawrence of Arabia." "I'd ridden a camel when I was a sprout running around with my dad in the deserts of Iran, but I was wearing camping clothes. When I had the robe, the cloak, before Desert Shield, I didn't have the camel."

In his memoir, he wrote that he was surprised to learn during his relationship building that Arab leaders didn't see Iraq as a threat; they worried far more about Iran's historic hostility against Arabs. It was a reminder that here, regional feuds originated in millennia of ancient ethnic hatreds and wars. The U.S. Departments of State and Defense thought that although Saddam Hussein had massed his army on the Kuwaiti border, he might only take the Rumaila oil fields but not actually invade. In July 1990, three days before the Iraqi invasion, the U.S. ambassador to Kuwait was told she could take her planned vacation.

On August 1, 1990, General Schwarzkopf briefed the Joint Chiefs of Staff, saying that the Iraqis would cross the border and could be in Kuwait City in six hours.

The next day, I was merging into early Thursday morning commuter traffic in San Francisco when National Public Radio's Bob Edwards announced that at two a.m., 100,000 Iraqi troops and 700 tanks invaded and were occupying the Gulf state of Kuwait. He said Kuwait was an oil-rich kingdom that, with Iraq, represented 20 percent of the world's oil reserves. Saddam Hussein, Iraq's fifth president, who'd been in power for 20 years, announced that a provisional government had been established in Iraq's "19th Province" and that he would turn Kuwait City into a "graveyard" if any nation sought to militarily challenge his takeover. The Bear and the leaders of the Middle East grasped that Saddam's taking of Kuwait opened the door to Saudi Arabia, whose riches would crown him as a modern-day Padishah sultan. After the Gulf states would come Israel, and after Israel, the true dreaming could begin anew.

Saddam Hussein used chemical warfare, murder, torture, and rape to control his own people. Now, Iraqis were doing to the Kuwaitis what Nazis had done to Poland and Europe, and what the Empire of Japan had done to Asia and the Pacific archipelago. In World War I, America had responded to German submarines sinking its merchant ships by declaring war on Germany. In response to Japan's invasion of China, America imposed a trade embargo on Japan, an act that Japan regarded as a declaration of war. I thought, It's war, and the Bear is CENTCOM CINC. It's a mess but he'll get it right. He'll be the man of the hour.

I didn't know that he would be the man of the decade.

Under direction of President George H.W. Bush, the CINC's staff enacted OP 1002-90 and assembled and deployed its disparate units from around the world. Operation Desert Shield was underway. Later, the U.S. ambassador to Iraq said, "I didn't think, and nobody else did, that the Iraqis were going to take all of Kuwait."

Iraq had the world's fourth largest army and had been armed by the Soviet Union to become a massive Arab force. It would fight with short supply lines in its own region. Its troops were combat-hardened, unafraid of 120° deserts, and would feel they were defending their homeland and the "19th Province" against a *kafir*, or infidel, and thus, a traditionally hated invader.

The United States had the world's seventh largest standing army, with headquarters eight time zones and 7,000 miles distant. It would have to transit mined waterways to reach inadequate ports and would be fighting with gear that had not been tested in combat while deploying a force that had been at peace for 16 years.

It is a popular notion that people and institutions cannot change. H. Norman Schwarzkopf disproved that notion in my life, and historical precedents supported him. Whenever I witness organizations resist necessary changes, I remind myself that in 1853, Japan had been powerless when modern foreign warships sailed into Yokohama Harbor. Japan resolved to change, and in 41 years it converted itself from an illiterate feudalist state into an industrialized world power, albeit without considering the benefits of democracy. In 1975, the U.S. Army ignominiously retreated from Saigon. The Army resolved to change, and in 15 years transformed a nearly-million-soldier institution from a state of brokenness and even lawless disorder into one of the most effective combat forces in the world.

Into the 1980s, senior general officers like Fred Franks, Creighton Abrams, Donn Starry, William DePuy, and Carl Vuono had fiercely fought institutional inertia and human resistance to bring sweeping changes. They altered two change-resistant features in human nature: behaviors of character and behaviors of relationship.

Army leaders would be required to change themselves and thereby inspire change in others. The Army's defensive mentality was being replaced by Air-Land Battle, a bold, maneuver-based doctrine based on the classic principles of war. It depended upon unit leadership, initiative, and rapid, coordinated actions on the enemy's flanks and rear. Theory becomes reality by hours of practice and by dress rehearsals; the Army practiced the doctrine, with many initial failures in its many training sites, to include demanding maneuvers in the 114° heat of the National Training Center in the Mojave Desert.

Max Thurman's "Be All You Can Be" policy meant realigning the recruitment force with ethics, removing recruiters who cheated, and focusing on high school graduates while avoiding high-risk recruits. This had produced soldiers who, by a few percentage points, were better educated than the general American public. They were lean, athletic, and tough. With strong leadership, they were ready to find the enemy and destroy it. As Deputy Chief of Staff for Personnel, Thurman had selected Norm Schwarzkopf to be his deputy, and they had begun excusing ineffective officers and NCOs from the Army only a few years after the Connelly Investigation had removed unethical officers from the recruitment process. By the mid-1980s, it was becoming the army that the nation required.

It was this Army that CENTCOM called upon to defend the Arabian Peninsula. To block further Iraqi expansion, U.S. units, led by the Air Force, began flying into Middle Eastern bases in the largest air transport operation in history. The fourth stage of the CINC's war plan to evict the Iraqi army from Kuwait employed AirLand Battle doctrine, the principles of war, Sun Tzu, and the Battle of Cannae. If he executed AirLand Battle doctrine, then he would strike deep into the enemy rear to disrupt communications, lines of supply, and ability to maneuver. If he obeyed the principles of war he would maintain the initiative and rapidly concentrate at the point of decision. To be a *mentu*, a disciple, of Sun Tzu, Schwarzkopf would seek to deceive the enemy commander by appearing to attack at a key point that he would, in fact, ignore and instead strike massively where he would not be expected. Finally, to align with the lessons of Cannae, which he had long held in his thinking, he would employ stunning shock force—his armored formations—in a bold envelopment to pincer the Iraqi Republican Guard and permit its annihilation. Again, following Sun Tzu, who regarded protracted war as a means of defeat, the CINC would only act with an adequately sized force to rapidly and decisively end a war that the media was predicting could be a long, futile, high-casualty, Vietnam-like slog. He aimed for total military victory at minimal cost.

Sun Tzu placed prime importance on spies and battlefield intelligence. Most armies, including America's, traditionally fail to understand the enemy's capabilities. The British grossly underestimated the American colonists and their leadership, and thus the world's greatest military power was defeated. The Union and the Confederacy each assumed it would achieve victory in the Civil War in short order, and they combined to kill more Americans than all the other wars in which the United States has fought. America presumed it could easily defeat the Japanese, North Koreans, Viet Cong guerillas, and North Vietnamese regulars, and instead found itself fighting to avoid defeat. In Desert Storm, other than the Republican Guard formations, the Iraqi army proved to be far less effective than projected. It was a happier miscalculation.

I was in the Army Reserve but was not assigned to a unit, which made it harder to be deployed. I got a phone call from Bob "More Beer" Lorbeer, my company mate and roommate from A-3. He was now a full colonel at U.S. Army Forces Command, FORSCOM. Bob was activating Reserve units for CENTCOM.

"You want in?" he asked.

"To serve under the Bear!? I'm in!"

"Gus, I can't promise I can get you into the Gulf. I'm making assignments and can't even get there myself. Call you at home ASAP, out."

I cancelled appointments and rushed home. I didn't get called up, and Bob didn't make it to the Gulf. While Bob "Moon" Beahm, Tommy Pence, Bill "The Truck Master" Nash, and other classmates served gallantly in Desert Storm, they'd have to win it without More Beer and Gustavo on the ground with them. The Army now had night vision devices, so I could theoretically see at night, but they depended on having good vision. I'd undergone two radial keratotomies and remained impaired.

Saddam Hussein did not expect a strong U.S. response to his invasion of Kuwait and calculated that U.S. Army elements could not win a desert war. Iraq had defeated Iran in 10 years of desert combat, and Iranians knew the desert better than Americans. Further, Saddam held that no Arab states would support an infidel America.

With his earlier, theoretical, four-stage plan to eject Iraqi forces, General Schwarzkopf persuaded the White House that liberating Kuwait would require greater forces. President Bush agreed to apply immediate maximum force, a direct departure from the gradual parceling of resources in Vietnam, and the president and Secretary of State James Baker began to live on airplanes to build a 33-nation military coalition. It joined Syria, Afghanistan, Pakistan, and Yemen with Great Britain, France, Bangladesh, Niger, and Denmark. It was General Schwarzkopf's job to form from this polyglot assembly of very different people a unified military formation.

Because the coalition force was outnumbered and the attacker should, by doctrine, outnumber the attacked, the National Security Council and Joint Chiefs of Staff estimated 20,000–30,000 U.S. casualties in the liberation of Kuwait. Trevor Dupuy, a noted military expert, estimated 100,000 American casualties in the first phase of the war as Saddam threatened burning fire pits and masses of American dead in the "mother of all battles."

General Schwarzkopf later told me he was thinking about Hannibal Barca as CNN carried news flashes. The star on a new world stage of cabled immediacy was not a sovereign leader, chairman of the Joint Chiefs, actor, or telegenic reporter. On the screen for all the world to see appeared a big, larger-than-life American general in a common utility desert camouflage uniform. He was dressed like a common soldier and spoke with the fixity of purpose of Ulysses S. Grant. The big man was giving a news briefing as if he were in a West Point engineering section room, complete with Academy pointer and charts. Behind the presentation was a military mind that remembered the axioms of Sun Tzu and the lessons of Cannae.

I'd seen photos of him over the years as I'd held his lessons in my head. Seeing him and hearing his voice sent shock waves through heart and brain, reminding me that I was his acolyte. Memory took me back to that time when he fiercely fought for my character, and I could not breathe. It was like returning to that rare moral space where the battle rages on between what we are and what we should be. He had been my guide in that contest, and now, watching him, I remembered and treasured those times when he was a professor and I was his pupil, and, had the internet then existed, you could Google either of us without registering a hit, for he was just being introduced to the entire world. When we were at West Point in the 1960s, he was already who he was, and I was already trying to secretly imitate him.

General H. Norman Schwarzkopf was telling the world the way it was. While my heart lifted to see and hear him, glad that he was in command, confident that he'd do the hardest right thing, and would win the war quickly with minimal casualties, I also experienced stabs of pain. I should be with him. I loved my family and would sacrifice all material goods for them, but I wanted to trade all my civilian pay and rank to simply be one of his soldiers in a remote corner of the battlefield.

He appeared 50 pounds heavier than he ought to be. But CENTCOM wasn't a troop command in which he'd be up at 0500 to run three miles with 15,000 lean and fit, chanting troops. He was a general officer in the world's worst hotspot while locked in a cheerless headquarters building, eating hot dogs and ice cream on the run, and sleeping like Max Thurman, who didn't believe in sleep.

His voice was low and raspy; he'd been using it to reach hundreds of thousands of troops in his commands during the past 35 years. I'd been a drill sergeant for only one year, and my once resonant voice had never fully recovered.

He gave an incisive and controlled grasp of a complex situation. He showed his force of will, humor, and decency. He was making a sensational impression on the watching world. It should scare the wits out of Iraqi Republican Guard commanders, who now knew that a very tough warrior had them in his crosshairs and was unafraid of their vast numbers, home-field advantage, ranks of combat veterans, and their threats to soak the desert in a sea of American blood.

The last American general whose presence had entered public consciousness was General William C. Westmoreland, who had not presented Washington with a winning war plan in Vietnam and had failed to inspire confidence in the American public.

Norman Schwarzkopf's confident, personable, and informative briefings assured a worried America that our soldiers were in good hands and that our strategy was sound. By not exaggerating gains, by appearing authentic and accessible, and by demonstrating a sense of humor, he represented a presence that was an abrupt departure from the many less-than-credible briefings during the Vietnam War.

Behind the scenes, the CINC had gathered the senior officers of the Coalition into a secure briefing room in Riyadh. In the company of his generals, and in the fashion of Dwight David Eisenhower revealing the plan of Operation Overlord to his coalition commanders, and the personal touches the warrior-king Edward III on the eve of the Battle of Crécy,

Norman Schwarzkopf took the stage and pulled back the curtain. A map of the region depicted the plan of Operation Desert Storm.

General Barry McCaffrey, Commanding General, 24th Infantry Division (Mechanized), a major component in General Fred Franks' VII Corps, was in the room. A member of the West Point class of 1964, the folks who graduated a month before my class reported for Beast Barracks, he'd been badly wounded in Vietnam and had received two Distinguished Service Crosses, the second highest valor award after the Medal of Honor, and two Silver Stars. Grievously wounded, he assaulted an enemy machine gun position and attacked it relentlessly while under fire until he'd killed the enemy. Courage in all things for him had become habitual.

I have spoken with General McCaffrey. I greatly admire his strong reputation within the profession as a leader of wisdom and incredible toughness. He said that when the CINC unveiled the attack plan in the Gulf, he almost gasped and that an electric thrill ran through the senior officers in the room.

The generals, he said, had failed their soldiers in Vietnam in vision, in forceful advocacy, and in speaking truth to authority. Now, in that conference room, it was clear that General Schwarzkopf had changed their world. His plan had the Army, Marines, Air Force, Navy, and Coast Guard using bold maneuver, misdirection, and deception—all the things that we as a military had forgotten to do in Vietnam. It was thinking aligned with character and competence, enacting the proven principles of leadership and war. It was rare generalship of the first order.

McCaffrey said in a leadership lecture series at West Point that "The boldness of the plan inspired us because it wasn't going to be a massive bombardment followed by a frontal assault. It would brilliantly outflank the enemy and save the lives of our troops." In the minds of those tutored by the Bear, he was restating the lesson of the Pyramid—save your people—and the principle of bold maneuver—concentrate and envelop. Don't repeat World War I trench warfare. Candidly tell your superiors what is needed to produce victory. Your stars and approval by others be damned. It's about leadership, and it will always be about leadership, and that means it's about your character, and not your politics of self-advancement.

Hannibal prepared for Cannae by deeply studying the tactics, tendencies, strengths and vulnerabilities of the Roman Legion. Iraq was the Soviet Union's primary military client; its military equipment and operational philosophy made it an imitation Red Army, so the CINC prepared for Desert Storm by first reviewing his deep understanding of Soviet Army doctrine. He then studied the Iraqi army's performance in its long war with Iran. Where Hannibal had made a long and rapid journey across Western Europe to reach deep into the Italian peninsula, the CINC rapidly assembled his formations from the United States and Europe to position them on the Kuwaiti and Iraqi borders. Hannibal knew the Roman commander, Gaius Varro, feared hills and valleys, so Hannibal chose a flat and broad plain. Varro would aggressively crash into the coalition center, so Hannibal directed his center to gradually fall back. Once the Roman army was sucked inward, Hannibal would signal to bring in his wings to envelop the enemy.

The CINC knew that Saddam Hussein was preparing trenches and emplacing his armor in revetments, so the Bear would boldly sprint his formations on a flat, open, and seemingly uncrossable desert to envelop the static Iraqi formations. He and Hannibal began the engagement by cutting off the enemy's supply lines, confusing the enemy commander, and deploying an effective coalition force.

Hannibal's army at Cannae consisted of Gauls, Spaniards, Nubians, Africans, and Carthaginians, all of whom had learned to fight as a cohesive whole.

Schwarzkopf's coalition included Afghans, Argentinians, Australians, Bahraini, Bangladeshi, Belgians, British, Canadians, Czechs, Danes, Dutch, Egyptians, French, Germans, Greeks, Italians, Kuwaitis, Moroccans, New Zealanders, Nigerians, Norwegians, Omani, Pakistani, Poles, Qatari, Saudi Arabians, Senegalese, South Koreans, Spanish, Syrians, Turks, United Arab Emirati, and Americans, most of whom had not even previously spoken to each other, much less teamed under deadly fire.

Hannibal knew that Varro would likely be reckless with his two-to-one numerical advantage, and tried to fill Varro with even greater overconfidence. In the August heat and summer dust created by 135,000 soldiers of both armies on the march, Hannibal deftly concealed his disciplined cavalry behind his infantry center, making his coalition force appear even smaller. The CINC knew that Saddam Hussein feared an amphibious attack on Kuwait City from the Gulf and would increase his strength there to resist it. To encourage Saddam's anxieties, he created the appearance of a vast and imminent assault from the sea, and Saddam kept depleting his right flank—where the actual coalition attack would focus—to destroy the Marines who never landed.

Hannibal's final stroke came from his heavy, mobile cavalry, which had earlier crossed the Alps, and then adeptly divided to execute a double envelopment of the Varro's Romans on both wings. The CINC's decisive blow came from General Franks' VII Corps of fast-moving heavy tanks that performed a single wing envelopment (forbidden Iran was on the other flank) of Saddam's main force.

Of the 86,000 Romans who marched into Cannae, 75,000 died. The Iraqis awaited an amphibious landing that never occurred, and were defeated by the VII Corps' left hook they never expected. Most of the Iraqi army died or surrendered in the envelopment. They abandoned Kuwait and the survivors fled the Coalition forces.

Hannibal had formed a personal relationship with each group and deployed them at Cannae based on an intimate understanding of their relative strengths. Before Desert Storm, the CINC knew the capabilities of his units and deployed them with geometric logic for optimum communication, movement, and fire. He personally connected with the foot soldiers, who were inspired by his obvious personal and operational care for them, allowing his confidence in them to become their trust in him. Reporters learned that from the moment the Bear landed in Saudi Arabia on August 26, 1990, he routinely worked 15-hour days, seven days a week, ate meals in the war room, and slept four or five hours a day.

"The troops revered him," wrote journalist Rick Atkinson. Staff Sergeant Justin Smith said that "when he came to Dhahran, we just swarmed around him. He was like a father." Roger Cohen, a *New York Times* reporter working the European desk, wrote that "Schwarzkopf liked to mingle freely with his men in the desert, shaking their hands, embracing them, chatting with confidence about inevitable victory, and reveled in his nickname, 'the Bear.'"

Fifteen years after Gulf War, while delivering leadership training at Fort Benning and Fort Carson, soldiers told me that they had loved the Bear in Desert Storm. One related how the Bear had hugged him, completely swallowing him up in his big arms, "just like he was my dad." They felt enormous affection for this big man who had moved among them like a take-charge gunfighter. They believed he used his general's stars, his high rank, not for his advancement or book deals, glitz, or a political future. He committed his stars to work tirelessly for their safety and for a quick victory "so we could go home." While I was delivering leadership training to the staff and faculty at the United States Army Sergeant Majors Academy at Fort Bliss, a senior NCO bitterly opposed the notion that the CINC, as an advisor in Vietnam in 1965, had actually crossed the Cambodian border. "He wouldn't do that," he maintained. "Not the CINC."

In his memoir, the Bear wrote that during Desert Shield, the operation to defend Saudi Arabia from invasion, and before the UN-set deadline for Saddam to leave Kuwait was passed, he asked his wife and children to constantly pray for peace. Years before in his BOQ, he had done a sing-along of the lyrics to "Do You Hear What I Hear": "Pray for peace, people everywhere." Permanently scarred by the loss of soldiers under his command, and prepared for war, Norman Schwarzkopf prayed for peace.

Meanwhile, the Bear was steadily encouraging the soldiers of his coalition as King Edward III had done before the Battle of Crécy, on 25 August, 1346. He wasn't a remote commander on a distant hill. He shook their hands, hugged them, loved them, and accomplished what Sun Tzu had prescribed for generals 2,000 years earlier: He had delivered to them the undying affection and deep personal commitment of the good father. Using his knowledge of the military art, he would lead them to victory.

The ground war was ended after less than 100 hours of combat. The U.S. military lost 149 dead and 849 wounded for a total casualty count of 1,143.

Because it was America leading the Coalition, the killing was stopped. In this regard, the Bear revealed himself to not be a classic warrior of 2,200 years ago, for he admirably did not complete a modern, annihilating Cannae. The CINC estimated that the Iraqi military lost 20,000–30,000 fatalities and 75,000 wounded. Kuwait was liberated with far fewer casualties than imagined and thousands less than Hannibal Barca's coalition suffered or had inflicted on its enemy. Not since Jehoshaphat faced the armies of Ammon, Moab, and Mount Seir at Tekoa, near Bethlehem, and Joshua took Jericho, the fortress of palms and the worship of the moon, had such a great enemy been so decisively routed with so few allied losses in so short a time.

H. Norman Schwarzkopf had executed a battle plan that would cause generals and future generals to study Desert Storm with great care. Marshal of the Soviet Union Viktor Kulikov, former Commander-in-Chief of Warsaw Pact Forces, in his review of the Gulf War, wrote, "The military operations between the coalition forces and Iraq have modified the idea which we had about the nature of modern military operations." In a totalitarian state in which the capitalist West could never be reported as besting the awesome weapons and superior thinking of the proletarian state, Kulikov wrote, "One point is already clear; the Soviet Armed Forces will have to take a closer look at the quality of their weapons, their equipment, and their strategy." While no single battle or engagement captures all the principles of the art of war, a study of Desert Storm teaches many of them.

While Marshall Kulikov would not name the CINC, he concluded that the preeminent factor in the Gulf was "the human factor."

It's always about leadership.

General Schwarzkopf returned with his forces to dramatically emotional accolades the nation had not expressed since the end of World War II. He was lionized, thanked by the president of the United States, awarded by Congress, knighted by the Queen of England, and given more awards than he would ever consent to wearing.

Prior to Iraq's invasion of Kuwait, President Bush's approval rating stood at 60%. After the war, it soared to 90% as national confidence and approval of the military climbed out of the aftermath of the Vietnam War.

Rick Atkinson wrote in his book *Crusade*:

> Kuwait was liberated, Saudi sovereignty assured, Persian Gulf Oil secure. An army touted as the world's fourth largest had been smashed. Saddam had been stripped of his conquest, his pretensions, and much of his arsenal. Euphoria swept the United States, renewing the national spirit and reviving an indomitable zeal. As Schwarzkopf stood astride the battlefield, so America seemed to stand astride the world.

Rarely can a Western leader inspire confidence in the Middle East. Yet, fourteen Muslim nations had joined the American coalition to free a fellow Islamic state from a Muslim aggressor. As the British component commander, General Peter de la Billière said, Schwarzkopf was "the man of the match."

Queen Elizabeth, in granting him Knight Commander, Order of the Bath, said that General Schwarzkopf had acted as one of the fabled knights, the men of iron who sacrificed their unmatched strength to save victims of oppression.

H. Norman Schwarzkopf, who'd been in a follow-orders military environment since childhood, could now choose, in the manner of a civilian, to be anything he wanted. In a replay of Dwight Eisenhower after World War II, there was tremendous pressure on him to run for office on either side of the aisle. This was in contrast to General Douglas MacArthur, whose ambitions for personal glory and the Oval Office became public while he still commanded UN forces during the Korean War. The Bear declined the offer to become Army Chief of Staff, retired from the Army after 39 years in uniform, and began considering what to do with the rest of his life. Leading commentators confidently predicted that a man with such talent and popularity would not long remain out of the corridors of power.

That year, I received a letter from the Bear, with the final words written boldly in his familiar, engineering-precise, left-handed calligraphy:

October 3, 1991

Dear Gus,

Thank you very much for your wonderful letter. I have wondered what happened to Cadet Lee in the last two decades. I am very pleased to see that you have a beautiful family, much happiness, and great success. Of course, I knew back in 1968 that all this was coming your way and no one is more pleased than I to see that my beliefs were well founded.

Your commencement address to the College of Letters and Science this past spring was absolutely superb. I thoroughly enjoyed reading it and there is no doubt that your young audience benefitted tremendously from your sage advice. Words cannot express my appreciation for the acknowledgment in your book and the character of Na-men Schwarzhedd. I look forward to reading "China Boy" in the near future.

Again, thank you for your warm letter and the personalized copy of your book. Very best wishes to you and your lovely family in the years ahead.

Stay in touch!
Sincerely,
H. Norman Schwarzkopf
General, U.S. Army, retired

There wasn't a hint of rebuke from this world-famous, four-star general for my not having stayed in touch.

32

Remember to Sing

The caged bird sings with a fearful trill
of things unknown but longed for still
and his tune is heard on the distant hill
for the caged bird sings of freedom.
Maya Angelou

In 1996 I was on an author tour for my third novel. It was based on discovering enemy spies in our forces in Korea and incorporated some of the Bear's details about combat in Vietnam. My author appearances intersected with the activities of a rock band in which Amy Tan alternated as the lead singer. Because of our friendship, I became a temporary performer, or perhaps, more accurately, a mascot, to the Rock Bottom Remainders, a talented body of mega-level best-selling authors who also had genuine musical abilities. Amy Tan could play piano, Stephen King and Dave Barry played bass guitar—you get the idea. The Remainders included Cynthia Heimel, Sam Barry, Ridley Pearson, Scott Turow, Joel Selvin, James McBride, Mitch Albom, Roy Blount, Jr., Barbara Kingsolver, Robert Fulghum, and Matt Groenig. They were fulfilling what so many red-blooded Americans wanted to experience: being a rock star to crazily enthusiastic concert crowds.

"Come up on stage with us," said Amy, whose generosity of spirit knows no bounds.

"I don't think that's a good idea," I said. I'd rather jump out of an unstable airplane onto a concrete runway.

Kathi Kamen Goldmark, founder, manager, and Earth Mother of the band, whom I knew as the owner of a media escort company that drove authors to their appointments during tours, said, "You're crazy to not go up there. It'll increase book sales."

"I don't think so," I said. "It'll probably end my writing career. My musical abilities don't go past playing the radio."

"Gus, you must play piano."

I nodded. "Yep, smart Chinese people, like my sisters, play piano. I don't."

"Well, you seem to have a nice voice," said Kathi, "you can sing."

"The director of our church choir invited me to join . . ."

"Great!" said Kathi. "See?"

"He said to bring a bucket, so I could carry a tune. I got kicked out of Seventh Grade Vocal class. When I was singing in a black church, a little girl told me I didn't have to sing every hymn."

Other than not being a mega-best-selling author, not possessing a single fiber of musical talent, being tone-deaf, and never wishing to be a performance artist, I fit in perfectly.

I was in a rock band and I was in Florida. Light bulb.

I called Norm Schwarzkopf who lived in Tampa. His secretary for his cleverly named business, Black Summit, put me through. My heart slugged, and I tried to organize my thoughts. I'd seen him on television, but hadn't spoken to him in decades.

"To what do I owe the honor?" It was him.

"Sir, I'm wondering if you have any hot dogs left?"

We caught up on family and work as if he hadn't changed world history, uplifted the confidence of the nation in the style of Atlas lifting the planet, and become a leading global luminary.

"General, I'm in Florida and I thought I'd invite you to an event of exceptionally high culture."

"Let me guess. You're giving Hamlet's soliloquy while juggling knives and singing the Alma Mater."

"Close, sir. I'm part of a rock band of big-name authors, and the big number is 'Soul Man.' They're called the Rock Bottom Remainders."

I awaited a guffaw and got silence. I said, "Remainders. It's what happens to unsold books. They get remaindered in big box stores at a discount."

"No wonder I never heard of remaindering," he said.

"That's right. You sold out your entire stock of 10 million with nothing left to remainder. I forgot that getting books remaindered only happens to us guys in the lower engineering sections. But the band has raised over two million dollars for charity. They're your kind of musicians." I rolled off their names like a master of ceremonies.

"Where are you?"

"I'm at the Miami Book Fair, put on by Miami Dade College."

"Gus, that's almost 500 klicks from Tampa. Don't tell me you're using that broken slide rule of yours to calculate distances, and that you think Florida's a little state."

I was trying to convert klicks to miles.

"It's about 280 or 285 miles," he said. "Gus, you have time to drive up? Wait a moment. I remember you had a distinct reputation for not being able to sing. And now you're singing on stage for the public? That's pretty funny. I'm the one with a voice. You know I led the Cadet Choir when I was a Firstie."

"Then sir, you drive down here to get up on stage and perform. I'm just here because of the kindnesses of friends, and I'll probably cause a civil disturbance."

"Good talking to you, Gus. Call me when you're closer. Just being in the state of Florida doesn't count."

We signed off. My heartbeat was almost normal. I remembered a conversation, many years ago, about music. I'd said something scornful about West Point's chapel service, and he'd quietly said that he had loved leading the Cadet Chapel Choir, being part of a powerful chorus of men's voices.

"Military drums," he said, "drilled formations at march, and the same drums marched formations into battle. Music lifts spirits but singing lifts hearts. We could be in the middle of Gloom Period, that wicked wind whipping off the Hudson that would cut through our heavy wool uniforms to the bone as we marched to Chapel. We'd troop into the choir loft and I'd get the sign and we'd sing. Suddenly, it wasn't cold anymore and the gloom of winter was gone and the light would come through the stained glass windows and we were lifting our voices, strong and melodic, to heaven. The best scotch in the world can't mimic that.

"Gus, I know you don't believe in God. But remember to sing."

I'd forgotten to tell the Bear that Maya Angelou was here with the band in Miami. Maya Angelou, an honorary member of the Remainders, was not only the U.S. Poet Laureate who could pen prose like poetry, but she had been a professional singer who could also dance. She had performed in hot spots like the Purple Onion in North Beach when I was a kid boxer a few blocks away in the nearby downtown YMCA. The Bear recited poetry, loved to sing, and had been an early supporter of civil rights. Perhaps he would've driven down to see her.

I posed with her and someone took our picture. I smiled, and she looked like a person who'd had too many cameras pointed her way.

"Your family been in America a long time?" she asked.

"First generation from China," I said. "I grew up in the Panhandle, the Western Addition. I was raised by the Downtown YMCA on Golden Gate, and was in the boxing program there about a mile away when you were performing at the Purple Onion. My first church, although I wasn't a believer then, was Zion A.M.E." The African Methodist Episcopalian Church had been founded by freemen of African descent in Philadelphia long before the Civil War. It used Methodist theology and order of worship and the Episcopalian form of governance with bishops.

"Lord, son, you grew up with the brothers."

"Yes, Ma'am. It was an honor. And you inspire the world by singing when the world doesn't go right."

"Which," she said, "is all the time. And writing. Did you write about being a Chinese boy in the neighborhood?"

I said I did.

"I was a stranger in every land I knew," she said. "You heard me speak of it. The years of being mute after being raped when I was a child. Writing, I find, is like singing, and it frees me from whatever tries to lock me in."

"Shakespeare could say that no better than you."

She smiled for a moment. "You're kind," she said. "Now let's go lift their spirits and spread some happy out there."

When she went on stage, the crowd roared and stood for her, and there was great love in that space. I natively didn't enjoy the noise and the clamor, but I was glad Amy and Kathi had welcomed me as an adjunct to their work of charitable music. Later, I played the kazoo and lustily sang, masked by the chorus of talent and the deafening roar of the audience.

I sang as if I had the voice of a great bear of a man, inspired as he had been by light streaming inward from stained glass windows, and I found the harmony and the pitch, my heart beating to the steady and reliable pulse of a drum of the spirit.

Discern the Harder Right

Right is right, even if none be for it, and wrong is wrong, even if all be for it.
William Penn

John Whitcomb sat on a British Airways Jumbo jet on Runway 10/28 in Delhi airport, pondering how to find clean, server-quality energy, the "good stuff" that wouldn't foul networks and induce electronic high-tech crashes for a Mumbai data center.

It was 1998, when Saddam Hussein evicted UN inspectors, President Clinton ordered airstrikes and approached his impeachment, the Unabomber was apprehended, "Saving Private Ryan" and "Shakespeare in Love" topped Hollywood, and Whitcomb wrestled with how to provide effective physical and digital security in a congested, compressed, and partially undeveloped urban space. Whitcomb designs data centers like Manet painted water lilies: brilliantly, artistically, and out of the box. He knew India's difficulties in supporting high-tech computing. America shared the problem.

In his methodical voice, he would tell anyone who would listen, "It's just flat-out dangerous to be on the grid, even in America. But our data centers have no choice. They have to use what's available, and what's available for advanced technology is crude and subject to brown-outs and sabotage."

He later told me that the idea struck him with almost physical force: Why not build a modern power plant that produces sophisticated, server-quality energy in a remote and naturally secure space and then build the data center around it? It would be a dedicated power plant removed from the consumer energy grid with independent jet-turbine backups! It was three years before 2001, when the term "9-11" simply meant an emergency call number in the United States, and not the never-known-in-the-West anniversary of an epic 17th century Islamic defeat.

Back in America, Whitcomb reached out to thought leaders in architecture, start-ups, technology, real estate, finance, government, and organizational leadership consultants to help build, organize, and advise a complex, multidisciplinary venture. He told them: "Fortune 500s, financial firms, Wall Street, the NSA, need to house their back-up mainframes on our SuperSite for safe power and security. Firms could cooperatively purchase security that, as my military friends would say, would equal a North Dakota Minute Man missile site."

He named the new firm SuperSite Colorado. It later became Endūr.

There was interest but no funding. Invited by a friend and captured by Whitcomb's vision, I became a leadership consultant to the start-up and, as others, worked without pay. I invited retired Colonel Charlie Murray, my former commander in Recruiting Command, a terrific entrepreneurial thinker, to join. He suggested I contact General Schwarzkopf. Charlie lived close to the General's home in Tampa; I could send the invitation through Lieutenant General Jim Ellis, a retired West Point classmate of Charlie's, who had been First Captain of the Corps of Cadets and was one of the Bear's closest friends. I knew and admired General Ellis, thanks to Charlie.

"Jim Ellis would be terrific," I said, "but why don't I go directly to the Bear?"

"Gus, if you lived in Florida, you'd know that everyone's after Schwarzkopf, and I mean, *everyone*. Both political parties. I don't know the man and even *I've* been asked to get him as a speaker for community events just because I was in the Army! Look, you've always been his guy, his friend. If I were you, there's no way I'd ask him directly for a business favor. Hey, Big Thunder, why am I telling you this? Didn't you invent the whole idea of saving face?"

"Good point," I said, still a son of *guanxi*, face, which requires trust and community respect. In *guanxi*, a go-between asks, saving the face of a person who will say, No. It was 2000, and Schwarzkopf mania was still alive.

Jim Ellis, son of a farmer, and Charlie Murray, son of a crane operator, had been top-tier West Point intercollegiate lacrosse players. Both were wounded in combat in Vietnam. Charlie became a colonel and was en route to general officer when he became a whistle-blower; this gave him the opportunity to become a successful entrepreneur and constitutional lawyer. Jim had enlisted in the Army out of high school, won an appointment to the Academy, topped his class in academics, athletics, and leadership, and became First Captain of the Corps of Cadets. Now a retired three-star lieutenant general, the square-jawed former CG of the U.S. Third Army (Patton's Own) and Deputy CINC of CENTCOM, had a Princeton graduate degree and was the CEO and president of Boggy Creek Camp for terminally and chronically ill children. The camp had been founded by Paul Newman and Norman Schwarzkopf.

The message came back from Jim Ellis that General Schwarzkopf would be honored to join Endūr, and he sent his greetings to me. I conveyed my appreciation back to him through General Ellis.

"Gus," said Jim, "the General wants a personal visit with you. Is that okay?"

Years earlier, in 1987, the phone rang in my office. I innocently answered it.

"I VERY ANGRY!" cried my father, jarring my Army-impaired hearing and causing ancient childhood shivers to run laps up through my circuitry. He screamed that he'd just been mugged and that he was too old to kill the mugger or even fight him. I managed to get him to report that he was physically unharmed, but emotionally distraught.

My father was a vigorous, 5-foot six-inch, 145-pound, 82-year-old. He was about to retire. I was shocked he hadn't killed the poor mugger. "Dad, I'm so sorry. Are you okay?"

"NO! NOT OKAY! NEVER EVER OKAY! GIVE WALLET, MONEY. HE GOT MY FORT BENNING RING! SHE HAVE KNIFE, I NO HAVE MY GUN! SO ANGRY, I THROW RING ON GROUND, MAKE HER PICK UP!" My father often confused second-person pronouns.

In China, he had hated the social corruptions of his native land and loved the distant idea of a free America with the passion of a Founding Father. So he valued his U.S. Army Infantry School ring, with its "Follow Me" bayonet shield, above all other possessions. Japan's attack on Pearl Harbor had made America and China formal allies in the war, and he had been a tough and combative 36-year old Chinese Army infantry major and fighter pilot who'd been given the rare privilege of completing the U.S. Army's Infantry Officer Course and Basic Airborne School at Fort Benning. The training he received at Benning and the ring it gave him were the highest honors of his life. In 1942, he had reverently squeezed the ring onto the third finger of his right hand. He had never removed it in combat or to bathe or sleep. After 44 years, its once-deep engravings had been worn smooth and the aquamarine stone had dulled, but the ring symbolized valor, patriotism, and the best years of his life. It was his Tolkien's One Ring; he loved its preciousness no less than Gollum was attached to his.

"I SO BROKEN HEART!" he cried. His sorrow swamped me.

"HAVE OLD PASS TO FORT BENNING, SIGNED, 1942 BY COMMANDANT! I GO NOW!"

It was 1987, terrorism was afoot, and given his ever-terrifying personality and capacity for violent rage, the MPs might arrest him, or worse. I asked him to wait. I called Charlie Murray. Did he know anyone at Benning through whom I could buy an Infantry School ring for my father? Charlie had stood by me when I was a hated whistleblower (but I repeat myself), and then he himself had blown the whistle on injustices and graciously accepted the fruits of moral victory— the end of a great military career. Maybe he could help save my father's spirit.

A week later, Colonel Jim Ellis, Chief of Staff of the Infantry Center, the former Army corporal who'd served three combat tours, received the Silver Star and the Purple Heart, and was Charlie's classmate and fellow lacrosse player, welcomed the former Major Lee, Chinese Army, to Fort Benning. He gave my father, who wore his snow-white VFW overseas cap, the VIP treatment complete with salutes, meals, and more memorabilia than a senior citizen the size of a light welterweight could easily tote. His escort was the Honor Graduate of the most recent Infantry Officer Basic Course, and the tough young lieutenant with a baby face shepherded my father as if he were Douglas MacArthur.

The first stop was the Post Exchange, where a fitted white-gold Infantry School ring, with "T.C. Lee" etched on the inner band, awaited him.

He phoned me. "I put ring on right finger. I cry like little boy. Like you used to."

The ring faces me from the base of a computer monitor. Its engravings are deep and the aquamarine stone brightly gleams. It is our version of Plymouth Rock, for it marks my family's landing in America and the turning point that granted us and our children new freedoms, new hope, and fresh opportunities that remain almost unimaginable in the older world from which we had come. The ring sits patiently, and awaits transfer to my oldest son.

It was now 2001, Muslim terrorists had killed 3,000 Americans in New York, the Nation's capital, and Pennsylvania on 9-11, and we were pursuing Osama bin Laden near the Pakistani border. General Jim Ellis had also joined our company. He was now on the phone.

"This is on close-hold, Gus," he said. "Special Ops troops in Afghanistan just took down a Taliban stronghold. They found pictures of *our friend*. They had drawn a sniper's crosshairs across his face." He paused. "You know what to do. We stepped up security at our friend's home. No, *our friend* refuses to wear a vest. Call me if you need help."

It was known that General Schwarzkopf and President Bush had been targeted by Islamic fundamentalists. In a week, the general would land at San Jose General Aviation airfield for an Endūr business meeting in Silicon Valley, where the Bear would appear as a new member of our board. Executive airports, rife with random people, equipment and movement, are sniper havens.

I contacted the deputy chief for investigations of the San Jose Police Department (SJPD) and alerted them. I identified myself and our organization.

"A very big VIP," I said, "is coming here in an executive jet in seven days. Threat level against him is high but he's uncovered. We're requesting security. If you agree to help, we need security 24/7; no one can mention his name to anyone; he won't be meeting the mayor or other luminaries; and he won't wear a vest."

"You going to tell me who it is?" asked the deputy chief.

"I won't say his name aloud, nor, I hope, will you when you figure it out. Here are hints: Big, Brown, Black, Grizzly, Papa, Porridge. A football play with a long heave into the end zone with seconds left." As CINC, he'd called Fred Frank's grand VII Corps left hook in the desert a "Hail Mary" football play. "His code name is, 'Our Friend.' Want to play?" They weren't the best hints in the world, but he got it.

"Oh, man. He's really coming here? Well, we're all in. Give me the particulars."

SJPD assembled a hand-picked eight-man team and detailed an Explosives Ordnance Disposal Canine Team. I met them for a walk-through.

"Sir," said the team leader, "each guy here is ex-Army or Marines. A few of us were in the Gulf with him. We took personal leave to guard a man we think is a national treasure. We want him to know that we'll take a bullet for him, no questions asked." The other team members nodded their heads.

"You his chief of staff?" asked another.

"Just one of his acolytes," I said. "But once his man, always his man."

It had been so long since I'd seen him. I fretted over what to say first. I memorized a Shakespearean warrior's greeting I thought he'd like.

When it happened, it was a warm California day, similar to the fall day at West Point when I met a broad-shouldered professor who would inspire me to change my life.

The day had become almost tropical. I'd shed coat, dress shirt, and tie for a polo. The sleek, gleaming-white executive jet made its approach. It executed a perfect touch-down and stopped. The security team had the perimeter, the team chief scanning outward as the rest of us gazed inward. Several aircraft produced continuous white noise. I was a middle-aged guy with thinning hair who felt like a kid about to make his first visit to Disneyland.

Norman Schwarzkopf exited. He wore a dark suit with a black shirt and an artistic multicolored tie with red and gold highlights. He warmly greeted Jim Ellis, two old war horses who had marched the long anabasis into enemy territory, taken wounds, lost comrades, and survived the law of averages. My pulse elevated, I came to attention and saluted. His face broke into a heart-breaking smile. He returned the salute, we shook hands and he gave me a bear hug.

"Hello, Cadet Lee," he said.

"Hi, sir," I said. "Thank you." I was too emotional to say more. He rubbed my shoulder and he was that guy with whom I ate hot dogs. Across the street wasn't Terminal C and there was no hint of Peninsula smog; rather we were in his BOQ, at Battle Monument, the river, with the Corps marching onto the Plain in full dress gray, at the Gothic Cadet Chapel on its high, perpetual overlook in the crystal-clear blue skies of West Point. We glanced at each other; we'd somehow grown older.

Security was anxious to move him. He got in the black Chevrolet Suburban first. Someone had a camera and quickly took a blurry photo of the General and me.

"You look great, sir," I said.

He beamed at me. "Liar," he said. "You've kept up in the weight room."

"I'd have done better if I had my former bench press spotter. He used to run around in gray Academy sweats." I quietly told him that his personal security detail had committed to protect him with their bodies. He didn't like it, and grimly nodded. I withheld saying that they thought of him as a national treasure. The security detail led the way and re-cleared a small conference room in Silicon Valley's Hyatt Regency. Schwarzkopf shook hands with the members of the security detail as he thanked them. They regarded him with the deep and unique love of soldiers who trust their general, at a higher plane than fans gazing at a rock star. He quickly won the heart of the German shepherd whose nose had declared the room safe of explosives.

"Reminds me of my dog, Bear," he said with a huge grin. "Being my dog, he'd get distracted by *that*." The General pointed to a cornucopia of fruit, nuts, and Breyer's mint chocolate-chip ice cream sitting on the side board of the conference room. He liked M&Ms, but I'd forgotten to request them. I remembered hot dogs but the hotel didn't carry them and wouldn't order out.

"Thank you, men," he said.

After 30 years of trying to meet his standards while being physically separated, and connected only by sporadic correspondence and phone calls, Norman Schwarzkopf and I sat down to talk. In the hallway, by the exits, stairwells, elevators, and on surveillance cameras, his security detail kept careful watch. In the garage and behind the building, two members were in full "battle rattle" for a sustained firefight against terrorists.

The two of us sat in luxurious chairs as if this were a normal, back-at-the-Academy confab in the Officers Club. All that was different was that he was among the most notable figures on the planet and I wasn't partaking of the copious amounts of available food.

Only 67 years old, he was the survivor of countless firefights, multiple wounds, many surgeries, and an excessive number of airborne landings. His former long stride and rapid movements, always compounded by a sorrowful back, had adopted a slight limp and a precision about where and how he placed each foot.

He asked about family. I bragged to him about Diane, Jena, and Eric. He spoke of Cindy, Jessica, and Christian—my heart sank. I'd always avoided Jessica's name, as I did with all people who bore the name of our first daughter.

I had never thanked him for setting the impossibly high ethical standard that had inspired me to be an Army whistleblower. His mentoring had prepared me to do the highest moral action regardless of risk to self-interest. But I'd delayed contacting him until I could deliver an ethics lecture at West Point. Then I could say I was a TOAD at the school where I'd failed. But the invitation from the Academy never came, and after Jessica's death in 1980, I was in too dark a place to reach out to anyone, much less him. It'd been seven years since we'd last spoken and 34 years since we'd last seen each other.

"Jim Ellis has kept me up to date about what you did in the Army, standing up to Max Thurman and your brigade commander. Proud of you. Tell me about you."

I confessed my struggles to be courageous. He listened with the attentiveness of an old friend.

"I'm so sorry about your daughter," he said. "Awful, awful bad luck." His face tightened with feeling. "But God gave her a great mom and dad. You gritted your teeth, stopped focusing on your losses, and muscled on. And now you have a beautiful family and three kids. It's just that you have one in Heaven. She's there with all our lost soldiers and heroes, where there's no pain and suffering. We all lose the dear people."

"Thanks, sir. I remember that you gave hints about faith, which I ignored."

"As I recall, you ignored a lot of my hints."

I nodded. "Ah, true enough. Weird thing is, I came to faith when I wrote *China Boy*. I realized that Christians had helped me, all my life. That included you. That's helped me with my family. Helped me improve on my weaknesses."

"Funny," Schwarzkopf said, "in combat, I accepted my fate; it was out of my control. Had many moments of saying, 'Ah ha, so this is how Schwarzkopf dies.' Even with my whole body puckering, I never got 'foxhole religion.' I had honored God before I put on my first uniform, before I took the oath, before I went into combat. But in the Gulf, with the lives of those troops in my hands, as the general who made the final decisions, I read the Bible and prayed on many sleepless nights. Kept the Bible on my night stand. I became more faithful when I was farthest from dying, but my soldiers were closest to it."

"Sir, that sounds like you, all over. It's what you taught us. Serve others, not self."

He smiled brightly in the manner of a young major, spreading pleasure through the room. His smile was Homeric and filled the parts of humanity that needed substance.

"Night before the air war began, I called in Dave Peterson, our CENT-COM chaplain, a great guy. I said I was committing troops to fight and some would die, on both sides. I needed him to pray for them, for our command. When he wrote and issued the prayer, I asked him for Communion for me and those who wished it. I used to do that when I commanded a battalion in Vietnam, every night before an op or a big decision."

"Didn't know that," I said. I knew past casualties had weighed on him; I sensed those losses had aged him.

"You know I was more nervous when I was about to be knighted by Queen Elizabeth than I was when I was being shot at, mortared, rocketed, and under attack by superior forces? Isn't that nuts? A member of the Queen's party asked how I was doing. I said, 'Well, compared to this, facing Saddam Hussein was a piece of cake.'"

"Sir, I can't imagine you being nervous for anything."

"You missed catching the tremor in my hands and voice. Gus, are you coming on the Board?"

"No, sir. With you and Generals RisCassi, Welch, and Ellis, and Admiral Arthur at the top, you have my corner of expertise covered."

"Well, that's too bad. I accepted the invite on the presumption that you were a Board member so I'd get to regularly see you. Do you want to join the Board?"

"Sir, I'm sorry for the misunderstanding. I'm a staff guy, kind of a G-1 and G-3 (Personnel and Training). I want to ask you a lot of questions to catch up. Can I do that?"

"Only if they involve Solid Mechanics." He cackled and I laughed.

"Ah, sir, that's pretty funny. So my big question is, is tangent the opposite over the hypotenuse?"

He grinned. "I'm pretty sure Euclid would agree with you."

"What I'd love to know is, back in the Gulf War, what do you think was the harder right, stopping the war early or going on to Baghdad?"

He almost dropped me with a severe look. He said it was a subject he seldom discussed. He said he'd tell me, but I wasn't to share his answer or put it in a book, and he gave his reasons. Methodically, he told me and explained why. It was a great lesson, and I thanked him.

Later, he gave the central part of his answer in an interview with National Public Television's "Frontline," which made his position public.

"Personally," he said, "of course I wanted to go to Baghdad, arrest Saddam Hussein and his government, hold a military tribunal, and hang the S-O-B for his rape and torture of Kuwait and really, for the crimes against his own people, the Kurds, the Iranians, and for even longer, his political enemies, the folks who weren't of the Tikriti clans. As a JAG, you could've been part of the prosecution team." He adjusted his watchband—now only wearing one—and looked down. "What he did to them, the mass torture of women and children—they acted like savages. He burned their oil fields, not to destroy their economy—most of their wealth is banking, but just to be a sonofabitch. I flew over those stinking, burning fields, the destruction of the air, of the environment. It was a replay of the Arab invasions of the seventh century.

"No question. He should've faced a trial for crimes against humanity, a Nuremburg, for his massacre of the Kurds, the brutalities of his secret police." His left hand made a quick, abrupt downward chopping motion.

"Kuwait was his opening gambit to take Saudi Arabia. Then he'd simply march down the Persian Gulf to scoop up Qatar and the UAE. He'd become OPEC, all by himself, and could claim regional Islamic Sunni leadership, trumping the hated Shi'a of Iran. He could dedicate Iraq to missile and nuke development and do what no Arab leader has been able to do since the Jews were cast into Diaspora from the Holy Land 2,000 years ago—destroy Israel." He went into an interior space, choosing words.

"Israel. Israel was a distraction in Desert Storm. Saddam was hitting their cities with Scuds but we had to keep the Israelis out of the war. If they came in, it would've busted the Coalition. Many Arabs don't like the West, but their deep hatred of Jews, even to me, who has familiarity with the region, is unbelievable.

"In many ways, Israel's the central question. The Muslim leader that destroys Israel will be hailed as sultan for a hundred years. But after that, they'll divide tribally and fight each other again, as they did before Islam and as they have since Muhammad. The fall of the Ottomans after World War I ended the caliphate and the *padishah* sultans. Then came the state of Israel and the emergence of Nasser, the Ayatollah, and Saddam Hussein, each competing with each other to end Israel."

"But I thought we were the great Satan," I said. "Ergo, 9-11."

"Well, our success as a nation reminds them of the failure of their states. We symbolize the infidel. Islam spread out of Arabia and darn near conquered the entire world. The first to stop them, as you know, were the Mongols, although some of them joined in. Islam renewed its conquests and ran into modern Europeans, and they haven't beaten a Western army for 300 years. But Arabs have been after Jews since Exodus, before the advent of Islam. They were fighting Jews when America was a forest. We're just a new enemy."

"What does that mean for us, going forward?"

"It means that it's too bad, really, in retrospect, that we didn't fully exploit the Iraqi retreat." He nodded grimly. "I hoped VII Corps with McCaffrey's 24th Mechanized in the vanguard would complete the envelopment and bag the fleeing Guard divisions, and even take out the 20 divisions that remained in Iraq. But if we'd kept going, our Arab allies in the Coalition would've stopped before the Euphrates. And the French would've stopped before the Arabs—and poof, no Coalition. I would've handed the American president a diplomatic bag of manure in his relationship with every capital in the Levant and with Paris and Brussels and then, with his political situation at home. But militarily, we'd have completed the encirclement.

"Had we taken Baghdad, we'd own Iraq and all its problems. We'd have to keep most of our 541,000 American troops in-country to occupy a nasty region that's really three separate ethnic groups that don't get along and have only been glued together by a totally oppressive secret police that was as bad as the KGB and the Stasi. We'd have to stay 10 years minimum to build a democracy like we did in Germany and Japan after World War II. Can you imagine what that would have cost? The commander-in-chief didn't want that."

"We'd have the oil reserves of Iraq to pay for it."

He made a dismissive gesture. "Iraq's run by a tyrant. The economy's broken by his spending everything on himself and his family and his Tikriti tribe and his palaces and that huge army. We studied their petroleum industry; it's not that sound.

"Anyway, when the Cabinet saw news video of Highway 80, the 'Highway of Death,' they asked if I had a 'military objection' to stopping our advance, meaning: Would stopping combat operations after 100 hours of ground combat put our Coalition forces in danger?"

The "Highway of Death" was littered with Iraqi military equipment and plunder-filled stolen Kuwaiti vehicles that our Apaches, A-10s, and Intruders had turned into a junkyard. Yet there were still hundreds of vehicles still streaming north. Continued attacks on retreating Iraqi forces—half military and half brigands—would appear to the public as slaughter, while the Bear knew that surviving Iraqi formations could prove to be totally lethal. The dilemma: how to secure victory *and* respect your enemy.

"I thought of Colville in the final hour at the Battle of Waterloo," he said. "One of his aides said the British Army was doing murder against

Napoleon's Old Guard, so Colville asked the French to surrender. They said, '*Merde!*' Well, in Iraq, we hadn't completed the exploitation, the envelopment, and the Republican Guard was mostly retreating but the rear guard was defiantly fighting. We were wiping them out, and these were the guys who murdered, raped, and pillaged by policy. Not only Kuwaitis, but their own people. We could've done a clean sweep."

"Cannae," I said.

"Yes, Cannae." He set his mouth. "Commanders need to break the enemy's will to fight, but the honest answer to the question from the White House was, No, stopping now wouldn't endanger our guys, and I said so.

"As I said it, I thought of McClellan's fatal hesitations. Montgomery's failure to bag the German Fifteenth Army in the Scheldt Estuary, Mark Clark not catching the German Tenth Army with the Anzio breakout." He sighed with the painful comparisons we'd studied at West Point, the failures to pursue and complete a victory.

"God, I hope I don't end up in some military treatise at Leavenworth about not stopping the rest of Saddam's formations. Damn, I would've happily done it, but it wasn't my mission. My mission was to liberate Kuwait. Everything after that would put me in the same general territory of MacArthur exceeding his orders in Korea."

"Jeez, sir! No one could make that argument about you."

"Well, you know some blamed Spruance for not pursuing the Japanese after Midway after he won the battle that turned around the war in the Pacific. And critics went after him again after the Battle of the Philippine Sea. Well, God, I hope they don't do that with me. You can't imagine the pressure I felt." He audibly exhaled and shook his head. "People keep asking me about my temper, and Safwan, and helicopters. Tell me you're not going there!"

Safwan airfield, deep in Iraqi territory, was where the Bear wanted to hold the ceasefire talks with the Iraqi ground commanders. After being told that Coalition forces held Safwan, he learned that the Iraqi army was still there in force. It was an embarrassing slip after a near-perfect campaign. Later, the Iraqi commanders requested permission to fly helicopters on humanitarian missions, and the Bear agreed. Instead, the Iraqi used their rotary aircraft to kill Kurds.

He was becoming unhappy. He didn't suffer foolish questions. I still wanted to know his thoughts.

"Sir, I didn't know you had a temper."

He sighed, shook his head, and smiled.

"How much do you worry about Islam?" I asked.

"Not much." He said that while the impulse for true and sustained *jihad* against the infidel world has never really died, the means of doing so has been stalled by the re-emergence of the West and a gradual moderating influence as the Middle East gained more exposure to the world. While he admitted that elements of Islam could destabilize regions and hijack airliners and cause wars, they could no longer threaten to conquer Europe.

"Islamic armies don't want to march on Vienna, Rome, Paris, Madrid, or London, like they did for so many centuries. They want to march on Tel Aviv. Of course, we can't let them do that, because, morally, Israel's our ally and we're connected in old and ancient ways, and they're the only functioning democracy in the entire region. If Israel fell, there'd be another holocaust and we'd be too late again, and then Islam would inevitably feel the need to turn their eyes to the West.

"Living in the Middle East showed me that history moves slowly there. It's like Asia, with the exceptions of Japan and Singapore. Europe and the West make history speed up. The Middle East has violent upheavals, but real change is slow. Forward reforms are usually met with violent reversals. When I think of that part of the world, I don't really expect change, or easy change, in the style of the Western tradition. So we should have limited expectations of our ability to bring visible changes through diplomacy, economic development, military alliances, or war."

"What about Islam's command to rule the world?"

"We have to be vigilant. More than that, we have to maintain real relationships with the friendly states in the Middle East in quiet times. We tend to only run to them when we need them. This has not gone unnoticed. America isn't an empire, but the way we treat ourselves and others can be haughty."

"Sir, it's so logical. Why don't we do that?"

"Because we, the soldiers, are the ones who see it, and our temperament is trained to be direct. The State Department doesn't like directness. To be blunt, the Defense Department doesn't either. We need officers who truly understand history and how our military interacts with it. We didn't understand that in Vietnam; you know, that the Vietnamese would fight for a thousand years to the last man and woman and we had generals who promised we could win in months. We still don't understand the Middle East and that there are great forces there that have been at work before Islam. We have to know why we're fighting or not fighting, and we have to accept that the principles of war still hold true and that we can't win on the cheap. I don't think we really understand the centrality of Israel to what motivates Islamic leaders. This is the most ancient of all ethnic divides. We have thousands of officers with advanced degrees in political science that actually think we—America and our policies—somehow caused the problems in the Middle East." He laughed. "Talk about hubris! We've only been here a few hundred years; they've been there with their really phenomenal regional wars for millennia.

"Worse, we have legions of officers who'll willingly risk their lives in combat but won't endanger their careers by speaking truth to the government or really, even to themselves. I think it's okay to be terrified that you might fail, but it's not okay to remain silent because you might lose approval or rank. General's stars are to be spent sacrificially for right causes."

34

Never Quit Serving

I was too honest a man to be a politician and live.
Socrates

Not for the first time, I imagined H. Norman Schwarzkopf standing in the Oval Office, considering the Potomac, preparing, as a chief engineer of global coalitions and multi-service jointness, to harmonize into Americans our splintered political parties and processes. I asked him the question that pounded in the heart. "Sir, if there were a veterans' movement to draft you to run for the presidency, would you consider the option?"

He shook his head.

"What if there'd been a veterans' movement right after you retired?"

He shook his head harder. "I'm repulsed by careerists and power-seekers. Come on, Gus! I hate politics! When I worked in the Pentagon—you were spared that—I'd walk those corridors and the rings and just seem to go nowhere. That's more than a metaphor. Those creepy 1984-styled spaces are filled by way too many office-seekers, and not William T. Sherman-type 'Give 'em hell' leaders who'll tell Higher (headquarters) the way it really is."

"What if you just respected all persons, especially the careerists and the office-seekers, and just gritted your teeth and did it . . ."

"Sport, there's a world of difference between respecting careerists when you meet them as singletons or as a small little mafia in your formations, and getting elected into a whole chamber of professionally committed careerists on the other! You know my Pop's great work in law enforcement was upended by an unethical political rival who got control of the governor's office. It haunted him and it'd haunt me."

I wanted him in government, and leaned forward, as if my gravity could move him. "But, as awful as that duty would have been, what if you were the right person at the right time, like you were in the Gulf? What if your calling was to do that, like Moses being called to return to Egypt, the last darn place he wanted to see again, with the worst mission imaginable? There's no leader like you around right now."

"Ha! Glad you weren't part of the press corps." He rose to make a snack dish, looking at the slowly melting ice cream. The cashews dropped onto the small plate like heavy monsoon raindrops on corrugated metal roofs in East Asia. "My friends saw me do global diplomacy to form the Coalition against a notorious tyrant. For that, I can wear the top hat and the *thaub* robe and play the role of diplomat, and even dance the dance of seven veils. Heck, it's why you invited me onto the board of this company, to go out and meet and greet to help get backers for us so we can protect the Republic. I can do that. But I'd rather hunt with my dog Bear and shoot skeet and tell war stories with good Scotch and make occasional fun of the Navy.

"Gus, I don't have that grinding patience and a tolerance to dance political *lambadas* for a living. We're supposed to improve on our weaknesses, but Great Scott, Gus, in a target-rich environment like Washington D.C., with violations of ethics leaping around like 12 lords of Christmas, I'd go apoplectic and end up smashing pointers, ordering them to stand at attention, and heaving chalk at them! Hell, I'd end up throttling someone. Remember when I used to do that, throw chalk?" He laughed.

"So why not accept the offer to become Army Chief of Staff?"

"A tougher question. The fall of Saigon, April '75, I was deputy brigade commander of the 172nd at Fort Richardson, Alaska, and I saw on the news North Vietnamese T-54 tanks bust down the gate to Independence Palace in Saigon, while our last Marines had to retreat from the U.S. Embassy, trying to pull kids out of the soup. God, that was terrible." His eyes teared and his bullet-shaped head seemed to harden.

"That day, my resolve to repair the Army became an obsession. The government had led us into a mess, but we can't do anything about that.

Fact is, the generals had let us down. They were the military experts and they showed neither mastery of the military art nor the guts to accept we weren't winning, nor the moral resolve to change our damn direction. We talked about this. We had to stand by the South Vietnamese as they fought their war as Asians fight wars, not take over the war and do it our Western way and then realize too late we'd then have to stay there for a hundred years. Okay, so it took us the next 15 years to fight our own dumb inertia and Washington and the careerists in uniform who were trying to look good instead of do it right. It was as hard as war and harder because we were fighting in mush against our own kind." He chewed some nuts, crunching them.

"You saw what our soldiers can do if they're trained, equipped, and led—1991 was a big year. We beat an imperialist dictator who wanted to conquer the Middle East and wipe out anyone who opposed him, and the USSR and the Cold War and the looming threat of global thermonuclear war just evaporated. There should've been celebrations like V-J Day, and President Reagan remembered as the guy who helped pull down the Berlin Wall, but there weren't. But I guess, that's the way we are now.

"Gus, whoever replaced Carl Vuono as the chief would have to downsize the Army, reduce our officer ranks, and break down our incredible fighting formations. We'd be ordered to demobilize, as America always does after we painfully build up the best military, ripping it apart just to save money. People who don't know war and passionately argue that we don't need an army because we can talk evil men into acting peaceably, while most of us struggle to get along with co-workers. But we disarm too fast, too politically, after every war, which makes us jump through burning hoops and take early casualties in the next one. Heck, when I was saying good luck to the Long Range Recon Patrols before they stepped off into Iraqi-controlled space, I was so moved by their courage and worried for their safety that I couldn't speak. You think I'd take a job so I could just fire them later? That's what the Chief of Staff job called for." He was quiet for a while, shaking his head. "Let someone do it who won't cry his guts out every day."

I wasn't sure what to say.

"So, Gus, you're doing leader development now."

"Sir, I'm using the content you taught me. People are paying me to repeat it. They never seem to ask me for engineering consults."

"Good thing! Well, you had leadership before we met. You were the responsible squad leader who won a sergeant major's approval. Not easily done. Do you enjoy it?"

"I think it's important. People don't believe me, that I get nervous when I present. I do the stuff you told me long ago: take a deep breath and still myself, and something comes over me and I become this other person who's just freighting a message that we all need, and I present and can do it without notes."

"It makes sense to do that in preparation," he said. "I kind of do the same thing, and then I warm up to the audience as I go, but I don't remember telling you that."

"I was giving an OMI (Office of Military Instruction) talk. Your advice resulted in my receiving an outstanding cadet presentation award."

He smiled.

"Leadership," I said, "is essential. But getting people to change is hard. It was easier to teach leadership as overhead slide lectures than asking them to change who they are by changing their ways."

"Isn't that the truth!" he said, slapping his knee. "People still think that leadership means brains. Leadership's the hot topic out there. It's like the weather: Everyone talks about it but few do anything about it. You know the only way you get people to change is by moral example. Motivation and influence and carrot and stick don't really work. You inspire them by modeling what you want and then, practice, practice, practice."

"That's it, sir." I looked at my list. "Are you going to write a leadership book?"

"Considering it. I thought about you and your book, *China Boy*, when I was writing my memoir. Steinbeck said writing 'makes horse racing seem like a solid, stable business.'"

He smiled and I laughed. "I didn't know that one. Mark Twain said writing was easy—just sit with the blank page until blood comes out of your eyeballs. But it's easier," I added, "when the publisher gives you an advance royalty that would buy an aircraft carrier."

"You bought an aircraft carrier with your royalties?" he asked.

"Kinda talking about you, sir," I said. He'd gotten five million in 1991 dollars.

"But you kind of ticked me off when you told me your first book only took three months to write."

"Aw, sir, that book wrote itself. Really, it was Providence. Your principles—well, your singleton principle— that it's always about leadership, and your two laws you're now calling 'Rule 13 and Rule 14'? They're close, but not identical to what you taught us at West Point. I've been trying to write down the essence of what you taught me in book form, but it's not been easy."

He smiled. "I say there's one principle—it's always about leadership—and two rules: if in command take command, and do the right thing. Principles are based on truth and Rules guide you to act on it, right? I call them Rules 13 and 14; that's easier to remember than 'Rules 1 and 2.'"

"Well, except for those of us who are mathematically challenged."

"Hey, that's thinking rather highly of yourself! As I recall, you weren't even good enough to qualify as 'mathematically challenged'!"

"Ha!" I said, and we laughed, he laughed harder, and I brayed like a donkey. Catching an elusive breath, I bent my fingers towards me, inspected my fingernails, shrugged my shoulders, and said. "Well, I don't want to brag," imitating a Charlie Murray mannerism.

He laughed again, causing me to laugh anew.

"Sir, what happened to Schwarzkopf's First Law of Leadership: 'Judgement to do the Harder Right Whatever It Costs'?"

"I decided we know the right thing to do, it's just hard to do it."

I rubbed my face. "Sir, I don't agree. I think a lot of the folks I work with no longer know the right thing to do and don't even want to figure it out. They're getting paid to produce short-term results that don't get them in trouble and make them look good. It's turned a whole bunch of us into what you used to call 'candy-assed managers.'"

Later, I remembered that he'd told me in 1966 that values in America were changing, and that his generation wasn't thinking the way his father's had.

"I don't remember the expression, but it sounds like me. You may be right."

"Didn't you find that a lot of people, particularly superiors, lacked what you called, 'fine judgment'?"

He nodded. "Okay, you keep telling people out there that part about judgment, and I won't worry about it and won't have to modify my rules. When will you write your leadership book?"

"I haven't even figured out the title. But it'd just be a cognate of your work."

"Not true. You're synthesizing it. And including parts I presumed people know."

"Sir, you have other plans?" It was the question the press asked him, all the time.

"Just keep serving. After the Army was a question mark. I wouldn't do politics, and wouldn't just play golf and shoot skeet. But I want to get you out shooting with us when I can go. I'm working in conservation, serve on boards, and do some public speaking." He stood to stretch. I did as well, remembering his bad back in the weight room.

"A few years ago, Paul Newman contacted me. I'd seen him in movies and especially enjoyed *Exodus, Cool Hand Luke, Butch Cassidy and the Sundance Kid*, and *The Sting*. Learned he was a World War Two radioman-gunner in the Pacific. He asked me to run a camp for terminally and severely ill kids. I was really drawn to that, but I knew my buddy Jim Ellis was exactly the right man. So Jim became CEO and ran the Boggy Creek Gang and I backed him up with fund-raising and caring for those little kids." The Bear had personally given the Camp over a million dollars.

"Look at these kids—they're just little kids—with terrible, terrible illnesses where they're bed-ridden, suffer amputations, and hear 'No, you can't do that' all their lives. They come to the camp and hear 'Yes,' and swim and ride horses and go up climbing walls. I tell you, when they hug you and thank you, it just breaks me down." He coughed. "Weren't you raised by the YMCA and then you did youth work for them?"

I nodded. "They saved my life. Jim's talked about the kids at Boggy Creek. He says that the kids really love you and like to climb on you like a Jungle Jim."

"That's funny," he said. "That's what the kids call *him*. It's very good to see you, Gus. I loved your family Christmas cards. Your wife and kids are beautiful."

"Yes, sir. Thank you for this time with you." I started to rise.

"Remember my best military assignment?"

I sat. I was tempted to quip: When you were a TOAD at West Point.

"Sir, you got to do Cannae in the Gulf. You used the principles of war and Sun Tzu and won the biggest campaign with the least losses."

He shook his head.

"Sir, it was being an advisor to the Vietnamese Airborne."

He nodded. He leaned forward and I inclined toward him, as I'd been doing since I was a junior at West Point. He reminisced about that year in which he learned that not only could he remain calm and lead others by example under enemy fire, but that his reading of history, his comprehension of the military art, his love for his soldiers, and his respect for all persons had formed in him a unique capacity to lead in war.

He brought it into the immediate present, speaking not about paratroopers in Vietnam in 1966, but to leaders everywhere, today.

"You do it not to be loved but out of love for your soldiers. You do anything—ANYTHING—to keep them alive. Best soldiering experience of my life. Small-unit action with your brothers against the enemy in sustained battle, whispering, screaming at each other in my bad French, outsmarting an enemy that's mastered quick movement in his own terrain. I love that language because it was the language of my brothers.

"Terrifying but inspiring; life to the maximum. I had to use everything I had to stay alive so I could help keep others alive while knocking the fight out of the enemy. It was always the Battle of the Pyramid. Remember that lesson in class? How to take the objective without losing any of my guys? Damn, it's good to see you!"

"Ditto, sir. I remember the Pyramid. The puzzle: how to accomplish mission with a minimum loss of life. No one in history did that better than you in the Gulf."

I looked down, an old Asian habit in the company of an elder. "I've missed you. I always thought you adopted me because I reminded you of your South Vietnamese paratroopers, but you said I was closer to being Gomer Pyle than I was to one of those guys."

"Hah! That sounds like me. But you *did* remind me of them, my men. You had that quiet sense of attention, of absorbing your environment. That kid-like sense of humor. I liked your upper body strength— something, with my size, I never really had. Anyway, you gave me the sense I hadn't totally ditched them. Which I had, though it was *entirely* against my will. You still remind me of them. Westerners look you in the eye when they say something important. My paratroopers, to save my face, would lower them when they said something that was important to them. You did the same thing."

I looked up at him.

"When I was at the Pentagon working for Max Thurman in Personnel, we did a lot of radical stuff. Made it easier for women to have equal promotion and training opportunities. Encouraged development of minority and female officers, and for effective officers to extend in combat when appropriate. Did you ever get to meet him?"

"Sir, I liked General Thurman, even when he deliberately tormented me to change my position. Turned out it was just a test of my convictions. He reminded me of a TOAD I knew at West Point."

"You know, he was the only guy who didn't seem to need sleep. Or food." We began to eat the very soft ice cream.

"Before the Pentagon, I returned to Vietnam as a battalion commander, and contacted the Vietnamese 1st Airborne and reunited with some of them. Now, many are dead—some, because we ditched them after we said we'd stand by them."

For the first time, I heard the quiet hum of traffic in the street below.

"Sir, one of Jim Ellis's classmates," I said, "was also a mentor to me. He asked Jim to invite you to this company. Colonel Charlie Murray gave me air cover when I blew the whistle on my brigade commander. Charlie was swamped as chief counsel to the Connelly Investigation and had to report to Congress, but he got on the net and got the Inspector General to parachute onto our position. Charlie's in our company. You'll meet him at tomorrow night's dinner. He says, 'Remember we're just passing through, to do the best we can with the time that we're given.'"

The Bear nodded. "I'll look forward to meeting him."

"Sir, when I discerned the highest moral action and how hard it would be to do, I sarcastically thanked you, but the gratitude was real. You helped me act like a man and not just a male protecting his own skin. That's who I am, rather naturally."

"You've changed. Visit me in Tampa, Gus, so Brenda can meet you and we can discuss history. We'll talk about your dad. Did you ever make amends with him?"

"Sir, I did, and I never thanked you for your advice. Never forgotten it. Diane and I moved him to Colorado to live near us. He was 91. In his last months, he surrendered his anger. I actually liked him. In his last version of himself, he was kind and considerate and honored everyone. He had a heart attack and slowly, over two days, he just gracefully melted away. He'd spent his life around a fair amount of agony. In his last months with us, he was physically comfortable, without pain, and freed of that incredible anger of his. I read to him from his favorite books, Keegan's *Six Armies in Normandy* and Allen's *Anthony Adverse*. One of our ministers prayed over him, and I read to him from the Book of Luke. I actually miss him, now."

In his memoir, the Bear had made public his unlimited love and admiration for his father, whose passing had deeply affected him. One of the things that separated me from many of my Academy peers is that I felt no loss when Edith died, and less loss than I would've wished with the death of my father. I looked at the Bear, and knew, deep down that which I'd known from the moment he gave me eight hot dogs in Quarters 39, that I'd placed on him a moral mantle of relationship that my father had long ago decided to not wear.

At the dinner, I introduced General Schwarzkopf to the audience. I said that who we are is in no small measure due to our teachers and mentors, and that this was particularly true for me. I gave an appropriate introduction.

He took the stage to a thunderous and cheering standing ovation that had become his customary greeting by Americans, western Europeans, and Arab members of the Coalition. With his well-used voice, he thanked everyone.

"If you add up," he said later, "the GNPs of Japan, Germany, Great Britain, France, and China, they don't quite measure up to ours. Our economy, and some our precious life blood, have not been used to conquer nations, but to protect the world from tyrants.

"Our economy is the result of our Constitution, our free enterprise, and our hard work. Protecting this economy, and the key intelligence and military computing assets of the United States, in an era of increasing terrorism, has been essential since engineering opened the digital age." He grinned at me. Then his mouth became stern.

"The events of 9-11 have punctuated this truth. This company's solution, to create high-security, independently powered data-processing campuses that could survive a 9-11 type attack, is the wave of the future, and each person here can say, 'I was there at its creation.'

"Now, let's get it right."

35

Keep to the High Narrow Ridge

What lies behind us and what lies before us are
tiny matters compared to what lies within us.
Ralph Waldo Emerson

"What the @#%!! do you think you're doing?!" roared Endūr's CEO, pounding the conference table. "Didn't I tell you that those factors are off the table!?" It was half a year after the banquet in San Jose. The Bear had at times lost his temper to inspire us to be better leaders. It wasn't the best approach, but I never questioned the nobility of his purpose. The CEO's anger came from an inner rage that sought to punish; ultimately, it produced humiliation.

The staffer who was the object of anger tried to nod his head in feeble accord.

At the first break, I gathered Frank Ramirez, a top senior executive, a man of historic intellect and business insight who had functionally founded the company, and asked the CEO to join us. Years before, Frank had played a key role in helping me make a change in my values. We huddled on the cool Italian marble floor of our building's modern foyer. It was so brilliantly lit in Colorado's bright, high-altitude sunlight that we needed sunglasses.

"It's normal to feel anger," I said. "I'm better at quick anger than most. Did you two men promise the company and its people, in writing, to govern your anger and to be in masterful control of it, particularly in respecting the least of us?"

Frank nodded; the CEO looked away and shifted on his feet, getting ready to leave the conversation or order it to end.

"Was the guy who just received a ration of anger in there big in rank or small?"

"Our youngest associate," said Frank, licking his upper lip and glancing nervously at the CEO.

"A few months ago," I said, "you each signed the Anger Covenant that each of us carries in our wallets. The Covenant is aligned with our corporate core values. The signatures say we're accountable to each other for our behaviors. Am I following the Covenant so far?"

Frank nodded. The CEO's face began to turn red.

"The deal was that if any of us expressed the anger that we naturally feel, we'd gather and give each other Buddy Checks."

The CEO swung at me; I blocked him with my left arm. His fist struck my watch, which exploded and fell on the unforgiving floor in several pieces with small metal clinks echoing against high walls.

Frank had quickly taken three giant steps away, his eyes agog, a hand covering his mouth in shock with a hint, in his look, of pleased amazement that someone had stood up to our increasingly angry boss. I kept my eyes on the CEO, who was glaring at me, chest heaving, face scarlet, shaking his unhappy, vulnerable, unwrapped, and unconditioned knuckles. I didn't think he'd try again. I felt sorry for him; for a person with such a dramatic lack of self-governance would find himself struggling mightily at leading a principles-based enterprise designed to protect the Free World.

I'd been swung at and hit many times, but the amateur punch hadn't caused me to lose consciousness, so I kept speaking.

"What triggered you to yell at our junior associate in the meeting? Good to know our points of ignition. I'll ask you about what you just did with me, later." At some level, I wasn't shocked. I'd recognized the CEO's tempestuous nature and his ability to suddenly rage at colleagues as preconditions to physical violence that had defined my childhood and adolescence. On the other hand, I'd never expected him to express it to those of us who had maintained some degree of physical fitness.

"I know you have a temper," I said quietly. "How can I help you maintain self-discipline?"

There followed a long pause. "I'll get back to you," he said and swiftly left.

"You owe him a watch," called Frank.

John Steinbeck had once said that no one wants advice, only corroboration.

At a later staff meeting, which the CEO did not attend, Finance reported that the CEO and some of his new hires were making unauthorized purchases, to include unnecessary real estate transactions. Verifications confirmed both the impermissible expenditures and their significant scope. I'd been taught to travel in bandit country by some of the bravest men in American history. As gossip is unprincipled, one must go to the source, and one begins by respectfully asking questions of the responsible party.

"Not you," said Frank. "He hasn't liked you since that incident in the lobby. I'll do it if you insist," he said. "But our CEO won't change. It'll be a futile gesture."

"So my question is, What's the highest right action, the hardest right thing? Regardless of outcome? We didn't pick pragmatism as one of our corporate core values. If we did, we shoot for immediate, practical results. But dummies that we are, we picked integrity, which is a bear. What does integrity require us to do?"

"Act for the right," said Chris Armstrong Kay, a highly ethical executive, "regardless of risk to self-interest." The room agreed. I had taught them the Bear's lesson on acting for the harder right, what I had begun calling the "Highest Moral Action." The lesson was hard to ignore, since General Schwarzkopf sat on our Board.

"Right. So the CEO has to be told to stop and reverse these expenditures," said another.

"And when he doesn't change?" asked one.

"We don't quit," I said. "We keep after it. Who does the CEO answer to?" The Board.

"But he," said one, referring to the CEO, "selected a lot of the board members so he can pull the votes to protect himself."

Andrew Jackson said that "a single person in the moral right represents the majority." The board included General Schwarzkopf. Confidence in the right can overcome worry. I asked, "What is the highest right thing to do?"

One suggested that one of us speak to the CEO and give him a chance to admit and correct the expenditures. Another urged that we hire an auditor to monitor to make sure corrections are made. If the CEO didn't comply, then the matter should be referred to the board. We agreed to proceed on those points, and I thanked them for getting it right.

Norman Schwarzkopf and I drank coffee. We were seated in a conference room in the Mayflower Hotel in Washington D.C. after colleague John Prosser, one of Colorado's top architects, had received a standing ovation for his talk. The Bear had been the first to stand and applaud.

"I'm proud of you for taking on the CEO," he said. "Talk is he assaulted you."

"Sir, you once said that people who try to walk the high narrow moral ridge will not only get attacked; they'll get persecuted. I've been picked on for being weak and a chicken, and I paid a big penalty as a cadet for being prideful and cowardly. I guess, all in all, I'd rather get punched for trying to do the right thing."

"Well, just don't make a habit of it. It's one thing for *me* to contest higher authority. I was kind of built to be an SOB to the top brass. But it makes me nervous as hell when one of my captains does it." He smiled. "Firing the CEO for those expenditures, those bad hires, and for attacking one of our officers has caused predictable problems. He was very convincing, an amazing salesman. In his absence, some of our leading client prospects are now questioning our proposition. And our burn rate on our first investment tranche has to be slowed. But we do the right thing regardless of outcome. If the enterprise fails, the risk to the nation increases and I just stop coming to board meetings. What will you do?"

"I'll go back to consulting. You know, teaching your stuff. You should get a royalty."

His mouth thinned. "Our system of government is based on principles and on the willingness to defend those principles. American business thrives as a result. You know that people are already saying that 9-11 could never happen again. But raiding and piracy have been part of the human landscape since Biblical times."

As we struggled to find customers, our company's orientation shifted from service delivery to a heightened sales consciousness. In that vein, others encouraged me on general principles that I leverage my relationship with Norman Schwarzkopf. Conscience instructed me that the effort to have me socialize with the Bear was not based on principles but on their opposite.

Our business enterprise partner and funding source was a Fortune 500 energy firm that was the ninth largest electricity producer in the world. In 2001, it was riding a four-year, $17 billion growth curve and was a darling of Wall Street with shares above $50.

That year, Enron's illegal pipeline shutdowns and unethical manipulation of energy transaction prices shook Wall Street and world markets. A Western drought produced the California energy crisis and resulted in deaths, rolling blackouts, and desperation for citizens and businesses. Our partner was headquartered in California. Enron's subsequent collapse nearly sank the energy industry, damaged the national economy, and put our partner into lifeboats. Bankruptcy took Pacific Gas & Electric, narrowly missed Southern California Edison, and cost the state $40 billion. Our prospective clients couldn't consider a multi-billion-dollar investment in an innovative, secure data campus and our energy partner looked shaky even if a client gave the green light. Our partner, a principled and ethical business, sadly slid into bankruptcy, but has since recovered.

Another enterprise bought the remains of our company. Hope persists that the concept, whether as a direct offshoot or as an unrelated corollary to John Whitcomb's vision, will someday be adopted for the secure computing of our primary national and business organizations. Since then, one company, using a large underground nuclear bomb shelter from the early days of the Cold War, has advanced the concept.

Meanwhile, the Bear invited me to join his hunting and shooting parties, and I was tempted. I tried to discern.

At West Point, we'd operated in his BOQ and we worked out in the gym, largely by coincidence, shot a few hoops, and had one meal at the Officers Club. But we'd never double-dated or played tennis, which were the activities he had shared with fellow officers.

I therefore graciously declined his invitations to shoot skeet. We had an official relationship that was built more on the past than the present. I was absolutely one of his men, and I would do anything for him. But he was my life mentor and I his acolyte; our proximity was of the heart, and I was one of many honored visitors in his life. I would not presume upon his greatness of spirit by crossing the line that had drawn us together and had made possible his generous fortification of my capabilities. There was a clear boundary between our lives, and I, as the recipient of his gifts, would be the one to honor it.

My shooting buddies in law enforcement and the military know I love the smells and music of a firing range: the hot, acrid, nose-cutting scent of gunpowder—what we mistakenly call "cordite," the metallic snap of racked rounds, the barks of gunfire, the pings of ejected cartridges, and the commands of range safety officers. It brings back days of youth on Army firing ranges and the pleasure of hitting 500-meter targets on a hot summer day when your weapon is zeroed-in, winds are calm, you know you can't miss, and the ammo cans are full. The Bear and I never shot together at the Academy's ranges. Diane wondered if I should keep declining.

"Babe," I said, "he's a four-star general and CINC, and I'd always be . . ."

"A lesser person?" she asked.

"A captain," I said. "Good catch. I'm not in his peer group. The lowest-ranking guy he hangs out with is a retired three-star general."

Then, I felt secure in my decision.

Today, I regret it. It was based on thinking that we had many years remaining in our connection.

I didn't get that one right.

36

Courage: The Backbone of Leadership

Leadership is character plus competence.
If you can only have one, take character.
H. Norman Schwarzkopf

"To lead I must have character, an inner goodness," said Don Shaw, company president. "I have to smile and greet our employees even when I have crushing budgetary issues in my head, and some of them have been acting against company interest. And I do this because respect is unconditional. Unlike trust, which has to be earned."

I nodded.

"And I learn all this by first stopping my worst habits and then practicing courageous communication."

Don's company, ISEC, Inc., is a national specialties-based construction firm that helped build Denver International Airport and laboratories around the world. This conversation occurred in 1998, at the beginning of my consulting relationship with them.

"Is there a book that tells us that?" he asked.

I shook my head. "It's mostly from bitter experience, auguring into the earth, and being mentored by great leaders. I'm just the guy who took incredibly careful notes."

"Don't you, like, write books?" he asked. "How come you haven't written it?"

It was a good question. I'd been trying to write the leadership book for 10 years. It was like trying to write a dictionary without an alphabet, or, in ISEC terms, building a structure without a blueprint. I had an embarrassment of knowledge but lacked the buckets to organize it. Aphorisms, axioms, parables, and principles that I understood in isolation had in the conglomerate become piles of warm, inter-tangled spaghetti. My most meaningful lessons had come in the form of endless Army testings, so the attempts at outlines marched in step from chapter to chapter, chanting reveille run cadences, while dropping for push-ups and bellowing for more injections of forced marches. After four novels, I could easily create fictitious names and would concoct more to protect the guilty. I energetically wanted to point out what was wrong to emphasize what was right, as this would conclusively demonstrate that I was not only gifted in insight, but rather amazing. I eagerly would try to change the world with what half a century of work, life, a fortunate marriage, great children, and a fierce Bear had taught me. It's always about leadership, which is two things: character and competence. Do the right thing and take responsibility. How hard could this be?

It took 15 years to merge the Bear's life lessons with my resistance to change, lessons as a manager and leader, and the deeper instruction as husband and dad to practice and codify the behaviors of courage. It took Diane's insightful and patient organization to make it coherent. Courage is character at the testing point and backbone, habitual resolve, is needed to do the tough behaviors of character in order to advance character. As cowards armed with wishbones cannot lead effectively, we titled the book, *Courage: The Backbone of Leadership*.

Courage was our fourth book that referred to the Bear. Although he was working to support children in need and a host of other charities, he said that if I sent him an advanced copy, he would try to read it.

He quickly wrote to say that the book was superb and that he would send along some words. Here is what he wrote and sent to the publisher:

When it comes to leadership, Gus Lee has walked the walk and talked the talk.

Now in his latest book, he offers all of us who call ourselves leaders a primer on how to gain and maintain in ourselves and our organizations that critical element that makes the difference – courage!

H. Norman Schwarzkopf, General, U.S. Army, Retired

I read his words, again and again. I thought we'd written a useful book, full of operational truths that should improve leadership and organizations.

But being able to restate much of his leadership essence exceeded our hopes. I became giddy. I was unspeakably happy! Honored! Overwhelmed by his generosity! He was still helping me! I took a deep, cleansing breath and reminded myself of the Army axiom to demonstrate calm in the midst of raging excitation.

"DIANE! NORM SCHWARZKOPF SAID THAT COURAGE MAKES THE DIFFERENCE! HE LIKES THE BOOK! HE REALLY, REALLY LIKES THE BOOK!"

Diane and I danced around the room and I made several Chinese-Mongol war whoops that caused Pooki the Wonder Dog to first seek shelter and to then wonder if I needed a veterinarian.

After 40 years of association, the Bear had said by implication that I'd actually absorbed his mentoring.

"Courage," wrote C. S. Lewis, "is the sum of all human virtues at the testing point."

"If courage goes," wrote J. M. Barrie, the author of *Peter Pan* and an educator who informed an era, "then all goes."

"Cowardice seeks to suppress fear and is mastered by it," said Martin Luther King, Jr. "Courage faces fear and thereby masters it."

"Courage," said Claire Booth Luce, "is the ladder upon which all other virtues mount."

It's always about our courage, which is the basis of leadership, and leadership begins with unconditional respect. The rest is details.

"Thank you, sir," I said aloud.

Later on the same day, the publisher called with news. Warren Bennis, the founder of modern leadership theory, had also written an endorsement for *Courage*. I'd welcomed being an adjunct instructor in leadership at USC because Bennis was there and USC was where the Bear did grad school. Warren Bennis was a distinguished professor of leadership who had written its pathfinding works and in the years following World War II had shifted the nation's business discussion from management to this new field. He had consulted to the largest multi-national corporations and had done research at MIT and USC to deepen his understanding of what makes a leader. His book, *Becoming a Leader,* reflects leaders' need to undertake personal change, and it became a commonly read text in business, the military, government, and education.

He had said that of the thousands of executives with whom he'd worked, from Fortune 500 CEOs and football coaches to U.S. presidents, none had failed for lack of technical ability; all failed for lack of character. Even what appeared to be technical competence failures tracked back to fear or laziness or some other character flaw.

"It isn't lack of brains," said Bennis in a lecture I attended. "It's a lack of moral strength, of backbone and moral fiber. Managers need intelligence, education, and experience. Leaders need what managers have, plus integrity and character."

He and the Bear were in accord.

Professor Bennis and I had chatted about leadership and character when I was an adjunct at USC. We laughed at the idea that the Army had taught us everything we knew and that we owed our careers—he wrote 60 books—to doing a million push-ups in the mud and running with rifles and full packs up endless hills. Bennis had liked the fact that we'd both been Army infantrymen. Like most World War II combat veterans, he was reluctant to speak of those days, and like most Baby Boomers who had served in uniform, I yearned to learn from his experiences. Perhaps our shared veteran status, made gossamer-thin by the harsh severity of his service in contrast to the ease of mine, but fortified through my trust in his leader development work, led him to say that he'd grown up as a Jewish kid fearful of New Jersey's German Bund youth gangs. I realized that neither a cerebral world-class intellectual Jew nor a frail and fearful Chinese indoor lad had a background that suggested we'd become Army officers.

He spoke in a soft voice, the corners of his mouth always ready to smile, his eyes bright with gentility of spirit, his snowy white hair witness to hard, sustained combat. At the age of 19, Warren Gamaliel Bennis was the youngest American infantry officer in the Battle of the Bulge. He was a rare survivor of his unit and one of only a few Jewish-American combat officers to assist survivors of the Nazi death camps. He was now the leading authority in leadership, a field he had largely created and defined with reported research. Until Bennis began his leadership research and teaching at MIT, America had focused maniacally on management and education, intelligence, and exercise of authority.

Leadership had become the forgotten and almost discarded science of character and courage, of unconditional respect and trust, with roots going back to the days of Moses and David.

"Except in the Army," Bennis said. "The Army trained me to see that infantrymen are the harshest critics in the world. They'll judge us on one thing: Can we do the right thing the right way.

"So, you have two young men take command of side-by-side platoons. Both took the same basic officer courses and qualification schools. They're equal in brains and physical stamina; they even look alike. But in 30 days, one platoon won't trust their officer and will fantasize about killing him to save their own lives. The other platoon will willingly die for their leader, will carry him around on their shoulders, and name their kids after him. The differential is not intellect or strength or physical winsomeness or even education.

"The difference is character and moral courage. Here, at USC, I replace the word 'platoons' with 'shops and firms and corporations,' but the term 'officer' remains in play."

He said leadership was essential for modern life because it turns "vision," today's word for hope, into reality. We watched well-dressed Southern Cal students queuing up for Tea House coffee and sandwiches as they purposefully chased concepts of hope.

"The most dangerous leadership myth," Bennis said, "is thinking there's a genetic gatekeeper to becoming a leader. Officer training at Fort Benning proved that character and leadership are competencies that are acquired via tough practice. It disproved for me the belief that they're inherited traits. We learned that in a national emergency, such as being attacked by Hitler and Tojo, America can train leaders in one hard year. That's precisely what we did with our young people to beat the armies of the Third Reich."

He looked at the students, who seemed not to notice him. "Nothing in my life indicated that there was a leader in me that only awaited the training. Nothing in me suggested I could not only lead men in battle, but keep them alive while accomplishing the mission." I was comparing him to the thousands of lieutenants I'd known. I think he was wondering if I matched up to his instructors at Benning.

"I had top instructors with the winning equation: Practice doing the right thing under harsh training conditions and build the necessary competencies to lead infantrymen against a resilient and deadly enemy. I did it, like a million other American Army officers."

"Have you installed Fort Benning and the Infantry School here at Bridge Hall? Have you started actual skills practice in doing the right thing, like solving conflicts and giving what I call 'Buddy Checks'?"

He shook his head. "That's a bridge too far. After the war, I researched leadership. I thought I was on the verge of discovering the Rosetta Stone, the source of the Nile, the splitting of the atom. Some listened to the data but few people changed. I was on the faculty at MIT, Harvard, and Boston University. Students ask me what each taught me about leadership.

"I tell them that the best lectures at our elite schools can't top the best leadership lessons I got at Benning, lessons I had to quickly apply with my soldiers in World War II in Germany: Lead by example. Do that hard right thing when everything in you screams, 'Don't do it or they won't like you.' Survive in constant, miserable, life-threatening discomfort where you're cold for a year and you care more about your men not getting trench foot than you do about living. Never think about how the Nazis are going to kill you or your next promotion or what's in it for you. Correct things that are wrong, and do it immediately if they endanger your men, and so what if it means speaking truth to the boss. You know the old saw: What are they going to do, send me to Germany and make me fight Nazis?

"Most students listen, perhaps some accept it, but many forget and very few apply it. Old CEOs come as guest lecturers and tell them it's not about the money, but the students know the CEOs are wealthy, and the students don't believe them."

"There is some of that at West Point," I said, "the seemingly honorable cadet who avoids tough conversations, gossips, wants to use the free education to get rich and powerful, and is hooked on pornography."

"Yes, surrounded by humanity, aren't we? I surely liked pin-up pictures, but the Army didn't, so I gave them up. I tell students that I'm proof that leaders are made. I reported to Fort Benning an uncertain, nebbish little Jewish kid. An artist couldn't sketch me because my ethical boundaries were fuzzy. I was defined by playing lousy football and by my collection of Benny Goodman records."

"Tell me again what 'nebbishy' means? My Yiddish is not as good as it once was."

"Ah, you want to know the *nebbish*? The nebbish was sleeping when God handed out brains and guts; the nebbish reads Hebrew the way an axe swims. He's befuddled, pitiful, a victim of circumstance. I was nebbish: silly, foolish, superficial, and terrified that blonde Gentile girls would see the lamentable truth of me. What a way to *not* live! You know Benning. I tell my students that it and the Army were the perfect meritocracy.

"You could be rich and handsome and popular and fail; poor and ugly and awkward, but if you did the right thing, you'd succeed. If you were slow, you had to practice to be fast. If hesitant, they trained you to act decisively and always for the right, always for your troops and not yourself. They were just murder if you took advantage of others. If you cheated, they booted you without a second thought. Not like today. Now we're afraid of lawyers, no offense to you.

"If you weren't physical, you became fit. You had to practice shooting, passing tough obstacle courses, land-navigate, and call in artillery, all under enormous pressure until you learned to act calmly as the heart jumps from the chest." He was genteel, wise, and he smiled with his heart-felt memories of painful training. "They made you tough so you can lead when it becomes tough.

"If you couldn't *do*, they excused you to do something other than leadership. If you could do, you trained others to do, and they kept you until you couldn't. Oh, we talk about a meritocracy in higher education, but it's not; it's just intellect and brainpower without heart and character, so it's not truly about merit. Here we hope they arrive with character, but if they don't, we ignore it unless they're caught cheating. Even then, we're not as decisive as the Army was. The Army presumed we had to practice it to learn it. I can't say they were wrong, because they weren't.

"Truly, it was the best behavior modification training in the world. Every instructor believed in what he was doing and mastered what he taught. He'd give 10 minutes of theory and then came four hours of practicing behavior change with profanity for free. The instructors believed the American officer had to master these skills, or good wouldn't triumph in the world." He grimaced. "I saw Polish survivors of the death camps and knew the Benning faculty had been right. Without us in the war, there'd be global slavery and death.

"Higher education has reversed Benning. We only teach theory and research. Behavior modification sounds like mental torture, so we don't even give it 10 minutes.

"You know the most important lesson of all of OCS." He issued the flat, declarative East Coast question without wasting a breath on a question mark. He looked at me.

"Leadership," I said.

"Yes, oh, yes. I think they teach that at West Point. What class were you?"

What class was I? This necessitated saying I hadn't graduated.

"Well," he said. "You were obviously supposed to live. As was I. I should've died but didn't. I was at my best trying to keep the boys alive through our final push into Germany. I was complaining to Captain Bessinger, my company commander, a great guy, about resupply or the weather, how tired we were, our feet, you know, the complaining."

"He spat out chaw and said, 'Crap, kid, the other side has an army, too.'

"Ironically, I got a Bronze Star for threatening one of our tank commanders who tried to back out of supporting us in taking an enemy airfield. Do you teach that dichotomy between inspiring people and using the threat of firing people at the Academy?"

I said we had examples of both, and I enjoyed the following discussion. We both had classes to teach, and I no doubt over-thanked him for his time. "I liked lecturing at West Point," he said.

West Point had been my maddening unattainable dream, my lifelong standard of moral conduct, the asymptotic and unachievable bar of one who strives, however imperfectly, to live above the common level of life. It was the challenge that befalls every cadet and Academy graduate. It was my Waterloo, my retreat from Saigon, that site of crushing failure where the pang of dismissal never lost its sharp, acidic, self-inflicted stab in the gut.

I was therefore surprised when West Point selected my second novel, *Honor and Duty*, as required reading for Cow English, and even more surprised when Colonel Joe Cox of the English Department invited me to speak at the Academy. I learned that cadets could now choose between a wide array of science and humanities majors and were no longer required to take the two courses that I'd flunked. Instead of separating cadets, the Academy had instituted summer sessions to increase retention and allowed cadets to repeat a failed class. Paradoxically, the most difficult mandatory course, with the greatest number of academic failures for Cows, was now English. One of their challenges was a requirement to critically analyze my second novel.

I traveled to West Point intent on explicating the plot and letting them know the theme was simple: *Do the hardest right thing.*

I faced a thousand Second Classmen. I began by apologizing to them for producing a work that had not only become their required reading, but had been the basis for body-puckering final writs.

While I was referring to character in a novel about West Point, the Class of 1970 was preparing its annual West Point national ethics conference. They had been Plebes when I was a Cow and had recently endowed our alma mater not with a building, statue, or fountain. Instead, in accord with its motto of "Serve with Integrity," it gave West Point a living event—the annual National Conference on Ethics in America (NCEA). Colonel Cox told NCEA about me, and I was invited to speak there in 1995. West Point had come calling, and I became a regular feature. Since then, every autumn, I make a pilgrimage to the Academy to meet up with the now gray-haired and balding kids I'd once led when I was an upperclassman. They are now among my closest friends.

Colonel Doug Boone, an infantry officer who was the Director of West Point's Simon Center for the Professional Military Ethic, the center for character development, asked me to talk to the Academy's ethics and character instructors at the launch of the new academic year. No great pressure; there would be no general officers, and it would just be a small gathering of 300 folks in Robinson Auditorium, once called North Aud, the same stage upon which Harper Lee, Pulitzer Prize-winning author of *To Kill a Mockingbird*, had stood to address us when I was a cadet. I'd been transported by her goodness, enchanted by her love of all people, and her talk that night had triggered little baby thoughts in me that eventually became books. As I was introduced, West Point's three general officers, the Superintendent, the Dean of Academics, and the Commandant of Cadets, entered. The conjunction of the three generals seldom occurred outside of graduation or the appearance of the commander-in-chief or a chief of state. The last time I'd been in their offices had not been Cadet Lee's most wonderful day.

I told the character faculty that Edward III of England had made a difficult crossing of the Channel to land in France to fight a vastly superior French army. On the eve of the Battle of Crècy, on a hot August night in 1346, the king had walked among the simple campfires of his archers, giving them courage to fight bravely on the morrow against the larger and stronger force.

On the opposite side of the field, Phillip VI of France drank fine wines, ate *foie gras,* and caroused with his high-born cronies late into the night while imagining the great victory and riches that awaited them on the morrow

"You know what happened," I said. "The next day, the outnumbered English commoner archers destroyed the flower of French knighthood. They fought fiercely for the soldier next to them. They fought for their king, who had unconditionally respected them as men.

"This is now your job. It is your moral duty to fight fiercely for the character of your soldiers and cadets so they in turn can lend courage to their people.

"I'll give you some behavioral tools to help you do this." I thought it was well received.

Colonel Boone appeared from a side door. "I am authorized to offer you a position as a full Professor of Character. Congratulations, Gus, I'm very happy for you. Talk it over with Diane and get back to me."

The offer was stunning, but Diane and I were not willing to uproot and move to West Point. With pain in my chest, I declined.

West Point didn't fill the position. Instead, they offered me the Chair of Character Development, which would require half-time work without carrying a teaching load or moving to New York. I could make recommendations in the design of character development curriculum. I accepted. Colonel Boone retired, and I worked for Colonel Ron Clark (today, Brigadier General Clark) and later, Colonel Glenn Waters, two remarkable and highly decorated combat veterans of Iraq and Afghanistan. They liked the idea of teaching behaviors instead of drowning cadets in PowerPoint presentations, but we lacked the requirements and resources to attempt change. I was able to associate with Professor Emeritus and retired General Fred Franks, one of the Army's most beloved leaders, who had led the mailed fist of VII Corps's massive left hook in Desert Storm to shatter the Iraqi Republican Guard and win the history-making 100-hour ground war.

I called Charlie Murray, now practicing law in the Tampa area, to let him know that West Point had essentially readmitted me.

"Great, Gus. You can now do your long-awaited Firstie Year."

I laughed. "It is sort of like that, isn't it?"

I was teaching at West Point. I stopped in front of Lincoln Hall, the former BOQ, where the Bear and I had spent our Saturdays. I stood at Trophy

Point at the River, where he'd spoken of the eyes of George Washington and of Benedict Arnold. I remembered his limp from many wounds and too many jumps. Just thinking of his lifetime of pain seemed to put a crick in my knee, which had seen far less wear than his. Every day, for my three years as a cadet, I'd passed Henry Kirke Brown's statue of our tall and strong commander, General George Washington. I had often paused to gaze upward at him atop his war steed Blueskin, his upraised arm pointing me toward the infallible True North. I imagined the Bear standing next to me, encouraging me to get it right.

I awoke in my BOQ, which used to belong to Ladycliff, a small, Catholic, all-female college founded by the Franciscan Sisters. I hadn't dreamt about returning to West Point for Firstie Year. I felt an enormous relief, and the dream hasn't returned. Because I was old, vain, and slow, I took my solo West Point morning reveille runs early. Thus, my snail-like plodding, which we used to call an Airborne Shuffle, wouldn't impede teams of frighteningly fit cadets as they sprinted on Thayer Road along the river.

One morning I got a late start and found myself in a pack of fast-moving cadet runners. I speeded up to not impede them and felt a sharp pain. Being the same guy who tried to lead night patrols while being unable to see, I did a sprint while stepping off the sidewalk to get out of their way. My knee collapsed so quickly that I didn't fall—I folded like a limbless giraffe. The last thing I wanted occurred: The cadets stopped to help me. It was West Point, overflowing with Eagle Scouts and cadets who know how to apply emergency first aid and battle dressings.

A knee scope and crutches brought me another honor beyond belief: a Military Police pass that allowed me to park in the middle of Central Area. It was like getting a lifetime meal ticket to 58 Tour Eiffel in Paris, where dinner costs the same as a medium-sized luxury vehicle or a small house on Lake Como. My office was on the ground floor of stately Nininger, the nerve center of the Academy, the last standing, traditional, crenelated granite tower from the ancient days of West Point. In other words, from my era.

"Hi, Lynn," I said. "This is Gus Lee. May I please speak to the general?"

"Well, Gus Lee," said the Bear, "how is my favorite cadet?"

"Sir, I'm fine. And you?"

"Gus, I think I need to get back to the weight room."

"Sir, I can meet you there in six minutes. I'm calling from Nininger Hall, Building 747, in the middle of Central Area, facing the clock tower."

"Do they have you facing inspection and walking punishment tours?"

"I think that's tomorrow. I'm very proud to tell you that I'm now West Point's first Chair of Character Development. I'm in the absolute heart of Post. I'm trying to insert your teaching into the curriculum, but I've heard change isn't easy. I'm here because of what you taught me."

"Gus, that's just great. No one better to do it."

"Thanks, sir. But before you give me an impact promotion and too many warm fuzzies, let me tell you the bigger truth."

"I can't wait to hear it." I could feel his amusement.

"Sir, I'm in a transient faculty assignment. In other words, sir, I'm Temporarily on Academic Duty. I'm a TOAD. I wrote T-O-A-D on a whiteboard not too long ago to remind the cadets that, as Charlie Murray would say, we're all just passing through."

We laughed.

"I really hated being a TOAD," he repeated.

"Sir, I'm honored to be one because you were one."

"Okay, Gus, with that, Sport, I'll stop saying I hated it."

I was home, and Norm was smiling because of what I had said.

37

Practice, Practice, Practice

I hear and I forget. I see and I remember. I do and I understand.
Kong Fuzi, Confucius.

The importance of actively and constantly practicing specific skills to develop competence is an ancient human habit. Recent research by K. Anders Ericsson proves that 10,000 hours of sustained kinetic practice are required if one is to master a complex skill. Doing the 10,000 hours is no guarantee of mastery, but mastery will seldom occur without them.

Strengthening the need for kinetic and dynamic practice is a newly discovered truth from researcher David A. Sousa: After 24 hours, people retain only 5% of what they hear. Before the flood of technology, the retention percentage from passive classroom attentiveness was higher.

Sitting in lectures and seminars, we quickly forget 95% of what we heard. But sustained practice of skills with expert coaching tends to produce mastery. Separated by 25 centuries, Schwarzkopf's, Bennis's, and Socrates' experiences as foot soldiers led them to become teachers of wisdom and, thereby, to do what they deeply wished—to provide betterment for others, for the public and the polis.

Forbes magazine has concluded that the expensive U.S. commitment to leader development programs has resulted in a failed return on investment. At an estimated cost of $170 billion a year for the past 20 years, our nation's leader development programs have failed to produce effective leaders.

I have been part of the leader development industry that delivers increasingly expensive content with promises of quick high returns. While clearly advancing participant knowledge, valuable personality insights, and innovative experiential learning, it has failed to produce a steady stream of leaders of character, grit, and ethical courage.

I have seen the bitter truth: Lecturing about ethics, exhorting people to do the right thing, improving psychological understanding, and explaining the intellectual components of courage, character, and management produce few, if any, effective leaders and moral heroes. I've been reminded that the brilliant Admiral Hyman Rickover believed that leaders were born and not taught.

General H. Norman Schwarzkopf and Professor Warren G. Bennis knew that we're all born with innate abilities, but held that rigorous training in character produces leaders of character. "All must," said the Sage, "consider the cultivation of the person as the root of everything." Socrates, Plato, Aristotle, and Kong Fuzi discovered these truths in facing, 2,500 years ago, the human weaknesses that bedevil us today.

As an Army football player, Norman Schwarzkopf knew that the better-practiced player was likelier to make the team and to defeat the skilled opponent. As a student of history, he knew that the commander who consistently practices the principles of war most wisely is likeliest to achieve victory. The U.S. Army practiced AirLand Battle again and again in the burning sands of the Mojave and won the fastest war in modern history in the western deserts of Iraq. When I trained in the Mojave, I wanted to leave before I got there. So it is when practicing anything worth learning.

I've asked executive audiences how many hours they spend a year practicing the habits of aerobic and anaerobic physical fitness. The average answer is two hours a week, or 100 hours a year, or 1,000 hours a decade. This aggregates to 30,000 hours across the span of a career.

Many have been youth soccer coaches, overseeing an average commitment of two hours a week for ball-handling, passing, dribbling, kicking, and blocking before a weekly one-hour game during a 12-week season. This provides 36 hours of skills and tools practice a year. Added to 100 hours of private play, a child soccer player will have gained 400 hours of soccer skills practice in three seasons.

I ask executives, "In the same style of going to the gym, how many hours a week do you practice the specific skills and tools of doing the right thing under pressure, of respecting people you do not admire, and of communicating courageously with the toughest personalities in your organization, to include hard dialogs with your superiors?"

The average response is zero, which aggregates to zero hours a week, zero hours a month, zero hours yearly, and zero hours across a career—an avoidance of the essential areas in which managers and organizations struggle and even perish. We inadvertently are imprinting into our national psyche the behaviors of avoidance, justification, blame, gossip, disrespect, and fear—the discordant children of the Greek god Ares and the classic elements of cowardice.

Character skills training was once the monopoly of democracies. Socrates taught the behaviors of self-sacrifice, Plato advocated the actions of justice, and Aristotle instructed in practiced habits of character. These became keystones in the arch of modern civilization. But these instructed behaviors, actions, and habits of character can now only be found in the rarest of places. We no longer kinetically practice the practical behaviors of character that we need in relationships and work. The cost of a gradual recallibration of the nation's moral center, caused in no small part by focusing on consumption of ever-increasing gigabytes of knowledge while avoiding the practice of character competence, has become painfully evident and increasingly costly.

In 1967, Major Schwarzkopf tried to tutor me to speak respectfully to Courtland Difford, a cadet captain and hugely popular beau ideal. In truth, the man was going off his moral rails as he deepened his habits as a shameless and soon-to-be criminal sexual harasser and rapist. Against this, his excellent brain, good looks, social charms, athleticism, and photogenic personality would prove to be meaningless.

I was 20 years old and I knew this. It was Saturday after parade. The major and the members of the Corps used all the hot water in showers, we'd doused ourselves in Aqua Velva, and guys were tossing footballs on the playing fields of West Point. He and I were in his Quarters 39. The Bear moved his chair to directly face me.

"Did you speak to Cadet X, that Big Man on Campus, the Firstie womanizer who insulted your sister, like I said you should?"

I had a sudden itch to lie about my silence with Big Diff Difford. But members of the Corps operated under an unrelentingly strict Honor Code. Reluctantly, I shook my head.

262 • WITH SCHWARZKOPF

"Going to talk to him?" he asked.

The answer was, *No.* "Probably not, sir."

"Okay. What were the words I suggested you use with that guy?"

I scrunched my eyes together. Nothing in the memory bank. "Sir, I don't remember."

He pressed thin lips together and nodded. "Prepare to listen."

I concentrated to memorize his next words, which were: "'I don't appreciate you disrespecting my sister.' Say it."

I repeated the words.

"Good. Now let's call this roué of yours, 'Eutychus.' He was the guy who dropped dead at Troas when he heard the spoken truth, which is probably what's going to happen to your guy when you talk to him like an officer should talk to a problem."

"Eutychus? From one of the plays of Aeschylus?" I asked. "Euripides?"

He shook his head. "Stay on course. Now, I'll play Eutychus, the womanizer. You play yourself, armed with the great words I just gave you. Unless you've forgotten them already."

"Sir, it's okay, I get it! I understand, really. We don't have to do this."

"You're right. Only *you* have to do this. Look, if you don't practice it, what's the chance you'll ever use it? Character's just like boxing or the bench press. Can you box if you never practice punching and parrying, movement, if you never spar in the ring?"

"Sir, that's different."

"Negative, Sport, it's not. Courage is muscle memory. It's a practiced discipline, not an abstract idea that you remember and pull out of your ear when you need it or a trait you pull out of a memorized list of qualities. It's a behavior that you *do because it's a behavior you practiced*. You rehearse assaulting a fixed position at Buckner. Next thing you know, you're doing it under real fire. But you'd better rehearse it, again and again, and make tons of stupid mistakes and get corrected on the spot by Sergeant Rock before you try it for real. Singing, courage, football, and war—they all require practice, hard practice. It's doing Warren Truss bridge problem calculations, again and again. We do it in engineering but we don't teach it in character. Practice, practice, practice!"

"Sir, I'll use them."

"That's right, Sport, you're going to use them. *Right now.*"

I squirmed, not wanting to look stupid by trying something I hadn't mastered. Conscience said I was being cowardly, but my futile vanity won out. "It, it's just role-playing, it's not real. It's why they call it *playing*. So I can't do it for real. It'd just be fake. It's too uncomfortable. It's touchy-feely."

His jaw jutted. "You calling me *'touchy-feely'*?"

I gulped. "No, sir, but you're not so great at this yourself, or you wouldn't yell."

He put his face into mine and roared. *"All right, Lee!* What the hell are you doing gossiping about me!? You have some beef with me about what I said about your sister, you'd better be man enough to tell me straight to my damn face! *Got it?!"* His face was red. He was really angry, furious at my passivity, my chicken-heart, and I recoiled, face flushed, body bristling, wanting to cover up, jump up boldly, and leave. He had pinned me, forked me on the character chessboard. In Chinese chess, it was called, *fēn chā de qi*, movement causes exposure. Forcing myself to stay seated, I took a breath.

"I don't appreciate you disrespecting my sister," I said with the verve of Barney Fife.

"What of it?" he snapped.

"It's not right," I said, a statement broad enough to embrace the Bear making me do a stupid, embarrassing role-play.

"So what?" he snapped. "You got something to say?"

"So," I said slowly, my brain whirring, "every time you disrespect her, you'll hear from me."

"Oh, wow, man." He made a taunting face. "Wooo-ooo! That's scary! So it's okay with you if I disrespect other females."

"No, Eutychus." I found some spine and pointed at him. "That's just as wrong. But you act like a gentleman and a scholar, like you're supposed to, you won't hear from me."

"You're full of crap," he said.

"Even if I am, I'm onto you. I'll coach you every time you slam women."

The Bear grinned. His huge left hand clapped me on my shoulder. I saw it coming or he would've unhinged me. Dang, he was strong. Fighting him would be like punching out George Washington's statue, only worse. He's on your side; don't fight him.

"Great! Just great!" he cried, rubbing his palms together. "See, you can do it! Practice whatever's scariest and you can master it. Don't practice and atrophy in place."

I resumed breathing.

"Let's do it again. Now, get it right." And we did, just like his engineering problems.

He later said, "I told you I'm not great at this, myself. Don't ever let your own faults stop you from teaching your troops what they have to know to be their best. I have a temper but I can teach you to not use yours. And I only raise my voice at the privileged few, and you cadets, although you think you're beset by overwork and stress, are definitely privileged and, compared to being in combat, damn-near coddled. Am I right?"

I was getting the best education in the world for the price of a little perspiration.

"You're right."

"Do you get it?" he asked. "Respecting someone means you'll accept nothing less from him but his best. So I put a little pepper in it. You guys in the bottom sections had demonstrated a very low care factor. It's like I asked if your indifference bugged you and you said, 'I don't care.' I had to shake you like knocking walnuts from a tree, but you finally made a maximum effort in Solids. I think every one of you is going to pass the course.

"Doggone it, Gus, you're supposed to fight fiercely for the character of others. Not many do that. There's a cap to brain power and only so much you can do to improve. But character is virtue; it has no ceiling in practice or development. And it determines all outcomes. With it, you can be happy. Without it . . ." He shook his big head.

"We're all wired to do right or wrong. What we are is a result of what we practice, what we *do*, and not what we hear.

"You can't have too much courage. That's where West Point is ahead of the world."

I accepted the intellectual truth of the lesson.

The Bear was fighting for my moral worth. I was defending my small chance of being popular, of expending minimal amounts of spiritual sweat, and avoiding trouble with people whom I did not admire. Ultimately, I refused to believe the truth that the Bear offered because I never spoke to

Big Diff Difford, the womanizing Firstie that the Bear had dubbed Eutychus, the man who died when he heard the truth.

The story of young Eutychus, who was so indifferent to the teaching of wisdom that he fell asleep and fell from a third-story window, was good. I later learned that when we kill our worst behaviors, we make room for what Lincoln called the better angels of our nature. I was happy to later learn that Eutychus came back from his coma, or was resurrected, gaining the opportunity for new life.

The Bear's teaching was altering who I was, but I was filled with stubborn pride and filed the lesson about practicing, practicing, and practicing the behaviors of right conduct in my over-packed Locker of Forgotten Wisdom.

I wish I'd faced my fear and spoken my heart to Big Diff. He might have yelled at me, reduced my cadet rank, and hurt my feelings. It might have made no difference in his behaviors. But my silence, my avoidance, and my flight from mere discomfort diminished his chances to straighten out, heed his conscience, and avoid his later shame, and it made a coward of me.

The key lesson about practicing the behaviors of courage remained in storage for a decade until, as a captain, I earnestly and passionately spoke to my commander, Colonel Willoughby, about the one subject he did not want to discuss. I could Buddy Check him because the Bear had poured instant imitation courage into my tank when I was a cadet. Because I was slow, "instant" took 10 years.

Driving to the airport and flying to Las Vegas for the meeting with Colonel Willoughby, I had rehearsed an imagined courageous and respectful conversation with a man gifted with anger and authority. I didn't have the specific courageous communication tools that have been given to me since, but I knew the one principle, that it's always about leadership, and I knew the rules about respecting all and taking moral responsibility for outcomes. The rules equipped me to go forward into certain conflict with a sense of peace and calm.

When Colonel Willoughby opened the door to his hotel suite, I had already faced my fear and had abandoned flight as the lousiest option. I took a deep and silent diaphragmatic breath, projected unconditional positive respect from my eyes and my heart, and spoke practiced words in alignment with True North, on the high and narrow ridge of the highest moral action. I didn't do this because I was courageous; I did it because I could imitate the behaviors that a courageous mentor expected of me. If I thought I had to do it entirely on my own, without an earlier moral example, I probably would've muffed it.

When my bosses, from Norm Schwarzkopf and SGM Keila Solomon to D. Hamilton Willoughby and the angriest CEO in the world, expressed ire toward me, I had in my brain the grooved-in habits of responding with a calmness I did not feel and a courage I had always lacked. Courage is demonstrating habits of rightness in the face of fear to forthrightly do the highest moral action. I am proof that even the most frightened and timid among us can show the fortitude of lions.

The Bear had required that I rehearse the skills I would need for the rest of my life. Those rehearsals helped me be of use to others, and showed others more capable than I how to lead.

Farewell, TOAD

The object of war is peace . . . if the campaign is frustrated,
the resources of the state will not be equal to the strain.
Let your great object be victory, not lengthy campaigns.
Sun Tzu

Not long after Endūr closed its doors in 2004, I was invited to present a leadership seminar in Aspen, Colorado. One of the other presenters was retired General Barry McCaffrey, who had led the 24th Mechanized Infantry as part of General Fred Franks's VII Corps crushing left hook, the Cannae pincer that was the essential maneuver in Desert Storm. General Franks was the Chair for the Professional Military Ethic, and I was able to confer and learn from him in my work at the Academy. "Teamwork includes," General Franks said to me at Eisenhower Hall, "among many other factors, that everyone on the team gets a voice, and that everyone on the team has a degree of genuine commitment or risk equivalent to their responsibility in leading."

I'd met General McCaffrey, one of General Frank's subordinate commanders, only once at West Point, and it was an honor to spend a few minutes with him at the seminar.

I smiled when he said, "It's good to share West Point's lessons, but it's hard to get people to change."

During my presentation, I cited H. Norman Schwarzkopf's emphasis on honoring all persons as a prerequisite to effective leadership. The audience had a fair number of young executives, and his name didn't seem to register with them.

"Who's H. Norman Schwarzkopf?" I asked with a smile. I could've asked them to compute a mind-bending Black-Scholes derivatives income problem—dangerous as it later proved to be when actually applied to the market—and they'd get the answer before I could adjust my glasses. There was an uncomfortable silence.

"Wasn't he a general or something? Or a secretary of defense?"

I was happy to tell them who he was and that what he taught me could be immediately useful to them.

At a break, General McCaffrey said, "People forget pretty quickly."

In the book of Exodus, God used Moses to free the long-enslaved Hebrews from Egyptian bondage. The Hebrews began crossing the great Sinai desert. Six weeks after their dramatic deliverance, they feared their new freedom and demanded to return to what they knew—the cruelties of Pharaoh's overseers and the whips and goads of slavery. Twelve years had passed since the CINC had commanded 800,000 troops in a 100-hour ground engagement, executed a sustained battle of maneuver, and ended a war before it could become a bloody, spirit-stealing, and heartbreaking war of attrition. The Bear had helped trigger national celebrations, ticker tape parades, and hopes for lasting peace. If people could forget the destruction of Pharaoh's army in less than two months, no wonder no one remembered the destruction of Saddam's army a decade ago.

I wrote a short tribute to the Bear, scribed on parchment by an expert calligrapher, and sent it to him.

In every age, a single leader's courage uplifts generations, inspires a nation, and alters the world. In the late 20th Century, America made money, but struggled to align its behaviors with highest principles. Cynicism and selfishness, fear and hesitancy, timidity, and worry slowed the national heart.

Then, a Babylonian crisis created historical inevitability. An American leader was needed. Providence needed him. He had led in combat and trained in peace. He had shaped us as cadets, as officers and non-commissioned officers, as soldiers, as an army.

He had taught us to be responsible to others, to be courageous in facing fear, to show character instead of serving ambition. He had followed the moral imperative to align himself with the highest principles.

He was the American warrior, *H. Norman Schwarzkopf.* He was the leader of a great global army, a savior to millions, an inspiration to his countrymen, and a source of hope to free people around the world. He was our mentor. We will be his troops to our last breath. We join the Republic in giving undying thanks.

In every age, a leader's courage uplifts generations, inspires a nation, and alters the world. As the world entered the 21st Century, that man was you.

Cannae   Iraq

Gus Lee and the other Norm's Boys
of the USMA Class of 1968

Amid his many charitable activities and a dramatically reduced speaking schedule, the General called me.

"It's in the center of my flags," he said, emotion tugging on his vocal cords. Upon retirement, general officers receive two flags—Old Glory and one with large white stars equal in number to rank on a field of bright red. He was saying, thank you.

In 2009, I gave a talk at Tampa University's Business School.

Jim Ellis and I met Norm at his office. The entrance was an alcove with the flag of the United States and his deep red general officer's banner with four brilliant white stars. Between the flags is a photograph of the Bear saluting with his trademark broad smile. Beneath the photo was the parchment that I'd sent.

He had lost weight and color. His appearance contrasted with the young, bullet-headed major with a tropical tan and buzz cut when we had met 43 years earlier. Instead of moving like an ominous downhill locomotive, his steps were studied with a new and even more deliberate method.

Jim Ellis took a photo of the Bear and me in the alcove. I was delighted to see him. I couldn't stop smiling.

We talked of family, associates, and history. I studied his presence and found myself memorizing the movement of his left, dominant hand. It used to describe larger arcs.

He said that our generals were again agreeing to minimum troop commitments in Iraq and Afghanistan in a disavowal of what President Bush had envisioned in Desert Storm. Not so long ago, the president had followed military advice and built the force so it could win a quick victory. Now, we'd returned to the days of minimalist efforts, of the agonizing indecision of the Vietnam War, in a difficult search for the winning national policy that had yet to be convincingly defined.

No one was thinking coherently about the Sunni, Sh'ia, and Kurds, the ancient ethnic histories that could not be restrained by mere military presence.

We had entered the weakest military suit of democracies: protracted war in which dribbled-in forces were exposed by political debate and failed domestic support while asymmetrical combat began violating the principles of war to produce erratic, chronic, politically unresolvable, and demoralizing warfare.

I remembered that the Bear had been fearless in the councils of government. Kings and superiors naturally dislike Biblical Nathans who truly do their duty by speaking truth upward. The reaction of kings is to demote generals who speak candidly and promote those who say yes because there are afraid to ask why. I remained fascinated that the Bear had spoken the truth to the top, and rose to high office.

"In sum, that's pretty depressing," he said, adjusting himself to sit straighter. I thought of his old back ailments, but I think what bothered him was poor military strategy, poor national vision, and a country failing to support an American war in the way that Americans traditionally had. It is not by saying "thank you for your service" to those in uniform as you pass them in busy airports, while you head for a meeting and they are in the business of bleeding for you, but by courageously joining some part of the fight.

"I want to tell you," he said, "that I'm really proud of you as a dad, as a husband. I have that superb Christmas photo of your family on my desk at home. I look at your kids and in a way, I'm connected to them."

"Yes, sir, you are, and they to you."

"You haven't done badly as a professional, either. You're now a C-level exec leading up an organization that's the size of a brigade or a minus-division. It's like you're a colonel or a two-star." His eyes glittered brightly.

"Next to telling me I was as stupid as shark poop, that's the nicest thing you ever said to me." We laughed. "In military terms, I report to the brigade commander, a very good guy, and I'm his XO (executive officer.) Sir, can I tell you a story?"

"Please," he said, sitting back in a great chair. "You can even make it about Solid Mechanics." He smiled, his body relaxing.

"After serving as a drill sergeant, I went back to school at UC Davis. They asked me to become a counselor for low-income minority students, and I agreed."

"Wait a moment," he said. "I thought you were the Cadet Brigade Commander of the ROTC detachment at Davis, and in law school and grad school. You mean they asked you after you finished school?"

"They asked when I was still in school, to be a part-time counselor, an assistant dean. It was like being a cadet you know, ridiculously over-scheduled. This new position required me to participate in admissions. One day an admissions clerk gave me a folder. 'You might find this interesting,' she said. It was my own UCD application.

"Inside was a long vertical Admissions Action Sheet. Under 'Grades' it said, 'Unsatisfactory: academic disqualification at last college; recommend No Transfer Admit.'

"Under 'Recommendations,' it said, 'Excellent, read the top letter.' On the bottom of the Action Sheet, it said under 'Decision,' 'Admit Conditionally, One academic quarter GPA probation.'

"I read the top letter of recommendation. It was from you. Your letter got me into college so I could get a degree and my advanced degrees. You'd said that you could've saved me from academic failure. But you *did* save me."

He nodded and looked down. In a voice of regret he said, "We never did go shooting."

"Well, that might be a good thing. I train with the Kansas City Police Department. The payment is letting me fire every weapon in their inventory and being a buddy of top sergeants and the armorer. Five years ago, I shot the 25-yard center bull with a tight group. I also hit a tiny little sideways-mounted Ten of Hearts playing card on the third shot with a nine-millimeter Glock 17 at 50 feet. This year, I almost shot the armorer, didn't qualify at the short distance, and thanked them for not mounting a playing card for me to miss. My vision's going and I'm still that guy who can't see a thing at night."

"Well, I'm not shooting anymore either." He told me about his family, and about his hobbies, and about his health.

We were quiet for a while, three older men resting in Florida sunlight in which danced young and light-hearted dust motes.

He cleared his throat. "Gus, you're now a TOAD, teaching in our alma mater. We've come full circle. You're now doing what I was assigned to do when we met." He thinly cleared his throat, as if he lacked the air to carry his words. "We TOADs have to stay together." He smiled.

I quietly breathed, trying vicariously to give him my air.

"Let's make this our farewell."

The words hit like a sledge hammer. I nodded, for a moment, unable to speak. Then, as easily as I had ever spoken the challenging English tongue, I thanked him for mentoring me, for being like a father, my heart full and voice clear, the message coming from my past and the hopes for our children and the dreams of a brave and democratic nation.

He smiled his great electric smile; the world brightened. He stood.

I put out my hand and he hugged me. It was hard and tight, the close grip of a commander who loved his soldiers; an aging man who, I think, was flattered that one of his cadets had tried to honor his lessons and loved him for who he was and for the goodness that he tried to pour into him. It was the clasp of a leader who had prayed for his men.

I saluted.

"Farewell, Gus."

"Good-bye, Sir. God bless you." As I left, I lost control of the muscles in my face.

Taps

Be strong and courageous. Do not be terrified; do not be discouraged,
for I am with you whatever you do.
Joshua 1:9

Jim Ellis was on the phone.

"Brenda has set the date. Our Friend is going to be buried at West Point. The Superintendent is sponsoring a reception and has invited me and one guest. Carol's not coming. Want to hang around a group of general officers with me?"

As a recovering coward, I'd long treasured God's message to Joshua as he stood, paralyzed, at the banks of the Jordan. Joshua was the most valiant of the 12 brave reconnaissance scouts who first entered the Promised Land. Under Moses's leadership, Joshua was a tough, combat-tested warrior who had fought in the deserts of the Holy Land and Arabia. Now, he learned that because Moses had never mastered his anger, God forbade this greatest of Hebrew prophets to cross the river; Joshua would now have to lead without his mentor of 40 years, and Joshua didn't think he could do it.

I'd been carrying H. Norman Schwarzkopf's life lessons in the cargo pocket of my heart for 47 years. When I felt fear, I turned to his principles to try to discern and do the highest moral action. Now this great and generous man had died. Part of me had followed him into an unknown space, and crossing rivers seemed harder. I accepted Jim Ellis's kind invitation.

I stood at Trophy Point and the river and remembered the Bear's words that rode the winds of the Hudson that kissed the bones and the viscera within. On January 27, 2012, one month and a day earlier, he had passed away in his home in Tampa, with Brenda, his children, and Lynn, his aide, and his inner staff by his side. General H. Norman Schwarzkopf was going to be buried today in the West Point Cemetery near the grave of his beloved father. In the wind I tried to remember his voice. I remembered him talking about one of his bosses.

"Gus," he had said, "you know Richard Cavazos, right?"

I had nodded. Cavazos was a legendary soldier who had fought and been wounded in Korea and Vietnam and, in the style of General McCaffrey, had received two Distinguished Service Crosses. He was an Audie Murphy type, constantly saving his men and bravely attacking superior enemy positions while laughing in the face of fear and the masque of death. Cavazos would become the first Hispanic American four-star general.

"Cavazos was my boss. He didn't much like my rambunctiousness, but he always backed me for the toughest assignments. He's the one who sent me to Grenada to tie together the services in another attempt at joint operations. He was leaving III Corps to go to FORSCOM and said he'd come say goodbye to my 24th Infantry Division at Fort Stewart.

"'No hoopla, no bands, Norm!'" he ordered, and man, he meant it.

"I'd ticked him off earlier. During the energy crisis, the Pentagon said no Christmas lights, no lit trees on post or in quarters. I could tell that DOD had just crushed the morale of our troops. So I defied the order and put up lights and allowed anyone who wanted to do the same. You're shaking your head at me—what, you don't like Christmas anymore!"

"Sir, I love it. I just don't know how you got four stars."

"Well, I don't either. Anyway, I called Cavazos and said I'd calculated the energy cost from the lights at $400 and had written a check to the U.S. Government for that amount, and that we were going to be acting in contravention of the energy order. Cavazos wasn't happy but said he didn't like the order either. He was also a softie for Christmas.

"So, now Cavazos has said farewell to my division and I take him back to the airfield. I got the 24th Infantry band assembled by his aircraft and he's about to ream me out for disobeying him for doing hoopla and I give the signal and the band strikes out with his favorite hymn, which is also mine. It's in your West Point novel, *Honor and Duty*. It was your mother's favorite hymn, the one that kind of brought her to be a Christian girl when she was a teen in China."

"'Amazing Grace,'" I said.

He nodded. "Well, Cavazos and I, these two old grizzled guys—he's a real two-fisted gunfighter, one of the toughest hombres ever—we're standing at attention on the tarmac and we both start singing the words to the hymn. Now, it's been said by some that I'm kind of an emotional guy . . ."

"Sir, you *are* an emotional guy."

"Well, be that as it may. Okay, I am, and I've told the world that. Anyway, we're singing and I'm using my old Cadet Choir tenor, and damn if we both aren't crying. That hymn, doggone it, I can't help it. Every time, it just tears me up. Same thing happens with the Hallelujah Chorus which, by the way, I know by memory."

I confessed to still stumbling over the melody of the "Alma Mater," which is close to admitting heresy.

"Amazing Grace" had been written by John Newton, a former slave trader who wrote the hymn to capture apology, atonement, forgiveness, and prayers for redemption. The Bear and General Cavazos had lived their lives in service, patriotism, and bravery with fidelity to their wives and families. But the hymn moved them as if they had been wretches who needed saving. He had cried for the hymn that meant the most to my mother. Long ago I had proudly declared that I loathed West Point's weekly chapel services. My scornful comment had to have hurt his deepest sense of self, but the Bear had softly replied that attending chapel had helped him organize his thoughts.

Later, as a father, an uncontrollable temper surfaced with angry beratings of my innocent, five-year old son. Therapy helped me understand the source of the anger, but the behaviors persisted. For that sad moment, Kong Fuzi had said, "Knowledge is easy, but action is difficult." In desperation to not become a carbon copy of my father, I tried the one thing I knew I would never trust and the thing in which Diane had been raised—a church. I found the core message of Scripture to be freeing, and the wisdom of sermons from the likes of Paul Watermulder, James Edwards, and Tim Keller proved to be life-changing. They were deeply consistent with Diane's love for our children and the Bear's teachings. My first turning point took place when I heard a reading from a best-selling book:

Go forth into the world in peace
Be of good courage
Hold fast to that which is good
Render to no one evil for evil
Support the weak, help the afflicted
Honor all persons

What followed was a miracle. In moments, overcoming the deeply ingrained habits of ten thousand or so controlling, dictatorial, and emotionally remote Chinese ancestor patriarchs from whom I'm descended, I genuinely apologized to my son and was given an inner authority to govern my anger. I asked for his forgiveness. He later told me that it saved our relationship. (He and his wife invited Diane and me to move near them in the Seattle area; our homes are five minutes apart and as I write this I'm having lunch with him tomorrow. We are active grandparents.) A blessing.

I painfully remembered how gently the Bear had carried his beliefs while I had freely broadcast my scorn of those with religious thoughts; I had looked down upon them as if they'd been first century lepers. I had openly violated his principle of honoring all persons by disrespecting those on a religious path, and then, I disrespected my own son. Executing this change had been one of my many essential moral river crossings. My moral faults were my turning points in the battle of life, and West Point was the great forge of character in which an officer had pounded on my weaknesses with Vulcan's fervor.

Here, at the point of the river where the Hudson turns dramatically to the west, I remembered his anecdote about Cavazos and how a hymn written by a slave trader could deeply unite men of German, Mexican, and Chinese heritages. Here, at Trophy Point, we had assembled in formation on our first day as cadets. We had removed the white gloves from our right hands to raise them in a solemn pledge to defend the Constitution against all enemies, foreign and domestic. The lightness of lifted arms contrasted with the gravity of the promise.

We had committed ourselves to the protection of the Republic and to fight its enemies to the death, informed by fearless military discernment, and based on the decisions of civilian authority, whether they be righteous or erroneous. West Point would seek to equip us, by day and by night, to render our commitment principled, moral, learned, rational, and effective.

Trawlers steadily pushed freight to Canada through the Hudson's thinning February ice. An Amtrak Empire Service train sped north on the east bank, its horn wailing a haunting version of the blues, forlorn, lonely, its sad notes evaporating in the frigid wind that was turning skin to numbness.

My chest ached as I crossed Thayer Road to rejoin Jim Ellis, who had invited me to attend the Superintendent's reception in Quarters 100, Jefferson

Road, West Point, the Federal-style building that is the oldest structure at the Academy.

Army helicopters clattered and whomped onto The Plain to deliver former Vice President Dick Cheney, former Chairman of the Joint Chiefs General Colin Powell, Army Chief of Staff Raymond T. Odierno, and former Army Chief of Staff Carl E. Vuono to Quarters 100. Retired General Fred Franks, my former senior mentor when I worked across the Plain, arrived by vehicle from the Simon Center for the Professional Military Ethic. Former Army Vice Chief of Staff General Jack Keane was already in the Superintendent's quarters. Colin Powell greeted and shook hands with Jim Ellis, who then ushered me inside. I was the only officer in the reception that was not a general. I listened to the party speak of Norman Schwarzkopf in the manner of siblings remembering their most illustrious brother. They were telling stories of him, some of which I'd never heard. The recurring theme was that he retired too soon, that he could have convinced Congress to reduce the dangerous downsizing of our defenses, that he would've had useful ideas about the Middle East, that he was missed, and would be missed.

"He could tell the truth to the top," said one.

He also, I thought, had that commanding and inspirational personality that could gain full support from our government, the trust of the president, form winning coalitions, and gain a lightning-quick victory in the historically perplexing Middle East.

I walked a thin line between being a guest and an interloper. I ate sparingly and left the brass and their private conversations to scan the Superintendent's library. The Superintendent joined me, and we discussed ethics, books, writing, and authors. He was about to leave West Point. I knew the feeling, and a momentary melancholy settled over a day already broken by sadness.

It was time to load onto buses for the Chapel memorial service. As a cadet I had found a strange affirmation of strength in the classical majesty of the neo-Gothic granite structure, its beautiful stained glass windows, and the irresistible sense of the supernatural. To enter its nave was to visit Europe, the continent from which so many of our American traditions had originated. Our stately chapel was where the Bear had come every week to organize his thinking. Today, it offered sanctuary for his spirit and for the grief of his family.

Jim Ellis and I entered the Chapel. In the entry was a large photograph of General Schwarzkopf in formal Army whites. I thought: Sad, so sad.

I was wrong. The first hymn was "Amazing Grace" and I sang, in my tone-deaf barking, with renewed joy. I could picture the Bear as a fresh-faced Firstie, the tallest member of the great Cadet Choir, singing with a young Cadet Fred Franks from Company L-1, leading their unified voices to praise the heavens. Thirty-five years later, these two four-star generals with angelic voices would smash a tyrannical and terrorist army in Mesopotamia. As his Academy roommate, his Desert Storm boss, his daughter, and the Post Chaplain spoke of him and his significance to the nation, I heard the Bear singing, "Do you hear what I hear" from down the hill at Quarters 39.

Retired Major General Leroy Sudduth, the tall, stately, and heavily decorated commander of 1st U.S. Special Operations Command, had been Norm's roommate for their four cadet years. He said Norm had spent more time tutoring others, "especially us boys from the South," than he did on his own studies. "He was not just a bright light in the Long Gray Line. He was a strong supporter of the Starlight Foundation, an organization dedicated to rescuing children from abusive situations. He was a champion for the wounded warriors and Nature Conservancy . . . and a national spokesperson for cancer awareness. He never wavered from a life of Duty, Honor, Country and his love of soldiers always took precedence over politics and business, and soldiers could always trust him. He was one of the brightest lights, and we will miss him."

Retired General and former Secretary of State Colin Powell stood before the crowd that included officials of the Kuwaiti government and of the Bear's Desert Storm coalition, and told stories about Norman from the Gulf War. "H. Norman Schwarzkopf has come home to a place he loved, and now he forever marches to the cadence of Duty, Honor, Country. This West Point is our North Star, where standards are set, and principles and virtues are taught."

Cindy Schwarzkopf said, "How do I do honor to my father, a man of exceptional gifts, in 10 minutes? My grandfather came to school here and my father taught cadets in these halls and he met my mom, and 44 years ago, they married in this chapel." She spoke of her dad with a love and a passion that placed us in their living room at Christmas. We smiled as she recounted their laughter and glee at her father's magic tricks, his wearing a clown outfit at their birthday parties, and his deep and warm love for his children. Her father wasn't the man in uniform known to the world; he was their dad, and his life principle of integrity was his gift. "He made us laugh, and sing with Pavarotti and then Johnny Cash. He was more comfortable in a tent, was our 'Jeopardy' champion, unbeatable in poker, the best hunter and fisherman, the man who helped us take our first steps, taught us to ride bikes, to ski, cheering us at our swim meets.

"Doing right was his guide," she said, projecting the Schwarzkopf family persona into our inner selves. Those who knew him nodded in the certainty of her statement. "He was no nonsense—get it done and get it right."

The Cadet Choir then sang the West Point "Alma Mater," the final stanza of which rang in the tall Gothic rafters.

And when our work is done
Our course on earth is run
May it be said, 'Well Done
Be Thou At Peace.'

At the West Point Cemetery, space had been saved for the Superintendent's party, of which I was a minor part. Cadet Company A, First Regiment, which was the Bear's, marched out in full dress gray as the honor guard.

The reveille cannon that roused us when he was a bachelor and I was a cadet now fired 17-guns for a four-star general who would never leave Post again.

Family, friends, and comrades held fast and wept. Flanked by generals and his family, I thought the small urn couldn't contain a man who had unified a coalition stronger than Hannibal's; had liberated a helpless kingdom; defeated the army of an infamous, fascist tyrant; had won one of the fastest ground war victories in military history; had inspired and lifted a doubting nation by demonstrating courage and superior competence in the face of a dreaded foe; and in quick order, had relieved the world of its fear of a long and terrible war.

He had not been a careerist, seeking approval for the next promotion. He had always spoken truth and willingly accepted the consequences. He sacrificed much of his personal life to be a full-time patriot, to protect his soldiers, and to do the hardest right. He knew his better nature. By becoming a man that was scarcely predicted in an unathletic and approval-seeking adolescent, he had achieved the Cervantes outcome—a victory over self. Now, his body was being returned to the hard soil and black granite of West Point. "Be ashamed to die until winning a victory for humanity," said Horace Mann.

General, I thought, closing my eyes. How free you must be from shame, and how long your victory over weakness will inspire others in this school to do likewise.

The ailing children he had served since retirement had called him their friend and regarded him as their hero. The young residents of Camp Boggy Creek had known his heart of gold through his generosity and through Jim Ellis's leadership. I imagined, in this hallowed grove of weeping European beech and flowering dogwood, of Carolina silverbells, great oaks, and winter King Hawthorns, the happy laughter of the thousands of children he had served.

A solitary bagpiper stood apart, and all knew his tune, which had lifted us in the chapel and now haunted us as we gathered at the river. I now murmured the words to the lilt of the piper. "I once was lost but am now found, was blind but now I see."

There was no escaping the penetrating words of that famous hymn, used by the world for multiple purposes, and played twice, today, with great feeling.

The sharp report of rifles and the mournful play of "Taps" punctuated his absence and created remembrances of previous memorials for dead comrades. All those accumulated bereavements seemed to have been given to Brenda Schwarzkopf, whose tears reminded us of our small proportion of loss. Brenda, Cindy, Jessica, and Christian had sacrificed precious time with him so he could serve the nation and the cause of freedom.

Through blurred eyes, I looked upward into steel gray clouds and transmitted a heart-felt prayer for a brave soul who had lent me strength when I was weak and had bolted a backbone into me where I had sported wishful thinking. When I had most needed character, he had generously poured from his cup into mine.

I could see the Corps march past us in review to the West Point March, the upbeat bugles, happy fifes, and great drums lifting hearts as the ordered regiments turned eyes right with lowered gaily-waving yellow company pennons, presenting arms to a general who had epitomized the selfless courage, the high character, and the ferocity of principled resolve possessed by great leaders of history.

Somewhere nearby, perhaps from the thick branches in the stately Chinese lacebark elms, came memories of his long-dead Vietnamese brothers, the men with whom he'd been a company-grade officer in the intimacy of a small, depleted combat unit engaged in continuous battle on the other side of the world. The wind moved through Oriental oaks as they might have whispered, *Aller doucement, mon capitaine*, Go softly, my captain.

I would miss my friend.

Echoes

Courage is more exhilarating than fear and, in the long run, it's easier.
We do not have to become heroes overnight, just a step at a time, meeting
each thing as it comes, seeing it is not as dreadful as it appeared.
Eleanor Roosevelt

*T*áoyě qingcāo, to forge character. Developing leaders is like human metallurgy. The forge requires dedication, sweat-inducing labor, and gutsy recoveries from failure to produce leaders of true inner steel. Thusly forged, leaders inspire others to right action when they are faced with harsh moral tests. Forging character accompanies the old Eastern truth: "Calm seas do not make good sailors."

The counterpart Western axiom is: "No one comes to character without suffering."

Because the Bear helped lend a courageous purpose to my life, and his principles percolated into me despite resistance, Diane and I have *táoyě qingcāo* in our small family forge. Our natural and adopted children lead lives of service for the common good in missions, the Army, non-governmental organizations, and education. Most importantly, three of our children have married, and married persons of character. Wonderfully, two are now parents.

H. Norman Schwarzkopf's brutal honesty regarding one's weaknesses and practicing habits of courage are echoed in the school that helped form his roots and are in the soil in which he only technically rests. For today's leaders to courageously solve mind-bending and increasingly complex moral and social problems, they must first know how to discern and courageously fix their own. This requires guts and behaviors, tools, and habits of unwavering character. He didn't view these skills as hard; he believed they flowed naturally from loving his soldiers.

Every fall, Sully, Whitey, and I—three men influenced by the Bear when we were young—walk along the river road at West Point. Cadets playing hard athletics fill the great marching Plain to our left as we pass Lincoln Hall on the right. The Bear's BOQ now houses the Department of Social Sciences. From the window of an upper room, Quarters 39, he once labored for his students, a giant would-be Asian iron worker forging character from weaker metals.

It was at West Point where we lucky few learned so many essential lessons. We pass the breathtaking, familiar panorama at Trophy Point to pay our respects in the subdued grove of our fallen. Whitey salutes the white markers of his parents; Sully salutes the markers of classmates; I salute at my mentor's grave. I report to him about principles, the conduct of my family, my fight against my inner challenges, and the state of character development. I thank him. I remember his amused smile as I sought to imitate his best qualities, the greatest of which was his moral courage.

We admire the heroic individual who by brave example seems to lift our deepest hopes of being honorable and courageous, unbefuddled by a difficult world, and equipped with that rare resolve to do the hardest right regardless of risk.

Lincoln, it was said after he was taken from us, belongs to the ages; the Bear is but a part of a shorter span of history. In my mind, he belongs to the river of this great and verdant valley and to the enduring rock that is West Point. He also belongs to all Americans and to all the people of the world who honor virtue above self.

The Hudson is compelled by nature to take a hard and radical turn around this admirable and intrusive western rock. In a like fashion, the Bear accepted West Point's daunting challenge to make hard turns in his own persona to fight against self-interest. Instead of earning personal awards and practicing advancement, he tutored others.

The 1960s had spawned a new generation that revered brilliance, force, power, charismatic oratory, and entertaining action. The Bear appreciated knowledge but hungered for wisdom. He avoided publicity and found no reassurance in popularity or the approval of men. He could easily have trumpeted his size, mental acuity, and drive, yet he did not compare himself to others, but tested himself against the requirements of highest principles. He accessed a deep strength in fighting against his own nature to consistently do the highest right action.

How could I not cry for the loss of such a leader?

The wind, our winter enemy, now plays in the trees. Sully, the boxer and helicopter pilot, speaks softly to our dead. Whitey, the Infantry colonel and warrior, gently cleans the graves of his parents. If I become still in quiet gratitude for an unmerited life, and if I think about singing difficult and principled notes beyond my range, I can place myself in an officer's small bachelor quarters, and sometimes I can hear the memory of his imperative and affectionate voice.

I know what the voice instructs, powered as it is by his undying love for his soldiers and the commitment of his life to right behavior. He wants me to do what he wishes for all soldiers and all citizens of the world—to seek moral outcomes despite manifold fears, to be strong and courageous in everything we think, say, and do, regardless of risk to puny self-interests. I take that deep breath.

Come on, he says to me, you can do this. You must do this. Let's get it right.

Cadet H. Norman Schwarzkopf, Company A-1, West Point class of 1956, in his *Howitzer* yearbook photo. A cadet captain who played intercollegiate football, soccer, and wrestling, he led the Cadet Choir, had been in the Weightlifting and German Clubs for four years, and was known as "Schwartzie," which was also his dad's nickname when he was a cadet.

Kindergarten, Fremont Elementary, San Francisco Panhandle. I'm in the 2nd row, far left. Toussaint, my first friend in life, now Dr. Toussaint Streat, M.D., is 2nd row, second from the right. We're both smiling because my mah-mee was still alive and Too's father was still at home.

Steve Childers and Gus Lee in front of Sylvanus Thayer's statue, Plebe year, 1964. For the moment, we're smiling, for we are neither bracing nor being hazed.

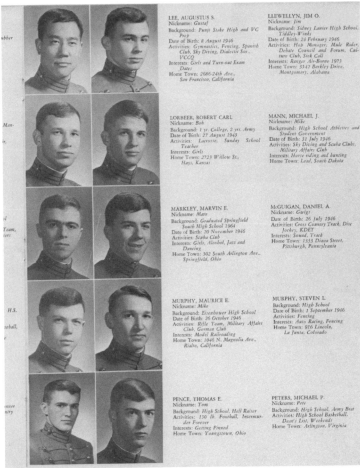

LEE, AUGUSTUS S.
Nickname: *Gustaf*
Background: *Punji Stake High and VC Prep*
Date of Birth: *8 August 1946*
Activities: *Gymnastics, Fencing, Spanish Club, Sky Diving, Dialectic Soc., VCCQ*
Interests: *Girls and Turn-out Exam Dates*
Home Town: *2686-24th Ave., San Francisco, California*

LLEWELLYN, JIM O.
Nickname: *Jim*
Background: *Sidney Lanier High School, Tiddley-Winks*
Date of Birth: *24 February 1946*
Activities: *Hop Manager, Male Rider, Debate Council and Forum, Culture Club, Sick Call*
Interests: *Ranger Air-Borne 1973*
Home Town: *3542 Berkley Drive, Montgomery, Alabama*

LORBEER, ROBERT CARL
Nickname: *Bob*
Background: *1 yr. College, 2 yrs. Army*
Date of Birth: *27 August 1943*
Activities: *Lacrosse, Sunday School Teacher*
Interests: *Girls*
Home Town: *2723 Willow St., Hays, Kansas*

MANN, MICHAEL J.
Nickname: *Mike*
Background: *High School Athletics and Student Government*
Date of Birth: *31 July 1946*
Activities: *Sky Diving and Scuba Clubs, Military Affairs Club*
Interests: *Horse riding and hunting*
Home Town: *Lead, South Dakota*

MARKLEY, MARVIN E.
Nickname: *Marv*
Background: *Graduated Springfield South High School 1964*
Date of Birth: *20 November 1946*
Activities: *Scuba Club*
Interests: *Girls, Alcohol, Jazz and Dancing*
Home Town: *502 South Arlington Ave., Springfield, Ohio*

McGUIGAN, DANIEL A.
Nickname: *Gwigs*
Date of Birth: *26 July 1946*
Activities: *Cross Country Track, Disc Jockey, KDET*
Interests: *Sound, Track*
Home Town: *1353 Diana Street, Pittsburgh, Pennsylvania*

MURPHY, MAURICE E.
Nickname: *Mike*
Background: *Eisenhower High School*
Date of Birth: *26 October 1946*
Activities: *Rifle Team, Military Affairs Club, German Club*
Interests: *Model Railroading*
Home Town: *1046 N. Magnolia Ave., Rialto, California*

MURPHY, STEVEN L.
Background: *High School*
Date of Birth: *1 September 1946*
Activities: *Fencing*
Interests: *Auto Racing, Fencing*
Home Town: *916 Lincoln, La Junta, Colorado*

PENCE, THOMAS E.
Nickname: *Tom*
Background: *High School, Hell Raiser*
Activities: *150 lb. Football, Intermurder Forever*
Interests: *Getting Pinned*
Home Town: *Youngstown, Ohio*

PETERS, MICHAEL P.
Nickname: *Pete*
Background: *High School, Army Brat*
Activities: *High School Basketball, Dean's List, Weekends*
Home Town: *Arlington, Virginia*

Ten of Company A-3's 31 Cows, 1966. From top: Gus Lee; Jim Llewellyn, smart, poetic, top athlete in our class, was a rifle company commander in Vietnam; Colonel (Ret) Bob "More Beer" Lorbeer, master of encouragement, wounded in Vietnam as a rifle company commander, awarded the Bronze Star, and is a successful attorney; "Smilin'" Mike Mann, one of our best, awarded the Silver Star and Bronze Star in Vietnam and became a corporate senior executive and power projects expert; Marv "Guppy" Markley, smart and humorous, served in combat and became a top oil industry expert; Danny "Gwigs" McGuigan, runner and musician; Lieutenant Colonel (Ret) Mike "Murph the Surf" Murphy, awarded Silver Star, Bronze Star, and Purple Heart in Vietnam, corporate logistician, now volunteers extensively in community; Steven L. Murphy, fencer and racing enthusiast; Colonel (Ret) Tommy Pence, humorous wrestler and raconteur, awarded the Bronze Star in Vietnam, and was CENTCOM comptroller; Colonel (Ret) Mike "Tree" Peters, good-humored, intellectual man of faith, awarded the Bronze Star for valor in Vietnam, became West Point's Chief of Staff, Chief Operating Officer of the Council on Foreign Relations, and president of St. John's College, Santa Fe.

Department of Mechanics faculty, 1967. The Bear is in the 3rd row, 5th from the left, with his trademark smile from not being with his Vietnamese paratroopers. Major James L. Dozier, 1st row, second from right, was the Bear's classmate; he was kidnapped by the Red Brigades in Padua, Italy, in 1981. He was freed by special operations forces after 42 days in captivity, was one of my excellent professors, and rose to major general.

The Cows, or juniors, of Company A-3, 1967. I removed my glasses. When told that I looked tough, I admitted that I was squinting and pretending I could see.

The Bear and one of his favorite cadets, San Jose, California, 2001. Many wanted their picture taken with the Bear, so I didn't even bring a camera. A member of the Bear's San Jose Police Personal Security Detail nervously took this shot. We'd been informed that the Taliban had targeted ex-President George H.W. Bush and the Bear for assassination, so I assembled the security detail.

The Bear and I in his Tampa office, 2009. The certificate I wrote for him sits below his photo and between his flags. Lieutenant General (Ret) Jim Ellis thoughtfully brought a camera and took the photo.

His values live. James Patrick "Sully" Sullivan, USMA Class of 1970, and I at the Bear's gravestone, West Point cemetery, Fall 2014. Colonel (Ret) Lawrence Kermit "Whitey" White snapped the photo. Whitey's parents' gravestones, and those of the members of the classes of 1968 and 1970, many of whom died in battle when we were young and soldiers, are nearby.

Appendix

★ ★ ★ ★

Here is what became of the West Point classes of 1968 and 1970, Gus Lee's Plebes, the Lee Family, Lieutenant General (LTG) (Ret) James R. Ellis, Professor Warren Bennis, and General (Ret) Frederick M. Franks.

THE WEST POINT CLASS OF 1968

Killed in Action or Died of Wounds

DAVID L. ALEXANDER	DONALD R. COLGLAZIER	PETER M. CONNOR
KENNETH T. CUMMINGS	JOHN E. DARLING	WILLIAM F. ERICSON III
JAMES A. GAISER	HARRY E. HAYES	RICHARD A. HAWLEY
DENNY L. JOHNSON	WILLIAM F. LITTLE	DAVID T. MADDUX
WILLIAM F. REICHERT	JEFFRY R. RIEK	DAVID L. SACKETT
LOUIS J. SPEIDEL	HENRY M. SPENGLER III	DONALD F. VANCOOK, JR.
DOUGLAS T. WHELESS	DONALD R. WORKMAN	

Class Officers: President, D. David "Dutch" Hostler, Colonel (USAR Ret); Vice-president, Daniel J. Kaufman, Brigadier General (BG) (Ret); Secretary: Charles "Chuck" S. Mahan, Jr., Lieutenant General (Ret); Treasurer: Myles J. Crowe; Historian: David "Dave" W. Gerard, Major (Ret); and Information Systems Officer: Surrey P. Everett, Lieutenant Colonel (Ret).

The 1,000 members of the class of 1968 that took the oath to protect the Constitution and the Republic on July 1, 1964, became 706 graduates who renewed their oaths 47 months later as Regular Army second lieutenants on June 5, 1968.

Classmate Jim Bodenhamer, a Bronze Star recipient from combat in Vietnam, reported that 217 members of the class volunteered after graduation to become Infantry platoon leaders in Vietnam. One in 10 died and 40 percent were wounded; others later died of wounds. Many were disabled.

Members of the class of 1968 were awarded three Distinguished Service Crosses (DSCs), 62 Silver Stars, and 110 Purple Hearts, 15 receiving more than one. Bill Peplinski earned four Purple Hearts, a DSC, two Silver Stars, and three Bronze Stars for valor in Vietnam, was medically retired for wounds, and became a physician serving veterans. Five classmates, Colonel (COL) (Ret) Charles Beckwith, Jr., COL (Ret) John McDonald, Lieutenant Colonel (LTC) (Ret) Robert A. Adams, COL (Ret) Charles F. Besanceney, M.D., and LTC (Ret) Joseph R. Henry, each received the Soldiers Medal for saving lives under dire conditions.

Eleven classmates became general officers (GOs); three became GOs in the Army Reserve. BG Dan Kaufman was awarded two Purple Hearts and the Bronze Star for valor, earned a master's degree and a Ph.D., became West Point's 12th Dean of the Academic Board, and a college president. Ninety-nine classmates retired as COLs; 120 retired as LTCs, and 42 achieved those two ranks in the Army Reserve or National Guard.

Forty-four classmates became physicians; 53 became presidents or CEOs; 66 were vice-presidents; 157 earned Juris Doctors (J.D.s) or MBAs; 20 earned Ph.D.s; 21 obtained professional degrees; and five became priests and ministers, including Mike Cerrone and Tom Margrave, both of whom had personal connections to the Bear. The vast majority of the class earned master's—many earned more than one.

Most of my Company A-3 classmates served in combat in Vietnam. Bob "More Beer" Lorbeer, George "Kent" Williams, Bob "Moon" Beahm, Mike "Murph the Surf" Murphy, Tim "Bouche" Balliett, Barry "Curve Wrecker" Hittner, and Jim "Fork" Fourquerean survived their wounds. "Smilin'" Mike Mann and Mike Murphy were each awarded the Silver Star; George Williams, two Silver Stars.

Arthur "Arturo" Frank Torres received the Bronze Star and other valor awards as a company commander with the 4th Infantry in Vietnam. Arturo passed away just before Thanksgiving 2013.

Steve "Ping" Childers served in Germany and in combat in Vietnam, became a CPA, and was the CFO for FIFA World Cup Soccer.

Bob "More Beer" Lorbeer was a top platoon leader in the 1/506th Infantry, 101st Airborne, awarded the Bronze Star for valor and Purple Heart, earned an MBA and a J.D., was recalled to duty for the Gulf War, retired as a COL.

Larry "Rap" Rapisarda served in Vietnam and Korea, earned a master's and a Ph.D., became an Electrical Engineering professor at West Point, and retired as a LTC.

Jim "Pastor" Adams served as an Infantry officer in Vietnam, became a Green Beret, and operates an engineering business in Fayetteville, NC.

Mike "Tree" Peters received the Bronze Star for valor with the Armored Cavalry in Vietnam, served in Operation Just Cause in Panama, fought in the first Gulf War under General Schwarzkopf, became Chief of Staff at West Point, retired as a COL, and is president of St. John's College in Santa Fe.

Bob "Moon" Beahm was awarded the Bronze Star with a "V" for valor and a Purple Heart in Vietnam and a Legion of Merit in Desert Storm/Provide Comfort for saving thousands of Kurds' lives, and retired as a BG from the Army Reserve.

Jim "Moose" Altemose became a top Air Force fighter pilot, and was awarded the Distinguished Flying Cross (DFC).

Jon Anderson served as an Infantry officer in Germany and Vietnam, and earned two master's.

Tim "Bouche" Balliett was twice wounded in Vietnam with the 1st Cavalry, earned a master's, managed combat vehicle programs, and supports Operation Helping Hand to aid soldier's families in Florida.

Antone "Tony" Cerne was a combat engineer with the 82nd Airborne in Vietnam, earned a master's, and became a nuclear regulator.

"Cousin Brucie" Bruce Erion was awarded the DFC, three Bronze Stars, and other valor awards.

Jim "Fork" Fourquerean led two rifle companies in Vietnam, was wounded, earned a master's, and works in systems analysis in California.

Jon Gardner was a Combat Engineers company commander, served in Korea, and earned two master's.

William Joseph "Billy Meatball" Higgins III was a platoon leader and company commander in the 1/506th Infantry, 101st Airborne, in Vietnam, earned a master's, and retired as a LTC.

Barry "Curve Wrecker" Hittner received three Bronze Stars and a Purple Heart as a combat engineer in Vietnam, and earned a master's and a J.D.

Bob Hunt served as an armor officer in Germany.

Charles "Freddy" Klein received the Bronze Star in Vietnam and earned a Ph.D.

Jim Orvis Llewellyn was a rifle company commander in Vietnam.

"Smilin'" Mike Mann was awarded the Silver Star and Bronze Star with the 101st Airborne in Vietnam and earned a master's.

Marv "Guppy" Markley served in Germany, Vietnam, and Korea, and earned a master's.

Maurice "Mike Murph the Surf" Murphy served in combat as an armored cavalry officer, was awarded the Silver Star, Bronze Star, and Purple Heart, and retired as a LTC.

Steven L. Murphy served in the Infantry.

Thomas "Tommy" Pence was awarded the Bronze Star in Vietnam, earned an MBA, and served as CENTCOM comptroller during Desert Shield and Storm.

Lewis Robertson served with the Air Force's 16th Survival Squadron in Alaska, became a constitutional lawyer, and passed away in 2011.

Louis Speer served in Europe and Vietnam, was awarded two Bronze Stars, and earned a master's.

Werner John "Plots" Stolp was in some of the hardest combat of the Vietnam War and earned a graduate degree.

George "Kent" Williams received two Silver Stars, two Bronze Stars, and a Purple Heart in two consecutive combat tours in Vietnam, earned a master's and a Ph.D., taught English at West Point, became the Air Force Historian, retired as a COL. He passed away in North Carolina in 2015.

David "Snake" Lee Sackett received the Silver Star for saving the lives of four of his men who were wounded and pinned down by enemy fire. He later died while leading his platoon in a firefight 23 miles north of Saigon in October 1969, and is buried in Arlington National Cemetery.

William "Big Ace" Bill Reichert was killed in Vietnam in 1971 and buried in Long Island National Cemetery.

Richard "Rick" Aspinall Hawley, Jr., an officer in 2/501, 101st Airborne, was killed in Vietnam, and is buried in the West Point Cemetery.

William Ross "Wrinkles" Irvin was awarded two Bronze Stars for Valor as an Infantry officer in Vietnam, earned an MBA, and retired as a COL.

THE WEST POINT CLASS OF 1970

The 749 members of the West Point Class of 1970 generously fund the Academy's National Conference on Ethics in America, a function that aligns with its class motto of Serve with Integrity, and reinforces the life lessons of the Bear. Class members who have actively supported NCEA operations at West Point include:

George "Barney" Forsythe who served in Germany and Korea, earned a master's and a Ph.D., became the associate dean at West Point, and retired as a BG.

Patrick Scully was a Ranger School instructor, president of EDS Japan, and a member of the EDS team of veterans that conducted the gallant Tehran hostage rescue operation described by Ken Follett in *On Wings of Eagles*.

William "Billy" Cater served in the Field Artillery, earned a CPA, and serves as NCEA's financial advisor.

James "Sully" Sullivan, an Army helicopter pilot with the 101st Airborne, earned a Ph.D. and serves as the unofficial class historian.

William "Watty" Wattendorf served as an Infantry officer in Berlin and Korea, earned a master's, taught at West Point, and retired as a LTC.

Gary "Gummy" Steele, Army star wide receiver in the Army Sports Hall of Fame, was drafted by the Detroit Lions, but chose to command Infantry units and retired as a COL.

Robert "Bobby" Brand served with the 173rd and 101st Airborne in Vietnam, was awarded three Bronze Stars, and retired as a COL.

David Lee Brown, class president, began in Field Artillery, earned a medical degree, and retired as a LTC.

Earl "Toby" Quirk served in Germany and in Special Forces and retired as a LTC in the Army Reserve.

Frank Monaco served in the Field Artillery with the 82nd Airborne and in Korea, earned a master's, taught at West Point, and retired as a COL.

Kerry Lawrence was an Armor officer in Germany and earned a J.D.

Phil Doleac became an Army dentist who served in Germany and Alaska and retired as a COL.

Lawrence K. "Whitey" White served with the 11th Armored Cavalry Regiment in Vietnam, was awarded the Bronze Star, served in Iraq and Afghanistan, earned a master's, was a West Point tactical officer and chief of staff at Ft. Benning, and retired as a COL.

Don Blakeslee was, along with Mike Bain, among the first West Point graduates to go directly to medical school. After retiring as a COL, he was recalled to active duty following 9–11 and serves at the Keller Army Community Hospital at West Point.

Many other classmates have served NCEA over the years, including Steve Wilson; Don Meinhold, Gus's bunkmate on the DMZ; Gilbert "Gil" Harper III, BG (Ret); Julian Burns, Jr., MG (Ret); James "Jim" McHone, COL (Ret), who passed away in 2015; David "Dave" Rosenblum; Bruce Peltier; Richard "Rich" Measner, LTC (Ret); William "Bill" Malkemes, COL (Ret); Bill Trivette, LTC (Ret); and Richard "Rich" Rutledge, COL (Ret).

THE PLEBES IN GUS LEE'S SQUAD

All 10 of the squad members of the class of 1970 graduated. Six achieved high rank, three became COLs; and three became LTCs.

Louis "Lou" Descioli served in the Southern European Task Force.

Larry K. Henderson served with the 101st Airborne in Vietnam, was awarded the Bronze Star, and passed away from cancer in 2014.

William "Bill" Malkemes was decorated for combat in Vietnam, earned two master's and an MBA, taught mathematics at West Point, and retired as a COL.

Richard "Dick" Martin became a Combat Engineer.

Paul R. McDowell earned a master's and retired as a LTC.

Thomas "Tom" Page served in the Infantry in the Berlin Brigade, earned a master's and an MBA, taught mathematics at West Point, commanded the 1/26th Infantry, and retired as a COL.

Thomas "Tom" Rozman served in the Infantry in Korea, earned an MBA, and retired as a LTC.

Louis F. "Tim" Sauter served in Field Artillery in Korea, earned an MBA, and retired as a LTC.

William "Bill" Spracher served as an Armor officer in Germany, earned a master's, taught at West Point, served in the western Sahara and the Southern Hemisphere, and retired as a COL.

Michael "Mike" Warren Bain an informal member of Gus Lee's Plebes, earned a medical degree, was on the medical team to care for the Tehran hostages, and retired as a COL.

THE LEE FAMILY

Da-tsien Lee, Gus Lee's mah-mee, was born in Suzhou, China, in 1906 to an aristocratic, scholar-gentry family. She attended St. Mary's Hall in Shanghai, where she excelled in English and became a devout Christian. She refused match-making to wealthy older men and chose the wild boy next door, Tsung-chi Lee. She remained faithful to him after he abandoned her and their children. She fled Japanese-occupied China with three surviving daughters to reach India and the United States, where she reunited with her husband in an unhappy marriage and died from cancer in 1952.

Tsung-chi Lee, Gus Lee's father, was the son of a nouveaux-riche family, rode a Harley-Davidson, and attended St. John's University in Shanghai, "China's Harvard," where he befriended the youngest son of the powerful Soong family. Instead of studying, he read the histories of the West and was expelled for deficiency in engineering after his junior year. He became a Chinese army officer and fighter pilot, fighting the Japanese Empire and the communists, and was in the United States when his wife and daughters found him. He married Edith Swinehart after his wife died. At 59, he began studying engineering, was hired as an engineer three years later and retired at 82. Surrendering his anger, he lived his final months in tranquility, dying at 91 without reconciling with his daughters.

Dr. Mary Lee, M.D., youngest of Gus Lee's three older sisters and only 12 when Edith banished her, lived with eldest sister Elinor and became the academic star, earning master's degrees, a Ph.D., and a medical degree. Mary forgave Gus for not standing by her when Edith evicted her.

Lee Hause, also known as Elinor and Lily, managed the flight of her mother and two sisters from Japanese-occupied China. To escape her father, she joined a nunnery but returned to attend her dying mother. At 23, Elinor rescued Mary, becoming her functional parent in Minneapolis. Elinor managed stores of distinction, was a highly-sought-after interior decorator, a stunning fashion model, and an accomplished pianist.

Ying Lee, Gus Lee's middle sister, worked her way through college, and became a public school teacher, community leader, and renowned political activist who was elected to the Berkeley City Council. In 2015 she was named Woman of the Year in the 15th Assembly District of California at age 83.

Edith Swinehart Lee grew up in Pennsylvania Dutch country, attended college, joined the U.S. Women's Army Corps during World War II, and became a poster girl for wartime bond drives. Deeply loved by Gus's father, she passed away in 1975.

Dr. Toussaint M. Streat, M.D., became an accomplished musician and entered medical school as many of his peers were entering the Army or the prison system, and continues to serve as a physician.

Lieutenant General (Ret) James R. Ellis was a corporal from rural Alabama who at West Point became First Captain, the top-ranking cadet. He commanded two Infantry companies in combat, earned a master's, taught International Relations at West Point, commanded the 10th Mountain Division and Third Army, and was Deputy CINC of CENTCOM. He received over 40 awards, including three Distinguished Service Medals (DSMs), the Silver Star, three Bronze Stars, and the Purple Heart.

Warren Gamaliel Bennis was a decorated World War II Infantry officer, receiving the Purple Heart and Bronze Star for valor. He initiated the academic study of leadership; based its development on character; disproved the myth of the born leader; and challenged a by-management-alone culture. An adviser to four U.S. presidents, he wrote over 60 books. He passed away on 31 July, 2014, at the age of 89.

General (Ret) Frederick M. Franks, Jr., class of 1959, served as an Armor officer in Germany, earned two master's, taught at West Point, was awarded the Silver Star, DFC, Bronze Star for Valor, Bronze Star, Purple Heart for the loss of his left leg, and 43 Air Medals. He remained in active service, and under his command, U.S./Coalition forces achieved victory in Desert Storm. He retired as a four-star general with four DSMs and many other awards and teaches at West Point.

COL (Ret) Charles A. Murray served two combat tours in Vietnam, was Staff Judge Advocate for the elite 82nd Airborne, USAREC, and CENT-COM, received two Bronze Stars, two Legions of Merit, and took an ethical stand that cost him his stars. He became a successful entrepreneur and a renowned Constitutional lawyer.

Acknowledgments

★ ★ ★ ★

To Mrs. Brenda Schwarzkopf for her blessing to write about her husband. To our children, Jessica, Jena, and Eric; son-in-law James Nardella and daughter-in-law Becky Lee and their children (as of this writing), Michael Brian Lee and Jude Francis Nardella; and our blessed "adoptive children," Danny Lee and Esther Lee Adams and her husband, Jeff.

To James R. Ellis, Robert Beahm, Lawrence Rapisarda, James Sullivan, Lawrence White, William Malkemes, Mike Murphy, Steven Childers, Mike Mann, Thomas Pence, Jon Gardner, Jim Adams, Bruce Erion, Jon Anderson, Ross Irvin, Charles Beckwith, Robert Lorbeer, David Clemm, Don Meinhold, my Company A-3 mates, and many unnamed members of the West Point class of 1968 for help with memory. To the West Point class of 1970, for West Point's National Conference on Ethics in America and for the peerless honor of naming me as an Honorary Member of the Class.

To my peerless agents and dear friends Jane Dystel and Miriam Goderich of Dystel & Goderich, New York, for your belief in me as a writer and for giving me the time to be the type of parent that my children required.

To the terrific people at Smithsonian Books, especially Director Carolyn Gleason for overall guidance and matching me to her staff: Christina Wiginton, Editor; book editor Mark Gatlin, and Editorial Assistant Raychel Rapazza, for their loving care and collegiality in helping to shape this book; Matt Litts, Marketing Director, and Leah Enser, Marketing Assistant, for their premier publicizing and marketing of the Bear's lessons to a larger world. Credit for a useful book belong to those above; all errors are mine.

To the faculty and staff and the U.S. Corps of Cadets of the United States Military Academy at West Point for their commitment to character, and to the soldiers and civilians of the United States Army, for love of country and for right action despite manifold fears.

To my coaches, teachers, trainers, bosses, and mentors, who did the brave deeds on the high narrow ridge. Of course, my love and thanks always to Diane, my courageous and beautiful wife, my blessing, soulmate, muse, and inspiration in everything.

To the men and women of the United States Army and the United States Armed Forces, for courageous service in the defense of enduring rightness, for sacrificing independence and self-interest to preserve principles of immutable rightness. Deepest gratitude to those who gave their lives in the cause of that rightness, and to the families that loved them in life and now care for them no less in their absence, that others might be safe.

Notes

★ ★ ★ ★

PREFACE

"IN 1963 AMERICA" According to the December 1973 U.S. Department of Health, Education, and Welfare report "100 Years of Marriage and Divorce Statistics: United States, 1867–1967," divorce rates grew from less than 3% to almost 7% from the late 1800s to the late 1960s. http://www.cdc.gov/nchs/data/series/sr_21/sr21_024.pdf. According to the Pew Research Center, using U.S. Census Bureau statistics, 40% of couples marrying in 2013 included at least one partner who was previously married. In 1960, the number of remarried adults was 14 million; in 1980 it was 22 million. Today, it is almost 42 million. Livingston, Gretchen. "Four-in-Ten Couples are Saying 'I Do,' Again: Growing Number of Adults Have Remarried." Pew Research Center, November 14, 2014. http://www.pewsocialtrends .org/2014/11/14/four-in-ten-couples-are-saying-i-do-again/; Wolfensberger, Donald R. Public Attitudes Toward Congress Over Time. Bipartisan Policy Center, January 24, 2014, p. 10. http://bipartisanpolicy.org/ /library/public-attitudes-toward-congress-over-time/.

"TODAY, RESEARCH REVEALS" http://www.gallup.com/poll/171992/americans-losing -confidence-branches-gov.aspx (accessed June 20, 2014); Center for Academic Integrity data presented at West Point, 2004, by founder Dr. Donald McCabe, professor of business, Rutgers University, and in conversations with the author.

"THE GOVERNMENT ACCOUNTING OFFICE REPORTS" Melendez, Eleazar David. "Financial Crisis Cost Tops $22 Trillion, GAO Says," *Huffington Post*, February 14, 2013; "Prosecuting bankers: Blind justice: Why have so few bankers gone to jail for their part in the crisis?" *The Economist*, May 4, 2013.

"EIGHTY-SEVEN PERCENT OF U.S. MANAGERS" "Report to the Nations on Occupational Fraud and Abuse: 2010 Global Fraud Study." The Association of Certified Fraud Examiners. http://www.acfe.com/uploadedFiles/ACFE_Website/Content/documents/rttn-2010.pdf.

CHAPTER 3

"I LEANED CLOSER TO HIM." MAJ Schwarzkopf cried and I was shocked; I didn't think men did that. Ulysses Grant cried unashamedly when he viewed the body of General James B. McPherson, commander of the Army of the Tennessee and a West Point honor graduate, class of 1853. Deeply religious, McPherson held that to be a soldier, a man had to forget the claims of humanity and to live above the common level of life. Bruce Catton, *This Hallowed Ground*. New York: Doubleday, 1955, pp. 422, 424.

"HISTORY INFORMED HIS FUTURE." Will and Ariel Durant said it was interesting that people are perplexed that world peace has remained elusive, when most people struggle to be at peace with family members, neighbors, and co-workers. "The trouble with most people is that they think with their hopes or fears or wishes rather than with their minds."

SCHOFIELD'S DEFINITION OF DISCIPLINE The discipline which makes the soldiers of a free country reliable in battle is not to be gained by harsh or tyrannical treatment . . . such treatment is far more likely to destroy than to make an army . . . to impart instruction and to give commands in such manner and such a tone of voice to inspire in the soldier no feeling but an intense desire to obey, while the opposite manner . . . cannot fail to excite strong resentment and a desire to disobey. The one mode or the other springs from a corresponding spirit in the breast of the commander. He who feels the respect which is due others cannot fail to inspire in them regard for himself, while he who feels, and hence manifests, disrespect toward others, especially his inferiors, cannot fail to inspire hatred against himself. Major General John M. Schofield, address to the Corps, 11 August 1879.

CHAPTER 5

"I WAS SURE HE WOULD WIN IT FOR US." My cousin Lee Lon-lon, the son of my father's brother, believed that *Dababa*, his uncle (my father) was a superman, for he rode a gigantic motorcycle, flew a warplane, had no fear of men or death, and was certain to defeat Japan by himself.

CHAPTER 6

MARY I was so cowardly that Mary's courageous resistance to Edith's abuse struck me as supernatural. Possessing the fighting spirit I lacked, she became a healer, and I became a soldier.

OUR CONNECTIONS Why did H. Norman Schwarzkopf maintain his interest in me? A possible reason is that he found me amusing. One of the ways I survived on the streets of San Francisco was to be funny. I can't recall what I said, but the Bear would laugh with me.

CHAPTER 12

"THE MORE YOU PRACTICE" The ability to overcome the desire to run and to instead charge uphill is a practiced competence.

CHAPTER 13

THE BEAR'S SURGERY The Bear had back surgery at the West Point Army Hospital in 1968 and spinal surgery in 1971 after his second tour in Vietnam.

CHAPTER 17

RIDGWAY'S SURVEY RESULTS Halberstam, David. *The Best and the Brightest.* New York: Fawcett, 1973, p. 177. Ridgway's team reported that victory in Vietnam would require as many as a million U.S. troops and draft calls of 100,000 a month in a long war in which, unlike in Korea, Vietnamese villagers would not welcome their rescuers.

CHAPTER 18

The Bear was probably quoting Honoré de Balzac.

CHAPTER 20
"DO YOU HEAR WHAT I HEAR?" Lyrics by Nöel Regney and music by Gloria Shayne Baker, performed by the Harry Simeone Chorale, Mercury Records, 1962.

CHAPTER 21
BLACK SUMMIT After retirement from the Army, the Bear would name one of his companies Black Summit, which was a play on his family name and a reference to the mountains of West Point.

CHAPTER 24
"LIKE A ROLLING STONE" Bob Dylan, Columbia Records, 1965.

SGT DOLONITZ After Germany surrendered, First Sergeant Dolonitz was assigned to guard the Nazi defendants during the Nuremberg trials. He stood behind Hermann Göring and faced U.S. prosecutor Edgar Bodenheimer, who would later become my mentor at UC Davis King Hall School of Law. After 31 years of service, Sergeant Major T.L. Dolonitz retired on September 30, 1969, receiving a full brigade Corps of Cadets pass-in-review. When I was a sergeant, I softly told a rowdy gang-leader draftee, "I learned this from my command sergeant major: 'Your soul belongs to God, but your body belongs to me.'"

CHAPTER 27
"WE WOULD RELIEVE 393 RECRUITERS" Pedron, Mark R. "Recruiting with Integrity: The Enlistment Standards Program," *Recruiter Journal*. April 2006. p. 8. http://www.usarec.army.mil/hq/apa/download/RJ/apr06.pdf.

CHAPTER 28
GENERAL DEPUY General William E. DePuy began his Army career as an enlisted man and was commissioned in ROTC from South Dakota State University. During World War II he fought at Normandy and in Germany and commanded the First Infantry Division in Vietnam. He was one of the chief architects who rebuilt the Army after Vietnam. He was awarded two DSCs, three Silver Stars, and two Purple Hearts. He died in 1992 at the age of 72.

CHAPTER 29
MAD MAX General Maxwell Reid Thurman was a principal in the Army's post-Vietnam reformation and credited with revamping the volunteer army that first appeared in Desert Storm. He held many commands and conducted Operation Just Cause in Panama. He died at the age of 64 in 1995.

COLONEL BELL COL Lawrence A. Bell was a 1956 graduate of The Citadel, became an Army aviator, served two tours in Vietnam, was awarded four Bronze Stars, and became the Inspector General for USAREC. He passed away at 79 in 2013.

CHAPTER 31

POTENTIAL WAR CASUALTIES Broder, John M. "U.S. Was Ready for 20,000 Casualties." *The Los Angeles Times*, June 13, 1991; "Potential War Casualties Put at 100,000: Gulf crisis: Fewer U.S. troops would be killed or wounded than Iraq soldiers, military experts predict." *Reuters*, reported in *The Los Angeles Times*, September 05, 1990.

APPROVAL RATINGS Smith, Tom W., "The Gulf War Produced a Jump in Patriotism and Support for Military," *The Baltimore Sun*, January 16, 1994. http://articles.baltimoresun.com/1994–01–16/news/1994016110_1_gulf-war-ground-war-invasion.

"THE TROOPS REVERED HIM" Atkinson, Rick. *Crusade: The Untold Story of the Persian Gulf War*. New York: Houghton Mifflin, 1993, p. 4.

AMERICAN CASUALTIES DeBruyne, Nese F. and Anne Leland. "American War and Military Operations Casualties: Lists and Statistics." Congressional Research Service, January 2, 2015. https://www.fas.org/sgp/crs/natsec/RL32492.pdf.

CHAPTER 36

BENNIS Bennis reflects on how the Army was better than college in developing leaders in his book *Still Surprised: A Memoir of a Life in Leadership*, San Francisco: Jossey-Bass, 2010.

CHAPTER 37

10,000 HOURS Ericsson, K. Anders, Krampe, Ralf Th., and Tesch-Romer, Clemens. "The Role of Deliberate Practice in the Acquisition of Expert Performance." *Psychological Review*, 1993, vol. 100, no. 3, pp. 363–406.

"KINETIC AND DYNAMIC PRACTICE" Sousa, David A. *How the Brain Learns*, 4th Ed. Newbury Park, CA: Corwin, 2011.

"LEADER DEVELOPMENT PROGRAMS" Myatt, Mike. "The #1 Reason Leadership Development Fails," *Forbes*, December 19, 2012.

CHAPTER 39

READING The reading is from a combination of verses, to include 1 Thessalonians 5, Romans 12:10, and 1 Peter 3:9.

CHAPTER 40

General (Ret.) Fred Franks taught me the expression of character as "the possession of inner steel and self-control."

Bibliography

★ ★ ★ ★

Ambrose, Stephen E. *Eisenhower: Soldier, General of the Army, President-elect, 1890–1952*. New York: Simon and Schuster, 1983.

Appleman, Lieutenant Colonel Roy E. *Ridgway Duels for Korea*. College Station, TX: Texas A&M University Press, 1990.

Arbinger Institute. *Leadership and Self-Deception*. San Francisco: Berrett-Koehler, 2000.

Aristotle. *The Nicomachaen Ethics,* Rackham, Harris, translator. Wordsworth Classics, 1996.

Atkinson, Rick. *Crusade: The Untold Story of the Persian Gulf War.* New York: Houghton Mifflin, 1993.

Axelrod, Alan. *Eisenhower on Leadership*. San Francisco: Jossey-Bass, 2006.

Baldwin, Hanson W. *Battles Lost and Won*. Old Saybrook, CT: Konecky & Konecky, 1966.

Barrie, J.M. *Courage: The Rectorial Address Delivered at St. Andrews University*. London: Hodder and Stoughton, 1922.

Bennis, Warren, and Burt Nanus. *Leaders*. New York: Harper and Row, 1985.

Bennis, Warren, with Patricia Ward Biederman. *Still Surprised: A Memoir of a Life in Leadership.* San Francisco: Jossey-Bass, 2010.

Benoit, Remy, editor, and members of the class of 1968. *The West Point Class of 1968: Both Sides of the Wall, Volumes I and II*, 2008 and 2013.

Bentley, James. *Martin Niemöller: The U-boat Commander Turned Pastor Who Defied Hitler, Survived Dachau and Became a Founder of the World Peace Movement*. New York: The Free Press, 1984.

Brookhiser, Richard. *George Washington on Leadership*. New York: Basic Books, 2008.

Bugle Notes. Staff of the Class of 1964, United States Military Academy, 56th Volume, 1964.

Carter, Stephen L. *Integrity*. New York: HarperCollins, 1996.

Catton, Bruce. *This Hallowed Ground*. New York: Doubleday, 1955.

Catton, Bruce. *Grant Takes Command*. New York: Little Brown, 1968.

Colwell, Jack L., and Charles "Chip" Huth. *Unleashing the Power of Unconditional Respect: Transforming Law Enforcement and Police Training*. Boca Raton: CRC Press, 2010.

Cohen, Roger, and Claudio Gatti. *In the Eye of the Storm*. New York: Farrar, Straus & Giroux, 1991.

Collins, James C., and Jerry I. Porras. *Built to Last*. New York: HarperCollins, 1994.

Confucius. *The Analects of Confucius*, translated by Simon Ley. New York: W.W. Norton and Company, 1997.

Connelly, Owen. *On War and Leadership*. Princeton University Press, 2002.

Coughlin, Con. *Saddam: King of Terror.* New York: HarperCollins, 2002.

Covey, Stephen M.R. *The Speed of Trust: The One Thing That Changes Everything*. New York: Free Press, 2006.

Davis, Paul K. *100 Decisive Battles from Ancient Times to the Present*. Oxford University Press, 1999.

Donald, Herbert Donald. *Lincoln*, New York: Cape Random House, 1995.

Durant, Will. *The Story of Civilization: Caesar and Christ*. New York: Simon and Schuster, 1944.

Edwards, James R. *The Divine Intruder*. Colorado Springs, CO: NavPress, 2000.

Edwards, James R. "Important Greek Words in the New Testament." West Coast Presbyterian Pastors Conference, March 31–April 4, 2008, Mount Hermon, CA. Lectures and conversations about rightness and German theologian Ernst Lohmeyer, and his heroic opposition to Adolph Hitler and Josef Stalin. http://wcppc.org/.

Esposito, Brigadier General Vincent J., and Colonel John Robert Elting. *A Military History and Atlas of the Napoleonic Wars*. Santa Barbara, CA: Praeger, 1965.

Fairbank, John K. *The United States and China*. Harvard University Press, 1961.

Fairbank, John K., Edwin O. Reischauer, and Albert M. Craig. *East Asia: Tradition and Transformation*. New York: Houghton Mifflin, 1973.

Fehrenbach, T.R. *This Kind of War: The Classic Korean War History*. Sterling, VA: Brasseys, 1963.

Fei Xiatong. *Xiangtu Zhongguo, From the Soil: The Foundations of Chinese Society*, translated by Gary G. Hamilton and Wang Zheng. Berkeley CA: University of California Press, 1992.

Fischer, David Hackett. *Washington's Crossing*. Oxford University Press, 2004.

Gladwell, Malcom. *David and Goliath*. New York: Little, Brown, 2013.

Greenfield, Kent Roberts, editor. *Command Decisions*. Washington, DC: U.S. Army Center of Military History, 1987.

Guinness, Os. *Steering Through Chaos*. Colorado Springs, CO: NavPress, 2000.

Halberstam, David. *The Best and the Brightest*. New York: Random House, 1969.

The Howitzer, The Annual Publication of the United States Corps of Cadets, for the classes of 1956, 1959, 1965, 1966, 1967, and 1968.

Jacobs, Colonel (Ret) Jack, and Douglas Century. *If Not Now, When?* New York: Penguin, 2008.

Keegan, John. *The Face of Battle*. New York: Penguin, 1976.

Keegan, John. *A History of Warfare*. New York: Alfred A. Knopf, 1993.

Kennett, Lee. *Sherman: A Soldier's Life*. New York: HarperCollins, 2001.

Kitfield, James. *Prodigal Soldiers: How the Generation of Officers Born of Vietnam Revolutionized the American Style of War*. Sterling, VA: Brassey's/AUSA Institute of Land Warfare, 1995.

Lee, Gus, and Elliott-Lee, Diane. *Courage: The Backbone of Leadership*. San Francisco: Jossey-Bass, 2006.

Thomas, Lewis, Fari Amini, and Richard Lannon. *A General Theory of Love*. New York: Vintage, 2000.

MacIntyre, Alasdair. *After Virtue*, 3rd Edition. South Bend, IN: University of Notre Dame Press, 2007.

McCullough, David. *1776*. New York: Simon and Schuster, 2005.

Miller, Walter M., Jr. *A Canticle for Liebowitz*. New York: J.B. Lippincott Publishing, 1959.

Mitchell, George C. *Matthew B. Ridgway: Soldier, Statesman, Scholar, Citizen*. Mechanicsburg, PA: Stackpole, 2002.

Mogan, Bill, editor. *Sons of Slum and Gravy: Stories of the West Point Class of 1962*. AuthorHouse, 2009.

Myrer, Anton. *Once an Eagle*. New York: Holt, Rinehart and Winston, 1968.

Niebuhr, Reinhold. *Moral Man and Immoral Society*. Scribners, 1932.

Nofi, Albert A. *The Waterloo Campaign, June 1815*. Combined Books, 1993.

Pappas, Colonel George S. *Prudens Futuri: The U.S. Army War College, 1901–1967*. Marceline, MO: Walsworth Publishing Company, 1968.

Perry, Mark. *Partners in Command: George Marshall and Dwight Eisenhower in War and Peace*. New York: Penguin, 2007.

Pink, Daniel H. *Drive: The Surprising Truth About What Motivates Us*. New York: Riverhead Books, 2009.

Plato. *The Republic of Plato*. Benjamin Jowett, translator. Cleveland, OH: World Publishing Company, 1946.

Pogue, Forrest. *George C. Marshall: Organizer of Victory 1943–1945*. New York: Viking, 1973.

Ridgway. Matthew B. *Soldier: The Memoirs of Matthew B. Ridgway*, as told to Harold H. Martin. New York: Harper and Brothers, 1956.

Ridgway. Matthew B. *The Korean War*. New York: Doubleday and Company, 1967.

Riker, John Hanwell. *Ethics and the Discovery of the Unconscious*. Albany, NY: State University of New York Press, 1997.

Ruggero, Ed. *Combat Jump: The Young Men Who Led the Assault into Fortress Europe, July 1942*. New York: HarperCollins, 2003.

Schwarzkopf, General H. Norman, with Peter Petre. *It Doesn't Take a Hero*. New York: Linda Grey, 1992.

Sorley, Lewis. *Honor Bright: History and Origins of the West Point Honor Code and System*. London: Learning Solutions, 2009.

Stilwell, Joseph W. *The Stilwell Papers*. New York: William Sloane Associates, 1948.

Sun Tzu. *Bing Fa, The Art of War*. Lionel Giles, translator. Harrisburg, PA: Military Service Publishing Company, 1949.

Studies in Battle Command. Fort Leavenworth, KS: Combat Studies Institute, U.S. Army Command and General Staff College, 2011.

Tan, Amy. *The Kitchen God's Wife*. New York: Putnam, 1991.

United States Military Academy. Register of Graduates and Former Cadets, 2007, Association of Graduates, 2007.

von Clausewitz, Carl. *On War*. New York: Dorset Press, 1968.

von Clausewitz, Carl. *Principles of War*, Hans W. Gatzke, translator. Harrisburg, PA: Military Service Publishing Company, 1942.

von Schell, Captain Adolf. *Battle Leadership*. Quantico, VA: Marine Corps Association, 2007.

von Schlieffen, General Fieldmarshal Count Alfred. *Cannae*. Fort Leavenworth, KS: U.S. Army Command and General Staff School Press, 1931.

Weintraub, Stanley. *15 Stars: Eisenhower, MacArthur, Marshall*. New York: Simon and Schuster, 2007.

Weller, Jac. *Wellington at Waterloo*. London: Greenhill Books, 1967.

White, Colonel Lawrence Kermit "Red". *Red White Memoirs*. Jacksonville, FL: Morris Publishing, 1999.

Williams, William Appleman, editor. *America in Vietnam: A Documentary History*. New York: W.W. Norton and Company, 1989.

Wong, Chester. *Yellow Green Beret: Stories of an Asian-American Stumbling Around U.S. Army Special Forces*. Amazon Digital Services, Inc., 2011.

Wood, Gordon S. *Revolutionary Characters: What Made the Founders Different*. New York: Penguin, 2006.

Wright, N.T. *After You Believe*. New York: HarperOne, 2010.

Index

★ ★ ★ ★

A

Adams, James R. (USMA 1968),
37, 59, 138, 286, 293
Adamski, Lieutenant Colonel Richard G., 157
Advanced Camp, 157–58
agoge, 63
Albrecht, Captain Warren Harry
Rudolph (USMA 1966), 24–27, 46
Alexander the Great, 43, 199
Altemose, Colonel James "Moose"
(USMA 1968), 123, 286
Ancient Greece: Achaemenids, 76; *agoge*,
63; Alexander the Great, 43, 199;
homothumadon, 51; Spartan training, 63;
Troy, 24, 64; Xerxes, 76. *See also* Socrates
Anderson, Marian, 79
Angelou, Maya, 215–16; freedom, 213
Arab world, 199–204, 208–10, 226–27,
273. *See also* Iran; Saudi Arabia
Archer, Major General Caleb J., 189–90
Aristotle, 63, 260–61
Army of South Vietnam (ARVN), 52–53, 113
Arnold, Benedict, 21–22, 92, 143
Art of War, The, 3, 14. *See also* Sun Tzu
Arvin, Captain Carl Robert (USMA 1965), 132
ARVN. *See* Army of South
Vietnam (ARVN)
Aufidus River, 20–21, 53. *See
also* Battle of Cannae
Augustine of Hippo, 7, 23

B

Baby Boomers, 5, 151, 250
Bachelor Officers Quarters (BOQ),
15–16, 120, 136, 166, 256–57, 282
Bain, Colonel Mike "Poo Bear" (USMA
1970), 290; family in Texas, 148; at
the Presidio of San Francisco, 166;
at West Point, 47–48, 69, 135, 159
Bain, Linda Leigh, 160, 166–69
Bank of Canton, 66–67
"Bastard Brigade" (29th Infantry,
Omaha Beach), 66
Battle of Cannae, 20–21, 207–10,
228, 237, 267, 269; Aufidus River,
20–21, 53; Schwarzkopf on,
66, 85–86, 126–29, 200, 203
Battle of Crécy, 117, 206–7, 210, 255
Battle of Duc Co, 80–83, 184
Battle of the Pyramids, 44–45, 209
Battle of Waterloo, 85, 227
Be All You Can Be, 179, 203
Beahm, Brigadier General Robert
"Country Moon" (USMA 1968),
138, 159, 204, 285–86, 293
Beatles, the, 5, 155–56
Beau Geste, 25, 149
Becoming a Leader, 249
behaviors: alignment with principles, 268;
behavior modification training, 253;
behaviors of character vs. behaviors of
relationship, 202; building character and,
90, 202, 248, 256; commitment to good,
283; confronting bad, 100, 265; corporate
accountability and, 242; courage and, 258,
265–66, 281–83; cowardly, 14; defining
honorable service through, 189–90; as life
standards, 59; persistence of bad, 275; self-
sacrifice and, 261; teaching, 256, 261–62,

265; war casualties from criminal, 158. *See also* character; courage; cowardice

Bell, Colonel Lawrence A., 179, 189, 297

Bennis, Warren, 249–54

Berlin Brigade, 101, 289

Bible, the, 37, 105, 224

Bishop Myriel, 91, 93–94

blessings, 59

Bodenhamer, James D. (USMA 1968), 285

Boggy Creek Camp, 219, 236

Bonaparte, Napoleon, 43, 51, 92, 126, 128, 141, 227–28

BOQ. *See* Bachelor Officers Quarters (BOQ)

borders: between Cambodia and Vietnam, 112; between China and Vietnam, 103–4; between Iraq and Kuwait, 200–201, 208; Schwarzkopf along the Cambodian border with Vietnam, 6, 77–78, 79, 112–18, 184, 210

Bowland, Colonel Warren F. (USMA 1968), 70

Brezhnev, Leonid, on war in Korea, 164

Buckner, Simon Bolivar, 86. *See also* Camp Buckner

Buddy Check, 30, 242, 252, 265

Bue, David (USMA 1968), 29

Bush, President George H. W.: approval rating, 211; Operation Desert Storm, 202, 204–5, 269; targeted by Islamic fundamentalists, 221

C

Cadet Chapel, 21–22, 56, 129, 215, 222

Cadet prayer, 54, 55, 56; quote from, 54

Caesar, Julius, 7, 71, 92, 126

Cambodia, 6, 77–78, 79, 112–18, 184, 210

Camp Buckner, 45, 56, 86–87, 99, 132, 136, 139, 151, 158

Camp Casey, 162, 164, 166

careerism, 82–83, 114, 116, 193, 231, 233

Carlson, Karin, 32, 75, 85; Christmas with, 123; last visit at Berkeley with, 155; separation from, 63–65, 69

Carlson, Lieutenant Colonel Richard G. (USMA 1968), 70

Carlyle, Thomas, v

Carter, Stephen, 22

Central Guard Room, 92, 142, 157

Cerne, Antone "Stoney" (USMA 1968), 8, 46, 286

Cervantes, Miguel de, 97, 279

Chamberlain, Neville, 89

character, 55–56; accountability and the Buddy Check, 30; assessing good, 162; behaviors of character vs. behaviors of relationship, 202; building by working at fears, 33; building through behavior, 90, 202, 248, 256; character development in curriculum at West Point, 255–58; conscience and, 55, 75; cure yourself, 55; Henry Beecher Ward quote on holding one's self to a higher standard, 13; leadership and, 2; as the possession of inner steel and self-control, 298; practicing until you can teach it, 56; Socrates on changing one's self first, 69; *táoyě qīngcǎo* (to forge character), 6, 63, 281

character development, 6, 11, 30, 33, 42, 54–56, 63, 152, 158, 281

Cheney, Dick, 277

Chiang Kai-shek, 61, 66–67

chih huo (matchmaker), 60

Childers, Stephen Douglas "Ping" (USMA 1968), 30, 37, 47–48, 69, 101, 131, 135, 137–38, 286

China Boy, 195–97, 212, 224, 234; advance royalties for, 196; Amy Tan quote in, 195; Christianity and, 224; Schwarzkopf reading, 212, 224, 234

China: Chiang Kai-shek, 61, 66–67; Great Leap Forward, 193; Great Wall, 65; H. H. Kung, 66–67; *Kuomintang*, 66; Long March, 66; Mao Tse-tung, 61, 66; Soong family, 66–67, 290; Sun Yat-sen, 66–67; Vietnam and, 103, 109. *See also* Chinese culture

Chinatown (San Francisco), 40, 61, 67

Chinese culture: *chih huo* (matchmaker), 60; *guanxi* (face), 74, 218; influence on Vietnamese culture, 60; *ji hui* (inauspicious talk), 132, 182; *jia* (the clan), 60, 155; *ren-che* (person who endures, *ninja*), 17, 25; Three Followings, 60–61; *yuing chi* (bad karma), 184. *See also* China; Confucius; Sun Tzu

Clausewitz, Carl von, 51
Clark, Brigadier General Ronald, 256
coalitions: Desert Storm, 278; Eisenhower's
    ability to build, 114, 199, 206–7; General
    Marshall's view on, 126–27; lack of
    true coalitions in Vietnam, 127
communications: about Vietnam,
    160; courageous, 247, 265; in
    military tactics, 43, 133, 203, 209;
    strategic systems in Korea, 162
Confucius: acting is understanding,
    259; emulating superior people,
    90, 125; failure to cultivate moral
    power, 31; knowledge is easy, action
    difficult, 83, 275; love and urging
    people onward, 24; Three Followings,
    60–61; Wen-lin (Forest of Pens),
    63. See also Chinese culture
Connelly Investigation, 175–76, 189, 203, 238
Connelly, Brigadier General Douglas, 175–76
conscience: in business, 244–45; character
    and, 55, 75; child's, 38; cowardice and,
    263, 265; good, 122; honor and, 75;
    Schwarzkopf as external, 1; stirring,
    102; troubled, 72; weak, 11, 22
contentment, 59; Baby Boomer discontent,
    151; with half-truths, 54, 56
core values: corporate, 242–43;
    Food, Avoid Pain, Play, 59
Cota Sr., Major General Norman
    (USMA 1917), 66, 82
courage, 247–51, 260–66, 282–83;
    addressing wrongs, 100, 163; always
    love your troops, 68; in battle, 255–
    56; behaviors showing, 258, 265–
    66, 281–83; biblical quote on, 273;
    courageous communication, 247,
    260–61, 265; David and Goliath, 37,
    183; Eleanor Roosevelt on, 281; fear
    and, 78, 249; as a hard decision, not an
    easy emotion, 122; Ke ji fu li (subdue
    self, do right), 41; Lao Tzu quote on
    love and, 162; Miguel de Cervantes
    quote on losing, 97; practicing courage
    like building muscle memory, 262,
    265, 281; quotes about, 249, 275; as

a requirement for leadership, 2; role
    of a single leader, 268–69; speaking
    truth to authority, 100, 106, 171, 207;
    West Point founded for people of, 38,
    264. See also character; cowardice
Courage: The Backbone of Leadership, 248–49
Cousin Brucie, 71, 286
cowardice: children's conscience knowing
    right from, 38; conscience and, 38,
    263, 265; as a danger to others, 78; as
    an easy emotion, not a hard decision,
    122; excuses are cowardly, 14, 18; God's
    message to Joshua, 274; inability to
    lead and, 248; mousing out, 35; role
    of fear in, 184, 249, 265; Wǔ shí bù
    xiào bǎi bù (the soldier who runs away
    jeers the one who ran a few paces
    more), 88. See also character; courage
Crécy, 117, 206–7, 210, 255
Cultural Revolution, 193
Cyrus the Great, 76, 127

D

David and Goliath, 37, 185
De Gaulle, Charles, 106
Demosthenes, 51
DePuy, General William E., 181, 202, 205, 297
Descioli, Lou (USMA 1970), 28, 289
Desert Shield, 201–2, 210, 287
Desert Storm, 1, 204–11; coalition of,
    278; General Fred Franks' winning
    maneuver at, 256, 267, 292; Israel
    during, 226; Schwarzkopf's nightly
    prayer during, 198; unlike Vietnam,
    203. See also Hussein, Saddam; United
    States Central Command (CENTCOM)
Dibenedetto, Captain Michael
    A. (USMA 1968), 70
Difford, Brigadier General "Big Diff"
    Courtland, 97–99, 101–2, 261, 254–65
discernment, 56
DMZ (Demilitarized Zone), 8,
    119, 162–64, 179–80
do the right thing, 25, 57, 71, 72,
    77, 78, 80, 114, 173, 243, 244

"Do You Hear What I Hear?"
123–24, 210, 278, 297
Dolonitz, Sergeant Major T. L.,
17, 145–46, 154, 169, 297
draft, 170–71
Duc Co, 80–83, 184
Dupuy, Trevor, 205
Durant, Will, 20, 98, 295
Duty Honor Country, 41, 75, 194, 278

E

Edward III, 117, 206–7, 210, 255
Edwards, Bob, 201
Eisenhower, Dwight D., 2–3, 92; choosing
not to intervene in Vietnam, 106;
coalition building under, 114, 199, 206–7
Elizabeth II, Queen of England, 211, 225
Elliott-Lee, Diane: advising on Gus Lee's
writings, 194, 248–49; first pregnancy,
172–74; full-time work, 193; marriage to
Gus Lee, 167–69. *See also* Jessica Michelle
(Lee's daughter) *under* Lee family
Ellis, Lieutenant General James Raiford
(USMA 1962): joining Endūr, 220, 222,
224–25; Schwarzkopf and, 218–19, 236,
238, 269, 273, 276–77, 280–81, 291
Endūr, Inc., 218–19, 221, 367
engineering: learning from Schwarzkopf,
31–35, 44; Lee Tsung-chi (Lee's father)
and, 121, 123, 290; Lee's difficulties
with, 8–9, 14, 46, 133, 134, 136–39, 142;
mandatory at West Point, 6, 8, 127–28;
tutoring from Rap, 136; usefulness
in military tactical problems, 44;
Warren Truss Bridge Problem, 33–35
Ericson, William F., II (USMA 1968), 159
Eschaton (the end of time), 14
ethics. *See* Willoughby, Colonel D.
Hamilton; United States Army
Recruiting Command (USAREC)

F

Fairbank, John K., 13
fear, 73–78; building character by working at
what you fear, 33; cowardice and, 249–50;
crossing one's own river of fear, 117–18,

284; doing right despite, 273–74; doing
the harder right, 54–56, 72, 78, 89, 100,
153–54, 187–88; Eleanor Roosevelt on, 281;
fear excused as a mental block, 33; Maya
Angelou quote on, 213; physiological
fight or flight response to, 9; reminds us
to use courage, 78; of social rejection and
isolation, 7, 101; Sophocles quote about, 73
Forest of Pens (*Wen-lin*), 63
Fort Ord, 148–49
fraggings, 170–71
Franklin, Benjamin, on conscience, 122
Franks, General Fred (USMA 1959),
202, 207, 256, 267, 277–78
Fua, Sergeant First Class William
"Rainbow," 172–74

G

Gallo, Tony, 23, 24, 69–70, 73
Gardner, Jon (USMA 1968), 8, 286, 293
Genghis Khan, 60
Gladwell, Malcolm, 183
gossip, 55, 99, 243, 252, 261, 263
Grange, Lieutenant General
David E., Jr., 164, 170, 180
Grant, General Ulysses (USMA 1843),
2, 22, 82, 92, 199, 205, 207, 295
Great Leap Forward, 193
Great Wall, 65
Green, Phyllis, 84
Guan Yu, 38
guanxi (face), 74, 218
Gulf War. *See* Desert Shield; Desert Storm

H

H. H. Kung, 66–67
Hannibal. *See* Battle of Cannae
harder right, 54–56, 72, 78, 89,
100, 153–54, 187–88
Harrelson, Keith "Hog" (USMA 1968), 8
Harry Simeon Chorale, 297. *See also*
"Do You Hear What I Hear?"
Hawley, Richard Aspinall (USMA
1968), 8, 159, 287
Hebb, Donald Olding, 42
Henderson, Larry (USMA 1970), 28, 130, 289

"Hey Jude," 155–56
Hickey, Colonel Pennell J. (USMA 1949), 139
Hittner, Barry "Curve-wrecker"
    (USMA 1968), 8, 159, 285, 287
Hoffer, Eric, 64
homothumadon (unique unity), 51
Honor and Duty, 254, 274
Honor Code at West Point, 108;
    conscience and, 75; cool on Honor,
    72, 175; Honor Code Representative,
    110; live it all your life, 187; lying,
    110; not honorable to tolerate
    cheating, 114–15; as training, 56, 72
Hotel Thayer, 84
Hugo, Victor, 91
Hussein, Saddam, 198–202, 204–5, 208–11;
    crimes against humanity by, 225–
    26; eviction of UN inspectors, 217;
    provoking Israel with Scuds, 226. *See
    also* Desert Shield; Desert Storm

I

Iaconis, Major Christopher S. (USMA 1968), 70
imaginary thinking (magical
    thinking), 80, 109, 129, 153, 182
incurvatus in se, 7, 23
Inmingun (North Korean Army),
    50, 163–64, 172
integrity: developing in others, vi; in corporate
    management, 243, 250; inflexible integrity
    of selflessness, 19; leadership and, 2;
    requirements of, 243, 250; serving with,
    95, 255, 288. *See also* Honor Code
Iran, 39–40, 62, 76, 125, 199–
    201, 204, 208–9, 225–26
Irvin, William Ross II "Wrinkles"
    (USMA 1968), 8, 44–45, 288, 293

J

JAG. *See* Judge Advocate General (JAG)
Japan: culture of, 60; invasion of China in
    World War II, 61, 63, 66, 201, 290, 291;
    invasion of Vietnam in World War II, 52,
    104; the "opening" of, 202; Pearl Harbor,
    10, 98, 219; after World War II, 227
Jean, Raymond (brother-in-law), 65

Jefferson, Thomas, 5, 7, 141
ji hui (inauspicious talk), 132, 182
jia (the clan), 60, 155
Jomini, General Antoine-Henri, 51
Joy Luck Club, 195
Judge Advocate General (JAG): Lee's
    time in Korea as, 162–63, 174–76; role
    in United States Army Recruiting
    Command (USAREC), 179–81. *See
    also* Murray, Charles A.; United States
    Army Recruiting Command (USAREC);
    Willoughby, Colonel D. Hamilton
judgement, 56
Jun tzu (man of moral rectitude), 98

K

Kai Tu, David, 195
Kay, Chris Armstrong, 243
Ke ji fu li (subdue self and do right), 41
Keane, General John M. "Jack," 277
Kennedy, John F., 31–32, 67, 120
Kim Il-sung, 164
Kong Fuzi. *See* Confucius
Korea, Republic of (ROK): armed forces
    of, 172, 174; Camp Casey, 162, 164,
    166; DMZ (Demilitarized Zone), 8,
    119, 162–64, 179–80; Imjin River, 163;
    Korean CIA (KCIA), 172–74, 180; Lee's
    time as Judge Advocate General (JAG),
    162–63, 174–76; *Pueblo* incident, 163–64
Krall, Diana, 107
Kulikov, Marshall of the Soviet
    Union Viktor, 210–11
Kuomintang, 66

L

Lao Tzu, 91, 162
Las Vegas, 183, 186, 188, 265
Lawrence of Arabia, 125
leaders of character, 2
leadership: doing the harder right
    (Schwarzkopf's First Law), 54–56, 72,
    78, 89, 100, 153–54, 187–88, 235; how it
    turns hope into reality through vision,
    251; inspiring others to be better men,
    95; it's always about, 53–57, 126, 158, 171,

211, 235, 248, 265; leading by example (I
can do it, so can you), 115; living above
the common level of life, 55–56, 111,
254, 295; Marian Anderson quote on the
needs of the led, 79; matching strength
to weakness, 53; as a sacred responsibility,
94; take no credit, take responsibility
(Schwarzkopf's Second Law), 56–58, 68,
80, 248; what you ignore you endorse, 100
Lee family: ancestral roots of, 40; Da-tsien
(Lee's mother), 6, 37, 62, 66, 191, 193,
290; Dr. Mary Zhu (Lee's sister), 37–38,
40, 62, 191, 193, 290–91; Edith Swinehart
Lee (Lee's stepmother), 7, 11, 32, 60, 65,
67, 75, 110, 121, 193; Elinor Hause (Lee's
sister), 62–63, 193, 290–91; Eric Michael
(Lee's son), 192; fear, 37–38; Gung-gung
(Lee's paternal grandfather), 19, 61; Jane
(Lee's cousin), 193; Jena Marie (Lee's
daughter), 192; Jessica Michelle (Lee's
daughter), 177, 179, 181–82, 190–92,
223; Jude Francis Nardella (grandson),
293; Lon-lon (Lee's cousin), 193, 195–96,
296; Lulu (Lee's cousin), 193; Mikey
Michael Brian Lee (grandson), 293;
Uncle Shen, 14, 41, 66, 88; Ying (Lee's
sister), 62–63, 193, 291. See also Elliott-
Lee, Diane; Lee Tsung-chi (Lee's father)
Lee Tsung-chi (Lee's father), 18–19, 34,
77, 123–24, 146, 193–96, 290; Bank of
Canton and the Soong family, 66–67; on
children, 168, 190; Daisy Tan and, 195–96;
engineering and, 121, 123, 290; joining
the U.S. Army, 7; marriage to Edith
Swinehart, 7, 11, 37–41, 53, 65, 67, 75,
110, 121, 193, 290; math tutoring, 34; as
Nationalist Chinese army officer in World
War II, 32, 66, 194; U.S. Army Infantry
ring, 219–20; working later in life, 123–24
Lee, Gus: dating life, 84–85, 88–90, 107–10;
deputy district attorney, 191; difficulties
with math and engineering, 8–9, 14, 46,
133, 134, 136–39, 142; early childhood
trauma, 38; fear of social rejection and
isolation, 7, 101; insights on Vietnam,
70–72, 75–77, 103–4; as Judge Advocate
General (JAG), 162–63, 174–76, 179–81;
letters from Schwarzkopf, 152–53, 212;
marriage to Diane, 167–69; medical
waivers, 6, 131–32, 142–43; struggles
with alcohol, 191–92; tasked with
investigating foreign recruitment in
Army, 172–76; Temporarily on Academic
Duty (TOAD), 160–61, 223, 238, 258,
272; time in Korea as Judge Advocate
General (JAG), 162–63, 172–76; tutoring
from Schwarzkopf, 31–35, 44–46; as West
Point's Chair of Character Development,
256–58. See also China Boy; Courage: The
Backbone of Leadership; Elliott-Lee, Diane;
Honor and Duty; Lee family; YMCA
(Young Men's Christian Association)
Lincoln High School, San Francisco, 63–64
Lincoln, Abraham, 26, 185, 265, 282
Lindbergh, Charles, 49
Lombardi, Coach Vince, 46
Long March, 66
Lorbeer, Colonel Robert C. "More
Beer" (USMA 1968), 1, 8, 10, 47,
101, 138, 159, 204, 285, 286, 293
Lost Fifties barracks, 92, 94, 96

M

MacArthur, General Douglas,
92, 199, 212, 220, 228
MACV. See Military Assistance
Command Vietnam (MACV)
magical thinking (imaginary
thinking), 80, 109, 129, 153, 182
Maillard, William, 63
Malkemes, Colonel William (USMA
1970), 28, 30, 289, 293
Mao Tse-tung, 61, 66
Marshall, General George C., 126–27, 129, 199
Martin, Richard (USMA 1970), 28, 289
McCaffrey, General Barry R. (USMA
1964), 207, 227, 267–68, 274
McCreary, William (USMA 1965), 47
McDowell, Paul (USMA 1970), 28, 289
Meinhold, Don H. (USMA
1970), 163–64, 289, 293

Middle East, 199–204, 208–10, 226–27, 273. *See also* Iran; Saudi Arabia
Military Assistance Command Vietnam (MACV), 43–44, 53
Military organizations. *See* United States Army; United States Army Recruiting Command (USAREC); United States Central Command (CENTCOM); West Point
Mongols, 40, 60, 65, 104, 226
Murphy, Lieutenant Colonel Maurice E. "Mike" (USMA 1968), 159, 285, 287
Murray, Colonel Charles A. (USMA 1962), 175–76, 178–82, 185–90, 218–20, 238, 256, 292
Myrer, Anton, 116–17

N

Nader, Frank R. (USMA 1968), 86–87
Nash, Major General William L., Jr. (USMA 1968), 204
National Conference on Ethics in America (NCEA), 95, 255, 288
NATO. *See* North Atlantic Treaty Organization (NATO)
NCEA. *See* National Conference on Ethics in America (NCEA)
NCOs. *See* non-commissioned officers (NCOs)
New Yorker, The, 194
Newman, Paul, 219, 236
Nimitz, Admiral Chester A., 199
ninja (person who endures), 17, 25
Nixon, Richard M., 170
Noll, Major Wallace (USMA 1953), 142, 145–47
non-commissioned officers (NCOs), 51, 61–62, 87–88, 170
North Atlantic Treaty Organization (NATO), 106, 127
North Korean Army (*Inmingun*), 50, 163–64, 172
NPR (National Public Radio), 201
Nunn, Senator Sam, 175

O

oath at West Point, 4, 15, 114, 169, 284–85
Odierno, General Raymond T. (USMA 1976), 277

Ofanto River. *See* Aufidus River *under* Battle of Cannae
O'Keefe, Mr., high school counselor, 64
Once an Eagle, 116–17
Ord, Major General Edward Otho Cresap (USMA 1837), 148–49
Orwell, George, 46, 177

P

Page, Colonel Thomas (USMA 1970), 28, 289
PAVN. *See* People's Army of Vietnam (PAVN)
Pence, Colonel Thomas E. (USMA 1968), 204, 287
People's Army of Vietnam (PAVN), 44, 81, 112
Peterman, Prof. Lawrence, 157, 159
Peters, Colonel Michael "Tree" (USMA 1968), 131–32, 138, 286
Phillip VI, 117, 256
Plato, 260–61
Powell, Colin, 277–78
practice, 73, 101, 127, 203, 252, 260-61, 265; 10,000 hours required to master a skill, 259; again and again, 152, 234, 259, 262; as behavior modification, 253; Bear required Lee to practice, 261-64; character requires, 58; makes perfect, 46; of courageous behaviors, 78; required in a meritocracy, 253; setting the example, 234; to codify behaviors of courage, 248; to form habits of courage, 90; we are what we practice, 264
prejudice, 86, 88
principles, v, 39, 114, 118, 158, 235. 242. 248, 268, 273, 280, 282, 283; conduct under pressure, 2, 190; West Point, 278
Pueblo incident, 163–64

Q

quod erat demonstrandum (QED), 33, 53

R

Ramirez, Frank, 241
Rapisarda, Lieutenant Colonel Lawrence Anthony "Rap" (USMA 1968), 8, 46, 134–38, 162–63, 286
rear echelon "personnel" (REMFs), 51

Reed, Randy, 156

Reichert, William F. (USMA 1968), 70, 284, 287

REMFs. *See* rear echelon "personnel" (REMFs)

ren-che (person who endures, *ninja*), 17, 25

Ridgway, General Matthew B. (USMA 1917), 106, 171

Riek, Jeffrey (USMA 1968), 8, 284

river of fear, 117–18

Rock Bottom Remainders, 213–14

Rogers, General Bernard William (USMA 1943), 171

ROK. *See* Korea, Republic of (ROK)

Romance of the Three Kingdoms (*Sanguozhi Pinghua*), 38

Roosevelt, Eleanor, 281

Roosevelt, Theodore, 22, 149

root cause solution, 89–90

Rosenthal, Herbert M., J. D., Lee's boss, 197

ROTC (Reserve Officers' Training Corps), 155–59, 271

Rozman, Lieutenant Colonel Thomas (USMA 1970), 28, 289

S

Sackett, Captain David Lee "Snake" (USMA 1968), 8–9, 56–57, 69, 284, 287

Saudi Arabia, 200–201, 208–11, 226

Sauter, Timothy (USMA 1970), 28, 30, 289

Schofield's Definition of Discipline, 25, 296

Schwarzkopf family: Brenda Holsinger (wife), 111, 198, 238, 273–73, 280, 293; Christian (son), 223, 280; Cindy (daughter), 223; Jessica (daughter), 223, 278, 280; Ruth (sister), 65–66; Sally (sister), 65. *See also* Schwarzkopf, Major General Herbert Norman (USMA 1917, Schwarzkopf's father)

Schwarzkopf, H. Norman, v–vii; accolades after Gulf War, 211; AirLand Battle commitment, 203; as Army football player, 260; on the Battle of Cannae, 66, 85–86, 126–29, 200, 203; Battle of Duc Co, 80–83, 184; Bear, his dog, 22; as a cadet, 17; along the Cambodian border with Vietnam, 6, 77–78, 79, 112–18,

184, 210; on careerism, 82–83, 114, 116, 193, 231, 233; as Commander-in-Chief (CINC) of U.S. Central Command (CENTCOM), 1–2, 198–211; charities for children with Paul Newman, 221, 236; comparing Desert Storm to Vietnam War, 203; death of, vi, 273–80; doing the harder right, 54–56, 72, 78, 89, 100, 153–54, 187–88; First Law of Leadership (do the harder right), 54–56, 72, 78, 89, 100, 153–54, 187–88, 235; "Five D's," 158; *It Doesn't Take a Hero*, 37; letters to Gus Lee, 152–53, 212; nicknames, vi, 50–51; nightly prayer during Desert Storm, 198; physical condition after Vietnam, 15, 31–32, 296; reading *China Boy*, 212, 224, 234; root cause analysis, 89–90; schooling, 49; Second Law of Leadership (take no credit, take responsibility), 56–58, 68, 80, 248; spending time at Christmas with Lee, 119–24; targeted by Islamic fundamentalists, 221; Tehran with his father, 68, 70, 76–77; on television, 1–3, 225–26; Temporarily on Academic Duty (TOAD), 10–11, 17, 114, 158; *Trau Nuoc* ("Water Buffalo") nickname, 50–51; tutoring Lee, 31–35, 44–46; Vietnamese Airborne, 43–45, 49–53, 80, 125–29, 237–38. *See also* character; courage; cowardice; leadership; Schwarzkopf family; Schwarzkopf, Major General Herbert Norman (USMA 1917, Schwarzkopf's father)

Schwarzkopf, Major General Herbert Norman (USMA 1917, Schwarzkopf's father): Crime of the Century, 39, 49; death of, 65; *Gang Busters* radio program, 39; as a source of courage, 39

"Sergeant Rock," 86–90, 99, 101, 136, 149, 262

"Serve With Integrity," USMA 1970 Class Motto, 95, 255, 288

Shaw, George Bernard, 103

Shen, Uncle S. Y., 14, 41, 66, 88

Sherman, General of the Army
William T. (USMA 1840), 2, 51,
82, 92, 148–49, 158, 231
Socrates: on contentment, 59; on faults,
125; on honest politicians, 231; on
human weaknesses, 260; on inner
beauty, 119; military experience of, 259;
on moving oneself, 69; on prayers and
blessings, 191; on self-sacrifice, 261
Solomon, Sergeant Major Kalei, 149–50, 154
Soong family, 66–67, 290
Spanish Moorish War, 104
Spracher, Colonel William
(USMA 1970), 28, 290
State Bar of California, 189, 196
Streat, Dr. Toussaint M., 62, 194, 291
strength: Lao Tzu quote on, 162;
matching strength to weakness, 53
Sudduth, Major General Leroy
(USMA 1956), 99–100, 278
Sullivan, James "Sully" Patrick
(USMA 1970), 90–93, 288, 293
Sun Tzu: applied to the Middle East,
203–4, 237; *The Art of War*, 3, 14; as
basis of guerilla tactics in Vietnam,
104; on confusing the enemy, 3, 14;
on intelligence gathering, 203–4; on
knowing yourself and your enemy,
15; on leadership, 1, 49, 112, 210;
on protracted wars, 203, 267
Sun Yat-sen, 66–67
SuperSite Colorado. *See* Endūr, Inc.

T

Tan, Amy, 195–96, 213
Tan, Daisy, 195–96
Táoyě qingcāo (to forge character), 6, 63, 281
Temporarily on Academic Duty
(TOAD), 10–11; Lee's time, 160–61,
223, 238, 258, 272; Schwarzkopf's
time, 10–11, 17, 114, 158
Thayer, Sylvanus (USMA 1808), 8–9, 92, 128
Three Followings, 60–61
Thurman, General Max Reid, 39,
178–81, 189, 206, 224, 238, 297
Tirey, Colonel James R., 157–58

TOAD. *See* Temporarily on
Academic Duty (TOAD)
Tolkien, J. R. R., 127
Torres, Major Arthur "Arturo" Frank
(USMA 1968), 8, 15, 36, 47, 69–
72, 99, 101, 135, 138, 285
torture, 173–75; during the Vietnam War, 80;
for intel, 80, 173–75; Japanese occupation
of China, 66; by Saddam Hussein, 201,
225–26; in South Korean Army, 173–75
Toynbee, Arnold Joseph, 98
Trinkle, Mike, U.S. Army advisor, 77–78
Trophy Point, 4, 15, 20, 22–
23, 143, 273, 276, 282
True Believer, 64
trust, 45
Tu, David Kai, 195

U

Union of Soviet Socialist Republics
(USSR), 233; Gorbachev's *glasnost*, 199;
involvement in Vietnam, 52, 104; Korean
War and, 164; in the Middle East, 200,
202, 207–8, 233; Red Army, 101, 127
United States: disease of short-term
thinking, 85; key to success in World
War II, 126; in the 1960s, v;
public confidence in, v. *See
also* United States Army
United States and China, 13
United States Army: Airborne School, 174,
219; AirLand Battle doctrine, 203, 260; the
draft army, 170–71; General William E.
DePuy, 181, 202, 205, 297; lead reformers
in, 204–5; National Training Center, 203;
9th Infantry Division, 160; Ranger School,
146, 158–59, 174; reform and rebuild after
Vietnam, 171; 2nd Infantry Division, 162,
170; as seventh largest standing army
in world, 202; 24th Infantry Division,
207, 274. *See also* United States Army
Recruiting Command (USAREC); United
States Central Command (CENTCOM)
United States Army Recruiting Command
(USAREC): Armed Services Vocational
Aptitude Battery (ASVAB), 172; *Be All*

You Can Be motto, 179, 203; Captain Rob Van Hooser, 179, 190; Category IV volunteer Army recruits, 175; role of JAGs, 179–81; 6th Brigade, 171–72, 175–76, 189. *See also* Murray, Charles A.; Willoughby, Colonel D. Hamilton

United States Central Command (CENTCOM), 1–2, 198–211. *See also* Desert Shield; Desert Storm

University of California, Berkeley, 62–63, 154–56

University of California, Davis, 156–60, 271; Adamski, Lieutenant Colonel Richard G., 157; Advanced Camp, 157–58; ROTC (Reserve Officers' Training Corps), 155–59, 271; Tirey, Colonel James R., 157–58

University of Southern California (USC), 31, 157, 249–51

USC. *See* University of Southern California (USC)

USMA (United States Military Academy). *See* West Point

USSR. *See* Union of Soviet Socialist Republics (USSR)

V

Vietnam War, 5, 7–8, 203–10; Army of South Vietnam (ARVN), 52–53, 113; Battle of Duc Co, 80–83, 184; breaching the greater principles of war, 129; Chinese cultural influence on, 60; end of the draft, 170–71; fall of Saigon, 232–33; false projections and media smokescreen, 3; French ruling class in, 65; Lee's classmates and plebes' service in, 286–92; Lee's insight into, 70–72, 75–77, 103–4; longstanding hatred of the Chinese, 103–6; Military Assistance Command Vietnam (MACV), 43–44, 53; no true coalition in, 127; Peers Investigation of My Lai, 175; People's Army of Vietnam (PAVN), 44, 81, 112; public opinion and protests against, 48–49, 170–71; rear echelon "personnel"

(REMFs), 51; Schwarzkopf along the Cambodian border, 6, 77–78, 79, 112–18, 184, 210; Schwarzkopf's physical condition after, 15, 31–32, 296; Viet Cong (VC), 50, 77–78, 80, 199, 204; West Point faculty and graduate rotation with tours in, 136

Vietnamese Airborne, 43–45, 49–53, 80, 237–38; Colonel Kha, 43, 50–51; Colonel Truong, 43–44, 51, 81; courage, 51–52; Sergeant Hung, 36, 50

Villanueva, Hector, 62

virtue, 5, 72, 264, 282

vision: John Whitcomb's vision at Endūr, 218, 245; lack of, contributing to failure in Vietnam, 207; as a principle of war, 85, 270; true higher moral purpose, 51; turning hope into reality, 251

Vuono, General Carl E. (USMA 1957), 202, 233, 277

W

warfare: magical thinking (imaginary thinking), 80, 109, 129, 153, 182; principles of war, 85, 129, 202–3, 237, 270; protracted wars, 105, 203, 270. *See also* Ancient Greece; coalitions; Confucius; *specific battles and conflicts*; Sun Tzu

Warren Truss Bridge Problem, 33–35

Washington, George: cutting down the cherry tree, 114; Horatio Gates and treachery, 143; refusing kingship, 114; Revolutionary War strategy, 21; West Point and, 7, 143, 257, 263

Waterloo, 85, 227

Waters, Colonel Glenn A., 256

Wellesley, Arthur, Duke of Wellington, 85

Wen-lin (Forest of Pens), 63

West Point: Army football, 46, 260; Beast Barracks cade training, 20, 25–26, 28–29, 56, 70, 92, 137, 207; Boarders Ward, 74, 141, 144; Building 720, 145; Cadet Chapel, 21–22, 56, 129, 215, 222; Camp Buckner field training, 44–45, 56, 86–87, 99, 132; Central Guard Room, 92, 142, 157;

West Point (*continued*)
character development at curriculum
at, 255–58; Class of 1965, 47, 132;
Class of 1968, 137, 269, 284–88, 293;
Class of 1970, 95, 255, 288–89, 293;
Crap Magnets, 46; First Class Trip,
134, 137, 143; oath at, 4, 15, 114, 169,
284–85; for people of courage and
valor, 38; Recognition Ceremony,
136; Recondo training, 132–33; slugs
(punishment), 94; Sylvanus Thayer,
father of, 8–9, 92, 128; Thayer Hall,
21–22, 139, 144; Trophy Point, 4, 15,
20, 22–23, 143, 273, 276, 282; walking
a narrow path at, 186; Written Final
Reviews (WFRs), 133, 134–35, 139.
See also cadet prayer; engineering
WFRs. *See* Written Final Reviews (WFRs)
Wheat, Colonel Clayton E.,
West Point Chaplain, 54
Whitcomb, John, 217–18, 245
White, Colonel Lawrence K., Jr.
(USMA 1970), 92–93, 289, 293
Williams, Colonel George K.
(USMA 1968), 159, 285, 287
Willoughby, Colonel D. Hamilton,
171–72; ethics violations under,
177–81; investigation into, 183–90, 187,
265–66. *See also* United States Army
Recruiting Command (USAREC)
Wilson, Steven D. (USMA 1970), 28, 47, 289
women: absence of at West Point,
23; Japanese occupation of China,
66; in military service, 39, 238;
Saddam Hussein's attack on, 225–
26; women's rights, 62–63. *See
also* dating life *under* Lee, Gus
World War II: Chinese immigration
to the US and, 7; draft after, 170;
French Army leadership in, 65; Gulf
War compared to, 211–12, 227;
key to America's success in, 126;
Schwarzkopf's father in, 39; West
Point faculty and staff and, 170
Wren, P. C., 25, 149
Written Final Reviews (WFRs),
133, 134–35, 139

Y

YMCA (Young Men's Christian
Association): Coach Tony Gallo, 23,
24, 69–70, 73; Mind, Body, Spirit,
194; teaching Lee to box, 7
yuing chi (bad karma), 182